# We the Dead

# We the Dead

Preserving Data at the End of the World

## Brian Michael Murphy

THE UNIVERSITY OF NORTH CAROLINA PRESS

CHAPEL HILL

*This book was published with the assistance of the
Authors Fund of the University of North Carolina Press.*

Designed by Richard Hendel
Set in Utopia and Real Text Pro
by codeMantra
Manufactured in the United States of America

*The University of North Carolina Press has been a
member of the Green Press Initiative since 2003.*

Cover images: filing cabinet and skeleton © iStock/CSA-Printstock; binary
code © Shutterstock/Tavarius; children from "The Middleton Family at
the New York World's Fair," Westinghouse ad, *Life*, April 17, 1939.

Library of Congress Cataloging-in-Publication Data
Names: Murphy, Brian Michael, author.
Title: We the dead : preserving data at the end of the world /
Brian Michael Murphy.
Description: Chapel Hill : The University of North Carolina Press, [2022] |
Includes bibliographical references and index.
Identifiers: LCCN 2021058924 | ISBN 9781469668284 (cloth) |
ISBN 9781469668307 (ebook)
Subjects: LCSH: Archives—Collection management—United States—History. |
Records—United States—Management—History. | Storage facilities—United
States—History. | Data centers—United States—History. | Data warehousing—
United States—History. | Digital preservation—United States—History.
Classification: LCC CD3021 .M87 2022 | DDC 027.073—dc23/eng/20220128
LC record available at https://lccn.loc.gov/2021058924

*To Nadia*

This is how one pictures the angel of history. His face is turned toward the past. Where we perceive a chain of events, he sees one single catastrophe which keeps piling wreckage and hurls it in front of his feet. The angel would like to stay, awaken the dead, and make whole what has been smashed. But a storm is blowing in from Paradise; it has got caught in his wings with such a violence that the angel can no longer close them. The storm irresistibly propels him into the future to which his back is turned, while the pile of debris before him grows skyward. This storm is what we call progress.

—Walter Benjamin, "Theses on the Philosophy of History" (1940)

# Contents

# Illustrations

# Introduction  I Will Survive?

*I'm just here to look at some old photos.* I slide my driver's license onto the silver tray below the bulletproof glass, then to a gun-hipped guard, a row of six assault rifles on the wall behind her. She keeps my ID and passes me a security badge, saying, "Clip this to your shirt. Return to your car, and someone will drive out in a few minutes. Follow them in."

I walk back to my rented Mazda and sit, stare straight ahead to where the road leads directly into, and under, a small mountain. Soon enough, I see a red car emerge from the tunnel; its driver waves at me and pulls a U-turn. I follow her to the security checkpoint, and after she's allowed through it's my turn to enter the cube of chain-link fencing. The Kevlar-clad security guard gives the trunk and back seat a cursory search, asking whether I have explosives or weapons. He's quite genial, almost cheery.

"You're going to Corbis, today?" he asks as he pops open my glove box.

"Yes," I reply.

"What an interesting place, huh? It's amazing they have all those old photos down there, isn't it?"

"Yes, it's amazing."

"Are you doing some research, errrrr . . . ?"

"Yes, I'm writing a book."

"That's great. Well, have a great day. You're gonna love it down there."

"Thanks."

He waves me through, slaps a button that raises the wall of fence in front of me and lays flat the row of yellow steel spikes on the road ahead. I then wait for a green light to raise yet another security gate protecting the entrance to Iron Mountain's National Data Center in Boyers, Pennsylvania. Formerly a limestone mine, the site was converted into a secure records and data storage facility during the Cold War. Now it consists of roughly 150 underground acres of vaults filled with ordered avalanches of paper, miles of microfilm, and digital servers forming a part of what we collectively, inaccurately, refer to as a cloud.[1] For the data we preserve around the clock doesn't live in the sky; it is a place on the ground, and underground. And at

Iron Mountain, one of over 2,600 data centers in the United States alone,[2] the entrance to the cloud is what military strategists call a choke point: a stone archway wide enough for only a single vehicle to pass through, easy to barricade, difficult to penetrate, one of the reasons this place has a security rating of four. To put that in perspective, the White House and the Pentagon are rated five.[3]

I have come here to do research at the Corbis Film Preservation Facility (CFF). Created by Microsoft founder Bill Gates for his image resource company, Corbis, the CFF is one of many vaults in Iron Mountain. The CFF contains a 10,000-square-foot refrigerated vault, located 220 feet underground in a limestone cavern, where Gates stores his collection of 20 million photographs. Corbis makes money by licensing images for use in commercials, greeting cards, magazine ads, documentaries, websites, book covers, and anywhere else images are deployed in the pursuit of revenue. Though journalists, or documentarians like Ken Burns or his assistants, have visited the CFF often, the facility is notoriously difficult for academics to access. I sent emails and made calls to whomever I could find on the Corbis website, over and over, for about three years. I had basically given up when I received an email from Ann Hartmann, the manager of the CFF. I'm not sure how or why I got in.

But the fact that academics have a hard time accessing the CFF makes sense, because the richest man in the world built it not for research purposes, but for profit. Corbis began as Interactive Home Systems, founded by Gates in 1989. The billionaire had imagined that people in the digital age would eventually have wall screens in their homes rather than TV sets.[4] Gates thought that once we all had screens for walls, whoever held the digital rights to images—whether historical photographs or iconic pieces of art—would stand to make a fortune.

Gates began buying massive amounts of art and numerous image archives. He snapped up the digital rights to art in the Hermitage Museum in St. Petersburg, Russia, the Philadelphia Museum of Art and the National Gallery in London, long before most museums, artists, and lawyers even knew what digital rights were. He bought one of Leonardo da Vinci's notebooks, known as the Codex Leicester, not to mention the digital rights to all of Ansel Adams's photographs, and some of the most important photography archives in existence. Gates's acquisitions included the Bettmann Archive, which contains over 10 million photos and illustrations, the entire United Press International Archive, and iconic photos like Albert Einstein sticking out his tongue, Marilyn Monroe having trouble with her skirt on a Manhattan sidewalk, and a row of construction workers perched on a steel beam floating fifty stories above the out-of-focus metropolis.[5] The originals of these highly valuable photos are actually stored in a special deep freezer in the CFF, at negative four degrees Fahrenheit. According to Henry Wilhelm, designer of the CFF and the leading expert in the field of image permanence, the refrigerated, humidity-controlled vault will effectively preserve the photographs and film in it for 10,000 to 15,000 years.[6] Without such measures, photographic negatives will naturally decay within a century or so.[7]

I pass through the choke point, my excitement building though I'm forced to drive excruciatingly slow on the underground roadway. Fifteen-mile-per-hour speed limit signs are posted everywhere in the limestone tunnels. As I wind along the pristine asphalt I see people walking on a path that runs alongside the road, others on golf carts, fire extinguishers attached to the stone walls here and there.

I park my car just outside the CFF, where an Iron Mountain representative named Debby greets me and offers to give me a guided tour of the larger facility. We hop into her golf cart and take off, and she begins to list some of the features of Iron Mountain. This underground city of vaults and offices has its own fire department—"There are the trucks!" she points out as we speed past four bright red fire engines. In addition to in-house emergency services, Iron Mountain has the backup supplies of any respectable doomsday bunker: the 2,000 people who work underground at Iron Mountain could survive for months under a total lockdown, without any contact or reinforcements from the world above.

We ride past a set of doors with a Warner Brothers sign beside them. "That's where the studio stores original masters of its classic films," Debby says. "*ET, Back to the Future, Jaws*, they're all inside. Just around the corner is an unmarked vault. There are a bunch of unmarked ones and most of them, I'm not allowed to tell you what's in there. But in that one"— she points to a set of black doors—"are all of the original reels of Steven Spielberg's interviews with Holocaust survivors. He's one of our private clients."

I learn that all of the original records of the U.S. Patent Office are somewhere down here, as well as the black box from United Airlines Flight 93, and numerous other artifacts in rooms without signs over the doors, their contents classified. As I ride the golf cart with Debby, I flash back to being five years old, watching the last scene of *Raiders of the Lost Ark* on Betamax. Now I'm speeding, on a golf cart, through a real-life version of that warehouse where they stored the Ark of the Covenant as the credits rolled. The fictional warehouse, like this one, is an almost boundless archive of materials, some of them secret, that we painstakingly preserve and protect, materials that exist in a kind of necessary oblivion just below the surface of everyday life. And like the Ark of the Covenant, we attribute to these materials a kind of supernatural power and treat them with reverence. Only a select few can approach them or touch them, on pain of death. Debby stops the cart and takes me into the HBO vault, a cold storage room with seemingly endless rows of shelves that rise twenty-five feet to the stone ceiling. "There you have it. Everything HBO ever produced. Every movie, every show. All of the masters." Then we climb back into the golf cart and ride past an office where herds of workers are returning from their lunch break. The facade of the cubicled space is plain, with a sign that reads, rather benignly, "U.S. Office of Personnel Management." But this office is one of the main reasons for the doomsday security measures at the facility, as it houses all of the records from security clearance proceedings.

We check out another vault, this one tidy and endless, and just as cold. We open up a box of microfilm backups of Nationwide Insurance policies. "Are these old?" I ask. "Why are they on microfilm?" She smiles, replying, "No, they're not old. These boxes just arrived. Microfilm is still the archival standard for permanent records. Digital files aren't considered permanent, so a lot of corporations and government agencies still keep backups on microfilm. For certain kinds of records, you have to, by law."

As if to drive the point home, Debby takes me down the road to a media lab where old paper files are being digitized, but in the other half of the lab, technicians in white coats are creating microfilm copies of PDFs. It's the blatant reverse of what popular culture and ads for digital technology tell us—namely, that we make progress by shifting to new data formats. But in that moment in the digitization and microfilming lab, I realized that media history is like all of history: a cycle, a whirlwind of human successes and failures much more disparate and haywire than any story we tend to tell about it.

She drops me off at a music and media production studio. The rooms of the studio have the same cave walls as the other vaults, but they have been painted a shimmering silver like something out of a 1960s sci-fi flick set in the 1990s. At some point an Iron Mountain decision-maker thought painting all of the stone walls of the underground caverns silver would be a good idea, something about reflecting light and heat in the sunless underground rooms. Only a small part of the facility was painted, though. This silvery cave contains every type of surviving media playback machine in the world. You have an old Edison wax cylinder you want to hear? A two-inch quadruplex videotape reel of news footage from the 1960s you need digitized? A nitrate film documentary from the 1930s? The studio technicians can pull up the sound or the images for you.

That is, if they can be pulled up. There are horror stories of master recordings being unplayable due to decay or malfunction. And these stories are not all, or even mostly, about the older recordings, but about the newer digital ones. According to Garrett, my tour guide of the studio, hard-drive failures can shut down an entire project and render any future projects involving that music impossible: "I remember we were supposed to re-master a Kanye West recording, which couldn't have been more than about 10 years old. We pulled the hard drive out of the vault, popped it in, and it just wouldn't spin. So that original material is lost."

Beyond the work of contemporary artists, Iron Mountain houses some of the most valuable recordings in history, including master tapes of Frank Sinatra and Elvis Presley. As Garrett tells stories of coaxing sound out of fragile artifacts, a studio engineer who looks like Dana Carvey's Garth from *Wayne's World* interrupts to inform me that I am standing in the same room with the original recording of Gloria Gaynor's "I Will Survive." He is running the tracks into the sound editing software ProTools for a disco version of *Guitar Hero*. "I bet you never noticed this superfunky guitar underneath everything else," he says to me as he presses a couple of buttons, and suddenly all of the tracks drop out except the guitar. He's right; I hadn't noticed the guitar before. And it is, indeed, superfunky.

Only later would I notice how strange and haunting it was that the recorded voice of Gaynor was shouting the phrase "I will survive!" even as it underwent preservation, like a protest against the decay and inevitable entry into oblivion that ultimately awaits even the most guarded of human artifacts. The pleading in the voice is both adamant and vulnerable, reminding us that one can desperately seek survival, but survival can never be guaranteed.

Then into the photo editing room we go, where a worker customizes Corbis images for licensing clients. She removes dust and hairs from the digital scan, as well as other noise. She also manipulates the image. Not just wrinkles or cracks in the emulsion, but also pieces of furniture or people can be removed from an image—at this moment she's erasing a podium from a photograph of Eleanor Roosevelt to make the photo more balanced. This is standard procedure for every digitized image, but it reflects a tricky truth: preservation may promise to keep everything the same, but it always changes that which it preserves.

Outside, Debby is waiting on the golf cart.

"How'd it go?" she shouts over the sound of air compressors and jackhammers.

"Very interesting," I reply at the top of my voice. Workers in yellow suits are perched on mechanical scaffolds across the road, widening one of the limestone caverns to make space for another storage space or office.

"Let's get you over to Corbis," she says and cranks the golf cart to full speed.

Elsewhere in the mine, she tells me, is a natural underground lake. Iron Mountain uses the water not for drinking but for cooling. A room full of servers gets very hot, as computers put out heat constantly as they preserve our digital documents and photos. Iron Mountain pumps the cold water of the lake through pipes running through the ceilings of the server rooms, which cools them down and heats up the water. The hot water is then returned to the other side of the lake, where it is naturally cooled by the stone cave. And the process starts all over again.

Finally, I reach my destination. I am here to see as many images as I can, but I am mostly interested in the Bettmann Archive. Bill Gates bought the Bettmann for an undisclosed sum in 1995, and at the time it was stored in a New York City office that was too hot and too humid to preserve the collection.[8] He originally planned to digitize it but soon found out just how much time digitization takes. After the first hundred thousand images, it was apparent that by the time half of the overall archive was digitized, many items would have deteriorated beyond recognition, breaking down in a process that archivists call the "vinegar syndrome," where the chemicals in film negatives release gasses that smell like vinegar as they decompose.

Gates decided to separate the most important and valuable images—which the Corbis archivists refer to as the "Very Important Photographs," or VIPs—and placed them in deep freeze (negative four degrees Fahrenheit) to halt their decay. To digitize them, the pictures first have to be thawed in a process that takes hours, as they have to be moved to progressively warmer temperatures to avoid condensation on their surfaces that would cause irreparable damage. The rest of the images are stored in the larger vault, set at thirty degrees Fahrenheit. Though it isn't quite as cold, the archivists still keep a coatrack of parkas by the door to the vault and put one on each time a client requests an image, whether of Holly Golightly smoking a cigarette, or of Kim Phúc the "Napalm Girl" running naked, screaming, down Vietnam's Highway 1.

As I step into the giant vault and look down the long rows of filing cabinets filled with tens of millions of photographs, I begin to wonder: How did Americans become so obsessed with trying to save photos, paper documents, sound recordings, moving images, and digital files? And how did we become obsessed with saving them forever?

## The Mummy Complex

In his essay "The Ontology of the Photographic Image," the pioneering French film critic André Bazin offered the most compelling universal theory on what motivates humans to preserve data. Bazin cofounded the influential journal *Cahiers du Cinema* and mentored French New Wave directors such as Francois Truffaut, who called Bazin's book *Jean Renoir* "the *best* book on the cinema, written by the *best* critic, about the *best* director." Renoir, for his part, elegized Bazin as "the incarnation of one of the saints in the Cathedral of Chartres who project a luminous and magical vision through their stained-glass representations."[9] Bazin died at the untimely age of forty, and his theory of preservation is not only that—it is also a meditation on mortality and the fleetingness of life. He penned this theory in 1945, in the wake of the unprecedented death toll of World War II, a war captured in photography and moving images in vivid and devastating detail. According to Bazin, humans attempt to ward off time and death by preserving images of themselves that will outlive their physical bodies. At the center of all this human creativity is a "mummy complex." Universal and transhistorical, practiced in all cultures and at all times, this psychic structure finds expression in all the "plastic arts," from painting to sculpture, from death masks and taxidermy to photography and cinema, not to mention ancient Egyptians' mummification of the dead—hence the "mummy complex."[10]

Yet Bazin could never really explain why preservation practices are so intensive and extensive in some cultures and not in others. Nor did he have an answer for why the scale and technological sophistication of preservation increases at one moment in history as opposed to another.[11] When we preserve, we manifest our mummy complex and tell ourselves that no matter what happens in this uncertain world, that no matter who is left alive when a war or economic meltdown or rash of terrorist attacks concludes, a trace of us will remain. This is the technological afterlife we seek, not unlike the Egyptians, who preserved the heart, liver, and lungs of the dead in earthen jars so that they could be used in the afterlife. But unlike the ancient Egyptians, we have made such extensive preservation necessary not only for the afterlife but also for our earthly life, as our financial lives, social lives, love lives, and all major economic and governmental institutions in our country rely on digital infrastructure to record, preserve, and redistribute the data that underwrites our everyday life. The Egyptians did not do this—so why did we?

*We the Dead* makes the case that the mummy complex has mutated. We have perceived success in our preservation efforts so often that we have made a way of life out of it. We Americans, we the dead, now have a new condition: the data complex. The data complex is both material, out there—in our libraries, archives, data centers, bombproof bunkers—and psychological, inside us—in our minds where we fear the progressions of time and decay, and place our faith in the bulwarks and technological magic of the cloud.[12] Emerging in the early twentieth century and developing and expanding through a series of crises, the data complex preserved more and more data about us and promised us security and a kind of data-based immortality long desired by the mummy complex. But now the data complex has become so vast, so automated by algorithms, machine learning, and artificial intelligence, that it has moved beyond preserving data about and for its human creators. The data complex now exists ultimately to preserve data for its own sake. The data complex's main purpose is to preserve itself.

Long-term, intensive preservation projects certainly exist in many places outside the United States, such as the Svalbard Global Seed Vault and other examples considered here, but the United States is home to a particularly dense concentration of key sites and institutions in the data complex. The United States outranks every other nation in the world with its 2,670 data centers; the United Kingdom and Germany are a distant second and third with 452 and 443, respectively.[13] Numerous companies now driving the expansion of the data complex are headquartered in the United States, including Google, Apple, Facebook, Amazon, and Verizon, not to mention Iron Mountain, the largest secure records and data storage company in the world, and Equinix, the leading data center colocation provider.[14] The United States is also the site of origin for global systems for organizing archives and repositories, such as the Dewey decimal system, which is still the dominant book organization system in the world, and the Library of Congress Subject Headings system, which is "perhaps the most widely adopted subject indexing language in the world."[15]

*We the Dead* accounts for why the data complex emerged so intensely when and where it did. Part of the reason has to do with a new "institutional matrix" that formed in the United States in the early twentieth century, aligning corporations, universities, government agencies, and large-scale philanthropic funding for research.[16] This institutional matrix would expand and transform over the course of the twentieth century as military interests were increasingly incorporated into it. Thus, the research driving, and simultaneously being driven by, the burgeoning data complex would change, too: Depression-era studies meant to establish the best storage conditions for paper and microfilm soon morphed into experiments determining which types of file cabinets could survive an atomic bomb.

## Human Biochips in the Corporate Cyborg

In the data complex's underground and remote vaults and caverns have accumulated the past century's attempts to preserve what Lisa Gitelman calls "the data of culture" in America: the "records and documents, the archivable bits or irreducible pieces of modern culture that seem archivable under prevailing and evolving knowledge structures, and thus suggest, demand, or defy preservation."[17] By the mid-twentieth century, every American not only had a physical body—what I call a "biobody"—but was also accompanied through life, and death, by a "data body." The Critical Art Ensemble defines the data body as the "total collection of records on an individual," and more provocatively as "a state-and-corporate-controlled doppelgänger."[18] We the Dead tells the story of the data complex, showing how it embodies the power of corporate, state, and cultural institutions to rule the American populace: their biobodies, their data bodies, and the entangled circuit of the two.

Over and over again, the data complex expanded in those moments when many Americans felt they were quite possibly living just prior to the end of the world, from the Depression and the hottest moments of the early Cold War, to this moment of human-induced climate change and ecological disaster. Americans now preserve more data—from paper documents to microfilm reels to digital files—than any other civilization in history. This book retraces our steps to show how we arrived here, from the first "permanent" time capsules, created during the Depression to preserve American culture for 5,000-plus years, to subterranean vaults in abandoned mines that now house artifacts of every information medium: etchings, rag paper magazines, magnetic tape, microfilm reels, wax cylinders, and digital hard drives.

As each generation of Americans took crises as opportunities to preserve more data in a proliferation of formats, the data complex grew from a constellation of records repositories into a prototypical cyborg. According to Sean Cubitt, "human beings with technological implants" are "fantasy cyborgs," whereas actual "cyborgs are huge agglomerations of technologies with human implants." Cubitt, drawing on the work of cognitive scientist and philosopher Andy Clark,[19] shows how human thinking and activities merge with vast technological systems like the internet, which now includes artificially intelligent software and overlapping networks of corporate and state power—both electrical and political. For Cubitt, humans are "bio-chips embedded to carry out specialist tasks" within the larger corporate cyborg,[20] their biobodies performing functions similar to microchips in the motherboard of a computer.

Cubitt's conception of the cyborg is actually quite consistent with the original definition of the word, coined in a 1960 essay called "Cyborgs and Space." Cowritten by Manfred Clynes, a Julliard-trained pianist and self-taught neurophysiologist, and Nathan S. Kline, a psychiatrist and director of a mental hospital, the article appeared the year before the first human flew in outer space, and it looked ahead to a future of limitless space exploration. The authors argued that humans shouldn't work to create Earthlike environments in outer space but should rather deliberately adapt the human body so that it can thrive in extraterrestrial conditions. According to Clynes and Kline, technological implants in human bodies do not, on their own, make a cyborg. Rather, a cyborg is born when those implants enable the integration of a biobody into a larger system that automatically maintains homeostasis in this new organism that combines human and machine.[21] In order to make possible "long-term space voyages, involving flights not of days, months or years, but possibly of several thousand years," a spaceship pilot couldn't be bothered with continuously "checking on things and making adjustments merely in order to keep himself alive." In such a scenario, the pilot would become "a slave to the machines." The purpose of the cyborg is "to provide an organizational *system* in which such robot-like problems are taken care of automatically and unconsciously, leaving man free to explore, to create, to think, and to feel."[22]

While much of the technology that makes up the sprawling cyborg of the data complex is new, this human-technological hybrid is a part of a longer evolutionary history of technogenesis—the process through which humans and their tools coevolve.[23] N. Katherine Hayles combines insights from paleoanthropology, evolutionary theory, and cognitive science to point out that human bodies can evolve quite quickly through epigenetic changes, which result from changes to our environment rather than genetic mutations. Because the brain can rewire its circuits in response to stimuli—a feature called neuroplasticity—new technologies can deeply change the nature of human being, thinking, and feeling in the span of a single generation.

Nicholas Carr famously details these changes to our cognition in his viral essay "Is Google Making Us Stupid?" and then in his classic book

*The Shallows: What the Internet Is Doing to Our Brains*. He explains how the smartphone, as a mobile computing device and social media interface, has become "the most interesting thing in the world." Smartphones have the ability to totally captivate us, "colonizing" the human brain's "salience network," the neural system that controls "the distribution of our attention." Carr cites studies that show that a smartphone, even if it is turned off, is such a distraction that it negatively impacts test performance by students in school, not to mention "the development of interpersonal closeness and trust." While one might contest the premises or conclusions of these studies, what is less contestable is the way that smartphones and other digital devices are crucial ligaments tethering our thoughts, emotions, and autonomic nervous systems into the circuits of the data complex. In a phrase that recalls the original definition of a cyborg, one behavioral scientist describes the salience network as "the interface of the cognitive, *homeostatic*, motivational, and affective systems of the human brain."[24]

Technogenesis has been ongoing for tens of thousands of years, at least since humans' development of stone tools and their gradual shift from moving around on all fours to walking upright. But even within that longer story, which spans the entire earth and all of the people who have ever lived on it, what we are seeing now in the merging of humans and their tools is unprecedented. We can now move beyond speculative questions of whether the machines will one day overtake us, or whether artificial intelligence will supersede human intelligence. Instead, we can look at the ways in which the machines have already taken over, the ways that human intelligence and artificial intelligence are already integrated into an expanding, deepening system I call the data complex. In the early twenty-first century, even the corporate imperative to generate profit is losing its primacy to the goal of proliferating, preserving, mining, and operationalizing data. The data complex is now so pervasive that we must ask whether the complex is actually serving its ostensible human rulers, or whether data is circulating through the complex—which includes human bodies and minds—ultimately in service to itself.

Certainly, humans' past decisions have built the data complex, and current human choices sustain it, but contributing to the creation and persistence of something is not the same as having control over it. There are rich and powerful human beings at the helm of corporations who shape the data complex in fundamental ways, but these tech titans are also subordinated to the thing they have created. In her book *Capital Is Dead: Is This Something Worse?*, McKenzie Wark convincingly argues that the most powerful economic class now is a group she calls the vectoralists, the controllers and owners of big tech companies and social media platforms like Apple, Facebook, Amazon, Alphabet (Google's parent company), and Microsoft. Even Walmart "has almost as many data centers as physical distribution centers, and they are about as large."[25] The vectoralists' aggregation and manipulation of data are powerful enough to make them a ruling class that subordinates other ruling classes. But even these elites, these rulers of rulers, who regularly populate *Forbes's* "World's Billionaires List," must serve and sustain the data complex by keeping it running, and growing, in order to maintain their wealth and power. In *The Age of Surveillance Capitalism: The Fight for a Human Future at the New Frontier of Power*, Shoshana Zuboff writes that the digital infrastructure has undergone a metamorphosis *"from a thing that we have to a thing that has us."*[26]

The vectoralists who tend to the data complex are rewarded with immense wealth for their efforts to the degree that they can repurpose the data complex as an "extraction architecture." Zuboff illuminates how companies like Google generate profits by selling predictions of consumers' future behavior, predictions based on the troves of data the company has collected about consumers' pasts: "e-mails, texts, photos, songs, messages, videos, locations, communication patterns, attitudes, preferences, interests, faces, emotions, illnesses, social networks, purchases, and so on."[27] The logic of surveillance capitalism, in seeking to extract data from everything that is happening, both inside and outside of our data bodies, at all times, is powerfully embodied in the Boston-based start-up Recorded Future. With financial backing from both Google Ventures and the CIA venture firm In-Q-Tel, Recorded Future "monitors every aspect of the web in real time in order to predict future events."[28]

The immediate prospect of fantastic profits drives such companies to expand the data complex further, at an astounding rate. The amount of data flowing over the internet "increased by a factor of 17.5 million over 1992's 100 gigabytes per day; 90 percent of the data in 2017 was generated in the prior two years; a single autonomous car will generate 100 gigabytes of data per second."[29] Whether the current economic system is best characterized as "surveillance capitalism," "platform capitalism," or some other term,[30] what is certain is that the profit-seeking efforts of the vectoralists expand the data complex's reach at every turn, rendering more and more of humans' lived experience as data. Thus, our data bodies now grow continually, even as our biobodies remain the same. Our data bodies continue to grow even after we die. On Facebook, a deceased person's account does not disappear but instead is "memorialized," a status that allows "friends and family to gather and share memories after a person has passed away."[31]

The limestone caverns of Iron Mountain are remnants left behind by extractive companies like U.S. Steel that recovered the accumulated minerals of bygone geological eras. Industrialists mined the past. Today's digital magnates fill those underground caves with servers, obeying the call of the data complex to constantly seek more space for aggregating, preserving, and analyzing data. The data complex provides the extraction architecture for the vectoralists who seek to profit from the lodes of data about what humans have done, by predicting what they will do. Vectoralists mine the future.

### Explorers of Infrastructure

The data complex encompasses not only our biobodies and our computers but also the infrastructures that link them together. My understanding of infrastructure draws heavily on the work of Lisa Parks, renowned media scholar and MacArthur Fellow, who defines infrastructure as "the material sites and objects that are organized to produce a larger, dispersed yet integrated system for distributing material of value, whether water, electrical currents, or audiovisual signals."[32] Parks analyzes media infrastructures, objects so large they can't be seen or otherwise observed all at once. Her work incorporates a wide range of artifacts, including "personal observation, photography, maps, video, art, drawings, and other visualizations."[33] She has issued a "critical provocation" to other scholars, namely that they need to go beyond analyzing media representations. To fully understand media infrastructures, she says, scholars need "to visit infrastructure sites and objects, observe infrastructural processes, and interact with infrastructure workers." This would allow them "to get as close as possible to these massive and dispersed things that always feel so unintelligible or so far away."[34]

When I first encountered Parks's style of research, I concluded that it must be difficult, logistically complicated, and utterly unpredictable, as she analyzes "physical sites and objects that are dispersed across vast territories."[35] And as I was just then beginning to try to figure out how and why the data complex came to be, it sounded like precisely the kind of research I wanted to do. In search of answers, I have visited the data centers and archives and bunkers of the data complex, following in the footsteps and thought patterns of my favorite explorers of infrastructure, a roster that of course includes Parks, as well as Nicole Starosielski, Tung-Hui Hu, Shannon Mattern, Tom Vanderbilt, Jenny Odell, Trevor Paglen, Jill Jonnes, Rebecca

Solnit, and others.[36] The historical sweep and technological scope of these thinkers never ceases to astound me and change me, shifting the way I see subway tunnels, fiber-optic cables, power lines, cell towers, and satellites.[37]

These infrastructural objects are often invisible to us, either because they are buried or simply easy to ignore as a part of the background. But their physical form reveals much about the outsize scale of human ambition: to reshape nature, to engineer our environments and thus redesign the niche our bodies respond to as we evolve. To see who we are now in the data complex, it is no longer sufficient to look in the mirror and gaze at our faces or our naked biobodies. The infrastructures of the data complex are now a part of us—we think with them, feel with them, remember our pasts, and thus compose our identities through them. We send love notes and messages on special occasions, from birthdays to bereavements, through their subterranean cables and invisible signals. To see ourselves now, we have to gaze at the data centers' multitudes of blue lights blinking on racks of servers or stand under their conduits, whose cool water carries away the heat generated by our teeming tweets, posts, and pins. We must scan the night sky for geosynchronous satellites that children, peering through toy telescopes, mistake for drifting stars.

The data complex, by design, outlives the humans who imagine and build it, and in it we have ended up preserving something other than just the traces of our appearance on Earth, our thoughts, activities, and vital statistics. In the storage spaces, media technologies, and infrastructures that preserve and distribute data, the hopes and fears of previous generations took on physical form. For instance, during the Cold War, bomb-proof bunkers embodied both the fear of nuclear annihilation and the hope that Americans could survive it. Through our own acts of preservation, our hopes and fears, too, become real and thus form part of the actual patrimony we pass on, if unwittingly, to the humans of the future. With its imposing facades and securitized facilities outfitted with surveillance cameras, steel gates, traffic spikes, and armed guards, the data complex is a paradox. On the one hand, these fortifications are forbidding—they repel any and all threats to the precious data of the past and present. On the other, they are welcoming. They invite future generations to deposit their data bodies, too, in the inner sancta where, perhaps one day, archaeologists will eventually break in. And as they catalog the contents of an underground bank vault repurposed to preserve old Hollywood movies, won't they wonder: *For what kind of society did these strange wheels of film serve as currency? What could one buy with these thin strips filled with black and gray ghosts?*

## Emergence of the Data Complex

The data complex is the protagonist of *We the Dead*. It begins to take shape in the early twentieth century as an outgrowth of historical processes kick-started at the end of the Civil War. Since 1865, the United States became increasingly industrialized, with population densities in urban centers rising as laborers flocked to new factories, steel mills, oil refineries, stockyards, and textile mills. Railroad tracks crisscrossed the country, and the modern corporation extended its footprint across vast swaths of land both in the United States and abroad, which required corporate managers to use paper records to oversee their profit-making enterprise. The federal government likewise expanded dramatically, the bureaucracy we know it to be first emerging in the 1870s to distribute benefits and pensions to Civil War veterans in the Reconstruction period.[38] The growth of record-keeping activities in governmental and economic institutions was so great in the late nineteenth century that Lars Heide refers to this period as an "early information explosion," debunking the myth that it was only with the advent of digital computers that we found ourselves drowning in data.[39]

All of these new records were crucial for the daily operation of American society by the early twentieth century, but these records happened to be printed on wood pulp paper—a media material that was sometimes quite brittle, depending on how it was stored. In fact, by the turn of the century, many antebellum newspaper editions, printed on much more durable rag paper composed of cotton fibers, were in much better condition than newspapers that were only a few years old. Modern wood pulp paper played a key role in precipitating the emergence of the data complex, as the medium's impermanence combined with its ubiquitous use by institutions meant to be our most durable produced great anxiety on the part of all manner of historians, archivists, and businessmen. The records required for historical research and legal proceedings, or for the reconstruction of accounts or vital records after a fire, the very archives that made modern American society possible were falling apart, their fibers undone by humidity, silverfish, pollution, and myriad other threats. Even by the late 1920s, no one had a definitive, foolproof means of preserving these materials.

Librarians were among the first to sound the alarm about the fragility of modern records, their collective voice only just then taking shape in the late nineteenth century. In 1928, Harry Lydenberg, the head reference librarian at the New York Public Library, convinced the Carnegie Corporation of New York to bankroll studies by the National Bureau of Standards (NBS) to determine with scientific certainty the causes of deterioration in paper and microfilm records, as well as effective technologies and techniques for preserving them. The studies, running from 1929 to 1938, coincided with the Depression, that decade-long global economic downturn that destabilized both capitalism and liberal democracy, as well as the scientific institutions that had been, up until that time, augmenting their influence and authority in public health, statecraft, and the practices of everyday hygiene and citizenship. The NBS studies established, for the first time, authoritative scientific knowledge about how to preserve paper and microfilm records indefinitely.

To stabilize capitalist power, businessmen sought solutions in the new science of data preservation, as well as the nascent scholarly field of business history. For instance, in 1937, Harvard business professor Ralph Hower wrote in the *Bulletin of the Business Historical Society*, "Much of the recent hostility towards private enterprise has arisen because the public has been told the mistakes and misdeeds of business, and there has been no one to supply corrective data on the other side."[40] Hower's confidence that modern records could even be effectively preserved was rooted in the facts found by the emerging field I call "preservation science."[41] He cited a recent article that appeared in the journal *Vital Records* and was written by Arthur Kimberly, a chemist who led the NBS studies and had recently been named chief of the Manuscript Repair Division at the newly formed National Archives. According to Hower, independent scholars could carry out research that helped combat the inaccurate propaganda that attacked businessmen and swayed public opinion against them. He thus encouraged the "systematic preservation of company records" as "an important aid in warding off unwarranted attacks upon private enterprise."[42]

That same year, one of Kimberly's colleagues, B. W. Scribner, published a similar article in the journal *Refrigerating Engineering*. In "Air Treatment for Preservation in Libraries," Scribner urged all libraries, if they were to properly and dutifully preserve their collections, to follow the recommendations of the NBS, as the National Archives and many other "important" libraries and repositories had already done.[43] Scribner's recommendations were transformative for libraries though not all the technologies were entirely new—air-conditioning was actually invented years before by Willis Carrier, in an effort to control the temperature of media materials. Making humans more comfortable came only later, after Carrier revolutionized the printing business by allowing printshops to maintain a steady temperature. Prior to his invention, temperature fluctuations caused paper stock to contract and expand while sitting on the print plate. Color images often required multiple passes through the printer, so when the paper expanded even slightly between passes, the layers of colored ink were misaligned, thus distorting the image or ruining it so badly that the whole run was thrown in the garbage.[44] Another early adopter of Carrier's technology was the Celluloid Company, where air conditioning eliminated humidity that otherwise caused "white specks to form on the film, which translated to white spots on the screen when it was projected." Carrier solved all of these problems, and thus paved the way for air conditioner usage in spaces of the data complex, such as libraries and archives.[45]

As most Americans did not read *Vital Records*, or *Refrigerating Engineering*, or other professional journals where NBS scientists disseminated their results, how did the principles and practices of the early data complex reach the American public? During the Depression, the first two "permanent" time capsules appeared, both projects attempting to preserve microfilm reels and other modern artifacts for over 5,000 years, both projects designed around the specifications published by the NBS. The first was the Westinghouse Time Capsule of Cupaloy, deposited at the New York World's Fair in 1939. The time capsule contained a "cross-section of American life" sealed inside a sterilized, glass-lined, airtight, helium-filled metallic tube buried 100 feet underground. The time capsule was a key part of the Westinghouse Electric Corporation's public relations effort to reconvince the American masses of the limitless value of "free enterprise," technological innovation, and corporate hegemony that would lead society to "A Better Tomorrow" (the theme of the fair). The vision of the future within the time capsule, and in the displays and advertising that accompanied it, revealed a very particular conception of the present, one that aligned "typical" American identity with whiteness, patriarchy, and the nuclear family structure so crucial to corporate health and stability.

The Crypt of Civilization, deposited in Atlanta, Georgia, in 1940, was a time capsule modeled after an Egyptian tomb, containing a version of American culture meant to be discovered by people living 6,173 years in the future. The crypt's creators were less optimistic than Westinghouse—they lamented the degeneration of the white race resulting from racial intermixture and increased immigration, not to mention the dysgenic effects of New Deal social programs that "rewarded the lazy and inefficient," and thus contravened Darwinian "laws" of nature.[46] From the time capsule and the Crypt of Civilization, which appeared around the same time, we learn that data preservation does not simply preserve existing materials, but is productive. Data preservation produces new technologies, artifacts, and cultural logics that do not assuage our anxiety about data loss, but rather stimulate more preservation, especially at moments when new crises emerge. As Nanna Bonde Thylstrup writes in *The Politics of Mass Digitization*, "The rationalized drive to collect is often accompanied by a slippage, from a rationalized urge to a pathological drive ultimately associated with desire, power, domination, anxiety, nostalgia, excess, and—sometimes even—compulsion and repetition." Drawing on the work of theorists Couze Venn and Slavoj Žižek, she argues that "no matter how much we collect, the collector will rarely experience their collection as complete and will often be haunted by the desire to collect more."[47]

Our obsessive permanent data preservation efforts in the Depression, on the surface, enabled us to render immortal portraits of the past and present for the sake of the future, so that those unborn civilizations can know who we were by digging up and opening the time capsules we buried in the earth. Of course, this aspect of our complex is a roundabout narcissism wherein we imagine future people not in their fullness and uniqueness, but as proxies looking back at us with interest and fascination.[48] In his "Address at the Closing of the Crypt of Civilization," Thornwell Jacobs, creator of the crypt, spoke in grand terms to the people of 8113 A.D. who would locate his time capsule and breach it with endless fascination: "We the dead, out of an ancient and forgotten past, salute you, the living, in the sunny hours of the future."[49] In Jacobs's vision, these future humans are reduced to mirrors, ghostly surfaces onto which we project our self-interest, and stroke our egos by imagining ourselves to be just that damn interesting.

The often unconscious aim of all this activity, however, is to manufacture a collective technological fantasy of immortal life through which we can repress our awareness of our mortality, our fragility, our inevitable ending. In his address, Jacobs goes on to embody this dynamic perfectly, as he suggests the possibility of actual human life extension through scientific or supernatural means: "If the laws of God permit, may there be some of us present with you when you hear these words." Elsewhere, in a speech he recorded on a metal LP and placed inside the crypt, he wonders whether the people of the future will have "the same hope of immortality" that he has.[50] For his collaborator, Thomas Kimmwood Peters, immortality was not a matter of hope but rather a certainty. Peters was an avid yoga practitioner who thoroughly believed not only in reincarnation but also that he would return to Earth in 8113 A.D. for the specific purpose of being at the opening of the crypt, where he would explain its contents to the people of that day.[51] To create a more tangible continuity between their moment and the future, Jacobs and Peters created metal tickets to the crypt-opening ceremony, meant to be passed down from father to son for the next 6,173 years.[52]

## Backup Loops

The objects examined in the book are among the most extreme cases of data preservation in their historical moment of crisis. As such, they condense and embody broader data collection and preservation practices, reflect hopes and anxieties that institutions and individuals invested in data at the time, and foreshadow transformations in the data complex that would occur during the next crisis. These cases were selected because they powerfully illustrate the range of key features of the data complex, while also revealing the material interconnections within the complex across historical moments of crisis. Each chapter highlights one feature of the data complex—from the toxicity of its technologies, to its bombproof architecture and telecommunications infrastructure, from its reshaping of human biology and consciousness, to its blurring of the boundary between life and death. The feature focused on in each chapter is the one most deeply related to that topic, though all the features are present to some degree in every chapter. With each new crisis, with each moment that Americans think their world—which they see as *the* world—is ending, the data complex shifts, expands, deepens. As the story progresses and the data complex grows and mutates, what was an extreme case of data preservation in a previous crisis becomes normal during the next one, or even comes to seem quite conservative. For instance, my one external hard drive of my personal files holds more data than the Crypt of Civilization and Westinghouse Time Capsule combined. The crypt alone was meant to represent the "accumulated knowledge of mankind," from the beginnings of ancient civilization to 1936.[53]

As a concept, the data complex encompasses both digital and analog data preservation efforts. It also illuminates how, historically and materially, these two types of data have been entangled. *We the Dead* shows that the practices of redundancy and backups across multiple media formats begin not in the digital age, or even the Cold War, but in the first permanent time capsules in the Depression.[54] Analog and digital are not opposites or stages in a progression, but two elements in a vortex of data preservation practices.[55] New data formats like digital files back up older ones like microfilm, even as new data formats are backed up by ancient ones like etching, to provide insurance in the event that the new ones are not as durable as our scientists and marketers promise them to be. I call these "backup loops," circuits of anxious duplication and dispersal that show our faith in new data formats to be both boundless and full of doubt.

The data complex is far larger than "the cloud,"[56] that overused, literally nebulous concept that mystifies the material existence of digital information. The data complex names a now normalized pathology wherein our frenzied data preservation efforts never actually produce the sense of security and peace they promise, but only provoke a desire for more intensive and extensive preservation. At this moment, we rely thoroughly on digital technology—the most ephemeral and unsustainable data format of all—and that reliance grows stronger all the time. The arrival of 5G, edge computing, and the pervasive automation of everything from public transportation to disease diagnosis drives and intensifies the data complex's need to expand. Many fear (or hope) that artificially intelligent systems will supersede human intelligence, or that the robots will rebel against their masters, or some other similarly Hollywoodesque scenario will play out if we continue to expand the role of machine learning in everyday life. But regardless of what the robots decide to do at some point in the future, the data complex is already approaching a moment where the end of humanity as we know it is possible, where the blurring of data and human life is so complete that the distinction no longer holds.

Scientists working in the field of synthetic biology have already figured out how to store digital data in synthetic DNA, a format that promises to be the most dense and durable ever created—the entire internet could fit into a shoebox-sized amount of DNA. The rise of synthetic biology means that backup loops now include genetically modified organisms, making data and biological life increasingly inseparable. According to Mél Hogan, DNA data storage is a watershed moment in the "coevolution of Big Data and DNA research," a development that contributes to our "condition of 'dataism'—the idea that data is more valuable than humans or that humans are somewhat useless without data."[57]

But one of the most revolutionary possibilities held out by DNA is its ability to not simply store data but also to create it. The holy grail of at least one leading researcher is to create DNA that records information about your body from within your body, information that could be read later, an innovation he calls "molecular ticker tape."[58] The data complex, then, is trending toward becoming more than just another cyborg, for even the machine side of the hybrid, and the data body it records, is becoming more biological.

In the early years of the data complex, preservationists feared that the loss of data would bring the end of civilization, the end of humanity as we know it. And so they created time capsules to protect and transmit a record of themselves to future people who would find it after the end of the world. Now it seems that the data complex may soon succeed in preserving so much data that human life itself is eclipsed. Whereas the data body used to back up human life, now human life, the biobody, would be the backup or the host for data that, unlike the human, will not die.

## The Biogeochemistry of the Data Complex

Now, I sit in the crown jewel of Iron Mountain's empire, the National Data Center in Boyers, Pennsylvania. The Bettmann Archive's 11 million photos are filed in manila folders stored in a 10,000-square-foot freezer with limestone walls, a cavern hollowed out by miners over a hundred years ago.[59] Each folder heading is listed in a big, black three-ring binder the Corbis archivists set on my desk, where I'll work for the week. I make a list of folders I'd like to see on an index card and hand it to the archivist, who puts on a parka and enters the freezer to retrieve them. "This might take a little while," she says as she walks away. "No problem," I reply. There is plenty to take in, and think about, while I wait.

The Corbis Film Preservation Facility, with its rotting celluloid strips, glass negatives, and cotton rag newspapers run through digital scanners in an abandoned mine turned bunker, is a media archaeologist's dream. The field of media archaeology encompasses a wide variety of approaches, but it nonetheless tends to cohere around several commitments. The one I most strongly adhere to is the idea that data is always *material*, no matter whether it takes the form of clay tablets, wood pulp paper and ink, or the magnetized surface of a digital hard drive.[60] This emphasis on the materiality of data means that data does not exist separately from the matter on which it is written, etched, or otherwise recorded—data *is* the material it is recorded on. In other words, from my perspective as a media archaeologist, the materiality of any given data, well, matters, as do the structures and sites in which we find that data.

Left alone in the Corbis office, I look over the surface of the white limestone walls and ceiling, thinking about the history of this cave. Before Iron Mountain acquired this facility, it was owned by the National Storage Company. One of its first clients was the U.S. Patent Office, backing up nearly 3 million pages of patents in triplicate, including the first one ever issued, signed by George Washington in 1790.[61] Another was the State Health Department of Pennsylvania, which by 1973 stored 4,000 rolls of microfilm duplicates of its files here. A magazine article from that year, called "Preserving YOUR Vital Statistics Records," described vital statistics records as

**Corbis Film Preservation Facility office.**

"data pertaining to births, adoptions, legitimations, deaths, fetal deaths, marital status and data incidental thereto." The health department's vault storing this "confidential data" was protected by a "bank-type steel door to permit access only to approved personnel."[62]

But in order to understand the data complex, we have to think about more than just historical chronology. One of the limitations of the mummy complex as a theory was that it couldn't account for why preservation practices intensify in a given historical period, or a specific place. What Bazin didn't fully explore is how the earth itself always played an active part in how and where new preservation practices developed. Bazin only hinted at this when he wrote that the "first Egyptian statue . . . was a mummy, tanned and petrified in sodium," a preservative action made possible by the desert itself. Before being wrapped in linen, ancient Egyptians' corpses were desiccated by being buried under the sand. Even further back, the practice likely derived from natural consequences of the climate, where a body that fell in the desert would dry up instead of putrefying, leaving it preserved. The tradition of mummification formalized something the earth's atmosphere and hot, sandy surface reflecting solar rays already did on its own.

So why did Iron Mountain, this facility of cave walls, cold storage, and computers, form where and when it did? Before becoming a facility to stockpile and protect data, this place was a mine for limestone. A versatile mineral, limestone has been used variously as fertilizer to replace nutrients lost from American soil during the Dust Bowl, as slag conditioner to burn in blast furnaces and bind with impurities from iron ore as it turns into liquid steel, as an aggregate for asphalt and concrete, and as an agent that separates cellulose fibers in wood to turn trees into pulp for making paper. But what about the story of this place before humans used it for their purposes?

For years, I've taught media archaeologist Jussi Parikka's brilliant book *A Geology of Media*. We often use the word "culture" to talk about media, which is a metaphor from biology, from the language of microorganisms, of soil and "cultivation," of life. Whereas Parikka begins with geology: the study of sedimentation and fossils that form across eons, of the ways time writes itself into matter. Inspired by his explorations, I have to ask: What would Jussi do? Perhaps he would think about the fact that the miners who dynamited and hauled out chunks of rock blasted these tunnels through an already buried world. Long before people found uses for limestone—long before there were people—the material that makes up the white walls of this data tomb was alive.

Over 300 million years ago, the land that is now western Pennsylvania was about ten degrees south of the equator, and under an ocean. Prior to this time, during the Silurian period, corals had been "very abundant and began to form reefs in the carbonate areas." Limestone is the result of all these corals and prehistorical life forms leaving behind skeletons that are then compressed in the crust of the Earth. Corals are like clocks in that they deposit "a thin layer of lime (calcium carbonate) on their skeletons every day."[63] These corals thus reflected cosmic events, their layers recording the rotations of the earth on its axis the same way the rings of a tree mark each trip the planet takes around the sun.

The growth rings of coral vary in size annually, and are used by scientists to estimate the lengths of years and days in past eras. These cave walls enclosing me 220 feet underground don't just come from a different time period, they come from a different *time*. When these petrified corals thrived, a year on Earth was 407 days long, each day lasting 21.5 hours.[64] Due to the friction caused by the ocean's tides moving it across the seafloor, the rotation of the earth has actually slowed down since then—hence the 24-hour day we all have (imagine how much we'd complain if it was still 21.5!). The day is still shortening, and the distance between New York City and London lengthening by an inch every year, because the earth is always moving, its plates shifting, compressing dead organic matter into minerals.[65] Bombproof facilities like Iron Mountain in many cases are placed where they're placed because of relatively low or no measurable seismic activity there, which also has to do with the movement of the earth, or relative lack thereof in zones where earthquakes nearly never occur.

Around the same time that corals flourished in the ocean of Pennsylvania, swampland stretched out, the biomass absorbing massive quantities of carbon from the sun and condensing into peat. Once covered by more fallen plant life, the peat, interred in the earth's crust and compressed, became the coal seams that fueled the steel mills of Pittsburgh and the foundries of George Westinghouse, who first made his fortune by inventing and manufacturing a fail-safe air brake for trains. The Boyers mine used to provide limestone for U.S. Steel, the conglomerate formed through a merger between the Carnegie Steel Company and two others, which made Andrew Carnegie one of the richest men that ever lived. The windfall from the merger funded Carnegie's subsequent philanthropic efforts, which included establishing the American public library system as we know it and bankrolling the NBS studies on the permanence of paper and microfilm.[66]

Even the wealth of Bill Gates, who hails from the Pacific Northwest, can be traced back to geology. The wealth that enabled him to purchase the Bettmann Archive and preserve it in this frigid tomb begins not with Microsoft, not with the two years he spent at Harvard before dropping out, not even with the Lakeside School where he and Paul Allen began programming computers in eighth grade. The story begins, again, with biogeochemistry, the combination of primordial sunlight captured and compressed in dead flora, the vast sheets of rock bulged and bent by rising magma, the black soil and relentless rain. The biome of the old-growth forests in the Pacific Northwest is more carbon rich than any other in the world, and that natural richness has been converted into accumulated wealth and industry.[67] George Moran founded the Lakeside School in 1905 with money he made in shipbuilding, a business that boomed in Seattle because of the exceptionally dense forests that surround it, a teeming wilderness out of which that sawmill of a city was cut. Around that same time, Bill Boeing came to Seattle and soon decided to launch an airplane manufacturing company there in the 1920s—airplanes were made out of wood back then, and the company also used to make wooden furniture. This meant that by the time World War II rolled around, Seattle was already as thick with technical workers as it was with trees, which in turn attracted more tech companies like the Computer Center Corporation, founded in 1968, through which Gates gained his 10,000 hours of programming time before even graduating high school.[68]

By 1979, the scene in Seattle was ripe for the upstart Gates to base his start-up there. Microsoft soon took the computing world by storm, and the cycle of wealth and technology in the Pacific Northwest continued. The rest, as they say, is history—the Seattle area now plays host to offices for Facebook, Amazon, SpaceX, Blue Origin, and many more tech companies. But the rest is also media archaeology—Gates's wealth as a tech titan, entangled with the literal roots of capital in the Pacific Northwest, begins with those trees and the soil in which they love to grow so tall and thick, and how those trees attracted loggers and manufacturers who deploy the term "raw material" to make living things seem like they were destined to be made into something else, destined to be made, ultimately, into money.

### Otto Bettmann's Photos of Photos

By the time the archivist wheels a truck full of thick folders out of the vault and toward me, I can't help but think about how much more fascinating this facility is than the Bettmann Archive itself. Though I haven't dug into the folders yet, I am certain that there's no way their contents can live up to Corbis's breathless hype about how the archive is "priceless" and "absolutely unique."[69]

But after flipping through the first folder, I realize I was wrong. There is, in fact, no superlative strong enough to describe the weird wonderfulness of the Bettmann. Each folder contains not just historical photos from United Press International or Underwood & Underwood, but reproductions that Otto Bettmann took with his own camera in his imperial effort to collect all kinds of images: engravings, pen and ink illustrations, blueprints, paintings and lithographs, even photos of other photos, each one more strange than the next. Whether the folder is labeled "Safes and Vaults," or "Chemical and Biological Weapons," or "Early Computers," or "The Border Itself," the images inside each one revise, on the spot, what you thought you knew about the subject.

There is one image in the Bettmann Archive that affected me more than the rest, though, and brought me to think about what darkness lurks under the foundations of the data complex: a librarian in California, wearing a three-piece suit and tie, perusing a rare book resting atop a cart full of them, as he prepares to roll these "literary treasures" into what the *New York Times* called a "lethal gas chamber for bookworms."

# 1

## Gas Chambers for Bookworms

Time loves a book—to fox its pages in lovely rust, tea,

sepia, and fecal starclusters; to brittle it, to riddle it with

pin-width insect labyrinths, to fade, chip, buckle, cockle,

scrape and in general tick eternity away by units of

wholesale decomposition; Time loves to suck a book

as clean as a chicken wingbone.

—Albert Goldbarth, "Both Definitions of Save"

In late spring 1928, as the orchids and camellias burst into bloom in the Huntington Library's gardens under the Southern California sun, librarians in the rare book collections noticed that something was feasting on the volumes in their care. Rail and utilities titan Henry E. Huntington had established the library in 1920, spending a small fortune to gobble up a number of the largest and finest rare book collections in a relatively short time, and creating a truly priceless set of artifacts.[1] The collection included one of only eleven surviving Gutenberg Bibles printed on vellum; a first folio of Shakespeare's plays, published in 1623 by the Bard's friends and colleagues just seven years after his death; a first edition of William Blake's *Songs of Innocence and of Experience*; as well as many irreplaceable newspapers, broadsides, and incunabula—books printed in Europe between 1455 and 1501.[2]

Though Huntington died in 1927, he intended his collection to live on long after him, but as the librarians discovered, the volumes were literally too full of life. The problem with assembling a massive collection of books—as was also the case for Huntington's magnificent botanical gardens—is that you necessarily collect the very organisms that feed on books, or plant leaves, or leather. Huntington's collection was infested with insects, foreign and domestic, bent on devouring the very books imbued with his spirit. These insects were steadily boring into the volumes from the outside, pausing to lay eggs somewhere in the dark heart of a closed Bible's illuminated leaves, turning the priceless treasure itself into a food-womb. The larvae then destroyed the same book from the inside out as they set out to colonize other tomes.

Huntington librarian Thomas Marion Iiams led the preservation effort. He was in a race against time, we might say. But what is time but insects, mold, bacteria, rust, dust? Time is, for the most part, a living force, microbial, bacterial, fungal, or basic plant forms that spread and devour and digest anything made with organic materials, such as book pages composed of rag paper or wood pulp, or leather covers or vellum documents, both made of animal skins. Thus toxic chemicals in the form of pesticides can combat time itself. Iiams was new to the librarian profession and was certain that more experienced overseers of fine collections would have a solution to his bookworm problem. In haste, Iiams wrote letters to much older libraries and repositories—the Huntington itself was only eight years old—to learn precisely how they ridded their precious books of the pest. He was alarmed to find that no one, not librarians at the Vatican nor at the oldest libraries in Britain, could offer a definitive prescription for how to protect books against the hardy insect. A number of the librarians he consulted thought bookworms to be a myth, and thus offered no help at all.

The letters, telegrams, and reading recommendations Iiams received mainly offered reasons why you can't kill bookworms. His colleagues elaborated from afar the bookworm's astounding resistance to traditional pesticides, its voracious appetite not just for book pages but for leather covers, for even the starchy glue that holds book bindings together. From those that did not doubt the bookworm's existence or tenacity, Iiams received suggestions that ranged from the highly toxic, such as spraying books with formaldehyde—which is effective for preserving dead humans, but a potent carcinogen for living ones—to the comical, such as sprinkling the shelves of the library with "a little fine pepper." Other correspondents suggested that the latter tactic would have been ineffective since, according to *The Principal Household Insects of the United States* (1896), bookworms are actually "partial to pepper."[3]

Variously known as *Anobium paniceum*, or the bread beetle, or drugstore beetle, bookworms had been known to eat their way through "druggists' supplies," from "insipid gluten wafers to such acrid substances as wormwood," from cardamom and anise to "the deadly aconite and belladonna." Even if arsenic dusted on books hadn't posed a mortal danger to human readers of those books, using such a drastic method would likely have been unsuccessful. According to Iiams, the bookworm displays a "universal disrespect for almost everything, including arsenic and lead."[4] One could understand, then, when Iiams published an account of his struggles in *Library Quarterly* and included two photographs of the bookworm on the same page, magnified 110 times, the top image shot straight on and the bottom one in profile—a microscopic mug shot.

Iiams continued to send letter after letter to librarians around the world, but his search for answers began to transform into a kind of fruitless commiseration. One of his correspondents was a librarian working in the tropics, where abundant insects and constant humidity wreaked havoc on books and manuscripts, and was in the process of planning a trip to Europe and the United States to learn more about preservation solutions. Iiams pointed out that he might find himself disappointed.

Even the Vatican, its library one of the oldest and wealthiest in the world, did not know how to ward off bookworms both effectively and efficiently. Since 1912, when the Vatican moved its books from wooden boxes on shelves to steel stacks, the bookworms had torn through its precious volumes faster than ever. Prior to the move, the bookworms could eat the wood of the boxes in addition to the books, so when the boxes were taken

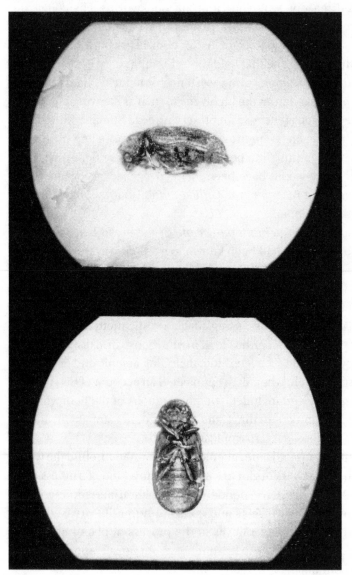

Mug shots of bookworm. From Iiams's essay "The Preservation of Rare Books and Manuscripts in the Huntington Library," *Library Quarterly*, October 1932. Reprinted by permission of *Library Quarterly* / Huntington Library and Gardens.

away, the little insects focused their rather voracious appetites on the books alone. Closer to home, the United States Bureau of Entomology responded to Iiams's query by admitting it had "never made a thorough study of insects affecting books." It had, however, fumigated libraries with hydrocyanic acid gas, but mainly to destroy "such external feeding pests as cockroaches and silverfish and such nuisances as bedbugs."[5]

Iiams grew up in Pasadena, just down the road from San Marino, and if he ever went to the Pasadena Public Library as a young man, he would have regularly used fumigated books. Amazingly, librarians considered the use of toxic fumigants to be consistent with a desire for "purified" air, probably because they were less concerned by air filled with toxins than the spread of contagious disease. As one epidemic after another swept through increasingly densely populated urban areas in the early twentieth century, public health officials newly empowered by a broader acceptance of germ theory sent notices to libraries when outbreaks occurred. These edicts forced libraries to close in some cases, to fumigate books in others, or even to burn books loaned to borrowers infected with yellow fever, spinal meningitis, scarlet fever, or bubonic plague. In 1908, Pasadena librarians took the precaution of fumigating "about 1200 of the most used books including any *suspects*."[6] Several years later, they would begin fumigating all of the library's books as a matter of course.

## Infected Books

From the beginnings of the public library system, the public and open nature of bookstacks provoked fear and the desire to purify the library's aisles and reading rooms, to exclude both disease and social undesirables. In 1883, the same year as Carnegie's first library construction grant, Charles Ammi Cutter, librarian of the Boston Athanaeum, opened the proceedings of the nascent American Library Association with an address called "The Buffalo Public Library in 1983." In his futuristic vision, he first enters the delivery room: "There was nothing remarkable about it save the purity of the air. I remarked this to a friend, and he said that it was so in all parts of the building; ventilation was their hobby; nothing made the librarian come nearer scolding than impurity in the air."[7] According to Cutter, these futuristic librarians vigilantly monitor the temperature and atmosphere in all the rooms: "Every one must be admitted into the delivery-room, but from the reading-rooms the great unwashed are shut out altogether or put in rooms by themselves. Luckily public opinion sustains us thoroughly in their exclusion or seclusion."[8]

The "great unwashed" were those poor and ill-clad individuals who did not conform to emergent standards of bodily hygiene. But cleanliness and purity and hygiene were terms that had deep biological connotations as well; they referred to a clean surface of the body as well as purity of character inside the body, at a time when many people believed vice and crime and immoral propensities to be inherited traits.[9] The social hygiene movement attempted to stem the spread of disease, prostitution, and other social problems, with many of its proponents also being eugenicists. Prior to Andrew Carnegie's funding a network of public libraries throughout the United States, most libraries were private and supported by subscriptions.[10] Cutter's dream of a purified library of the future, a "public" library characterized by exclusion, or seclusion, reveals a central difficulty of creating a truly democratic public space in an era where social Darwinism and eugenics shaped "public opinion." Up until the late nineteenth century, most libraries shunned lighting by natural gas because it was a fire hazard, not to mention bringing the risk of carbon monoxide poisoning. They "preferred daylight and thus closed their doors by dark," until the arrival of electricity. Light bulbs allowed libraries to stay open later, which brought in more working people,[11] some of whom would have certainly constituted Cutter's "great unwashed."

Reading and touching library books brought one into contact with the bodies, germs, and contagions of others. Books, like smallpox blankets, could be infected, and like people with contagious diseases, infected books were fumigated, treated, quarantined, and in some cases destroyed. One researcher experimentally infected books with scarlet fever and found that the dreadful germs could survive for eighteen days even in "lightly infected books." Public health officials compelled librarians, by law, to literally sterilize books during epidemics by closing libraries and fumigating the stacks with poison gas. The cover of the February 1915 monthly bulletin of the Los Angeles Public Library, *Library Books*, informed readers of borrowing policies on its front page, concluding with a sentence clearly intended to comfort visitors and allay fears: "The library receives notice of all cases of contagious disease. No book may be drawn or returned by anyone living in a house where there is a contagious disease until the house and the book have been fumigated."

In Portland, Oregon, after a spinal meningitis outbreak in April 1907, the library closed for two days for the fumigation of 7,500 volumes, and any books that had been loaned out were fumigated immediately upon their return by borrowers. At the public library of Toledo, Ohio, books in homes with smallpox, diphtheria, and scarlet fever were not to be returned, and if they were returned, they were destroyed. The Free Library of Saranac Lake, New York, had "travelling libraries" of twenty-five or more books each "loaned to boarding houses for sick people in the vicinity. The books in these collections," detailed a 1908 article in *Library Journal*, "are withdrawn permanently from general circulation and are never returned to the shelves of the library. Each time they are sent out they are carefully cleaned and fumigated."[12]

Books and magazines sent through the mail were also suspect. In an 1895 letter to the editor in the *British Medical Journal*, a public health officer named Charles Porter told of the case of an illustrated newspaper sent from Denver, Colorado, to a family in Stockport, England, which seemed to have infected their four-year-old child with spinal meningitis.[13] Upon reflection, Porter thought that valuable books didn't have to be destroyed, but could be kept for use "in the isolation hospital only," quarantined along with humans. Less valuable ones could be burned.

But neither the fumigation of individual books nor the toxic purification of a library's air had ever been demonstrated to kill bookworms as effectively as they sterilized books of typhus and other plagues. So, even if Iiams was familiar with fumigation techniques in libraries, they wouldn't have solved his growing bookworm problem. Ultimately for Iiams, preserving his books would require more than just the use of poison gas. He needed a technological solution that would infuse the poison deeply into the books to eradicate even bookworm eggs and larvae. Iiams's search for answers about bookworms was turning up one frustrating response after another. Scientists at the NBS were in only the preliminary stages of the first systematic scientific studies on the causes of deterioration in books, which at that point did not include specific experiments with bookworms. Thus, they could only feebly offer Iiams a list of references on the "insect enemies of books."[14]

In the absence of official recommendations, Iiams carried out experiments of his own. He wondered whether he could use a vacuum fumigation tank, previously employed by the California Department of Agriculture to fumigate plants, to force the poison gas to penetrate every square inch of infested books. He bought a tank manufactured by the Union Tank and Pipe Company of Los Angeles, which had previously manufactured a "California Floral Bulb Sterilizer" in the 1920s.[15]

Iiams was not an outlier among his peers. If anything, his efforts to obliterate life from the pages of books were perfectly in line with the practices of the developing data complex. As will become clear over the course of the pages that follow, the practice of data preservation is itself inherently

**Original caption: "Literary Treasures Saved by Book-worm Exterminator."
January 6, 1933. Reprinted by permission of Bettmann via Getty Images.**

toxic. The sterilization of data and the industrial technology solutions necessary for preservation were antithetical to life, if not outright poisonous. In Iiams's case, he was simply applying "an old method to a new problem" when he wheeled a truck of books into a gas chamber for the first time.[16]

## Gassing Paper and People

While the gas chamber was not an immediately obvious solution to Iiams when he first declared war on bookworms, the fact that he settled on it is not surprising in light of the wide use of both poison gas and gas chambers around that time. In 1924, even as the United States condemned Germany's use of poison gas as a war weapon, the State of Nevada carried out the first gas chamber execution, and other states soon followed. California's gas chamber would claim its first victims in 1938—two men who had killed the warden of Folsom State Prison in a failed escape attempt.[17] Sensational stories about poison gas appeared in newspapers regularly around this time, covering topics ranging from big cities using gas chambers to destroy stray dogs, to a desperately sad man sealing his doors and windows with tape, then dropping cyanide tablets in a bucket of acid to kill himself and his paraplegic wife.[18]

Still, Iiams needed to find "the ideal fumigant," one strong enough to kill the beetle, larvae, and eggs.[19] He experimented first with the popular pesticide hydrogen cyanide, also known as hydrocyanic acid gas, and later by its international brand name, Zyklon B. Americans widely applied this poison and others to exterminate perceived threats to the health or safety of the nation. U.S. Public Health Service (USPHS) officers fumigated dormitories at a yellow fever quarantine station in New Orleans, the outgoing mail of prisoners at a leprosy colony in Hawaii, and fruits and vegetables and plants arriving from foreign countries.

As public health concerns persistently blurred into eugenic anxieties and racism, Americans began fumigating people. Government officials fumigated the clothing of Mexican migrant workers in El Paso, Texas, at the headquarters of the Border Patrol, newly formed in 1924, the same year the Immigration Act restricted immigration from southern and eastern Europe, and Asia.[20] From August 1929 to February 1930, USPHS officers at Angel Island—the San Francisco Quarantine Station—carried out experiments, putting cockroaches in a 500-cubic-foot room and gassing them. Angel Island processed many Asian immigrants from 1910 to 1940, held them, and interrogated them in the same facility as this gas chamber for cockroaches.[21] When Nazi scientist Gerhard Peters argued for the use of gas chambers, or *disinfektionskammern*, in an influential article published in a

German pest science journal, he illustrated his text with photographs from the delousing station at El Paso. He would go on to become the managing director of DEGESCH, the company that supplied Zyklon B to death camps across Europe for genocidal atrocities that the Nazis referred to variously as "delousing the nation" or "disinfection" or "self-preservation."[22]

Though hydrogen cyanide was regularly applied to the clothes and skins of people, Iiams thought it was too dangerous to use on his precious books: it left a toxic residue on the pages that might poison librarians and readers in the future. After trying a couple of other poison gasses, and with the help of scientists at the California Institute of Technology, Iiams settled on a mixture of ethylene oxide and carbon dioxide that came to be known on the fumigant market as "carboxide." He went on to treat not only the infested volumes but all of the rare books in the Huntington's collection, all "foreign" books that entered its collections, and some of the Pope's bookworm-ravaged stacks in the Vatican.[23]

Iiams's innovative method soon attracted national attention. On January 1, 1933, a photo of the librarian landed on the pages of the *New York Times*. The headline "Lethal Gas Chamber for Book Worms" runs above an image of Iiams standing before a fumigation tank, a book held open in one hand as he examines it through a magnifying glass held in the other, a nearby truck of priceless books already loaded in the tank, their spines sparkling faintly as they await sterilization. There is no article accompanying the photo, only a short caption that credits Iiams with devising "this Gas Chamber in Which All Volumes Are Submitted Periodically to a De-Worming Process."

The photo was consistent with a broader public relations campaign by chemical companies to make the gas chamber appeal to the masses, and to convince more and more state legislatures to adopt the gas chamber as a capital punishment technology.[24] Proponents argued that the gas chamber was a humane and painless solution compared to the prevailing methods of hanging, the electric chair, and firing squads. In the view of many of its supporters, the gas chamber was not primarily a tool for punishment, but a vehicle for righteous pity and societal uplift. It ridded society of the unfit and mercifully put genetically inferior people out of their misery, since they were inherently unable to compete and thrive in modern society, and were thus destined for lives of crime, insanity, disability, and/or poverty.[25]

Under the sway of the eugenics movement and its principles of white racial purification—euphemistically known as "better breeding"—this rationale for capital punishment was popular among American elites, though not universal. One of the most prominent figures to resist this rash of support for capital punishment was Huntington Library board member

Paul Popenoe, who favored forced sterilization as the most humane means of ridding society of people who are "utterly unfit to hold their own in the world, in competition with normal people."[26] Popenoe was also the coauthor of *Applied Eugenics*, the most widely used textbook on the subject, as well as a board member of both the American Eugenics Society and the Pasadena-based Human Betterment Foundation, the most influential advocacy group for forced sterilization in the United States.[27]

Iiams's application of the gas chamber for book and document preservation spread much faster than the capital punishment technology. It addressed an increasingly widespread concern for the survival of data on paper. Iiams and his correspondents were among a small but exceptionally energetic group of preservationists, little known in their time and completely forgotten today, working at the cutting edge of a revolution in modern media and a broad transformation of business and government in America. Since 1870, the expansion of railway and telegraph networks allowed for larger "business units," as managers could travel long distances to far-flung sites of a business operation. This "new speed" of business "removed management from its old intimate acquaintance with details and increased the reliance upon records."[28]

Also, the prolonged economic depression of the 1870s, with its decreased demand for industrial products, led some factory owners to turn their focus from technology to organization, kick-starting the beginnings of the scientific management movement in American industry.[29] These new management methods, which would come to characterize corporate management within a few decades, required increased amounts of paper records. These records provided the benefit of leaving "a permanent trail" of orders, of costs of materials, time, and wages, in order to combat the "wasteful delay" in manufacturing caused by records being "too often kept by memory."[30] In this same decade, corporate lawyers succeeded in establishing the legal personhood of corporations.[31] The survival of the "corporate person" relied upon the survival of data on paper, but the paper comprising the bodies of these fictional yet powerful persons was brittle, ephemeral, its durability unknown.

The new reliance on masses of records changed the nature of modern memory and laid the foundation for the development of our data complex. National memory in modern nations, as Pierre Nora explains, is social and collective and is not only, or not even primarily, housed in brain tissue, but in the great repositories of paper records created by the state, corporations, and other institutions. Nora writes that "modern memory is, above all, archival." No longer located simply in the minds, communal stories, "gestures and habits," and "skills passed down by unspoken traditions," modern memory is "the gigantic and breathtaking storehouse of a material stock of what it would be impossible for us to remember, an unlimited repertoire of what might need to be recalled." We house this memory in "an autonomous institution of museums, libraries, depositories, centers of documentation, and data banks."[32] Written texts are not just aids to remembering; they are literally a part of our memory, the deep warehouse of information that we, as a society, would never be able to store entirely in our brains.

The operation of the U.S. government also required exponentially more records as the nation-state expanded. This situation was both ameliorated and exacerbated by the advent of information processing machines like Herman Hollerith's punched-card systems, first used for the census of 1890 and later adopted by banks, department stores, and many other corporations for accounting purposes. Hollerith went on to found the Tabulating Machine Company in 1896, later conjoined with a few other corporations to form International Business Machines, now best known by its acronym IBM. One contemporary scholar, Lars Heide, goes as far as describing the period between 1880 and 1945 as an "early information explosion," challenging the notion that the massive increase in both information and the importance of that information for the function of society occurred only recently in the digital age.[33]

### A Surgeon in the Library

Public health pioneer and polymath John Shaw Billings, whose name is little known today, played a decisive role in laying the groundwork for the data complex. His interests, experiences, and achievements foreshadowed a few of its key features: the proliferation and ordering of information, an emphasis on hygiene and sterilization, and an abiding, haunted awareness of human mortality. It was Billings who first suggested to Hollerith the idea of using punch cards to tabulate census results. As early as 1880, he imagined that statistical data relevant to both the living and the dead "might be recorded on a single card or slip by punching small holes in it, and that these cards might then be assorted and counted by mechanical means according to any selected group of these perforations."[34] Billings's idea prefigured the expansive data bodies that would accompany Americans through life by the mid-twentieth century, once the data complex was in full swing.

Billings had attended college at the age of fourteen and had finished medical school and entered the U.S. Army Medical Corps as a surgeon by age twenty-two, just in time to serve in the Civil War. From Gettysburg, he wrote a letter one evening to his new wife, describing himself as "covered with blood" and "tired out almost completely." The letter wasn't what one could call romantic, but it vividly reveals the intensity of his experiences in battlefield medical tents prior to physicians' knowledge of germs, antiseptics, or any kind of scientifically informed hygiene. It was a time when amputation was the best-known remedy for the kinds of misshapen wounds blasted into bodies by .69-caliber musket balls. Wishing he could sleep for sixteen hours, Billings told his wife that he had been "operating all day long," and had "got[ten] the chief part of the butchering done in a satisfactory manner."[35]

After the war ended, he was assigned to organize the medical records of the Union army, thus kicking off a lengthy career of innovation in the field that would later be called library science, not to mention the broader realms of information technology. As a leader of the short-lived National Board of Health, Billings traveled to Europe in 1881 to learn about "the most recent and best specimens of hospital construction, and also of museum and library buildings," and "to make special inquiry into the methods of obtaining and compiling vital statistics in England, Belgium, France, Germany, Switzerland, Austria, Holland, and Italy."[36] At the same time, he continued to write as an authority on hospital and library design and construction, publishing a series of "Letters to a Young Architect" in journals like *Plumber* and *Sanitary Engineer*, which would later be compiled into his book on *The Principles of Ventilation and Heating* (1884).[37]

Billings had no formal training in mathematics, but he was nonetheless so brilliant in the subject that he was hired as the head of the Vital Statistics Division for the U.S. Census in both 1880 and 1890. He also built the National Library of Medicine and invented an indexing system customized for medical periodicals. He served as a counselor of the American Library Association in its early years, and in 1883 he gave a speech at the same conference where Cutter offered his futuristic visions of an ultrahygienic public library. Billings's talk was called "Libraries in Washington," and in it he displayed a comprehensive knowledge of all national libraries' holdings, from the War Department to the National Observatory, from the Treasury Department to the Geological Survey, not to mention the library of the Surgeon General's Office, of which he was head librarian.[38] From the early 1870s, when Billings wrote two influential reports to the surgeon general—"Barracks and Hospitals" (1870) and "The Hygiene of the United States Army" (1875)—to the early 1890s, Billings "was regarded as the authority on public hygiene in the United States."[39] In 1895, Billings accepted a prestigious position as professor of hygiene at the University of Pennsylvania, but he resigned the following year in order to become the first director of the New York Public Library.[40]

Billings played a key role in the formation of the public library system in the United States. He had helped incorporate the Carnegie Corporation, the philanthropic organization endowed by Andrew Carnegie's massive steel fortune, and served as chairman of the board for a decade. It was Billings who convinced Andrew Carnegie to bring together the sixty-five free circulating libraries in New York City with the New York Public Library, and later to give millions of dollars to fund the construction of the public library system as we know it—the tycoon's construction grants paid for 1,689 libraries in the United States between 1883 and 1929.[41] In 1928, an endowment from the Carnegie Corporation of New York established the Graduate Library School at the University of Chicago. By 1931, the school's faculty had launched a professional journal, *Library Quarterly*,[42] which would go on to publish some of the most important articles in preservation science. The blend of articles related to records preservation, archival maintenance, database organization, and other concerns of librarians and records professionals.

Billings's professional interests and experiences embodied concerns that would animate the emergent data complex: public health and hygiene; the efficient, machine-assisted aggregation and ordering of information; a systematic approach to library design, classification, and indexing; a concern for the long-term material preservation of data; and scientific inquiry aimed at improving all these efforts. Like other figures who would soon shape the data complex, he had an intimate knowledge of human mortality. He had traveled to marine hospitals and quarantine stations across the country as he assessed their hygienic practices, facilities, and organizational structures. He had seen a multitude move toward, then pass through death's door on his operating table, and in the convalescent wards where he made his rounds. In one case at Gettysburg, a wounded officer asked Billings to check his pulse; he thought it was wavering and wondered whether that could be caused by a fever. Billings then felt the soldier's pulse, looked him in the eye, and "slowly answered, 'No, Mr. Abbot, there is no fever there. You are bleeding internally, You never will see to-morow's sunset.'" Billings then listened patiently to the dying man's response and asked whether "he had any messages to leave for his friends."

After the Civil War ended, Billings refused to ever speak or be questioned about his experiences at Gettysburg, Chancellorsville, Cold Harbor, the Wilderness of Spotsylvania, and other battles he had survived. But written accounts by others noted "his kindly face," his "tenderness he brought to a difficult service," and his deep familiarity with the fleetingness of life. One of Billings's early colleagues described him as "a highly gifted young life consciously drifting deathward."[43]

### The Problem of Perishable Paper

By the early twentieth century, the daily function of state, corporate, and historical institutions increasingly relied on masses of paper records whose durability and longevity were unknown.[44] While cheap paper had become "an absolute necessity," it was "not a quality product," and while the market for it constantly expanded, "this market [did] not include the printing of records designed for the use of future generations."[45] By the late 1920s, concern about the problem of wood pulp paper had spread among librarians, who were themselves dramatically increasing in numbers as more and more graduated from the Carnegie-funded library school at the University of Chicago. A number of concerned organizations formed committees to address the problem of wood pulp paper deterioration, including the League of Nations and the Technical Association of the Pulp and Paper Industry. In the 1930s, the expansion of federal bureaucracy through programs like the Social Security Act under the New Deal created even more state records. At the same time, new regulatory policies imposed on business required corporations to preserve certain records permanently, even before the NBS studies effectively established an authoritative meaning of "permanent."[46]

If we were going to date the emergence of the data complex, we would put it in the late 1920s, as Thomas Iiams confronted an infestation of bookworms, just prior to "definite facts" about paper deterioration being established by the NBS studies. Previous efforts to research the wood pulp problem had produced very mixed results and no conclusions. Various research projects were carried out by the Rag Content Paper Manufacturers, as well as "national government laboratories, and, separately, by a number of paper concerns." The American Library Association had also taken an "active interest" in the topic, and several newspaper publishers had begun printing "permanent" editions for storage in libraries.[47]

But such small-scale studies scattered across a few disparate groups could not solve the problem of perishable paper. More than any other single person, John Shaw Billings's protégé Harry Miller Lydenberg was the impetus for the NBS studies. While serving as head reference librarian at the New York Public Library, Lydenberg used his connections at the Carnegie Corporation to convince the foundation to fund studies of paper: why some papers deteriorate quickly, why others last, and how best to preserve them. Lydenberg had seen how, every night, under the globe chandeliers of the periodical reading room, librarians swept up sepia-toned chips of paper that littered the floor—sometimes sweeping up to four times per day to keep up with the fallout. Every day, hundreds of people passed through that room to read news both new and old, to stay current with rapid changes to life during the Roaring Twenties, to revisit the decisive battles of the Civil War as told by *Harper's Bazaar*, or to travel further back in time to the days when Indian and African slaves were still sold at a market on Wall Street.[48] As the librarians swept and returned bound editions of *McClure's Magazine* and the *New Amsterdam News* to the metal shelves, they began to notice that the brittle fragments of newsprint had broken off from the fringed edges not of the oldest papers but of the more recent ones.

Lydenberg came from humble circumstances but would go on to become one of the most influential librarians and book preservers in the country, eventually serving as the president of the American Library Association and the director of the New York Public Library. Growing up in Dayton, Ohio, his "boyhood gang had fights with the gang to which Orville and Wilbur Wright belonged." When Lydenberg was five years old, his father died from the effects of an old Civil War wound, "a tragedy that imposed upon [him] a need to work hard and live sparingly that remained with him always." He took on jobs "to help his mother maintain the family in genteel poverty," jobs that "introduced him to the world of books and printing." He delivered newspapers in the early morning darkness, which he would speak of "with pleasure" even "forty years later," and then worked as a page at the Dayton Public Library during his high school years.[49]

In many ways, Lydenberg was groomed for greatness, with direct work experience and mentorship from some of the leading lights of the field. In 1896, he graduated from Harvard after only three years of study, with highest honors in history and government, magna cum laude, Phi Beta Kappa, and all of this achievement "in spite of working long hours" in the library.[50] According to Keyes Metcalf, Lydenberg was "slender, rather short, and wiry and energetic physically, [and] he always climbed stairs two or three at a time."[51] Ralph Shaw, ALA president from 1956 to 1967, put Lydenberg in the top three practitioners of the library profession. Metcalf went all the way in his assessment: "In his sixty years of active library service from 1890 to 1950, [Lydenberg] was, all things considered, our greatest librarian."[52] Over a decade before jump-starting the NBS studies, Lydenberg had himself "made over twenty studies of methods of preserving paper stock that was deteriorating in a frightening manner." With John Archer, superintendent of the NYPL's Printing Office, Lydenberg "devised a laboratory for experimentation in preserving paper, especially newsprint, and books."[53]

One fateful day in 1927, an instructor from NYU named Robert Binkley brought his students to the New York Public Library to do research on the Spanish Armada. Because of their heavy use of the Public Records Office's documents "for the 1588 period," many items were "rapidly torn to shreds and tatters," and so a librarian brought it to the attention of Lydenberg. When Lydenberg then reached out to Binkley to discuss the issue of balancing the needs of present scholars with those of future historians, the men became fast friends. Like Lydenberg, Binkley was tireless. Lydenberg later recalled how one of their colleagues "completely described and summed up" Binkley and his exceptional enthusiasm: "One of his fellow workers said as we heard a door open and a brisk step charge down the hall, 'Here comes Binkley, all five of him.'"[54] After Binkley's untimely death in 1940, at the age of forty-two, Lydenberg wrote a memorial statement remembering their first meeting, wherein he immediately noticed Binkley's "zeal, appreciation of the other man's point of view, willingness to adjust himself to conditions, and at the same time confidence in his cause and insistence on its rightness."[55]

The data complex grew out the actions of individuals like Lydenberg and Binkley who shaped the institutions they served and led. These institutions themselves then reflected the ambitions, anxieties, and obsessions of those men, and became a means of passing on the data complex to subsequent generations. Both Lydenberg and Binkley thought that while the urgency of "the problem of perishable paper" had been up to that point articulated by librarians, the solution for the problem would come from chemistry. The topic received extensive treatment at the First World Library and Bibliographic Congress in Rome in June 1929, and Robert Binkley gave an address there wherein he proclaimed, "The records of our time are written in dust."[56] He also rightly asserted, "We do not know the chemistry of the decomposition of cellulose," and he described a study by the Royal Society of the Arts in 1898 that concluded that the quality of the rag fibers in the paper were the key determinant in the paper's longevity. The society printed a book called *Cellulose* on paper made according to their newly established standards. However, only thirty years later, according to Binkley, "the paper in this book showed early signs of rapid deterioration, probably because it was not free from acid and bleach residue."[57]

The data complex grew out of larger forces, such as the development of the railroad, but these key individuals, whose outlook was shaped by those larger events, in turn spurred major institutions into action to establish the new knowledge, practices, technologies, and cultural values that would become central in the data complex. The coming together of men like Billings, Lydenberg, Binkley, and Kimberly densely coalesced a set of personal convictions and professional values that would be institutionalized through their positions of authority and influence to form the early, sometimes invisible, increasingly pervasive structure of the data complex. These were men whose memories were thick with experience and expertise, men marked by the wars and epidemics of their time, by their culture's irretrievable losses and triumphs.

Similar to Billings, Robert Binkley is a paradigmatic example of an individual transformed by larger forces who then, in turn, reshaped those forces and the institutions that impelled them. While serving in an army ambulance unit in World War I, Binkley was wounded and "cited for distinguished and exceptional gallantry." During his time as a soldier, he had seen firsthand the wholesale and instantaneous destruction wrought by industrialized conflict. Immediately after the war he gathered documents, pamphlets, and propaganda from all over Europe as he assisted in the formation of the Hoover War Library, thereby becoming "acutely aware of the rapidity with which the sources for contemporary history are lost by destruction, dispersal, and decay, and of the urgent need for new techniques and a conscious and coördinated strategy on the part of librarians, archivists, and scholars."[58]

The energy Binkley applied to his task rivalled that of Lydenberg, making them a formidable pair in propagating the incipient features of the data complex. Prompted by the agitation of Lydenberg, the American Library Association and the National Association of Book Publishers successfully requested that the NBS carry out a study to assist in "the establishment of standards" for various papers "from the viewpoint of their use as records." So it was Lydenberg's initiative that launched the NBS studies on paper, and he would continue to contribute as the research developed, eventually serving as "chairman of an advisory committee for the bureau's research in the preservation of cellulose acetate film."[59] Just as Binkley proclaimed in his address in Rome, it would be chemists at the NBS, led by Arthur Kimberly, who would finally settle the question of paper's permanence. Kimberly's pursuit of knowledge about how to preserve paper would surpass all previous efforts in his drive for pure, hygienic, permanent data.

### Arthur Kimberly's Dream of Hygienic Data

Thomas Iiams had corresponded with Arthur Kimberly in the time leading up to the NBS studies, but the chemist could offer little help to the librarian then. Once the studies began, Kimberly did not initially focus on insects like bookworms because they actually weren't, in spite of Iiams's claims, the most serious threat to books and manuscripts. The supreme threat was human-made. By 1932, NBS researchers established that air pollution was the most serious threat to books. With the expansion of U.S. industry after the Civil War and a concomitant explosion of urbanization, the burning of fossil fuels for manufacturing, transportation, lighting, and heating in densely populated urban areas created unprecedented amounts of air pollution that hastened the deterioration of paper records. Industrialization was literally and figuratively an engine of the early data complex. It required massive amounts of paper records, but also churned out the sulfuric pollution that threatened to destroy those records.[60]

Big industrial cities like New York and Pittsburgh were among the first to see the effects of air pollution and dust on paper records. The first library built by Carnegie in the United States was in Braddock, Pennsylvania, nine miles north of Pittsburgh, and also the site of one of Carnegie's steel mills. Carnegie Steel actually owned the library and delivered the large amounts of coal necessary to heat its cavernous spaces, which included a gymnasium, a music hall, and swimming pool.[61] According to Kimberly and Scribner, it was the sulfur in the polluted air that broke down the wood pulp newspapers in the New York Public Library's collections. When sulfur dioxide combines with humidity and makes contact with book paper, it can become sulfuric acid, "literally burning the paper."[62]

Kimberly and Scribner insisted that this was a "new problem for librarians to face," and that "the preceding generation did not consider these things," evident in the fact that they printed "important records" on "impermanent paper."[63] The authors claimed that the 1930s were an exceptional period in the history of records preservation. The advent of modern wood pulp paper, which replaced the mostly handmade, relatively acid-free rag paper that preceded it, resulted in masses of paper records that were highly perishable.[64] Cheaper paper allowed for rapid dissemination of information, but it also "introduced, largely through the improper selection of papers, the problems of preservation of important records on impermanent papers, and the suitable choice of papers for permanent records." While librarians and archivists made efforts to preserve highly perishable wood pulp papers throughout the nineteenth century, all of these efforts ended "without very definite accomplishments."[65] The NBS studies sought to establish "definite data" about each factor that caused the deterioration of records.

Though the scientists carried out several studies related to air pollution, they noted that sulfur dioxide was only one of several "external agents

**Papers in a binder to be placed in a gas chamber.**
**From Jarrell, Hankins, and Veitch.,** *Deterioration of Paper*.

of paper deterioration."[66] The "organic constituents of books," such as "paper, cloth, thread, adhesives, and leather," were "susceptible to decay from chemical changes brought about by deteriorative components of the books themselves," or by "exterior influences" such as sunlight, humidity, heat, and temperature fluctuations.[67] But to overcome the effects of time and decay, the NBS would have to do more than just measure the damage already done to books and manuscripts. In order to figure out which kinds of paper could be effectively preserved, even permanently preserved, the scientists would have to measure the accumulated effects of these threats on books over the course of decades, or even centuries.

Scientists at the NBS had two options: invent a time machine and travel fifty years into the future to measure the deterioration of various types of paper, or simulate the passage of time. They chose the latter. NBS researchers thus had to fabricate an essential fantasy that supports the data complex: that one can *scientifically* simulate the passage of time. They used what they called "accelerated aging methods"—folding, heating, gassing, and scratching paper and film—to make claims about how long certain types would last under specific conditions. They measured the permanence of the various material components of paper: the inks; the acid content levels; the fibers, whether made of straw, wood pulp, or rags; the glues that held together the bookbindings.

In order to determine which papers were the most durable, Kimberly and his colleagues devised their own gas chamber experiments. For a duration of 240 hours, they placed fourteen samples of various commercial book and writing papers in a gas chamber filled with sulfur dioxide.[68] This study showed that some low-quality papers "suffered less from exposure to this gas than did high-grade papers," so an improvement in paper quality alone, while important, would not be sufficient to prevent the future deterioration of paper records. The scientists concluded that eliminating acid pollution in libraries through "the modification of library ventilating systems" was necessary to properly care for paper records. In their view, libraries now needed air-conditioning systems that washed the air in an alkaline bath to remove its acidity.[69]

Accelerated aging techniques create confidence and uncertainty in equal measure. On the one hand, we feel assured that we can preserve paper records permanently. On the other hand, we always know, in the back of our minds, that the permanence of those artifacts was established through a simulation, and that even though certain papers or films may be classified as "permanent," they require intensive care, specific temperatures and humidity levels, not to mention purified air with minimal acidity. All of the NBS's recommended environmental manipulations relied on a vast electrical infrastructure fueled by coal or hydropower, energy sources that themselves require stunning feats of engineering, constant maintenance, and political and social domination of populations living in areas from which natural resources are drawn. In short, our beloved permanence has been, from the beginning, contingent on a great number of factors beyond the library, the misalignment or breakdown of any one of which can make the permanent preservation of any book virtually impossible.[70]

Another problem with NBS scientists' assertions about permanence is that their methods were not very scientific. There is actually no scientific basis for the accelerated aging method's quantification of time, by which seventy-two hours in an oven at 100 degrees Celsius is the equivalent of several years of time passing, or what NBS scientists refer to as "natural aging."[71] In the case of one somewhat comical technique for simulating deterioration, NBS scientists placed a piece of film in a bottle partially filled with sand, shook it, and assessed the level of haziness that developed on the film emulsion.[72] But the preservation studies met such a dire need for answers about how to preserve our corporate and public memory that definite scientific facts were established nonetheless. The power and authority of both the U.S. government and the Carnegie Corporation certified the NBS studies as a venue for fact making, and the scientists who published their findings cited one another enough times that the specious empirical basis of accelerated aging studies was either forgotten or ignored. Once enough professional journals and mass media publications cited the studies and circulated their findings as facts, they became facts in spite of the questionable method of accelerated aging, which went unquestioned in every case.[73] The NBS had succeeded in establishing its "definite data."[74]

During the early years of the NBS studies, Iiams had shared his new knowledge about book preservation by gas chamber with Arthur Kimberly, who incorporated Iiams's technique into the authoritative list of preservation specifications for all libraries in the United States.[75] Kimberly played a key role in taking the NBS specifications nationwide and through them fundamentally shaping the data complex. Many libraries, museums, and archives across the country would adopt the NBS's specifications, including air conditioning, the installation of fluorescent lighting, and the routine use of gas chambers for sterilizing books and other objects. In 1935, Kimberly became the first chief of the Division of Repair and Preservation at the newly formed National Archives, where he ensured that every object that entered the stacks and shelves of the repository was first saturated with poison in a gas chamber.[76] And while vacuum fumigation was the best method for treating "a large volume of materials," he also recommended the fumigation of library stacks and open air.[77] He wanted to neutralize every threat to books and records, from insects and fungi to the volatile chemical and material components of the books themselves. According to Kimberly, dust had to be removed constantly from spaces where records were stored. The "angular particles of siliceous materials" are so small they embed themselves between fibers in the paper, and when the paper is flexed, they "cut the fibers" and also act as "nuclei for the condensation of acidic moisture."[78]

For Kimberly, however, gassing books and purifying the archive's air wasn't enough—he recommended making the books themselves thoroughly toxic in order to permanently protect them from insect predators. When repairing and binding books, Kimberly suggested that only the "highest quality adhesives" should be used when creating permanent records. In response to a request from an archivist at Maryland's Hall of Records, Kimberly sent a recipe for adhesive paste used to repair documents with Japanese tissue, the ingredients being "4 heaping cups of flour, 1 level tablespoon of alum, 1 teaspoon of formaldehyde, 3 pints of water." Generally, Kimberly saw book repair as an opportunity to add preservative toxins to archival materials, arguing that all glues and paste should contain "small quantities of phenol, thymol, or some other fungicide to discourage mold growth."[79]

Gas chamber at the National Archives. Original caption: "National Archives. Washington, D.C., Nov. 22, 1939. After the documents are enclosed in the chamber, all air is drawn out and the gas turned on." Photo courtesy of Library of Congress.

Toxic chemicals like formaldehyde and phenol kill microbes and insects and thus make preservation possible, preventing decay in a wide range of organic materials, in everything from dead bodies to books. Phenol, formerly known as carbolic acid, is a biocidal chemical extracted from coal tar, and by the 1930s it was established as a powerful preservative with wide applications. First produced in 1834 by a German chemist named Friedlieb Ferdinand Runge, who noticed that it preserved wood and dead animals quite well, carbolic acid provided a much-sought-after means for preventing wood rot in railroad ties, which were then being laid at a blinding pace between major cities in Europe. French chemists dubbed it "phenól," and it was soon used to preserve specimens on histological slides. When combined with arsenic, it served as the first truly effective preservative for animal skins in the practice of taxidermy. In 1846, decades before formaldehyde would revolutionize arterial embalming, English chemist Frederick C. Calvert convinced the medical school in Manchester to try out a new preservative method and found that an "injection of diluted carbolic acid preserved cadavers for up to a month, allowing for more elaborate dissections."[80] While the use of toxins in the preservation of corpses provokes no objections from the dead, the antimicrobial power of preservatives was also deployed in the battle to preserve public health: the same toxins were introduced into the bodies and environs of living people. Calvert and his colleagues went on to create a powder meant to improve public health and combat outbreaks of cholera and the like. Composed of a combination of carbolic acid, magnesian limestone, and sulfur dioxide, "McDougall's Powder" was dumped into sewer pools to treat and deodorize them, even into the River Thames during the "Great Stink" of 1858. The professor who treated Glasgow's sewage with the powder "saw that toxic doses of carbolic acid were hazardous to wildlife, notably the river's trout."[81] Several years later, he would teach Joseph Lister about the possibilities of carbolic acid for antiseptic techniques in surgery, and the Listerine namesake would use it to sterilize wounds and bandages, surgical tools and operating-room walls. He even diffused steam of the sweet-smelling poison in the air during surgery.[82]

Kimberly resembled public health pioneers in the way he sought knowledge from across professional fields and was microscopically meticulous in his desire for purified, sterilized records stored in a thoroughly hygienic space. A few years ago, I visited the National Archives and dug through Kimberly's papers. I found letters soliciting information from preservationists, as well as manufacturers of air conditioners, fumigation tanks, hydraulic presses for laminating documents, burglar systems and fire alarms, and other equipment he needed to make the National Archives the highest exemplar of the data complex. Kimberly wrote letters to Lydenberg, requesting a bibliography on insects' effects on books, and more details on his experiments with laminating newspapers between layers of cellulose acetate. He wrote to his colleague B. W. Scribner, chief of the Paper Section at the NBS, who would go on to invent the first paper comprised entirely of glass fibers (used as a filter in gas masks). He wrote to the American Radiator Corporation about a system that could maintain the proper moisture level in his "humidifying chamber," a windowless room with a door built for a bank vault, where he would "repair and recondition documents."

Kimberly wrote to Union Carbide, Terminix, the U.S. Bureau of Mines, the Celluloid Corporation, and to the Mine Safety Appliance company. He wrote requisition requests for books cited by Thomas Iiams, like *Les ennemis insectes des livres*, and for a long list of publications from the Department of Agriculture and the NBS, ranging from "Hydro-cyanic Gas as a Fumigant for Destroying Household Insects" to an article on the "Papermaking Quality of Cornstalks." He wrote a letter thanking someone for information on the "chemical treatment of water used in air-conditioning systems." Kimberly reached out to experts and other experimenters in preservation, even wrote a note to Thomas Iiams requesting a reprint of his article "Notes on the Causes and Prevention of Foxing in Books," and another thanking him upon its receipt.[83]

As Kimberly tried to maintain the purity of the space for data storage, he was concerned not only with the construction and design of the archives but also with the conduct of archivists themselves. Within a few months of arriving at the National Archives, he shot a memo titled "Lunch on the Premises by Employees" over to the director of archival services. Worded with an anthropologist's detachment, as if describing some exotic tribe, Kimberly wrote that numerous employees had "made it a practice to bring lunch with them to be eaten on the premises," a practice he found to be "very undesirable." He recommended that "some steps be taken to eliminate this custom as soon as possible," stating, "The presence of refuse from lunches is bound to attract roaches and other vermin which are undesirable in an institution of this sort."[84]

## Kleenex and Chlorine

Kimberly was perhaps the most extreme case of someone whose training, family background, and professional positions condensed the various facets of the early data complex. Kimberly could trace his roots all the way back to the Puritan immigrant Thomas Kimberly, who first brought the surname from England to America, and whose descendants would play a part in all the major transformations that shaped the new country, from the rise of the railroad and westward expansion to industrialization and war.[85] By the mid-nineteenth century, the prosperous Kimberly clan had fanned out across the expanding map of the United States. There are at least five towns called Kimberly, named for members of the family, in Minnesota, Alabama, Nevada, and Wisconsin.

In addition to railroad surveyors, flour mill and drugstore owners, canal and river lock developers, Kimberly was also related to titans in the paper industry. In 1872, his father's third cousin John Alfred Kimberly cofounded Kimberly, Clark & Co., building his Globe Mill on the Fox River, as its level banks made construction "easy and cost-effective." The Fox River also made the perfect preelectric energy source, as its "course out of Lake Winnebago north to Green Bay provided the steady flow necessary to make paper with consistent quality and thickness," all of these helpful geological features the remnants of glacial movement and retreat over 10,000 years ago.[86] In its first year, the company was producing two tons of newsprint per day, made wholly from linen and cotton rags.

By the turn of the century, the company was wildly successful and had made the shift to wood pulp paper and newsprint, founding a company town named Kimberly in 1889, and another called Niagara in 1898. They built the Niagara mill on the Menominee River, "where huge stands of Wisconsin and Michigan pulpwood were within economical reach and the water power was in ample supply."[87] That year, daily production levels dwarfed those of the early days—the Niagara mill produced 50 tons of manila, with the groundwood pulp mill and sulfite mill in Kimberly generating an additional 100 tons.[88] The now broadly diversified enterprise bought up old flour mills and turned them into factories that churned out book paper, printing paper, bond paper, and even the innovative new product on the scene: toilet paper.[89]

But Kimberly-Clark also made vital materials for hygiene and war. In World War I, cotton shortages allowed the company to obtain large government contracts to produce Cellucotton, a creped cellulose product that served as surgical dressings and that nurses adapted into sanitary pads that were superior to the other options at the time. Germans' use of poison gas provoked the need for a gas mask more effective than anything that had been created up to that point. The best "media"—the term for the substance in gas mask filters that absorbs toxins—was made of paper manufactured in Germany, which the United States obviously could not access. Kimberly-Clark began experimenting with Cellucotton for use as a gas mask medium, hoping to quickly find a way to protect American and British troops from yellow-green clouds of German chlorine.

But before the company could move into gas mask media production, the war ended. The government sold its surplus of Cellucotton to civilian hospitals, and Kimberly-Clark also bought back a substantial amount. In the 1920s, in an effort to make use of the stuff, the company created numerous now-standard products in American hygiene—Kotex, Kleenex, and Huggies diapers, brands still owned by the company today.[90] While Kimberly-Clark's gas mask venture stalled, the family's legacy in American warfare was nevertheless strongly established in World War I: Arthur Kimberly's father, Lieutenant Colonel Harry Standish Kimberly, served in the army and helped found the Chemical Warfare Service in 1918.[91] Later, he served as assistant to Secretary of Commerce Herbert Hoover, and continued in that role when the latter was elected president. The Department of Commerce houses the NBS, where Kimberly's son Arthur would start his career in government service as a chemist.

To be fair, Kimberly was not just obsessed with data purification due to some inborn compulsion—his job at the National Archives burdened him with an avalanche of documents that were nothing short of disgusting. These were not the illuminated manuscripts and pampered folios that Thomas Iiams safeguarded at the Huntington, aggregated from the curated collections purchased by the library's namesake.[92] The federal records now in Kimberly's care had been stored anywhere and everywhere bureaucrats and clerks had found space for them. In 1936, President Roosevelt heard that the Confederate war records were crammed into an auto mechanic's garage.[93] The burgeoning U.S. National Archives had to deal with the largest amount of records of any institution in the world, and these records had been left to molder and rot in a constellation of decay that prefigured in obverse the dispersed repositories of preserved materials within the data complex. Before federal records surveys carried out in the 1930s, the government didn't even know where all of its records were stored![94] In D.C. alone, the survey found 3 million cubic feet of records located in more than 6,500 rooms, and 35 million feet of film. Outside D.C., another survey, carried out by the Works Progress Administration, found an additional 5 million feet of federal records. If you put all these records in archival boxes and laid them side by side, they would stretch for 1,000 miles—you could walk on top of them from Boston to Atlanta.

Kimberly wasn't just finding ways to prevent things from happening to records in the future; he was receiving records that were covered with dust "and infiltrated with grit, fungi, and vermin." Somehow, all these accessions had to be fumigated and cleaned "quickly and safely."[95] And after each batch of records Kimberly purified, there was always another waiting to roll in behind it, an endless procession of library trucks that must have looked, to him, like the rock of Sisyphus.

While waging war against this empire of dust and pests, Kimberly also had to oversee much more delicate work. Many records had been folded for decades and needed to be flattened. This task was actually easier with records from before 1840, as most inks up to that time were not water soluble, so the documents could be misted and flattened more quickly than more recent records. Still, the task was gargantuan—one Works Progress Administration project employed several hundred people and flattened 100 million documents.[96] Kimberly's army of archivists ironed and fumigated documents, dusted and cleaned them with blasts of compressed air, and carried out the work-intensive and expensive process of "silking" documents to repair them by applying "crepeline with an aqueous adhesive to piece out or fortify paper or parchment."[97] Kimberly oversaw the lamination of paper documents with cellulose acetate, using the material base of film to preserve paper records, a practice of not just protecting one data format with another but merging them in a way that will appear again later in the data complex.

### Archives without Archivists

The good thing is that at the time of this deluge-like proliferation of records in the mid-1930s, there were not yet *any* trained, professional archivists in the United States![98] In 1934, when the first U.S. archivist, Robert D. W. Connor, and Robert Binkley began pushing for university courses that offered formal training to archivists, the word "archivist" was still quite uncommon in American English.[99] A photo of Connor distributed by a news photographer is captioned, "He's U.S. Archivist" and, underneath that, "No, dear children, an archivist is not a radical. He is one who preserves historical documents."[100] Solon Buck, the second person to be appointed archivist of the United States, would eventually make some progress in creating training programs for young professionals in his field. He taught a course at Columbia University in the fall of 1938 and the spring of 1939.[101] On the heels of this, the Carnegie Corporation funded courses at American University such as "The History and Administration of Archives" and "The Role of Records in Public Administration."[102]

Another challenge for Kimberly and his colleagues was the lack of adequate funding, staff, and equipment that plagued the National Archives from the beginning. Before its bronze doors—the largest in the world—even opened to the public, the National Archives suffered from the "backlogging condition," where archivists have an overwhelming amount of incoming records, leaving them unable to sufficiently classify and organize them, to separate the valuable from the worthless, the obsolete, the duplicates and triplicates.[103] So, under immense pressure and without sufficient funding or staffing, in the earliest years of the data complex archival work processes were being invented on the fly.[104]

In a spirit of desperate ingenuity, then, the United States sought to quickly pull together a national archive and thereby catch up with most other modern, imperial nation-states. France had established the foundational model for a modern national archive in 1789, and England had followed soon after with its own Public Record Office in 1838. By 1900, "most European countries had developed similar institutions, including the outstanding Dutch and German archives, and in Latin America twelve national archives had been established."[105] The data complex emerged in the early twentieth century in part due to this imperial impulse to document the nationalist past. In his classic study *The Past Is a Foreign Country*, David Lowenthal notes that while "instances of preservation can be documented from time immemorial," the tendency to "retain a substantial portion of the past is signally a latter-day goal." It was only in the nineteenth century that "European powers closely identified themselves with their material heritage," and only in the twentieth century that "they launched major programmes to protect it."[106]

While a wealth of professional knowledge accumulated from these various international institutions, the first archivist of the United States, Robert D. W. Connor, "knew that the National Archives could not apply the highly systematized European practices and training programs to its work because American records were so highly diverse and recent in nature."[107] Instead of simply borrowing from the wisdom of the past, these pioneers of the data complex generated new ways of organizing, sterilizing, and distributing data. In doing so, they reshaped Americans' relationship to the materials held in archives and repositories, providing the foundation for the rise of the data body. That aspect of the American self would take on more and more weight over the course of the twentieth century and eventually threaten to entirely take on a life of its own in the twenty-first. Similar to ours today, Kimberly's outlook was shaped by a reality where powerful institutions were constantly creating new agencies, new records, new repositories and backups of data. In his day, Americans began to have data bodies that continued to grow and thicken with records all the time, even as they slept, like mushrooms in the moonlit dark. Like people in the early twenty-first century, Kimberly was learning how to live in a world drowning in data.

By 1936, the data complex had begun to increasingly formalize the duties of archivists and dispel public confusion about their profession. That year, a small group of passionate preservationists founded the Society of American Archivists.[108] Perhaps even more importantly, the first Social Security Administration office opened, and the National Archives was flooded with requests for records. Across the country, people aged sixty-five and over wanted to apply for their benefits. Though birth registration was nearly universal by the 1930s, the federal government would still have to deal with uneven documentation of citizens' vital statistics for decades afterward. In her book *The Known Citizen*, Sarah Igo points out that even as late as World War II, "the citizenship requirement for working in defense industries uncovered the fact that a full one-third of Americans of working age had no proof of birth." As a result, the agency "had no other option but to accept alternative forms of proof: Bibles, baptism or census records, military discharge forms, and sometimes affidavits of witnesses." Some African Americans' only pathway for proving their age and accessing Social Security benefits was to locate and present "the paperwork of enslavement: ownership records or court notices of sales."[109]

These early years of the data complex were driven by a relatively small group of people like Kimberly—professional librarians, archivists, chemists, paper manufacturers, soldiers working in laboratories or experimental stations, historians, and even capitalists seeking what we would now call a "data-driven" approach to accumulating wealth.[110] But as the data complex would expand and extend itself across the country, the fears and strategies of this small group of specialists and enthusiasts would increasingly afflict everyday Americans, and so would their hope and faith in technological solutions that promised to make paper and microfilm data permanent.

These institutional practices of data preservation would eventually travel throughout popular culture and the cycle of consumer products, especially with the rise of personal computing, and become common practices among individuals.[111] As everyday people reproduced those practices, they absorbed the beliefs reflected in them—namely, that saving more data could save the world, that new media were improvements on old media but it's good to keep old media around just in case. In the event that the nation's monuments were razed by riots or its factories destroyed by war, if fire consumed vital documents, then data properly preserved and duplicated was supposed to give people the ability to restore what had been lost. The data complex offered a promise of power—to control the uncontrollable and ward off the inevitable, to undo catastrophe, like an explosion captured on film but played in reverse: billowing smoke and fire and shrapnel sucked back into a building, scattered bricks pulled together again into an orderly façade, then the reconstituted bombshell swiftly rising through the sky to the yawning bomb bay doors, which close slowly as the bomber flies tail first back to the airfield.

Of course, large-scale bombing and destruction, while broadly feared, never ended up striking the United States, but the data complex took hold in the lives of everyday Americans nonetheless. By the turn of the twenty-first century, it would be normal to have a few obsolete laptops or towers, external hard drives for backups, bankers boxes of paper records in closets, online storage in the cloud, and untold terabytes of digital files generated about every single person in the country, stored on corporate and government servers in far-flung data centers. But in the 1930s, only the people who were obsessed, or were paid to be obsessed, with data preservation thought as much as we do now about our data bodies. As with many other beliefs and behaviors within the data complex, what was considered extreme in one moment of crisis became normal in the next.

Kimberly's dream of a perfectly pure environment for books and records would materialize in the invention of a new technology: permanent time capsules. Armed with the preservation science generated by the NBS studies, and in direct consultation with NBS chemists, two men would each create a time capsule that aimed to preserve paper and microfilm for more than 5,000 years. The inner sancta of both capsules were sealed off and suffused with inert gas, which rendered the growth of mold or fungus or the survival of insects impossible, and made Kimberly's dream come true. But these preservationists also expanded Kimberly's vision. They thus enlarged the nightmares that haunted the work of preservationists as they meditated on the economic turbulence of the times, the nationwide upheavals around immigration and race, the threats to the traditional structure of the American family, and the prospect of the first war fought primarily through aerial bombing, one that promised to be more destructive than any the world had ever seen.

### The Toxic Afterlife of Paper

In 2012, Kimberly-Clark closed its paper mill in Everett, Washington, just north of Seattle. The decades of paper bleaching runoff left behind dioxin sediments in the East Waterway measuring "15 times higher than what the state considers safe." Dioxin was the key ingredient in "Agent Orange," one herbicidal chemical weapon among many that U.S. planes sprayed over vast swaths of Vietnam to kill crops, force rural populations toward cities, and thus deprive the communist opposition of its base. Agent Orange famously caused birth defects both in the next generation of Vietnamese and in the children of the U.S. soldiers who were exposed to it. The level of dioxin near the plant is not likely to affect humans, but dioxin is bioaccumulative, and thus can collect in the fatty tissue of fish, which, when consumed by humans, carry the disruptive toxin into human endocrine systems.[112] The accumulation of wood pulp itself has also had fatal effects, as it has coated the bay's bottom, "smothered sea life and created a 'dead zone.'"[113] Kimberly-Clark took control of the mill when it acquired its chief global competitor, Scott Paper, in 1995. The merged company tried to make some improvements to lessen its negative environmental impacts, but nothing could reverse the damage done by five decades of manufacturing facial tissue, toilet paper, and paper towels that would themselves be used, then "thrown away," likely to end up in some other body of water.

The same year Kimberly-Clark bought Scott Paper, researchers at the Library of Congress published a report showing that books and documents fumigated in gas chambers retained a residue of carboxide, then released it slowly over time, thus posing a risk to "unsuspecting and unprepared curators and other personnel who routinely service the fumigated materials." The materials also posed a danger to researchers and readers, although to a lesser degree, due to their more occasional interaction with the documents. And so all of the documents and books collected over several decades by the Huntington Library, by the National Archives, and by many other institutions are toxic.[114] Chronic exposure to carboxide can increase the risk of leukemia, brain tumors, and other cancers; it can cause chromosome damage and may also affect the reproductive system. Preservation rendered our national memory carcinogenic.

# 2

## We the Dead

Probably the persons who open the Capsule will have a physical appearance very like our own, except that they should have learned the principle of breeding a better race. . . . They should be, and probably will be, a race of supermen and superwomen, as judged by our standards; but only common men and women as judged by their standards. . . . This will be a healthy world governed by wholesome people. The abnormal will have no place in it.

—A. W. Robertson, Chairman of the Board,
   Westinghouse Electric and Manufacturing
   Company, 1939

I walk along the southern banks of the Allegheny River, through Pittsburgh's Strip District, passing brick buildings once owned by Heinz, Westinghouse, and U.S. Steel. The archives of Westinghouse Electric, as well as a replica of the Time Capsule, reside in a former warehouse, now known as the Heinz History Center. Named for an heir to the canned food and condiment juggernaut, the building bears a forty-foot-tall neon sign of a ketchup bottle, perpetually pouring out a stream of red light. I marvel for a moment at the sign, then enter and pay the admission fee. On my way to the Time Capsule exhibit, however, a wall display titled "Frozen in Time—the Story of Our Building" catches my attention. Apparently, this structure that now stores historical archives was originally built to store ice.

In the late nineteenth century, the Chautauqua Lake Ice Company cut chunks from the lake's frozen surface and loaded them onto a train bound for Pittsburgh, where four railcars at a time could pull into the company's warehouse and unload their giant blocks. The ice would then be broken down and delivered by horse-drawn wagon throughout the city. In 1893, the company's first warehouse burned down, and in 1898, the second one met the same fate when 2,000 barrels of whiskey ignited and caused a horrific explosion on an upper floor, killing five, including a man struck by falling telegraph and telephone lines and electric lights at a nearby street corner.[1] As I snap pictures of the display, I wonder whether the archives upstairs hold photos of the fires or clippings from a Gilded Age newspaper, the front page bearing a sketch of the strange sight—flames burning through a summer's worth of ice.

This warehouse, built just after the 1898 fire, is lucky number three, and it is now a climate-controlled records storage facility and conservation center preserving data in a space that previously stored ice used to preserve, well, everything else. Ice blocks inside the first refrigerators, known as iceboxes, preserved food in homes as well as perishable goods that traveled great distances by rail from farms to urban centers. By the 1920s, trucks with combustion engines replaced the iceman's horse-drawn wagon, and electrical refrigerators built by companies like Westinghouse dethroned natural ice. In 1952, the Chautauqua Lake Ice Company closed, and the warehouse then changed hands a few times, becoming storage space for a lumber concern, a seed company, and others. In the 1990s, the data complex repurposed it, as it did so many structures of brick and thick beams of timber from America's now mostly long-gone old-growth forests. The spaces that once chilled ice from lakes across western New York, now kept at the slightly higher temperature of sixty-eight degrees Fahrenheit, extend the shelf life of paper documents, microfilm, and photographs in the archives of the Historical Society of Western Pennsylvania.

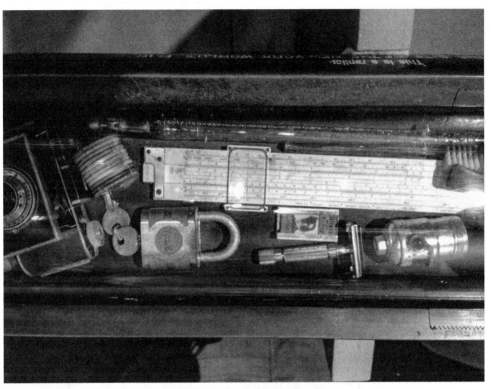

**Westinghouse Time Capsule of Cupaloy replica displayed
at Heinz History Center in Pittsburgh, Pennsylvania.**

The replica time capsule displayed at the Heinz Center is fitted with a cutaway glass panel to show the capsule's contents. This replica was first displayed at the New York World's Fair of 1939, where the original time capsule was deposited fifty feet underground in Flushing Meadows Park, directly in front of the Westinghouse building. The time capsule contained microfilm reproductions of encyclopedias and books, a miniature library that focused mostly on science and engineering knowledge. This record of civilizational knowledge was supposed provide a blueprint for setting humanity back on the path to civilization in the event that the human race degenerated in the next 5,000 years or the accumulated knowledge and dominant institutions of American society were destroyed. In the case of corporate records, which would be duplicated on microfilm en masse by the 1940s, microfilm backups would provide the basis for restarting a specific business in the wake of disaster, which would more broadly ensure the survival of corporate capitalism on a societal level.[2] Later, in the Cold War, the federal government would make extensive continuity-of-operations plans along these lines, too, with data preservation being central to these efforts.

The time capsule included only two novels—Sinclair Lewis's *Arrowsmith* and Margaret Mitchell's *Gone with the Wind*. These two Pulitzer Prize-winning novels embody the technological and racial fantasies and fears that informed the design of the time capsule. *Arrowsmith* tells the story of a young doctor from the fictional midwestern state of Winnemac—a place one literary critic called "more typical than any real state in the Union."[3] However, Winnemac is also home to a world-class futuristic university that supposedly puts Oxford and Harvard to shame, a school whose "buildings are measured by the mile," where students play on "a baseball field under glass." Every year it adds hundreds of new Ph.D.s to its faculty "to give rapid instruction in Sanskrit, navigation, accountancy, spectacle-fitting, sanitary engineering, Provençal poetry, tariff schedules, rutabaga-growing, motor-car designing, the history of Voronezh, the style of Matthew Arnold, the diagnosis of myohypertrophia kymoparalytica, and department-store advertising."[4]

Lewis's tone is certainly satirical, but it is also apt in its description of the kind of futuristic dreams Westinghouse harbored. The novel also speaks to the concern for defining what is typically American, the precise essence of American culture, and attempts by corporate science to establish popular faith in the power of capitalist innovation to bring about a better tomorrow. Other items in the capsule reflect the consumer culture of the day, tools of value calculation, and personal hygiene: safety razor, lock and key, camera, slide rule, baseball, swatches of fabric, toothbrush, matches. Most of these are recognizable even today, but one artifact likely is not—the Sterilamp bulb manufactured by Westinghouse, a device that supposedly killed germs with its red-tinted ultraviolet radiation.

To make sense of the time capsule, or any artifact, you have to look at its surrounding context. Towering over the time capsule display is a seven-foot-tall robot called Elektro the Moto-Man, a placard describing him as the "world's first voice-activated robot." His feats may strike us as unimpressive in this age of chatbots, holograms, sex dolls that breathe, and so much more, but Elektro's repertoire of abilities was astounding for the time, as he "smoked cigarettes, could count to 10 on his fingers . . . walked, talked, and could identify the difference between the colors red and green." Elektro's features and streamlined brushed aluminum exterior were a great improvement on the more humanoid, though dehumanized, "mechanical man" that Westinghouse exhibited in 1930—"Rastus the Mechanical Negro." Also referred to as a "mechanical slave," Rastus was molded in black rubber and could not walk, but he could certainly bow.[5]

Below the Elektro display, an information panel explains how Westinghouse created a fictional family called the Middletons who appeared in comic strip–style magazine ads and even a feature film shot in Technicolor to promote the company's fair attractions. In these ads, the Middletons, an idealized version of the "typical American family," meet Elektro, examine the time capsule, and stand in awe before the Singing Tower of Light. These ads were meant to inspire the readers of magazines like *Life* and the *Saturday Evening Post* and the *Country Gentleman* to travel to the fair and experience these spectacles.[6] The name "Middleton" is a reference to the landmark book *Middletown: A Study in Modern American Culture*, published in 1929 by sociologists Robert Staughton Lynd and Helen Merrell Lynd. *Middletown* helped to establish the figure not only of the average American but also of the average American town. The Lynds carried out their research in Muncie, Indiana, an overwhelmingly white midwestern town with "a small Negro and foreign-born population,"[7] contributing to a growing sense in popular culture that the average American actually looked like the fictional Middleton family in the film and comic strips produced by Westinghouse.

Alongside the reproductions of these ads is a historical document on newsprint called *Westinghouse Fair World*, which offers more detail and photographs of the aforementioned exhibits and others, such as the new technology of "television" and the *Microvivarium*, where magnified projections of microscopic bacteria show them "battling for existence" in several illuminated circles on the wall. Then, in what press releases described as an "execution," a white-coated technician flips on a Westinghouse ultraviolet bulb called the Sterilamp, and "these thrashing, fighting organisms . . . stop their wild gyrations, curl up and die—and science scores another victory."[8] The *Junior Science Laboratories* exhibit gave young people the opportunity for hands-on fun, and the *Kitchen Planning Section* exhibit showed the kitchen of the future, full of Westinghouse appliances that promised to save every homemaker abundant time and energy. The *Battle of the Centuries* exhibit pitted Mrs. Drudge versus Mrs. Modern in a dishwashing contest. Of course, Mrs. Modern, with her brand-new Westinghouse dishwasher, wins the battle every time. Not only that, she looks splendid by the end, her hair and makeup still pristine, while Mrs. Drudge is disheveled. Her apron soaked with suds, her hair fallen into her face, Mrs. Drudge has no time to read a newspaper and stay informed of current events the way Mrs. Modern does. Drudge does battle with an unwieldy stack of filthy plates that defeats her every time.

Where the librarians of the previous chapter sought to preserve through annihilation, the figures that populate this chapter take a different tack. As we shall see, data preservation doesn't simply save existing data—it is also productive. It generates new technologies, artifacts, logics, and fantasies that do not assuage our anxiety about data loss, but rather stimulate more preservation, especially at moments when new crises emerge. The Westinghouse Time Capsule of Cupaloy produced through preservation a streamlined version of American culture aimed at rebuilding white solidarity among the masses, in order to help stabilize scientific capitalist power during the Depression. The time capsule claims to simply preserve the essence of American culture for the future, and in actuality it produces a specific conception of that essence and reinforces it in the minds of fairgoers like the Middletons in the present. Preservation, in this case, is an act that functions to obscure the exclusions that make possible a monolithic conception of American culture. This logic corresponds to the flattening of the diversity of the American citizenry necessary to composing figures like the typical American, or the typical American family, that constitute the singular American "public."

## Technicolor Whiteness

I take the elevator up to the sixth floor of the Heinz Center, where the Westinghouse archives reside. I plan to spend a week here buried in gray boxes and manila folders, yellowed newspapers and carbon copies of memos, glossy promotional photos with purple mimeograph captions stuck to the back—a world of letterhead, rubber cement, and the illegible scrawl of powerful men's exquisite fountain pens, deciphered and typed by women confined to the clerical. But first I want to see the Westinghouse-sponsored movie *The Middleton Family at the New York World's Fair*, and I know from the finding aids that an original copy is housed at the archives.

"Can I watch it?"

The archivist shakes his head. "No, we don't screen it, because we don't want to possibly damage it or cause wear on it unnecessarily."

"Can I see it, though? Not view a projection of it, I mean, but just see the film reel itself?"

"No, we don't let the public access it. We have to keep it in the best condition we can. To make sure it's available for future users."

I think, But if we're protecting it for the sake of future users, once those future users arrive, won't they again be unable to view it or see it or touch it, in order to protect it for the sake of future users? I keep the thought to myself, though, having grown quite accustomed to such eternal deferments of access in archives. Instead, while waiting for a load of records to be retrieved, I search the Internet Archive, locate a digital copy of the film, and begin watching it anyway.

The Middleton family and their story are just as absolutely, positively typical as Westinghouse promised, which is to say it's all very fucking weird.

The first shot of the film shows us the world through the eyes of the Middletons as we travel in a car along a road, passing by sun-glazed, grassy fields bounded by rough-hewn fences. It is clear we are outside the city, and after several seconds we see a sign that reads, "Welcome to Huntington, Long Island." Traveling right to left, it's as if we're going back in time or memory, away from the city where the future is cultivated like crops, and toward something more traditional. The next shot is a familiar scene: a tree-shaded suburban street, all center-hall colonials and dormered roofs and gambrels. Several children, all white, making their way down the sidewalk, one riding a bicycle in the street. No adults in sight to supervise or otherwise protect these young ones. Huntington is clearly a safe and wholesome place.

Huntington. Is it a fictional place? I feel like I've come across Huntington, Long Island, before but can't think of where. I resist the urge to Google it, which would drop me down a rabbit hole that would probably lead me to learn numerous factoids about the founding, transformations, current census data, and famous residents past and present of Huntington, but ultimately would result in me looking up the current prices of baseball cards I sold off years ago, or classic Land Cruisers, or browsing (read: drowning in) the infinity that is clickbait gossip posts about the UFC, or, God help me, the hilarious and unending Babel of Twitter threads and memes commenting on gossip posts about the UFC. Then, all of a sudden, an hour and a half would have passed, and since I only have a week to be with these boxes of documents, I can't afford such lapses. The internet can wait.

The plot of the Middleton film turns on the transformation of the Middleton children, Bud and Babs. Bud is a playful but pessimistic boy who deeply questions the value of "free enterprise," corporate capitalism, and scientific innovation as he faces the dwindling economic opportunities of the Depression. The Middleton daughter, Babs, is attending art school in New York and has begun dating one of her instructors, an immigrant, Marxist abstract painter of Russian descent named Nickolas Mackaroff, whose arrogance and snobbery is exceeded only by his anticapitalist fervor. The family hopes to correct Babs's misstep by fixing her up with Jim Treadway, a hometown boy from Indiana who now works as a guide in the Westinghouse building at the world's fair.

By the end of the film, all the threats to America's future seem to be resolved through the changes in these two young people. Babs breaks off her relationship with Mackaroff and pairs with Treadway. Bud wins a letter-writing contest where he explains to a friend back home how bad off the world would be without the innovations of Westinghouse, and he reads the letter publicly at the awards ceremony, effectively turning into a copywriter or budding (get it?) PR man for American big business before our very eyes. A full-page color ad that appeared inside the cover of *Life* magazine put a finer point on Bud's redemption. In the ad, Bud interacts with teenage scientists in the *Junior Science Laboratories* of the Westinghouse building, after which he decides "to abandon his ambitions to lead a swing band in favor of an electrical engineering career." In an effort to connect the transformation of Bud to the transformation of prospective fairgoers reading *Life*, the ad asserts confidently, "You, too, will enjoy seeing and talking with these scientists of the future."[9]

The Middletons provided an important point of contact between Westinghouse and the American public it hoped to educate at the fair. According to Roland Marchand, "The defense of the economic system had gained priority on the corporate public relations agenda of the late 1930s."[10] As the emerging profession of public relations gained increasing influence in the 1930s, "the new experts in design and in audience response" warned corporations "that only increased showmanship would save their displays from obscurity at the great New York and San Francisco fairs of 1939."[11] Rather than educate the masses by illustrating the impressive processes of production that generated a cornucopia of modern consumer goods, as world's fairs had historically done, this fair would instead showcase technologies and products in order to "promote an appreciation of the company as an institution, not a systematic understanding of its processes of production."[12] These experts counseled corporations to simplify their exhibits because contemporary processes of production were far too complicated for the masses, afflicted with short attention spans, to understand.

As much as *The Middleton Family* occupies a place firmly in the past, the data complex has many ways of making the past current again, and the film remains relevant. In 2012, *The Middleton Family* movie was added to the Library of Congress's National Film Registry, marking it for long-term preservation and study. In the words of then librarian of Congress James Billington, "The National Film Registry spotlights the importance of preserving America's unparalleled film heritage. . . . These films are not selected as the 'best' American films of all time, but rather as works of enduring importance to American culture. They reflect who we are as a people and as a nation."[13] The Middleton family's journey is a microcosmic dramatization of Depression-era threats to the corporate capitalist economic order and the typical American family—framed by the film as being one in the same. Westinghouse intended to utilize its world's fair exhibits, including the time capsule, to reeducate the American public on a massive scale and produce a reorientation in American youths toward corporate capitalist values.

I still want to Google the town of Huntington, Long Island. Where have I seen that name before? Prudently avoiding the internet, I reexamine the first shot of *The Middleton Family*. Just before we see the "Welcome to Huntington" sign, there is another sign bearing an isotype-like image of the fair's architectural emblem, the Trylon and Perisphere, a 610-foot-tall spire and a 180-foot-diameter sphere, respectively, connected by the world's longest escalator. Lewis Mumford wrote that the Perisphere was like "the great egg out of which civilization was to be born."[14] Inside it, fair visitors could view a diorama showcasing a utopian city of the future. I spotlight search "Huntington" in my laptop's files, but nothing helpful comes up, just everything Thomas Iiams ever published, a bunch of old annual reports of the Huntington Library, biographies of the library founder, Henry E. Huntington, and an image of—that's it!

I click open a sepia-tone photo of an archive, walls lined with steel filing cabinets and hulking wooden units that look like overgrown card catalogs. It's a scene at the Eugenics Record Office (ERO), which was located in Cold Spring Harbor, New York, and written in white ink in the lower right-hand corner is "Sunden Studio, Huntington, L.I." The ERO was an archive held at the Station for Experimental Evolution, later known as the Carnegie Institution of Washington Department of Genetics.[15] The ERO was founded in 1910 by Mrs. E. H. Harriman and was initially financially supported by John D. Rockefeller (railroad and oil fortunes, respectively). But by 1918, the Carnegie Institution of Washington had assumed full financial responsibility for its operating budget, annually providing around $25,000 until the ERO was closed in 1939, the equivalent of about half a million dollars today. But why did Westinghouse set Grandma Middleton's home there? I finally break down and ask Google Maps. Oh, Cold Spring Harbor is not *near* Huntington; it is a hamlet *in* the town of Huntington.[16]

Why not just set the opening in Muncie, the actual site of Robert S. Lynd and Helen Merrell Lynd's findings for their book *Middletown: A Study in American Culture*? Is the film really trying to link the typical American family in some way to the worldwide epicenter of the eugenics movement, the site of the ERO, whose purpose Charles Davenport, director of the Carnegie Station and the ERO, described as an effort to

fill the need of a clearing-house for data concerning "blood line" and family traits in America. [The ERO] is accumulating and studying records of physical and mental characteristics of human families to the end that the people may be better advised as to *fit and unfit marriages*. It issues blank schedules (sent on application) for the use of those who wish to preserve a record of their family histories.[17]

It's probably just a coincidence that the above mission statement speaks directly to the film, wherein the Middletons work together to derail the engagement of Babs to an immigrant, a "near white" person whose utterly phonetic name Mrs. Middleton doesn't even attempt to pronounce.

The typical American family, corny and unbearably white though it may be, isn't really, in any fundamental way, related to eugenics, right? The augmentation of the data complex, the new technologies, artifacts, and practices it spawned in the 1930s were not fundamentally linked to attempts to preserve whiteness.

Right?

### The Conception of Data Bodies

In *The Middleton Family* film, the first thing the Middletons check out at the world's fair is the time capsule. More specifically, the family encounters a replica of the WTCC with a cutaway window—the same one I saw at the Heinz History Center—alongside a display case offering an orderly version of the jumbled contents stuffed tightly and vacuum sealed inside the cylindrical glass crypt of the time capsule. The Middletons provide an effective point of identification for viewers by helping them to understand the time capsule as an expression of corporate science's power to bring about "a better tomorrow"—the theme of the fair—rather than see it simply as a strange novelty. Bud and his father ask the questions; Mrs. Middleton giggles and gasps in amazement; and the grandmother watches passively, except for chiming in about how she "supposes cloth and things like that are included in it, too."[18]

The time capsule replica and display case viewed by the Middletons and other fairgoers framed its contents not only for future archaeologists but for contemporary audiences. The encyclopedias lined up side by side attested to the condensing power of microfilm and suggested an order and comprehensiveness of the knowledge preserved in the capsule, or, as Jim Treadway terms it, "the brains of the world done up in a small package." Microfilm's relatively compact format fit nicely with time capsule creators' claims that they accumulated records that constituted a representative cross-section of human knowledge, achievements, and lifestyle.

Dreams of immortality are, of course, as old as the mummy complex, as old as mediated humanity itself. But the time capsule pointed toward a shift in our relationship to data in its use of microfilm. The time capsule also showcased, like a magnified zygote, the conception of Americans' data bodies, reflecting the amassing of records on each of us that was then being centralized by the New Deal, the Social Security Administration, the Selective Service, and the Internal Revenue Service.[19] While Westinghouse consulted the NBS directly and designed its time capsule according to the bureau's specifications, academics in the emerging field of business history, as well as librarians and archivists of all kinds, referred to the NBS studies in their calls for the use of microfilm to improve corporate record preservation practices.[20] The National Archives, only recently established in 1934, had also adopted microfilm as a permanent medium for records, while other institutions, such as banks and insurance companies, had been backing up their records with microfilm since the late 1920s.[21]

In the Westinghouse archives, I found an issue of *American Banker* newspaper from 1938 containing an article that describes the use of Recordak microfilm in the Westinghouse Time Capsule. The article points out that this microfilm is "the same kind that banks use to record checks and valuable records." Indeed, Recordak survived the Depression and was available to Westinghouse because it revolutionized corporate record keeping, first in banking, then in department stores and insurance companies. The success of Recordak coincided with and contributed to the expansion of personal loans, installment plans, and consumer credit, all of which generated an avalanche of records for corporations to preserve and store. The newness of this vast credit system is evident in an article on the front page of this same edition of *American Banker*, one describing the profitability of debt. Bank executive J. P. Huston told "of his bank's success with a personal loan department and advised any bank which did not have one that they were missing very profitable business." Such record-keeping would expand exponentially across the span of the twentieth century and into the twenty-first, eventually leading to a situation where a human life could be overshadowed in significance, value, and certainly permanence by the data created about that life.[22]

Microfilm became the dominant data format for backing up corporate, financial, historical, and state bureaucratic records during the 1930s, partially because of economic concerns. Microfilm provided a space-saving mechanism for corporations and federal and state agencies looking to cut costs on office space during the Depression. New Deal policies caused a drastic expansion of the federal government and produced an unprecedented amount of records to maintain. The official definition of "records," offered in the 1939 Records Disposal Act as well as the 1940 Photographed Records Disposal Act, gave microfilm copies the same archival and legal weight as original paper documents. These acts also allowed originals to be destroyed and thus laid the foundation for the emergence of "records management" as a distinct field of expertise and enterprise.[23]

### The Book of Record

Of course, eventually, the concept of the typical American that fair planners and corporations like Westinghouse made would fade. At some point in the imagined progression of the next 5,000 years, the Middleton family line would break off, and Western civilization would indeed fall, and the direct memory of the time capsule would dissolve into oblivion. What then? To address this inevitability, G. Edward Pendray—a sci-fi writer, rocket enthusiast, and public relations pioneer working at Westinghouse—created *The Book of Record*, a guide that included instructions for locating the time capsule. The full title is *The Book of Record of the Time Capsule of Cupaloy: Deemed Capable of Resisting the Effects of Time for Five Thousand Years; Preserving an Account of Universal Achievements; Embedded in the Grounds of the New York World's Fair, 1939*. Pendray distributed *The Book of Record* to over 3,000 repositories: 466 public libraries, over 100 college and university libraries in the United States and 50 abroad, as well as the private library of J. P. Morgan. Over 200 North American museums and 70 abroad, as well as over 20 monasteries, 4 Shinto shrines, a few Buddhist temples, and 3 lamaseries in Tibet, all were sent a copy on rag paper rated "permanent" by NBS scientists.

In the acknowledgments section of *The Book of Record*, Pendray expressed gratitude to both Arthur Kimberly and his data preservation partner-in-crime at the NBS, C. G. Weber. The latter appeared personally in publicity shots with Groven Whalen, president of the fair, as they and a female assistant packed the items into the time capsule. The distribution of this "permanent" book so far and wide, high and low, aboveground and underground was a prophylactic against time, where time is not just the steady, slow, and inevitable destructive effects of erosion, wind, mildew, insects, and air, but also the flash and shrapnel of explosives, the hailstorm of incendiary bombs. Westinghouse's strategy, namely the idea that dispersing *The Book of Record* would protect against such destruction, prefigures the "safety in space," "industrial dispersion," and "target area" discourse of the Cold War to come, not to mention the digital age, where fallout shelters and data centers are placed in remote areas, away from population centers, imagined to be places far removed from where the next war will rain down on our heads.

In *The Book of Record*, the supermen of 6939 would find everything they needed to locate and interpret the time capsule. The U.S. Geodetic Survey provided the latitude and longitude coordinates to the thousandth of a second, precise enough to find the position of an object with a two-inch diameter anywhere on the earth's surface.[24] In the event that the earth's poles shifted, or that through geological processes the time capsule sank or moved from its point of deposit, the supermen could still find it "by the methods of electrical prospecting . . . used . . . for the location of minerals, water, buried metallic objects, and deposits of salt and soil."[25] Also provided was "A Key to the English Language," devised by John P. Harrington, a prolific ethnologist and recorder of Native American languages then being lost to genocide. The "key" included a diagram he called a mouth map, showing where all thirty-three distinct sounds in English are made by pressing the tongue against various locations in the mouth and on the teeth and lips. He changed the spelling of words in English to make them more consistent and logical, so that "mouth map," for instance, became "Mauth Maep." Harrington also included a kind of Rosetta stone in the form of "The Fable of the Northwind and Sun" by Aesop, written in standard U.S. English and in his own adjusted spelling system, and directed the reader to another pamphlet in the time capsule wherein translations of the fable were written in twenty-five languages.

The frontispiece to *The Book of Record* bears a photo that renders the time capsule a volatile, flickering symbol of both preservation and destruction, a licking flame of meaning. Above the heads of white Westinghouse scientists hangs the time capsule, a marvel of streamline design, admired by the smiling faces below it. The sleek, "bullet-shaped" exterior of the time capsule was consistent with the streamline aesthetic that shaped the visual appearance of many new technologies at the fair. According to Christina Cogdell's astounding book *Eugenic Design*, "Streamline design arose in part as a response to national inefficiency, in terms of increased sickness and hereditary degeneration, and in terms of the time it took women to clean their homes. Hence the style's nickname, given by [Henry] Dreyfuss, of 'cleanlined' design. Industrial designers worked with long-accepted and newly developed sanitary materials (wood, enamel, tile, glass, metals, chrome, sanitary paint, and plastics), replacing fabric and other dust-catching materials with smooth, impermeable, highly finished ones that could be easily sterilized."[27] Cogdell shows how the archives of designers such as Henry Dreyfuss, Norman Bel Geddes, Egmont Arens, and others "suggest that some designers did, in fact, correlate speed, intelligence, progress, and the reduction of drag with enhanced evolutionary progress."[28]

At first glance, the photo seems to capture the Westinghouse scientists' admiration for the marvelous thing they've made, but it takes on different layers of meaning when one considers that Pendray originally wanted to call the time capsule a "time bomb."[29] Upon reflection, he decided he needed to call it something else, and so he coined the term "time capsule" to christen his magnum opus PR project, "capsule" being, up to that point, a very rarely used word in American English. The time capsule in the photo, then, is also a time bomb. The very top of the capsule is obscured, and so what we're seeing could very well be interpreted as a high-speed photo of a falling bomb just before its moment of impact, a grim thought that can be read on the nonsmiling faces in the crowd. In Nick Yablon's astute interpretation of the image, he points out how the time capsule's similarity to an unexploded bombshell could even deter future archaeologists from opening it.[30] The photo embodies the fundamental paradox of technological progress—it leads to a better tomorrow where technology will have the capacity to preserve everything forever *and* destroy everything forever. This image of preservation and destruction circulated widely in publications such as the *New York Times* and *Popular Science*,[31] and it thus distributed

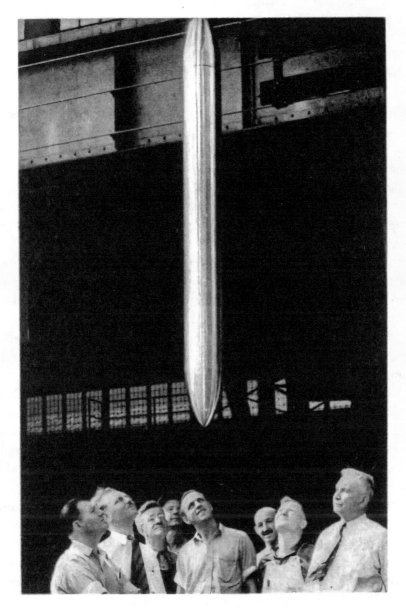

THE ENVELOPE FOR A MESSAGE TO THE FUTURE
BEGINS ITS EPIC JOURNEY

Frontispiece for Pendray, *The Book of Record*.
Reprinted by permission of Westinghouse Electric Corporation.

a powerful visual encapsulation of the anxious status of new technology within the data complex.

The polished cupaloy that forms the protective shell of the time capsule is a proprietary alloy created by the Westinghouse Corporation, but it is just as much an outgrowth of Pendray's sci-fi fantasies. In his fiction, Pendray captured the dominant fears of his day, of nonwhite races advancing technologically beyond white civilization, of invasion, of the end of whiteness. In 1929, under the pseudonym Gawain Edwards, he penned a novel called *The Earth-Tube*. The book belonged to a racist genre of fiction called "yellow peril," where an Asian race threatens to destroy Western civilization or white racial purity, or some other golden calf.[32] In the novel, a technologically advanced and bellicose Asian society has invented an alloy so strong it serves as both impenetrable armor and unstoppable artillery, capable of piercing any shield or barricade. Perhaps even more devastating is its use as a mining tool, one that the Asians use to dig through the center of the earth (I'm not kidding), surface somewhere near the western coast of South America, launch an attack of insectlike aircraft, and threaten to "wipe out all of the white population on both of the American continents."[33]

The yellow peril genre was fundamentally racist, but it was accurate in the sense that it precisely reflected the irrational fears white Americans projected onto Asians within the United States and without. Extreme adventures of the kind that animate plots in science fiction—whether one is going deep into the earth by mining, to the bottom of the sea, or into outer space—require superhard materials. Indeed, like the product of fictional Asian metallurgical wizardry, the cupaloy of the time capsule evokes both weapon and armor, its polished exterior a curved mirror distorting the reality that surrounds it.

In his 1939 essay "The Crucible of Change," Pendray imagined a future that is healthier, more sterile, more suffused with Westinghouse's technological wonders. He thought it was possible that "theatregoers of 1964 [would] get baths of invisible germ killing radiation, that during epidemics health commissioners, instead of warning against crowds, [might urge] attendance at irradiated public gatherings."[34] In the Westinghouse building, all seventeen toilets used the Sterilseat, a toilet seat equipped with a Sterilamp bulb, and all of the Gulf Oil stations in the vicinity of the fair likewise used the germ-killing seats.[35] The Sterilamp never did achieve the widespread use that Pendray imagined for it in the future, though the New York City MTA did make a prototype ten-car train that filtered the air and bathed riders in the sterilizing glow of Sterilamps. Nine of the ten cars were sold for scrap, though, in the lean budget years of the mid-1970s, and the only remaining car was put on display in the New York Transit Museum.[36]

For all the techno-utopianism filling its pages, *The Book of Record* concludes on a grim note, passing on to the people of 6939 not the voices of everyday people, but rather messages from "Noted Men of Our Time." The "noted men" were all Nobel Prize winners: physicists Albert Einstein and Robert A. Millikan, and German writer Thomas Mann. The Nobel Prize provided each of them with small fortunes drawn from a vaster fortune generated by the bequest of Alfred Nobel. Most famous for his invention of dynamite, Nobel also invented a smokeless explosive powder called ballistite, as well as "blasting gelatin," a standard substance used in mining for awhile.[37] The Nobel laureates' messages were not uplifting. Einstein noted, "Any one who thinks about the future must live in fear and terror." Even Mann's message, which referred to a kind of eternal spirit in humans and was in some ways the most hopeful, flew directly in the face of the fair's theme and the generally optimistic tone of *The Book of Record*. "We know now," he wrote authoritatively, "that the idea of the future as a 'better world' was a fallacy of the doctrine of progress."[38]

I couldn't have said it better myself.

Millikan, for his part, offered a thinly veiled eugenicist perspective. In his view, "the principles of representative ballot government, such as are represented by the governments of the Anglo-Saxon, French, and Scandinavian countries," were then "in deadly conflict with the principles of despotism." Millikan was the president of Caltech, where chemists developed Thomas Iiams's "carboxide," but he also helped to found the California branch of the American Eugenics Society, whose board counted the country's leading eugenicists among its ranks, such as Charles Davenport, Madison Grant, and founding president of Stanford University David Starr Jordan. Along with Huntington Library board member Paul Popenoe, Millikan was also a board member of the Human Betterment Foundation, a highly influential group that advocated compulsory sterilization of the "unfit." He "proudly considered" Southern California to be "the westernmost outpost of Nordic civilization ... [with] a population which [was] twice as Anglo-Saxon as that existing in New York, Chicago or any of the great cities of this country."[39]

Millikan was also the chairman of the board at the Huntington Library, where Thomas Iiams was fighting bookworms to save civilization, literally trying to sterilize books to preserve them. Millikan's racism reflected the cultural climate of San Marino, where restrictive covenants prevented minorities from living there and thus kept the town white, or, in Millikan's words, maintained its status as "the westernmost outpost of Nordic civilization." Even after the Supreme Court struck down such covenants, racial segregation was preserved through individual land deeds that flew under the radar of federal rulings. The desire to preserve whiteness was so strong there that even in 1970, sixteen years after *Brown v. Board of Education* mandated schools to desegregate, a judge found that the Pasadena Board of Education still "knowingly assigned" white and black students to different schools.[40]

### The Typical American Family Contest at the Fair

Fair planners went a step further than Westinghouse, hoping to clothe the comic strip and celluloid specters of the typical American family in flesh and blood. The planners held a typical American family contest, meant to be a fun and friendly competition that reinforced the eugenic ideals of race betterment and the "primacy of racial categories in determining citizenship in the world of tomorrow."[41] The contest tapped into a decades-old trend of eugenicists' exhibits that linked essential Americanness to whiteness. These were placed everywhere from international eugenics congresses and state and county fairs throughout the country, to century-of-progress expositions prior to World War I. There is no typical or average Americanness that is not rooted, ultimately, in eugenic whiteness.

In order to qualify as a "typical American family," relatives had to win an essay contest sponsored by their local newspaper. In these essays, families were supposed "to explain why they were typical." Corporate sponsors outfitted winners with various consumer products—they received a free ride to the fair in a new Ford, and they "lived on the fairgrounds in houses built by the Federal Housing Administration and sided with fire-resistant 'Asbestos Cedar-grain Siding Shingles' provided by the Johns Manville Company."[42] Families who won the contest were "to serve as representatives of the families of the nation."[43]

Among the families who won the contest were the Burdins of Miami, Florida. On the "Questionnaire for Selecting the National Typical American Family," Mrs. Burdin declared her occupation to be "housewife," like Mrs. Middleton, while Mr. Howard Burdin owned an office equipment company, similar to Mr. Middleton, who owned a hardware store. Thus, the Burdin family's livelihood rested on the demand for office equipment by corporate enterprise, and their gender responsibilities conformed to the corporate typical-family ideal represented in the Middletons. The typical American family had to be, ultimately, from nowhere. Similar to the typical Americans described in the *Middletown* studies, their typical and "native"

Americanness required a historical amnesia about their family's actual origins, which were necessarily located outside of America at some point in the past. On the questionnaire, which required them to "tell briefly the origin of the family," the Burdins' amnesia was apparently precisely the answer sought by the contest judges: "The ancestors of both parents lived in Alabama for so many generations that neither Mr. nor Mrs. Burdin ever heard where they came from. All were farmers." Finally, the family origin narrative also positioned the family more squarely, geographically, within the American nation than origins in Miami might suggest, as "Burdin's great-great-grandfather, who died at the age of 98 when Burdin was about 10 years old, had spent his whole life in Alabama. Mr. and Mrs. Burdin moved to Miami in 1925."[44] When New York mayor Fiorello LaGuardia met with the Burdins, he told them that they were more than just typical families, that they were the people "who make this country real."[45] The nation itself exists, lives, inside these typical, white, forgetful bodies, bodies that empty out the space they occupy. All the world is either wilderness or home, and in either case, it belongs to them. These are bodies bred to live, breathe, and be historical erasure itself. The Burdins forgetting "where they came from" was not an aberration but an integral part of the self-delusion involved in European immigrants becoming white, what James Baldwin called "the price of the ticket."[46]

The families who stayed the night in the Federal Housing Administration (FHA) model homes at the center of the fair indeed experienced the world of tomorrow, where federal programs like the G.I. Bill would provide economic privileges to white, heteronormative, patriarchal families, laying the groundwork for structures of economic inequality that persist to this day. The FHA program was a crucial factor in generating the privileges that constituted the material benefits and visible markers of whiteness in the postwar period. George Lipsitz explains that the Federal Housing Act of 1934 "brought home ownership within reach of millions of citizens by placing the credit of the federal government behind private lending to home buyers, but overtly racist categories in the Federal Housing Administration's (FHA) 'confidential city surveys and appraisers' manuals channeled almost all of the loan money toward whites and away from communities of color."[47]

The winners of the typical American family contest also literalized this symbolic ordering—their FHA model homes were located at the very center of the fairgrounds. Historian Bonnie Yochelson relates this symbolic centering to the streamline design style that shaped the visual appearance of many new technologies at the fair, including the sleek "bullet-shaped" time capsule. "Just as a seamless, streamlined form masked the complexities of

**The Burdin family of Miami, Florida, winners of the Typical American Family Contest at the 1939 World's Fair. Courtesy of the New York Public Library.**

a machine's inner workings," writes Yochelson, "so the ideal of the 'typical American' masked the complexities of American society. Despite its constant refrain of tolerance and freedom, the Fair proposed a future society that was homogeneous, exclusive, and harmonious by virtue of its shared heritage. There was no place for Americans who were poor, urban, non-white, or foreign-born."[48] The new order of the future presented to "everyday" Americans at the fair was meant to "preserve, not reform, asymmetrical power relations in society." The "everyday," "typical," or "average" American in this context served as the conduit for ideological imperatives aimed at the masses, imperatives that produced an idealized conception of the capitalist status quo, projected it into the future, and framed that act of production and projection as "preservation."

## Thirty-Six Tons of Air

The time capsule, *The Middleton Family* film, and, indeed, the entire fair, were each perched on the verge of a second Great War and inescapably haunted by visions of utter destruction. At the closing of the scene where the family encounters the time capsule, Jim Treadway refers to the underlying cultural anxieties that motivate such a grandiose preservation project—namely, that war or economic collapse or some other form of civilizational ruin will annihilate everything that is not preserved on microfilm, sealed inside a secure vault, and buried in a nearly inaccessible location. Jim says of the time capsule, "It's the most permanent exhibit of the Fair. It'll still be here when the rest of this place is nothing but dust." Mr. Middleton replies, "That's remarkable," then immediately changes the subject.

The time capsule, as the permanent data we desire, must be free of dust, because dust is an artifact of societal breakdown. Dust and dirt "constitute a kind of disorder, an inchoate state of being, and thus a type of moral defilement."[49] In his wonderful book *Dust: A History of the Small and the Invisible*, Joseph A. Amato details how in the early twentieth century "women especially fought a daily battle against dust and germs: it required attention to a very long list of things that started with nutrition and clothing, went on to exercise, and did not neglect sex and bodily excretions. In the home-front battle against disease, homeowners had to inspect lighting, heating, ventilation, and sewage systems, not forgetting eaves, troughs, and gutters."[50]

At the fair, visitors could look through a window into a model living room equipped with a Westinghouse Precipitron air filter system. With the press of a button, the Precipitron would suck all the dust from the surfaces of the furnishings. Several years later, *Life* magazine profiled the Precipitron in an article titled "Dirty Air," the first page featuring two cats snuggling each other, one gray and one white, with the following caption: "Cat at left lives in ordinary Pittsburgh house, is really pure white just like the one on the right which lives in Precipitron-equipped home." The dream of the dirt-free home, the dream of healthy air in a city built on industrial pollution, and the dream of pure whiteness are all very American dreams. From his Depression-era armchair, Pendray imagined that the housewife of 1964 would "have plenty of time to tune in on her television set, because dusting the house," with its plastic walls, its bathroom molded in one piece of plastic, would no longer be "a problem."[51]

The glass inner "crypt" of the time capsule was a microcosm of the sterilized, purified, dust-free environments of the future home in the world of tomorrow. Sealing artifacts inside a glass-lined, nitrogen-filled capsule takes the gas chamber for bookworms and renders it permanent, gassing the artifacts perpetually until the target opening date, which keeps the environment sterile. This biocidal environment that killed all actual life produced eternal life for data—the microfilm files, free of dust, mold, mildew, air, water, and heat, would, according to the NBS, endure for thousands of years. The time capsule's interior banished dust and the pathogens it carried; its smooth, streamlined exterior prevented the accumulation of dust and allowed air to flow around it with ease.

The Precipitron had migrated to the home from the realm of industrial production, where precision manufacturing had long required environments that were as clean as possible, and where dust could prove to be extremely dangerous, even deadly. Coal dust floating in the air occasionally caught fire in factories, causing death and serious injury, so often that a photo of the Precipitron factory assembly line made an appearance in a 1949 *Science News Letter* article called "Strikes Are Preventable." Workers in the photo ready machines destined for steel mills, where each one would "clean more than 36 tons of air every hour." In many factories, high-speed precision grinders and thread cutters vaporized and spun coolant oil into a thin mist that reduced visibility and coated the surfaces of machines, not to mention the floor, ceiling, light fixtures, walls, and wiring. According to some commentators, the Precipitron helped prevent strikes and labor unrest by improving safety and reducing the number of injuries among workers.[52]

The Precipitron was the precursor of the clean room, an invention that made possible the manufacturing of microprocessors and virtually every digital technology used today. While the clean room wouldn't arrive in its current form until the 1960s, Henry Dreyfuss—the designer behind the Trylon and Perisphere, the Westclox Big Ben, the iconic yellow-and-green

John Deere tractor, the Honeywell thermostat, and more—imagined the home of the future as a clean room *avant la lettre*. A vacuum-filtering system at the doorway to the home would remove loose dirt particles, "dust, bacteria, pollen and smog-fumes" not only "from your shoe leather, but from the fibers of your clothing, and to some extent from your hands, face and hair."[53]

Westinghouse would eventually combine the Precipitron with heating and air conditioning units marketed for use in typical Americans' homes. In this fantasy of freedom from dust, elaborated in a 1955 ad featuring Betty Furness in the *Saturday Evening Post,* the living room becomes the time capsule. For where there is no dust, no residue of life and movement and friction, there is no time, nothing to mark the endless deterioration of things, no thin layer of sloughed human skin cells and disintegrated insect husks to signal decay's march like the clicks of a clock.[54]

Similar to her surroundings, the typical woman is not supposed to age. She is preserved, embalmed by the very air she breathes, the home now both a time capsule and sarcophagus. She is an artifact protected against the threats of the world. I mean this literally. The Johns Manville Company manufactured the asbestos used to seal the steel canisters in the Crypt of Civilization; it also manufactured the asbestos cedar shingles that wrapped the walls of the homes at the heart of the fair, where families who'd won the typical American family contest resided during their visit. The same substance preserved typical Americans' biobodies and their embryonic data bodies against the threat of fire. But like the poison gas used to preserve data in gas chambers for bookworms, the practice of data preservation in this case was highly toxic, asbestos being one of the most potent carcinogenic contaminants employed by the engineers of "the world of tomorrow."

The three versions of the typical woman in the ad evoke a wife able to perform a superhuman amount of work, or a replicable android. She is ultraproductive and frugal, for the housecleaning days saved by the Precipitron "could easily pay for your entire Air Conditioning System." She is smiling a Stepford smile, eternally beautiful like Mrs. Modern, a beauty made possible because she has become a part of an assemblage with her Westinghouse appliances. When Westinghouse's *Kitchen Planning Section* set up its display in the *Hall of Electrical Living* at the fair, men and women who walked through it, gazing at a remarkably accurate prediction of how kitchens of the future would look, were not simply looking at appliances. They were looking at appendages. These were embodied in the so-called *Battle of the Centuries,* where the winning woman with the dishwasher, Mrs. Modern, keeps her hand on the appliance while it works, and the loser, Mrs.

"**COOLS** entire home all summer . . ."    "**CLEANS** air as never before possible" says Betty Furness. "Savings in house-cleaning help pay for entire air conditioning . . ."    "**HEATS** entire home all winter . . ."

# WESTINGHOUSE ANNOUNCES SAVINGS
# NO OTHER AIR CONDITIONING CAN OFFER

**One unit cools and heats entire home. A companion unit— PRECIPITRON—electronically removes over 90% of all air-borne dirt—*sharply reduces daily cleaning, yearly decorating costs.***

This new kind of saving puts year-round air conditioning into almost any budget.

A wonderful Westinghouse development, called PRECIPITRON, may now be added to your air conditioning. It keeps out the air-borne dust, dirt, pollen, that require daily dusting.

It also removes practically all air-borne grime that discolors walls, rugs, upholstery and ceilings.

If PRECIPITRON saves just one cleaning day a week . . . and only one painting job out of two . . . . it could easily pay for your entire Air Conditioning System.

Hay fever sufferers, especially, find a PRECIPITRON makes a home a haven of relief from pollen.

Get the full story of this new home PRECIPITRON, which actually isn't new. For over 25 years, PRECIPITRON has saved millions of dollars in industry—removing dust particles as small as a millionth of an inch, making possible many dust-sensitive processes.

**Mail coupon** at right for free 20-page booklet on Central Air Conditioning and PRECIPITRON.

YOU CAN BE SURE...IF IT'S **Westinghouse**

**PRECIPITRON®.** Completely Electronic Air Cleaner. Supplies purest possible air. Easy to install. Nothing to clog. No filters to change. No more current than 60-watt bulb.

◄**COOLING-HEATING UNIT.** Cools entire home. Heats in winter. Automatic or manual control. Oil- or gas-fired. Circulates healthful air, freed of excess moisture. Compact.

## $1075.00

Price includes 2 Hp gas-fired Year-Round Air Conditioner. It does not include PRECIPITRON unit, which is optional. Add installation and shipping costs.

**Westinghouse ad from the *Saturday Evening Post*, May 1955.
Reprinted by permission of Westinghouse Electric Corporation.**

Drudge, is a total mess at the end of the race. The woman in the Precipitron ad is the image of the wife as cyborg, her body incorporated within a circuit of machines she is locked into, or, so Westinghouse might say, freed from.

### The Backup Loop to Rule Them All

While Westinghouse was burying its time capsule in the ground, another more ambitious project was under construction in Georgia. In May 1940, Oglethorpe University president Thornwell Jacobs and his archivist Thomas Kimmwood Peters sealed the stainless steel door on the Crypt of Civilization in Atlanta, Georgia, a time capsule with a target opening date of 8113 A.D. Modeled after an Egyptian tomb, the subterranean vault contained microfilm reproductions of hundreds of books, as well as newsreels, all meant to represent "mankind's accumulated knowledge." According to a 1940 news article, Jacobs chose the specific site on campus because "of the vein of granite which runs very close to the surface on the Oglethorpe campus," so that "its foundation is bedrock."[55]

Though the crypt was completed after the Westinghouse Time Capsule, the former project actually began prior to and inspired the latter—G. Edward Pendray wrote the first magazine article about the crypt in 1936,[56] and he borrowed key features of the crypt to create the Westinghouse Time Capsule. Like the Westinghouse Time Capsule, the crypt stored its media artifacts according to the new research carried out by the NBS to establish the relative durability of various types of paper and cellulose acetate microfilm, more commonly known as "safety film."

However, the crypt's data preservation techniques worked to both reinforce and throw into question the supposed permanence of microfilm. On the one hand, microfilm served as a "permanent" backup for paper records. On the other, Jacobs and Peters knew that the NBS had established the relative permanence of microfilm through "accelerated aging studies," which simulate the passage of time. As microfilm's durability had never actually been tested across the passage of millennia, Jacobs and Peters also included in the crypt backups for the microfilm, the images not printed on cellulose acetate but etched into metal film invented by Peters himself.[57] However, the metal film functions not just as a backup for safety film but more broadly within a backup loop wherein hopes and anxieties materialize and circulate across data formats: the metal film was also coated with cellulose acetate, and thus preserved by it.[58]

Peters subjected microfilm to other preservative measures that further reflect an anxiety about microfilm's durability, an anxiety that belies his rhetoric about it being a "permanent" medium. Peters used the Vaporate

Film Treatment to protect microfilms from a variety of threats. Vaporate was a technology that increased the melting point of treated films and protected them against "heat, climatic action, abrasion, and excessive moisture." The treatment involved—what else?—placing films in a gas chamber, removing the air from the chamber and thus any moisture in the film, then replacing the atmosphere in the chamber with "certain chemicals" that coated the film with a varnish, making it both "difficult to scratch" and resistant to "oil or excess water" and "finger marks."[59] Once the microfilm was treated, Peters placed it inside a glass cylinder, and a vacuum machine again removed the air from the cylinder and replaced it with helium. Finally, he placed the glass cylinder inside a fireproof asbestos cylinder, sealed both ends, placed that inside a stainless steel canister, and soldered it closed.[60]

Jacobs had heard and thought much about what happens when worlds end. He had single-handedly raised money to revive Oglethorpe University in 1913; the institution had gone bust during the Civil War after investing its endowment in Confederate bonds. Campus buildings had been "used as barracks and hospitals and later burned."[61] Jacobs had seen society fall apart before in witnessing the aftermath of the Atlanta race riots of 1906,[62] and he saw another cataclysm ahead as tensions rose in Europe, bending white civilization's fate toward the "race-suicide" of another Great War. If the coming war didn't end white civilization, Jacobs imagined the deterioration of the "national stock" would. Like the eugenicists who created the "fitter families" contests and their offshoots that sought out typical Americans, Jacobs was concerned about the "degeneration of the average American citizen." He recorded a message titled "Greetings to the Inhabitants of 8113" and sealed it inside the crypt. Just as Westinghouse chairman A. W. Robertson hopefully imagined white supermen and superwomen would discover the time capsule, Jacobs communicated in no uncertain terms to people whom he clearly imagined to be his white counterparts in the future:

> It is almost a sure bet that, if nothing is done about it, the United States will, in a few centuries, become a nation of quadroons ruled by an upper class of Jewish blood. At present we are a conglomerate of whites from northern Europe, brownwhites from Southern Europe, yellows from Asia, indigenous reds, blacks from Africa, with our movies, radios and newspapers either owned or operated by Jews. With the single exception of science which is progressing magnificently, all the balance of our civilization—morals, politics, literature, painting, sculpture seem to be retrograding and, as I prophesied twenty years ago, we are face to face with another World War.[63]

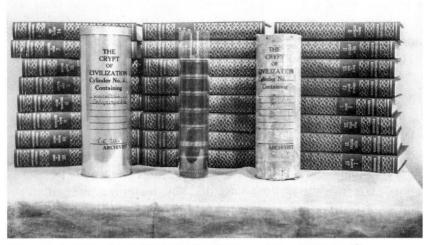

**Microbooks in the Crypt of Civilization. Thornwell Jacobs Collection, box 1, folder VA-176, Oglethorpe University Archives, Philip Weltner Library, Oglethorpe University, Atlanta, Ga. Reprinted courtesy of the Archives, Philip Weltner Library, Oglethorpe University.**

His perspective only grew more stark in the years that followed, particularly after the coming of the dreaded and predicted Second World War. By 1945, he editorialized in the *Westminster Magazine*, bemoaning that World War II was not a victory over the evil Nazi regime so much as an expression of white racial downfall on a global scale: "Yellows, blacks, browns and reds laugh as white nation slashes the throat of white nation and world power slips from the flaccid hands of the Aryan."[64]

For his archivist, Jacobs couldn't have chosen someone more experienced in filmmaking and film technology tinkering, more passionate about preservation, or more consistent in thinking with his own racist futurism than Thomas Kimmwood Peters. Peters's father and uncle were both Confederate captains in the Civil War, which he referred to in his writings as the "War Between the States." In 1915, Peters served as the historical consultant for D. W. Griffith's dastardly masterpiece *The Birth of a Nation*.[65] Working alongside his wife, Peters once spent 300 hours restoring a Confederate flag once flown by "Zachary's Rangers," a volunteer troop led by General Charles Thornton Zachary.[66] In an interview, he stated that he hoped to restore all thirty Confederate battle flags owned by the State of Georgia at the time. Among the preserved books in the crypt, Jacobs and Peters would include works by several Confederate luminaries, including *The Rise and*

*Fall of the Confederate Government* by Jefferson Davis, former president of the Confederacy; and, in a more bizarre vein, *Indo-Aryan Deities and their Worship as Contained in the Rig-Veda* by Albert Pike, former Confederate army officer and highly influential Freemason. Also included was Margaret Mitchell's 1936 smash hit of racial and historical delusion, *Gone with the Wind*, as well as an original script of the film version, donated by producer David O. Selznick himself.[67]

Peters was an inventor too, and his patents included a time-lapse camera, the first thirty-five-millimeter microfilm camera, and various rare gas and neon tubes. When Peters died in 1973, a profile in *American Cinematographer* magazine called him Hollywood's "most venerable pioneer of films . . . the last survivor of an age that saw the birth of the medium of film and the development of the art of film-making."[68] One of his inventions, never patented, was metal film. An expensive and highly impractical invention—for the purposes of cinema projection, anyway—metal film was the perfect solution for the Crypt of Civilization, for it provided permanent film newsreels.

There were no grounds for arguing that any film, neither nitrate nor the newfangled safety film, could survive centuries, much less millennia. Both technologies were less than fifty years old in 1938—they'd barely survived decades at that point. Though Jacobs and Peters cited research by the NBS to assert the permanence of their microfilm records, all of their evidence was based on "scientific" projections from accelerated aging studies. Only ancient materials such as papyrus, metal, and clay had empirically proved themselves to be permanent media. According to one 1940 news article that appeared just before the crypt was sealed, Jacobs and Peters included not only a microfilm copy of the Declaration of Independence but also a copy "etched in brass." The "voices of great men" recorded and preserved in the crypt were etched into metal phonograph records.[69]

Jacobs hoped that by that the time the crypt was opened, the sciences of diet, dentistry, and better breeding would lead to people living easily until the age of 150, and Peters was even more, er, optimistic. Peters told reporters that he believed in reincarnation and that he planned to be present at the crypt's opening in 8113 so that he could explain its contents to the people of the future. In perhaps their most intense moment of optimism, Jacobs and Peters even created stainless steel tickets for the opening of the crypt and intended them to be passed down from father to son through the generations until 8113 A.D.[70]

The time capsule and the crypt forced their creators to imagine American culture as ancient, as a set of artifacts discovered thousands of years in the future. This generated a paradoxical temporal position for preservationists. They constantly imagined themselves as advanced moderns, but they could only succeed in doing so by imagining the fantastic future success of their time capsule projects, a vision that again positioned them as primitive ancients in relation to the supermen that evolutionary thought and eugenic dreams led Americans to believe would inhabit the deep future. In an NBC radio broadcast recorded at Radio City Music Hall on April 18, 1937, Jacobs delivered a message to those who would find the crypt in 8113. He affirmed that future humans will likely be more advanced than us and thus will question the superiority complex of moderns like himself. He said, "We of the year 1937 looked back upon our remote ancestors as being savages and barbarians. Yet, we too, had wars among nations. We thought at the time that the principles for which we fought were important and yet, as you look back through the centuries you will perhaps in turn call us savages and believe that we lived in an uncivilized world."[71]

These preservationists, like later practitioners of backup culture in both the Cold War and the digital age, mediated risk perception by creating copies of files in multiple data formats, in multiple locations. The microfilm reels in the Westinghouse Time Capsule were actually copies of originals preserved in Eastman Kodak's vaults in Rochester, New York.[72] And according to his archived correspondence, Pendray had plans for a backup loop to rule them all. A copy of *The Book of Record* is preserved in Oglethorpe University's archives, located just above the Crypt of Civilization. Based on my research, including viewing the master list of contents in the crypt, Pendray's full plan never materialized. Still, for a media archaeologist such as myself, his imaginary data preservation effort is nonetheless significant, as it clinches yet another leg of the backup loops of both the crypt and the time capsule: Pendray planned to send Jacobs a replica of the time capsule to be preserved in the crypt.

So, the eugenically-engineered superhumans of the future who find the crypt would also find the time capsule. And in the backup loop to rule them all, Pendray included in the time capsule buried in New York a message that tells the futurians to travel south and excavate the Crypt of Civilization. There, they would find a replica of the time capsule. In this endless loop, what was supposed to be a definitive, clearly delineated record of American life, comes to seem more like a buried house of mirrors in which its bewildered discoverers will wander and spin.[73]

## Skyscrapers of Light

It is hard to predict the future. Nearly all of Pendray's predictions in his "Crucible of Change" essay were wrong. Jacobs did not imagine that the crypt would not be the only permanent archive to be created, that his project would spawn more projects like it. By the time the second Westinghouse Time Capsule was being filled with artifacts in 1965, the typical American man had aged a quarter century, postwar consumerism had shored up corporate power and profits, and the United States had become an economic powerhouse unprecedented in the history of the world. The United States was the "only major combatant of the Second World War whose productive capacities were left intact," its cities and towns unscathed by the bombing raids that leveled swaths of France, Germany, England, and Japan. Between 1950 and 1970, "Americans' assets—their houses, savings, and pension funds—quadrupled in value."[74] But the typical American was still anxious, even more so, still purifying what he loved against contamination, still sterilizing the air inside time capsules, still burying flags and Bibles for the supermen he hoped would descend from him.

Nowhere in all the futuristic speculation that fills the documents in the Westinghouse archives does anyone imagine that climate change might cover coastal New York in water. One scientist does address the unfounded rumor that New York City is sinking, only to dismiss it and assert that the grounds of Flushing Meadows will therefore be above sea level in 6939.

Flushing Meadows had long been a dump for the Big Apple, and by the time F. Scott Fitzgerald passed through the area in the early 1920s, during the writing of *The Great Gatsby*, the ash heaps there rose up ninety feet high. One of the titles Fitzgerald considered, before his legendary editor Max Perkins rejected it, was "Among the Ash-Heaps and Millionaires."[75] In the novel, Fitzgerald uses Flushing Meadows as a setting, describing it as "a valley of ashes—a fantastic farm where ashes grow like wheat ridges and hills and grotesque gardens; where ashes take the forms of houses and chimneys and rising smoke and, finally, with a transcendent effort, of men who move dimly and already crumbling through the powdery air."[76] When Robert Moses had all this waste removed a few years before the 1939 World's Fair, workers reportedly encountered "river rats the size of dogs."[77]

I remember reading *Gatsby* for the first time when I was much younger and wondering what he meant by a valley of ashes, what symbolic meaning it might have had, for I couldn't figure out why that many ashes would have existed in such gigantic heaps. Of course, I grew up in a house where heat came from a coal-free furnace and occasionally from a fireplace, so I really had no framework for imagining the massive loads of ash a coal-burning

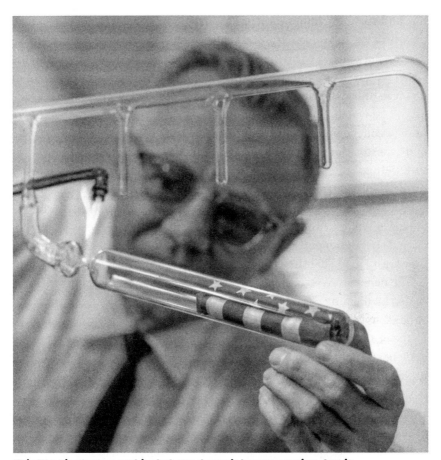

This Westinghouse archival photo doesn't bear a caption, but it must be from the second time capsule, deposited in 1965, based on other archival photos that show this flag sealed inside a glass tube. The photo is misfiled in the folder "Time Capsule 1938" in box 70, Photographs of the Westinghouse Electric Corporation, George Westinghouse Museum Archives, Heinz History Center, Pittsburgh, Pa. Reprinted by permission of Westinghouse Electric Corporation.

metropolis like New York must have generated. The scene of the ash heaps, forever lost to us in real life, paved over with the asphalt and the manufactured landscape of urban renewal, is temporarily immortalized in *Gatsby*.[78]

No one at Westinghouse imagined that the archaeologists of the future might ignore the time capsule altogether, and find much more interesting (as some archaeologists today already do) the ground around it—composed not of soil but of the remains of burnt trash, petrified horse manure, and coal cinders. Perhaps the time capsule creators of the past also dramatically underestimated future archaeologists. Perhaps these future explorers of dirt and rock will attain, or even surpass, the impossibly extrapolative, near-mystical investigative powers we now see displayed on shows like *CSI*, where a fleck of dust (which we find out is dead human skin, which contains DNA) yields a complete world and all the events that have happened in it. These futurians will shine their science through a grain of ancient cinder, and a whole New York City will flash up into appearance, skyscrapers framed with beams of light instead of steel. Unlike the inert microfilm reels and asbestos cloth swatches and safety razors ensconced in the time capsule, perhaps this projection of New York will pulse and move, and archaeologists will walk through it, encounter characters wearing Brooks Brothers suits and Tiffany diamonds, who smile and dance and truly believe they are alive. Will the archaeologists have the heart to tell them, as Fitzgerald once did, that beneath their rotgut radiance, their shimmering surfaces, they are all made of ash?

The near future is perhaps hardest to predict. Within decades of being sealed in, the time capsule and the crypt would turn out in many ways not to be exceptional at all, and thus to be of no great interest to archaeologists. By the 1970s, the crypt was all but forgotten when an Oglethorpe University student stumbled upon it and began publishing articles about it, bringing it back into scholarly and pop culture awareness. Nonetheless, in their designs these data preservation projects prefigured the future in a way their creators hadn't foreseen—the data complex would breed a constellation of sealed-off spaces, storehouses of records, of the memory and life of the nation itself. The Crypt shows us the structure of bunkers that would fan out across the country in the Cold War, haunted by the specter of nuclear destruction. Jacobs did not imagine that the crypt would typify the archives not meant to send a message to the future, but that became the basis for the function of everyday life by the beginning of the twenty-first century. The difference would be that the steel door would not be welded shut, but kept sealed by an armed guard who would control its opening and closing.

The Cold War would be defined not so much by visions of absolute annihilation (which are the opposite of visions), but by nightmare scenarios of surviving the end of the world. This survival would be made possible by spaces like the crypt, underground and secure but open, armed by guards in remote and sometimes secret installations built to protect our records, to protect the data that was becoming increasingly synonymous with our lives.

# 3

## Bombproof Cavemen

We were a peaceful town.

Show us a war, we'd say, and we'll show you

dust on the beakers. Dust on the hazard suits.

A fine thing to tell ourselves, beside the clock

and coffee shop, the Adirondack chairs.

In truth, we'd strew their fingers everywhere.

—Natalie Shapero, "Our War"

A little over 12,000 years ago in what is now New England, a massive glacier carved its way across the landmass, leaving behind a constellation of lakes and ponds, not to mention the river that would later be named after Henry Hudson, initiator of the conquest that opened the door to industrialization. The glaciers also created Boston Harbor, which would attract merchants, shipping concerns, and all manner of trade and capital accumulation. Unlike the mummy complex, which grew out of arid environments, in the United States the data complex sprang from carbon-rich, wet soils and the coastal and waterway formations bequeathed by the relatively recent geological past. The worldwide headquarters of Iron Mountain, now the largest secure records and data storage company in the world, is in Boston, and its first facility was in the Hudson Valley. These are not random sites within the history of capitalism, or of mining, or of information, but places poised by their geological formations and resulting ecology for the industries that later developed there.

In 1806, Frederic Tudor bought his first ship to carry ice cut from frozen lakes in New England to the tropical climes of the Caribbean.[1] Tudor's venture lost money for years, and he even ended up in debtors' prison a number of times. But he was so convinced of the profitability of natural ice harvesting and shipping that he persevered, and by the 1830s he was known as the "Ice King" and had made a sizable fortune by successfully shipping his ice around the world. In *Walden*, Henry David Thoreau comments on a gang of workers cutting ice for export from his beloved pond in the winter: "Ice is an interesting subject for contemplation. They told me they had some in the ice-houses at Fresh Pond five years old that was as good as ever." The icehouses were so well insulated, and the quantity of giant blocks so great, that the ice could last that long in storage and then survive the voyage to serve, in Thoreau's words, "the sweltering inhabitants of Charleston and New Orleans, of Madras and Bombay and Calcutta."[2]

Tudor tried to secure a monopoly on ice shipping, but he did not succeed, and those who followed him into the business transformed a network of New England ponds and rivers into manufacturers of cold. Building on the infrastructure created by Tudor, a bustling ice harvesting industry developed in the Hudson River valley in the late nineteenth century, with 135 icehouses lining the riverbanks between the Big Apple and Albany.[3] With increasing urbanization facilitated by railroads in the nineteenth century, the demand for fresh meat and produce increased as urban areas like New York City grew rapidly. Like Boston, New York City has a geological advantage: the Hudson estuary is one of the largest natural harbors in the world, attracting fort builders and invaders and traders, and ships carrying a wide array of goods. Commercial icehouses transported massive blocks on railcars and barges, the flatbed vessels pulled by tugboats down the Hudson, each one typically freighting between 400 and 800 tons of ice, often stored belowdecks to keep it close to the cold river water and prevent melting.[4] In 1855, New York City consumed 75,000 tons of ice, but by the 1880s, "this figure had reached approximately 2.5 million tons."[5]

However, with the invention of artificial refrigeration in the early twentieth century, combined with the pollution of lakes and rivers from urban industries, the ice harvesting companies of the Hudson River valley disappeared almost completely by World War I. But the ice companies did leave behind their large icehouses. These lay dormant for years: rotting, catching fire, being vandalized, and awaiting a new purpose.[6]

In the early years of the Cold War, Herman Knaust found the use these empty icehouses had been waiting for. Throughout the Northeast, Knaust was known as the "Mushroom King." He had worked his way up from literally shoveling shit on the banks of the Hudson River and nurturing mushroom spores in his cellar, to growing 300,000 pounds of mushrooms a year in abandoned warehouses left behind by the natural ice trade, not to mention the subterranean tunnels of defunct mines that provided the perfect combination of dampness and darkness. By the 1940s, he single-handedly supplied roughly a fifth of the mushrooms consumed in the entire country.[7] Eventually, Knaust Cavern Mushrooms grew to be the largest producer in the world.[8]

But after World War II, Knaust faced increased competition from Europe and Asia.[9] He needed a new direction and hoped to make use of a former iron ore mine he had purchased in 1936. It had once provided raw materials for Union bullets during the Civil War, and the Knaust family had grown some mushrooms in the mine for the World War II antibiotics effort, but the war was over now, and a truly huge operation would be necessary to make good use of the mine. An *American Magazine* profile of Knaust titled "Bombproof Caveman" explains that he came up with his new business plan while working with his church to relocate refugees who'd lost their identity documents during World War II. These refugees encouraged him to create a business that would protect vital records. So when the Russians tested a nuclear weapon, he went into action. He rented an office in the Empire State Building and installed underground vaults for paper and microfilm records in the caverns of his iron ore mine, 125 miles outside of Manhattan.[10]

In 1951, Knaust founded the Iron Mountain Atomic Storage Company (IMASC). The *Saturday Evening Post* called it "the safest place in the world."

It marked a new stage in the emergent practices in the data complex, which both persisted and intensified in response to the coming of the atomic bomb. As this chapter will show, a booming industry of bombproofing and securitization made possible the expansion of "open time capsule" design to a nationwide network of data preservation facilities. Banks, insurance companies, government archives, and state and local repositories moved microfilm backups of their vital records to these sites decades before the digital age, creating a backup culture (long before "the cloud") whose legacy still shapes the way we live today. If the goal of the time capsule was to condense an entire culture into a relatively small amount of data as a onetime communication to the future, then the aim of the constellation of open time capsules that emerged during the Cold War was to amass and preserve all the details, all the data that documented all individual American lives, that materially grounded identity and certified citizens' existence by the authority of powerful institutions, and make it accessible both before and after the end of the world.

### The Birth of Open Time Capsules

The East River Savings Bank and Loan, the first client of the fledgling IMASC, transported microfilm duplicates of its customers' account records in armored cars driven by gun-wielding guards to Knaust's small mountain in the Catskills, though the records would "in the main be just scraps of paper to thieves."[11] This intensely guarded, worthless shipment included "microfilmed records showing the bank balances of its 200,000 depositors, along with 200,000 duplicate-signature cards and a like amount of blank ledger sheets and devices to enlarge and read the microfilm."[12] The single entrance to the mine was 500 feet above river level and sealed by a bank vault door "heavier than the one protecting the nation's gold at Fort Knox." A round-the-clock security force of a dozen former police officers and state troopers "armed with .45s and tommy guns"[13] unlocked the door so that the boxes of microfilm could be hauled up a 900-foot-long corridor of steel-reinforced concrete, the floor of which was slightly inclined, making the mine effectively waterproof.[14] The individual subterranean vaults were fire resistant, air-conditioned, and, like the first permanent time capsules, built and maintained according to the specifications of the NBS. A diesel generator, tested weekly, backed up the electrical supply in case of a power outage, and the mine held emergency stores of food and water.

Corporate and state records were transported and stored under armed guards and constant surveillance because the continuity of corporate capitalism and liberal democratic government relied on the survival of these microfilms. Within the data complex then, records took on a peculiar form of value. The corporate microfilms and paper documents preserved at IMASC were both valueless and, in another sense—as a collective archive underwriting the everyday financial, social, and institutional transactions of American life—priceless. For instance, global sporting goods and excursion outfitter Abercrombie and Fitch sent microfilm backups of the charge account records of 80,000 customers to IMASC, as well as the collection history of every "derogatory account."[15] Every night, Abercrombie and Fitch workers microfilmed every sales check from that day and sent the miniature duplicates to IMASC by registered mail.

Each of the 400 vaults at IMASC was a time capsule: sterilized, purified, buried underground, protected from the insects, dust, and other natural forces of time and decay. But unlike the permanent time capsules of the Depression, sealed off from the world by a steel door welded shut or an immortal well filled with pitch and capped by a stone pylon, these Cold War capsules were open. These securitized vaults obeyed the preservative logic of the time capsule, but rather than delivering data to the future, they served as an ongoing backup for the present. Whereas Egyptian tomb builders used curses and incantations (and huge rocks) to block violations of their timeless sancta, and the time capsules of the Depression basically did the same with the inscriptions on their site markers, the vaults of Iron Mountain guaranteed eternity with guns, surveillance, the "bombproof" architecture of steel-reinforced concrete, and combination locks that were on both the bank vault door at the entrance and each of the inner rooms' doors lining the corridor of the mine.

Iron Mountain was at the forefront of a broad shift in the data complex. During the early Cold War, corporations and the federal government sought to preserve their ability to bounce back from a nuclear attack, and began backing up all of their important records on microfilm copies stored in remote "bombproof" storage facilities. IMASC was the paradigmatic open time capsule, its geographical isolation, bank vaults, armed guards, and bombproof concrete construction embodying the primary features of the data complex's rapid expansion in the mid-twentieth century.[16] The First National Bank of Boston "built a concrete and steel bunker in Pepperell, Massachusetts, to hold microfilms of its own records as well as the records of nine other banks leasing space." The bunker was equipped with an air filtration system "to eliminate radioactive particles" as well as "a shower where bankers could decontaminate themselves." One entered the bunker through a former bank vault door that weighed 16,000 pounds.[17] Chase also had "emergency corporate headquarters," and a remote storage facility built inside of a former bottling plant. Beginning with a shipment of 1,200 tons of records in 1951, the depository grew to the point that it was receiving 2 miles of microfilm per day, and 19,000 references were added to it each month.[18] Standard Oil had alternate headquarters in Morristown, New Jersey, with "its own electric generator, artesian well, and a sprinkling system on the roof" that would wash fallout from the building after a nuclear attack.

Other companies that took the precaution of storing microfilm records in alternate locations included Bell and Howell, Minnesota Mining and Manufacturing, International Harvester, International Business Machines, and McGraw-Hill Publishing. The New York Stock Exchange was storing records in the Adirondacks,[19] and even the Huntington Library built a bombproof vault 30 feet belowground where its precious manuscripts and paintings could be rushed to safety during a nuclear attack. At a cost of $250,000 ($2.5 million today), the vault was equipped with a 17-inch-thick door that, combined with its reinforced frame, weighed 30 tons.[20]

While microfilm had existed as long as daguerreotypes, it was only in the 1930s that its institutional use grew so widespread that it became a routine medium for the duplication of paper vital records, and eventually became itself a medium of vital records.[21] An April 1951 article in *National Safety News* called "Microfilm Safeguards Vital Records" describes a preservation effort by the Ford Motor Company. Beginning in 1948, Ford microfilmed over 1,250,000 of its "vital designs and engineering tracings which would be essential in putting the company back into operation in the event of a major disaster."[22] Consistent with the broader tendencies of the data complex at this time, Ford placed negative copies of microfilms in "fireproof storage vaults in Dearborn while the positive copies [were] stored in bombproof underground vaults far removed from [Ford's River Rouge plant]."[23] Up until the time of the microfilming, "many of engineering's 1,000,000 tracings, 50,000 of which [were] considered active, were stored in basements and other out-of-the-way places. They were subject to loss by fire, flood or other damage, and were taking up some 4,000 square feet of much needed floor space."[24]

The advent of atomic bombs could have provoked the collapse of the data complex, an abandonment of any dreams of preserving data permanently in the face of such an annihilatory device. Instead, the data complex intensified. The United States never built a nationwide network of bomb shelters to protect American lives from a nuclear attack. Instead, it built a constellation of vaults, invented a bombproof geography and architecture, gathered and buried the equivalent of billions of Westinghouse Time

Capsules of microfilm, and lined libraries and archives with gun-wielding guards, all to protect Americans' "data bodies," that newly solidified aspect of American lives that wedded them to data, and to the powerful institutions that collected and controlled it. By this time, the data body was comprised of "education files, medical files, employment files, financial files, communication files, travel files, and for some, criminal files."[25] Just as NBS scientists scrambled to define "permanence" during the Depression, civil defense planners, engineers, and architects needed to create specifications whereby buildings, safes, vaults, or even filing cabinets could be considered "bombproof."

And the first step in figuring out what will and will not survive a bomb was to simulate the data complex's destruction: Haul everything out to a fenced-off expanse in the desert and place it inside an assortment of structures, cinder block and brick and stick built. Place cameras on tripods and equip an army of men with clipboards and hazmat suits. Then drop bombs on everything you brought and built there. Take notes, measurements, photographs, and collect samples of sand—turn the obliterated remains into data. The resulting scientifically validated concept of bombproofing would make possible a widespread, if shaky, faith in the efficacy of the data complex's new stratum of securitized facilities and in the durability of the power structure and data bodies of the nation it preserved in the face of atomic bombs.

Still, as significant as the Bomb was in spurring the invention of bombproofing as a science, the serious investigation of bombproofing actually originated earlier, just after the United States entered World War II, in studies on how to ensure that bombs caused more destruction, not less.

### Typical German and Japanese Cities

Just west of Salt Lake City, Utah, an evaporated sea has left behind flatlands where only desert vegetation like pickleweed, greasewood, juniper brush, and bud sage can grow. No long-timbered pines or redwoods to be made into ski chalets or picnic tables, no corn or wheat, no grass for cattle grazing. This flatland's deep geological past destined it for something else. Tectonic plates folded into mountain ranges all around it, catching the moisture from storm systems that might otherwise move over the basin, leaving the land arid, fruitless.[26] Its empty clarity is what it had to offer, a place where data can be conjured clearly in the mirror of the sand's steaming hot surface, where detonations' shock waves can travel uninhibited across its vast flatness. So, in the wake of the Japanese attack on Pearl Harbor, the U.S. military turned this area into a weapons range called the

Dugway Proving Ground. It is a place built for the rehearsal of destruction, a place that is now larger than Rhode Island, spanning 800,000 acres.

On the other side of the world, the primordial shifts of landmasses and bursts of volcanic activity that created the Japanese archipelago left it with no petroleum deposits. The attack on Pearl Harbor was in direct response to a U.S. oil embargo that blocked Japan's access to fuel—when the United States and others prevented oil importation into Japan, the country lost over 80 percent of its usual supply. The surprise attack on Pearl Harbor was meant to be a decisive blow that would delay or prevent the United States from entering the war, and thereby allow Japan to continue taking over parts of Southeast Asia, where it could exploit the petroleum deposits there.[27]

Standard Oil took less than two months to erect the "typical" Japanese and German homes for bomb tests at Dugway in 1942. The resulting report, *Design and Construction of Typical German and Japanese Test Structures at Dugway Proving Grounds, Utah*, published by the Standard Oil Development Company in May 1943, includes several haunting photographs of the finished, empty-aired, utterly undisturbed home interiors just before their firebombing. These images of "Typical German Furnishings" show things that were crafted with extreme care so that they could be destroyed and thus flood spreadsheets with data, from the "Credenza, Chairs, Table and Settee in a Typical Dining Room Arrangement" to the "overstuffed sofa" in the "Typical Crowded Living Room in Workers Quarters." The most thoroughly chilling image is plain and dim, and bears a caption that glows darkly: "Beds, Crib and Bedside Table in Bedroom."[28]

The Dugway tests were as much a study of how architecture resists destruction by bombs as a study of how to destroy homes and factories. Early in World War II, Winston Churchill had wanted the United States to supply him with 500,000 anthrax bombs so that he could devastate six major German cities. Franklin D. Roosevelt refused to give Churchill the anthrax.[29] Instead, the president promised to deliver a more effective incendiary bomb, a type of weapon that had shown limited effectiveness against the masonry construction characteristic of urban areas in Germany.[30]

When FDR made his promise to Churchill, thereby setting the stage for the creation of Dugway, bombproofing wisdom was still rudimentary. Best practices were basically little more advanced than digging a hole in the ground beneath the hardest stuff you could find, such as a mountain, or burrowing into a hillside and covering it with stone or concrete. The concept of "bombproofing" still hadn't been backed up by data that proved which materials could withstand a certain amount of blast force and fire. A quick search in the Library of Congress's online holdings shows two black Union soldiers posing in an 1864 photo, seated in front of what looks like a rough version of a hobbit house built into a hill: the "bomb-proof quarters" of a "Major Strong" in Dutch Gap, Virginia.[31]

In the 1940s, "bombproof" was more of a cultural construction than an empirically verifiable attribute of architecture—as it still is today. As new weaponry develops constantly, and bombs can detonate aboveground, belowground, or in other ways that are impossible for civil defense engineers to predict, belief in bombproofing requires a constant renewal of faith through more tests of more materials. And as these tests continue, the data complex grows, thickens, lengthens its half-life further into the deep future.[32]

The Chemical Warfare Service teamed up with Standard Oil to fulfill FDR's promise to make a most effective incendiary bomb, but it wouldn't be easy. Prior to 1942, American and British incendiary bombs' key components were rubber and magnesium. Supplies to these materials were cut off by Japan's military presence in the Pacific and its capture of rubber plantations in the East Indies and Malaya, so a new material was needed.[33]

Louis Fieser at Harvard was working on toxic gas, but when that was discontinued, he put his energy into finding an alternative incendiary material. What he came up with was a "gelled-fuel" solution, what we now know as napalm.[34] The new weapon was tested first at the Jefferson Proving Ground in southern Indiana, where the military had bought farmland and over 400 houses in the area, giving people a month to move and get their belongings out. The military also disinterred the dead and moved the cemetery of St. Magdalene Catholic Church, but it left the deconsecrated church structure in place so servicemen could bomb it and observe napalm's infernal effects.[35]

But to be certain that carpet bombing the most populated cities in Germany and Japan would cause absolute devastation, the military needed to test its new incendiary—now named the M69—against structures that were similar to the ones in those cities. The architects and designers who served as consultants for the bombing tests considered the wooden eaves of the attic the "Achilles' heel" of German architecture. The M69 didn't just explode upon impact—it was designed to penetrate the roof of a German dwelling, landing in the attic, which was the only part of the home built out of wood, where it would spew a jet of gelled gasoline and white phosphorous, igniting fires that were difficult to put out. When white phosphorous lands on human bodies, it causes "severe thermal and chemical burns, often down to the bone, that are slow to heal and likely to develop infections." The bandages on wounds must be changed daily and the dead flesh scraped away, an indescribable level of pain that one surgeon compared to being "flayed alive." If burn treatments don't succeed in removing all of the white phosphorous fragments, they can reignite when exposed to oxygen. Doctors have reported the healing process taking months, because when they tried to "scrape the dead tissue" away from the burn, "flames leapt out."[36]

The military hired consultants expert in German architecture and consulted RKO Pictures' art department, as the company had recently re-created authentic German interiors for its hit film *Hitler's Children*. Because there was no wood below the attic level, the custom-built furnishings were very important to re-create accurately, for they would serve as the primary fuel for the fires ignited by the incendiary bombs. So the faithful simulation of civilian homes wasn't just to accurately represent German life; it was about seeing whether the bomb could start a fire fierce enough to spread to the rest of the house through the upholstery and guts of the furniture.

The section of the Standard Oil report on Japan begins with "Figure 18: Aerial Views of Typical Japanese Cities" and shows the rooftops and smokestacks of industrial sections, including workers' quarters, in the cities of Osaka, Nagoya, Kobe, Yawata, Kyoto, and Tokyo. Even as U.S. soldiers were stripping Japanese Americans of their homes, land, art collections, heirlooms, and cash assets, and cramming them into nondescript shacks of concentration camps in Tule Lake, Minidoka, and Manzanar, the bomb testers were building the most authentic Japanese homes that they could, down to the tatami floor mat. According to the report, the "Tatami floor mats are the most important item of Japanese furnishing since they greatly influence bomb penetration as well as the inflammability of the test structure."[37] Where the military could acquire originals, made in Japan, it did, but it supplemented these with imitation mats made with istle, found to be similarly penetrable and combustible to authentic ones.[38] I can't help but wonder whether some of the tatami mats "acquired" in San Francisco came from homes of Japanese Americans forced into internment camps.

### "The Bombsight Mirror"

Just as the tests suggested, the firebombing of Japan proved devastating. The damage was far more destructive and deadly than the two atomic bombs combined. In a single night, Curtis LeMay's command burned to death 100,000 Japanese civilians. In Errol Morris's documentary *The Fog of War*, former secretary of defense Robert McNamara says U.S. bombers killed 50 to 90 percent of the people in 67 Japanese cities. In a matter of five months in 1945, U.S. incendiary weapons killed over 1 million Japanese people. "This was all before the atomic bombs, which were also dropped LeMay's command, by the way," McNamara reminds viewers emphatically.[39]

It's impossible to communicate the horrors of firebombing, though Richard Rhodes's descriptions of it are unforgettable. In his monumental book *The Making of the Atomic Bomb*, he describes the bombing of Hamburg, so intense it turned into a conflagration—a fire so expansive and violent it lashes out for more oxygen with force sufficient to cause a firestorm.[40] Hamburg's downtown was hit with the equivalent of hurricane winds, even as the fire burned so hot it melted glass in the windows of streetcars. A nineteen-year-old woman witnessed a scene like something out of Dante, where the asphalt of the street had melted, and people who ran across the roadway "without thinking" had gotten their feet stuck, and "then they had to put out their hands to try to get out again. They were on their hands and knees screaming." A fifteen-year-old girl who survived the firestorm told of how people's "brains had tumbled from their burst temples and their insides from the soft parts under the ribs," how the morning after, small children "lay like fried eels on the pavement." People who managed to get off the street and underground before the bombs fell fared no better, for as Rhodes writes, "Bodies of the dead cooked in pools of their own fat in sealed shelters like kilns." At least 45,000 Germans died that night, "the majority of them old people, women and children."[41]

In his essay "War against the Center," Harvard historian of science Peter Galison explains how researchers at the United States Strategic Bombing Survey (USSBS) both analyzed German and Japanese infrastructure during World War II in order to locate the best bomb targets, and, at the end of the war, analyzed the damage of U.S. bombing campaigns, interviewed survivors, and wrote reports about the destructive effects of bombings on both industrial production and human populations.[42] These researchers were haunted by these experiences on the ground, and they could not help but imagine the same kind of devastation wreaked on American cities. Their reports were highly influential, and by 1951, President Truman made a speech that urged industrialists to disperse their production facilities so that no single bomb could strike a concentrated area of industrial production and severely diminish American economic and military strength. Galison calls this haunting effect on Americans' understanding of their own infrastructure (which, ironically, had never been bombed) "the bombsight mirror": "Bombing the Axis economy and dispersing the American one were reflections of one another."[43]

The National Security Resources Board (NSRB) quickly transformed President Truman's imperative into simplified, graphic propaganda that disseminated and legitimated the logic of industrial dispersion to local communities. In a publication called *Is Your Plant a Target?* the NSRB urged local leaders to form committees that would identify likely "target areas" in their communities, such as factories or power plants in urban zones, and make plans for dispersing concentrations of industrial production facilities to areas on the fringe of their cities, effectively driving suburbanization.[44] Communities were to create "dispersion reports" that mapped the areas most likely to be bombed. Galison argues that these "self-targeting analyses" translated the haunting of bombsight mirroring from the perceptual frames of USSBS officials and military leaders to the self-perception of everyday Americans. Beyond appeals to patriotism and national duty, the NSRB also persuaded communities to create self-targeting maps by making them a required component in applications for "certificates of necessity" for industrial companies, which gave them tax breaks, and facilitated "the approval of defense loans and the securing of defense contracts."[45] Throughout this process, which transformed the "architectures of infrastructure, computation, highways, and factories lay the remarkable practice of training Americans to see themselves as targets."[46]

## Operation Time Capsule

Much like the NBS scientists whose findings were cited in a wide variety of professional journals, researchers at the National Records Management Council (NRMC) called for the construction of fireproof and bombproof vaults for corporate records similar to those of IMASC. The NRMC provided influential guidance to corporate and state records managers on how to keep records organized in order to aid historians writing the history of business, to increase corporate efficiency, and to ensure the swift reconstruction of businesses in the wake of a nuclear attack or other disaster. Founded in 1948, the NRMC consisted of representatives from business, government, archival, and historical professions, and it "emerged from and carried on the work of the New York Committee on Business Records, the Society of American Archivists, the Business Historical Society, the American Historical Society, and the Economic History Association." The NRMC "published guidelines that set industry standards for filing systems, records centers, and engineering documents, . . . compiled the first index to Federal records retention requirements," and "sponsored the first conference on records management in 1950, which was held annually for about a decade." Its early clients included "the City of New York, E. I. DuPont de Nemours

& Co., Bethlehem Steel, the Rockefeller Family, and the states of Rhode Island and Illinois."[47]

NRMC researchers published reports and articles in journals such as *Business History Review, American Archivist*, and *Credit and Financial Management*, wherein they cited numerous instances of businesses overseas that survived World War II because their records were properly preserved, though bombs had heavily damaged or completely destroyed their factories and equipment. Even American businesses that suffered the minor fires that were rather routine in the first half of the twentieth century sometimes had to close shop as a result of severe water damage caused by firefighters' hoses. While their buildings and equipment received light or even no damage, their records were utterly destroyed. Thus they had no records of their accounts, of how much they owed suppliers or how much their clients owed them, no engineering drawings and blueprints, no financial records for tax purposes, etc., and consequently could not continue to operate.[48]

In the September 1955 issue of *Business History Review*, senior vice president of the NRMC Arthur Barcan published "Records Management and the 'Paperwork Age,'" in which he made the case for records management as a "new science."[49] According to Barcan, the work of the "records veteran" is to fight the "Battle of the Bulk," the mass of corporate records routinely generated in the course of business, most of which is not only not vital but useless to both the corporation itself in future planning and to the historian.[50] The main strategy for winning this battle was a records management system called "Operation Time Capsule," a term that weds war imagery, normalizing the securitization of records under armed protection and 24/7 surveillance, to the logic of the time capsule—namely, that a tiny cross section of scientifically selected records can effectively index a given historical period. But whereas the Westinghouse Time Capsule and the Crypt of Civilization were sealed and inaccessible until a date in the distant future, the records preserved through Operation Time Capsule were always changing, being added to or subtracted from. Accessible through securitized channels, they would provide for a more immediate resurrection of civilization by reviving specific businesses and state agencies.[51] The open time capsule, then, was not only a material practice in facilities like IMASC but also a master metaphor deployed to imagine how businesses could lose 95 percent of their records, and yet retain the memories essential to revive and regain their wealth and power, even after, and as soon as possible after, the end of the world.

As Arthur Barcan worked to establish the field of records management, he also aided the military in their bombproofing investigations. Formerly a captain in the U.S. Army, Barcan would apply his two primary areas of expertise in a military exercise code-named Operation Teapot.

## Two Hundred Suns

No one talks about this atomic bomb test. In the Nevada desert, a technician recorded the distance between the plotted ground zero and a file cabinet, a three-drawer tower like a hopelessly angular totem pole representing generations of men whose personalities and lives were exactly the same. A safe, another file cabinet, this one slightly protected behind a half wall of concrete, all this office equipment scattered across nested invisible perimeters mapped onto the sand. Then a ten-megaton bomb detonated and dented, flattened, and scorched metal file cabinets that were supposedly fireproof, safes built not for banks but for everyday American offices, their shelves holding the precious documents and secreted cash of fictional lives pulverized, or sheltered and awaiting the fallout, in a cascade of divine fire, steely strongboxes like barrels surviving the plunge down a cataract of plummeting brimstone.

From February to May 1955, the NRMC and the Safe Manufacturers National Association, after accepting an invitation from the Federal Civil Defense Administration, carried out Operation Teapot at the Nevada Test Site. The report of the tests was titled *Effects of a Nuclear Explosion on Records and Records Storage Equipment*, and it described the yield of the "Apple II shot" as equivalent to approximately 30,000 tons of TNT.[52] The report reproduced the emerging language of records as both the mind and body of corporations, stating, "Business records are the memory of an organization. Preservation of important business records in a disaster can help ensure survival of managerial direction and continuity of enterprise."[53] All of the cabinets and safes contained "typical records and records materials such as correspondence, paper samples, documents, microfilm, and sample telegraph messages."[54] Operation Teapot was the superlative version of the "accelerated aging" experiments used in the NBS studies— the flash from the bomb detonation was, according to one journalist, 200 times the brilliance of the sun, like nearly a year's worth of daylight experienced in an instant. The test site scientists even went to the trouble of printing and placing in safes fake stock certificates and bonds issued by imaginary corporations, like substantial ghosts created to be bombed from nonexistence to nonexistence, so that every aspect of their fantastic journey could be measured and reduced to data. The data complex expanded and transformed in response to these engineered nuclear spectacles and their resultant specters.

The Operation Teapot bomb test embodied the particular anxieties that cohered around data and technology in the early years of the Cold War. The nuclear test subjects—file cabinets and safes in this case—were numbered, and depending on their distance from ground zero, and whether they were "shielded" or "unshielded" by a wall or concrete basement or wooden house, they either remained whole and intact or were blown open, their inner records exposed or torn and twisted in misshapen masses. These images point to the fact that dispersal was not the only response to the nuclear threat. Not all data could be stored in bombproof locations like IMASC, far from target areas, so "a concurrent strand of thinking was to fortify the everyday environment."[55] The notion that the most mundane of everyday objects, such as file cabinets, need to be reinforced against the blasts of war highlights the extent to which the imperatives of civil defense successfully infiltrated everyday life in America. A couple of years later, Operation Plumbbob tested the Bomb against a Mosler bank vault to see whether it could resist the blast and protect its contents. The safe and vault manufacturer had made much in its ads about the fact that one of its safes survived the atomic bomb dropped on Hiroshima, but nuclear weapons had grown stronger since then. Nevertheless, after the test, the "vault interior was well protected," and "the vault contents were only slightly disturbed by the blast."[56]

These results reveal how, even as early as 1955, the entire practice of bombproofing was deeply saturated with fantasy. By that time, the hydrogen bomb had already existed for three years, so political leaders, scientists, and corporate officers at companies like Mosler were well aware of its surpassing destructive power, a force too violent for anything built by humans to survive. A direct hit would certainly demolish even Mosler's most stalwart designs. The first hydrogen bomb, tested in 1952, virtually erased the island of Elugelab in the South Pacific and replaced it with a 1,500-foot-wide crater in the ocean floor. The "Mike Shot" proved to be 500x more powerful than the bomb dropped on Hiroshima, exploding with "twice the power of all the explosive power of all the bombs used in World War II."[57] As Garrett Graff explains, "Cities would be leveled and excavated by a hydrogen bomb, destroying any benefit from a basement shelter."[58]

### "My Career Is in Films?"

In the effort to preserve the life of business and government by bombproofing data, individual Americans' data bodies were also preserved. A 1944 advertisement for Recordak microfilm—the company that first innovated the use of microfilm in banking, insurance, and department store records—powerfully illustrates the way in which microfilm records were vital to the corporation, the state, and the individual, beginning in the 1940s. The ad frames microfilm as a format whose durability and secure storage guarantees the perpetuation of individual identities that materialize in their vital records. The ad also implies that microfilm records constitute a duplicate self, yet one without which the self itself would cease to exist. This body of records, this data body, contains bank and department store accounts, selective service numbers, social security records, and life insurance policies. It is seemingly located in the ether, not in a specific location subject to threats of destruction, but rather in a kind of nonlocation made all the more secure because you do not know where it is. The scattered distribution of the records makes them seem safer because they cannot be destroyed by a single bomb strike or comparable disaster. The ad encourages readers to feel an increased sense of security that their individual identities, their "careers" as human beings, are recorded, preserved, and duplicated to prevent their total loss.

All this documentation of the average American was a relatively new development, only recently normalized. As Sarah Igo points out in her book *The Known Citizen*, in the nineteenth century it was members of the middle class and upper crust of society that were "undocumented"—not subject to state surveillance and monitoring and recording of their activities. Americans only became more comfortable with universal registration of their births and deaths and documentation of their lives when the government began to require such data in order to access entitlements, like social security payouts. Less than two decades before the founding of IMASC, many Americans had associated the heavy documentation of one's life with criminality, or questionable character, or being under the thumb of a totalitarian regime.

But by the early 1940s, the government, as well as corporations like Recordak, was disseminating publicity aimed at helping more Americans warm up to the idea that the data body was a solid, sprawling thing that certified and enhanced their lives. Several businesses across the country dedicated themselves to making metal social security nameplates. *Billboard* magazine offered a free calfskin billfold with your social security number, name, army or navy insignia, and address engraved in gold plus a free bonus gift: a "beautiful three-color lifetime Identification Plate" that carried "your full name, address and social security or draft number." These backup loops of paper, microfilm, metal, and even leather betrayed the uncertainty attending the new medium of microfilm even as it ascended to archival dominance. In a few cases, the backup loop included the body as well, as some men had their social security number tattooed on their arm, or even etched into their dentures.[59]

A resistant reading of the Recordak ad, however, might interpret the subject as ensnared in a web of permanent records, a web that ensures his subjection to the powerful institutions that preserve the records that define his identity, require him to pay his debts, to serve and die in wars, to buy bonds to pay for those wars, to consume in department stores, to cover his checks. His body comprises these records swirling around his floating head; his subjectivity is fragmented, as he is subject to a multiplicity of institutional powers. His clean-shaven, white, and symmetrical middle-aged face is a visualization of the typical or average American in all its various yet highly circumscribed embodiments, from the Middleton family in the ads and film of Westinghouse, to Elmer the Typical American, who was the mascot of the World's Fair, to the widely publicized winners of the typical American family competition held by fair organizers.[60]

The Recordak ad also tries to obscure the paradoxical status of microfilm as a medium that represented both a guarantee of national and individual preservation and a threat to the nation. In "Microfilm, Containment, and the Cold War," Auerbach and Gitelman explain that microfilm was a medium that "promised preservation and destruction, security and risk."[61] Spaces of preservation like IMASC contained mundane department store account records and the like, but also held state secrets and sensitive information that might pose a risk to the nation if they fell into the wrong hands. Microfilm's ability to condense information and render it easily transportable made it "important as a storage medium, national in scope," but also "made it vulnerable to illicit appropriation. While microfilm could act as a safeguard against falling bombs, it might also be the very thing to cause those bombs to fall."[62] Most people don't think much about microfilm these days, but back in the early days of nuclear weaponry, those dense black rolls or tiny dots loomed larger in the public imagination. We now know that "something as complex as a nuclear bomb" could not be "reduced to a single text or mysterious formula that then might be smuggled out of the country," but in the early Cold War there was a common misperception that losing track of important microfilm "would be to risk the security of the nation-state itself."[63]

The vital records of the average American—a typical symbolic stand-in for the nation itself in American popular culture—became inseparable from the vital records of the corporation and the state. In microfilm records such as those stored at IMASC, then, institutional and individual interests in records preservation converged, and the securitized protection of

**Your Selective Service number—** with the exact time and order of its drawing—was photographed the Recordak way.

**Your V----Mail letters** to your boy overseas—and his to you—travel on Recordak microfilm exclusively ... for the V----Mail system, with its speed, space saving, and assurance of delivery, grew out of Recordak.

**Your Social Security** record—"the world's biggest bookkeeping job"—is safeguarded by Recordak ... files that would occupy acres are condensed to a few small cabinets.

**Your Life Insurance** policies, or the records relating to them, are filmed with Recordak by many insurance companies—thus files are condensed, made error-proof, tamper-proof.

WHO...ME?

MY CAREER IS IN FILMS?

**Every check you write—** if your account is in one of thousands of the country's progressive banks—is photographed by your bank, using Recordak ... protecting you and simplifying banking.

**Your War Bond purchase** records, bearing your name, are photographed by the Treasury, which uses the Recordak System to insure you against loss.

**Your Hospital "case history"—** even your hour-by-hour temperature chart —may be safely tucked away in "capsule size" in your hospital's file-on-film. Leading hospitals have adopted Recordak.

# Kodak's Recordak System safeguards
## the vital records of everyone's life

TAKE a nation of 135,000,000. Millions of them writing checks every day. Millions with insurance policies. Millions buying War Bonds, carrying Social Security, and being counted in the Census ...

What a chance for "mix-ups." Even if every clerk in every bank, department store, and government bureau were *perfect*—imagine the endless piles of accumulating records!

Then came bank-perfected Recordak— "photography in a nutshell." It brings an Insurance Policy down to postage-stamp size. It photographs canceled checks at the rate of 100 a minute. Being photographic, it puts on film the *exact* image of whatever it shoots.

Only a few of Recordak's applications are shown here. There are hundreds of others.

Filing space? With Recordak, it averages one per cent of that needed for the original documents. This photographic tool of banks, industry, business, and government, developed by Kodak, is "keeping the walls from bulging."

EASTMAN KODAK COMPANY
ROCHESTER, N. Y.

REMEMBER THE U. S. S. ALCHIBA ... not a warship, just a cargo vessel?—how, landing desperately needed supplies in the Solomons, she was struck by a Jap torpedo—and with her decks a hell of flame—her crew stayed by and saved both ship and cargo?—A stern example for us at home.
BUY MORE WAR BONDS

**Your Account Record** In many department stores ... is now kept on Recordak microfilm.

## Serving human progress through photography

**Your U.S. Census record—** the last time you were counted, and every other time —is now on Recordak microfilm ... along with the hundreds of millions of other Census records, going back to 1790.

**When you** lose a document that is important to you, it takes but a few minutes to locate it in the Recordak file, and bring it up to "life size" in the film reader. There's your lost Insurance Policy—or War Bond—or the Check with which you paid that Income Tax!

Recordak ad, 1944.

such universally vital records became a justified and logical strategy for preventing the destruction or theft of those documents. Microfilm was a "technology of miniaturization [that] offered a material way of measuring and visualizing the tensions between active human agents and larger impersonal structures of state that organized, domesticated, and jeopardized them. It depended upon the dual potency of information compressed and nation preserved."[64]

By the early Cold War and the founding of IMASC, microfilm records were not merely backups for paper records, as the Recordak ad suggests. Rather, they were constituent elements in a backup loop in which anxieties about the possible loss of original paper records led institutions to preserve duplicates in microfilm, and anxieties about the possible loss of microfilm led institutions to store reels in bombproof and fireproof securitized facilities while also continuing to preserve original paper records in other locations. Microfilm and paper documents were thus *mutual* backups in a circuitous fashion, and together they, in a loop, preserved nation, corporation, and citizen. Microfilm and paper duplicates were often stored at a distance from each other, a strategy of dispersion meant to prevent all the copies of any single record from being destroyed by bomb, fire, flood, or other disaster, and thus meant to preserve the nation itself and corporations against the same threats.[65]

### The Darlings of Doom Town

In 1955, legendary newscaster Walter Cronkite donned a pair of blast goggles, preparing to witness the worst that Operation Cue had to offer. The bomb test would generate data about which housing structures could survive an atomic attack as the fireball and shock wave decimated Doom Town, the nickname for "the tiny hamlet built to be destroyed in the atomic explosion."[66] All along "Doomsday Drive," single-family homes sat silently and patiently, populated by unblinking white mannequins arrayed around coffee tables. In one house, the mannequin family of Paul Darling spent their final minutes together sitting stiffly, staring blankly at one another, or at an empty span of drywall, all of them ignoring the brand-new console TV on the floor. The caption of the photo calls them "the typical American family," and indeed they are. The family dreamed up in the *Middletown* studies, and the eugenics exhibits at county and world's fairs, and the contests held by newspapers across the country, took on flesh in all those venues only to be transmuted into plastic for the purpose of providing data about what an atomic bomb could do to the typical people that, as Fiorello LaGuardia said, "make this country real."

The bomb that destroyed typical Americans in mannequin form—the Apple II shot—was the same bomb that destroyed file cabinets, safes, and fake stock certificates. Operation Cue was carried out as a smaller exercise within the overarching program of Operation Teapot. It was a dress rehearsal for the death of the two entangled halves of the American self, both the biobody and the data body. The same test meant to establish the bombproofness of Americans' data bodies simulated the destruction of their biological bodies with mannequin stand-ins. Beyond the plastic people, waiting to be destroyed were all manner of consumer products, from cars to radios, chicken potpies buried in the ground and other foodstuffs lining trenches, not to mention "typical infrastructure" providing electricity and other utilities to the suburban dreamworld of Doom Town.[67] Where Westinghouse had pristinely preserved consumer goods, the bomb test destroyed them; where Westinghouse had gathered them and sealed them into an airless capsule, the bomb test pulverized them, then spread the radioactive dust they'd become on the desert winds.

The bomb test that destroyed Paul Darling, his home, his typical American family, and all the data that documented their social and financial lives was an inversion, a radioactive mutation of the Westinghouse Time Capsule, like a newborn with exomphalos—its internal organs formed on the outside of its body. I draw inspiration for this metaphor from a 1951 essay that appeared in the journal *Credit and Financial Management*, titled "Will One Fire . . . or Bomb . . . Ruin Your Company?"[68] The essay compared businesses to biobodies and vital records to "certain vital organs absolutely necessary to existence." Emmett J. Leahy, coauthor of the essay and director of the NRMC, was fond of comparing the data body to the biobody in vivid ways—he also originated the influential concept of "a life cycle of records."[69]

The inversion of preservation in destruction is a part of time capsule logic and is embodied in the practice of bombproofing, where the rehearsal (through nuclear bomb tests) and imagination of atomic disaster evokes the obliteration and dispersal of all that the time capsule encloses and preserves. At the New York World's Fair, the winners of the typical American family contest took up temporary residence in model FHA homes, separate from the condensed cross section or "snapshot" of American culture that resided in the Westinghouse Time Capsule. The setting of the Darling mannequins, their J. C. Penney's clothing, and all the consumer products, from new cars to frozen food to home safes, were likewise a snapshot, a stilled moment in the nuclear diorama of American life at midcentury, complete with plasticized flesh molded from the very petroleum that powered it all, dressed in synthetics as if the swatches in the Westinghouse Time Capsule were seeds that grew into full garments. Indeed, the fabrics worn by the mannequins were meant to be representative in the same way the contents of a time capsule are, with "every type of fabric manufactured in the country today" being included. Also, the mannequins—"20 representing men, 20 simulating women, two boys and two girls, and six toddlers"—were specifically arrayed to "[represent] clothes for every occasion, work or play," the fabrics including "woolen goods, cottons, rayon, nylon, orlon, dacron and orlon fleece." An interview with Hillman Lee, manager of the Las Vegas J. C. Penney's store that donated the clothing, noted that mannequins "representing children [would] wear school clothes," and one toddler mannequin would be "clad in a baby's sleeper."[70]

In the bomb test, the Bomb stands in for all technology, replaces all the gadgets and gizmos featured at the New York World's Fair, from Elektro the Moto-Man and his dog Sparko to Sterilamp bulbs and color television. For the Bomb condenses the possibilities of all future technology into itself, pressurizes all corporate scientific promises of "a better tomorrow," and implodes them.

And yet the mannequins did not die but went back to work after the blast, like any good American. After their injuries were transmuted into data, J. C. Penney's displayed the forms in their department store windows, complete with their flash-burned polyester clothes stuck to their skin. A sign informed passersby, "These mannikins could have been live people, in fact, they could have been you."[71] Penney's even took out an ad in the *Las Vegas Review Journal*, complete with "before and after" photographs of the Bomb-burnt mannequins—women, men, and children—and encouragement that readers "volunteer now for Civil Defense" and, of course, stop by Penney's, where the fifty mannequins were on display.[72] The mannequins thus did their part to embed the data complex, in its bombproof fantasy iteration, in the minds of the public while they shopped, an activity that counted as leisure time in the new postwar hyperconsumerist society.

These postapocalyptic mannequins were not still as stone statues are still, but were more like taxidermy, an art meant to make dead things look alive, reanimating them under the pretext that their motionlessness is not evidence that they're lifeless, but actually just a frozen moment of their movement. The taxidermist stretches a poisoned pelt over an armature of bones, foam, and molded clay to provide a snapshot, or, more precisely an early version of bullet time, offering a three-dimensional, 360-degree view of an object, suspended. In this way, taxidermy not only mutilates a carcass but also vivisects time, and it thus presaged photography the way photographs foreshadowed time capsules.[73] Photography could create stills of

Original caption: "4/27/1955—Yucca Flat, Nevada: 'Operation Cue,' the name given to the atomic test at Yucca Flat which was postponed today because of an unexpected turn for the worse in the weather, finds everything in readiness in 'Doom Town,' the tiny hamlet built to be destroyed in the atomic explosion. Photo shows a 'typical American family' of mannequins which will be subject to the test." Reprinted by permission of Bettmann via Getty Images.

any body in motion; time capsules could capture a moment in time across an entire culture, a snapshot of all its knowledge and habits and desires through a curated amalgam of the typical. At the fair, the living bodies of Elmer, the event's mascot, or even the actors in *The Middleton Family* film, vivified the idea of the typical American, gave literal life to the data of culture in the capsule. At Operation Cue, the mannequins became imitations of those living bodies, their extruded skins made for the registration of damage and extraction of data about what bombs would do to real people.[74]

For the Egyptologist, archaeology is about finding broken things and putting them back together, whether shards of clay pots or dynastic chronologies, an active process that Elliot Colla terms "artifaction."[75] The bomb tester also created artifacts, blasted culture into fragments in the name of data, in order to learn how to protect us through bombproofing, through sealing our bodies and belongings inside vaults of steel or reinforced concrete. The bomb test, too, was an open time capsule, unsealed and unprotected,

American culture staged and flipped inside out, the enactment of the very end of the world feared by the time capsule creators of the 1930s. It's as if the bomb testers pulled the typical cultural objects out of the time capsule, used them as props to populate a doomed movie set, wrangled the typical American family from their FHA home, sat them on the couch and with a fossil-fueled Midas touch turned them to plastic, then bombed all of it toward oblivion in practice for the apocalypse. The dust of obliterated typicality—glass, Bakelite, wood, polyester, leather, fiberglass, asbestos, paint—mixed with the radioactive atoms to form fallout, uncontained, drifting on the wind, carried across state lines to places where typical Americans would breathe it in, drink it, eat it in their breakfast cereal, style it into their nests of hair.

The rehearsal of destruction stimulates the desire to preserve more intensively and extensively, and thus the data complex expands wider across the earth's surface, deeper beneath it. The data complex bombproofed the nation's industrial capacity and Americans' data bodies, but another task was just as vital: bombproofing the mind. The postattack scenarios of civil defense would build on the bombproofing of architecture, office equipment, and infrastructure, extending the material existence of the data complex yet again into the neural circuitry of the biobody. Civil defense propaganda harnessed visions of destruction and dreams of survival to modulate adrenaline and affect, conditioning us to feel anxiety about the Bomb and meet that feeling with preparation, not succumb to the paralysis of panic.[76] Joseph Masco has convincingly argued that "the primary goal of what was publicly called 'civil defense' was not to protect citizens from the exploding bomb but rather to psychologically reprogram them as Cold Warriors."[77] In Masco's definition, "Cold Warriors" were citizens that belonged to a public that was newly "constituted and militarized through a tailored vision of totalizing threat." The U.S. government deployed a carefully selected set of images to access the emotional life of citizens, who learned to "fear the bomb" and "to fuse that fear with anticommunism,"[78] in an obverse affirmation of corporate capitalist rule and its ever-expanding data complex.

## "Preservation Family from the Atomic War"

In the Corbis office, I flip through the cold files of the Bettmann Archive, photos of safes and bank vaults, shots of Fort Knox and rooms with walls lined floor to ceiling with gold bars, and stills of civil defense drills that simulated the moment right after the bomb blast. But civil defense drills weren't just a snapshot; they were more like a tableau vivant, with mannequins and sometimes actors representing the wounded and dead.[79] In Olney, Maryland, civil defense training took place on "Rescue Street," an attack simulation project authorized by the Federal Civil Defense Act of 1950. According to the caption on a 1952 photo from the United Press, Rescue Street "simulate[d] a typical United States city block, with frame dwellings, brick row houses, a three-story office and apartment building, a five-story business structure, and a two-story theater building with shops. The buildings [were] designed to simulate 'bombed-out' living and working structures, thus giving utmost possible realism to the training of defense personnel in advanced fire-fighting and rescue techniques."[80] People came from across the country to learn there, then return to share their new knowledge with peer professionals in health care and emergency response. In another photo, in the biggest air raid drill ever held in the country up to that point, civil defense workers help "casualties" walk down the stairs of a building in Times Square. Another photo shows a casualty pinned under a tree with someone removing it and a priest "comforting" the "victim," while another is carried from the rubble on a stretcher, the fictional bomb having detonated not too far away in the Bronx, at 165th and Jackson. In some of these exercises they even flew the mannequins away by helicopter as if life flighting them to the nearest level-one trauma center.

Just as some people enjoy reenacting battles from the Revolutionary or Civil War, this is war *pre*-enactment. The civil defense training drills took real people who fit the typical mold set out by actors in *The Middleton Family* film and turned those average people into actors. In a photo called *Disaster Scene*, an overturned bus is surrounded by a smattering of children playing dead or critically wounded while lying on the street in rural Wisconsin. Their faces and bodies are made up with fake blood and latex lacerations, and they are waiting for hazmat-clad first responders in training to put them on a stretcher and haul them to a makeshift hospital tent, where they would, soon enough, be told to come alive and smile for the cameras.

This is all strange. It is all also normal. For the early Cold War forged a new kind of social contract through civil defense, one based "not on the protection and improvement of everyday life but rather on the national contemplation of ruins." By the mid-1950s, Cold War paranoia meant that to associate with anyone even suspected of having communist leanings somehow put the nation at risk of utter destruction. At the same time, civil defense called on citizens to serve their country by participating in exercises that forcefully imagined that destruction. The living dead children spilling from the overturned school bus were performing the "public ritual" of "imagining one's home and city devastated, on fire and in ruins,"

**"Disaster Scene." Pewaukee, Wisconsin, June 14, 1966.**
**Reprinted by permission of Bettmann via Getty Images.**

fulfilling a new kind of "civic obligation to collectively imagine, and at times theatrically enact, the physical destruction of the nation-state."[81] World War I certainly brought a new level of devastation that inspired Europeans and Americans to imagine the end of the world in unprecedented ways,[82] in part laying the groundwork for the first permanent time capsules, deposited in the 1930s. But in the Cold War, on the heels of World War II's firestorms and atomic bombs, Americans made the end of the world not just something that might happen in the future, but a part of the present. Since the early 1950s, the end of the world has been a mundane feature of everyday life.

In another archival photo from Texas, the town of Lampasas is invaded by "foreign" enemies who pen the adults together like pigs. While they perform being "interned," a little girl cries at how absolutely real the scene is for her.[83] Named Operation Longhorn, the 1952 fantasy invasion by communist hostiles called the "People's Republic" had other very real effects: 221 paratroopers from the Eighty-Second Airborne were injured, and one of them died, as high winds swept across the jump zone.[84] In another photo, Val Peterson, director of the Federal Civil Defense Administration, is crouching with a group of children in Las Vegas, where the school district became the first in the nation to issue "dog tags" to its 15,000 children so that their bodies could be identified after a nuclear attack.[85] Dog tags were also handed out to children in New York, San Francisco, Seattle, and other American cities, favored over another proposed corpse identification solution—tattoos. Tattoos were rejected due to their negative associations with the Holocaust and prison camps, and because a severe burn could remove them.[86]

A key aspect of bombproofing both biobodies and data bodies was to locate them far from target areas. Civil defense planners disseminated target area discourse through fake newspaper stories that accompanied civil defense air raid drills. In his book *One Nation Underground: The Fallout Shelter in American Culture*, Kenneth Rose theorizes what he calls "the nuclear apocalyptic": "a distinctive subgenre of speculative literature" written by philosophers, novelists, science-fiction writers, journalists, and civil defense planners that reflected a widespread belief that "nuclear weapons had brought humanity near the final apocalypse."[87] Stories of this subgenre appeared in newspapers, widely read publications like *Good Housekeeping*, *Playboy*, and *Collier's*, and in tracts published and circulated by federal agencies like the Federal Civil Defense Administration, as well as, eventually, state and local civil defense offices. In the below example of a fake front page written by the New York City Office of Civil Defense and printed by the *New York Journal-American* newspaper, fictional A-bombs strike New York, Buffalo, Albany, and Philadelphia. The "enemy armada" strikes during the lunch hour, a typical feature of nuclear apocalyptic narratives, where the ordinary town is usually going about its everyday activities, and citizens are unsuspecting that any attack is about to occur. The ostensible goal of such fake front-page news editions was "to make you more conscious of the need for Civil Defense."[88]

The news story on the fake front page titled "Thousands Flee into Westchester" points to the ways in which fears of racial contamination fused with nuclear terror. In the story, "homeless refugees" engage in rioting and mob tactics in the overwhelmingly white, affluent county of Westchester. The suburban zone survives the atomic attack, but the urban center is devastated, an outcome consistent with much of the speculative fiction in the nuclear apocalyptic subgenre. In his book *Fallout Shelter: Designing for Civil Defense in the Cold War*, David Monteyne writes that civil defense planners, "like social reformers before them, viewed dense urban neighborhoods as spaces of unpredictable difference and nonconformity to the ideals of a white American republic." Monteyne points to several different civil defense publications from the 1950s to show how "crowded, poor,

# 2 A-BOMBS HIT CITY

## Killed 1,104,814 | Injured 568,393

Special Edition — Journal NEW YORK American — FRIDAY, SEPTEMBER 25, 1953

## We Retaliate:
### Bombers Attack Enemy

## East Side In Ruins, 1,690,000 Homeless

Two A-bomb blasts turned vast areas of New York City into wastelands of flaming debris in seconds today, with an estimated 1,104,814 dead in the fiery ruins in Manhattan and Queens.

Early estimates listed 568,393 injured and 1,690,000 homeless, wandering through the city looking for shelter.

An enemy air armada, sweeping down into northeastern United States despite heavy losses to our Air Defense, dropped two 50-kiloton bombs at 12:45 p. m., marked by blinding flashes of light and towering clouds of smoke and dust.

The first bomb exploded 2,500 feet above Essex and East Broadway, while a few seconds later—indicating the well planned enemy attack—the second burst at the same level over Little Neck Parkway, near Hillside ave., Queens.

Reports were that the Empire State Building and numerous other skyscrapers withstood the blast, although suffering heavy damage to upper floors. Hundreds of blocks of tenements were turned into rubble.

A-bombs were also dropped on Buffalo, Albany, Boston and Philadelphia, according to information received by New York City Civil Defense Director Herbert R. O'Brien from State Director Lt. Gen. C. R. Huebner, shortly after the attack here. No estimate of casualties in those cities is yet available.

### Eisenhower Calls Congress

WASHINGTON, D. C., Sept. 25.—Swift and terrible retaliation is being taken on enemy cities and military installations by U. S. Air Force bombers, which took off from advance bases in England and North Africa immediately following President Eisenhower's declaration of a state of National Emergency.

The President has summoned Congress to meet in joint session at noon tomorrow, to ratify a formal declaration of war.

Senators and Representatives, most of them at their homes when the surprise enemy attack was launched, are now flying to Washington for tomorrow's joint session.

ATTACKERS DOWNED.

Nationality of the enemy was established by examination of wreckage of the attacking bombers, two of which were shot down by our interceptor planes north of Philadelphia.

The two A-bomb carrying bombers which penetrated our defense screen to attack New York City, were shot down over Bridgeport, Conn.

Another crashed in flames south of Buffalo. Two were destroyed over South Boston.

At U. S. Air Force headquarters in the Pentagon and at U. S. Navy and Marine headquarters, reports indicated that the main body of the enemy air armada was destroyed en route.

Sufficient planes managed to get through our defense screen, however, to reach the main targets, New York City, and the secondary targets of Boston, Buffalo, Albany and Philadelphia.

THE WOOLWORTH BUILDING, City Hall and surrounding skyscrapers felt the full force of the A-bomb dropped by the enemy today. While the buildings did not topple, their upper floors received considerable damage, windows were smashed, the steel girders buckled, fires broke out and debris falling into City Hall Park killed hundreds of bench sitters. In the Support Area. There, whose homes were only slightly damaged will be sent back to the right, after they have recovered from shock and fear. City Hall, an ancient landmark, was completely demolished (foreground).

### Thousands Flee Into Westchester

WHITE PLAINS, N. Y., Sept. 25.—Thousands of dazed and frightened homeless men, women and children .were making their way across the city line into Westchester County today.

In a complete state of panic, they converged on Yonkers, Mt. Vernon, and Pelham Manor, camping on lawns, packing in fields, begging for food and seeking shelter from the inhabitants of the area.

In Pelham Manor, the worst affected of the three towns, constabulary and housing were reported with conditions deteriorating as the stampeding thousands poured completely out of hand.

150,000 REFUGEES.

Civil Defense Director William J. Slater estimated that more than 150,000 refugees had poured into the area within three hours after the A-bombs hit the Metropolitan section.

"We are doing everything in our power to her border," said Slater. "But if the rioting and mob tactics continue, we will be forced to ask that martial law be invoked."

Some of the New Yorkers seeking shelter are being temporarily taken care of at Reception Centers by the Welfare Service. In many such centers the lines stretched three and four blocks long.

The arrival of injured has overtaxed the hospitals in the area to the extent that ambulatory patients are waving their beds to make room for the more seriously hurt victims of the A-bomb.

Arrangements were being made by Civilian Defense authorities to move some 50,000 whose homes were completely demolished in the explosion area, farther north.

### Trains Halted:
### Blast Disrupts Transit System

Severe damage to the Consolidated Edison Power Plant at Hudson ave., and to the Kent Avenue Power Plant, Brooklyn, has stopped service on IND trains in Brooklyn and Queens, and IRT Division trains in Brooklyn.

The IRT Division's two power plants at 59th st. and Hudson River and 74th st. and Hudson River escaped damage, making it possible to maintain service on the following lines:

BMT DIVISION—Astoria line operating from 42nd st. and Broadway to Ditmars blvd., Astoria, Queens.

IND DIVISION—"A" line trains operating from 59th st., Columbus Circle to 207th st., Washington Heights; "AA" trains operating from 59th st. to 168th st.; "D" trains from 59th st. to 165th st. and Grand Concourse, The Bronx.

IRT DIVISION—Flushing line from Times sq. to Main st., Flushing, Queens; Broadway-7th Ave. Expresses operating from 96th st. and Broadway to 242nd st. and Broadway and to E. 180th st.; Broadway Local trains north from 96th st. to 242nd st., trains running north from Grand Central Sta.; 42nd st.-Shuttle trains; Third Ave. Elevated trains running north from 129th st. to Gunhill rd.; Dyer Ave. Line.

### State of Emergency

Governor Dewey, notified at his farm in Dutchess County of the A-bomb attacks, declared a "state of emergency," invoking provisions of the Defense Emergency Act of 1951 to put Civil Defense regulations into effect. Mayor Impellitteri also announced a "state of emergency" placing all city departments actively into the defense plan.

The A-bombs exploded during the lunch hour, shaking the entire city. Brilliant flashes of light blinded people who happened to be looking toward the blasts. Great billows of smoke and dust rose in mushroom-shaped plumes high into the sky from Ground Zero of the two explosions.

In lower Manhattan the terrific force of the blast ren-

Continued on Next Page

### It Could Happen
#### ----But Didn't

A-bombs did not fall on New York today. We hope and pray they never do.

The material for this page was prepared by the City of New York Office of Civil Defense. At its request the New York Journal-American has printed it as a public service.

It's alarming . . . almost frightening.

If it has made you more conscious of the need for Civilian Defense, it has served its purpose.

**"2 A-Bombs Hit City." Reprinted by permission of Bettmann via Getty Images.**

derelict, multiethnic urban neighborhoods were destroyed in hypothetical attack scenarios."[89]

Industrial and urban dispersal were not designed to save everyone, and in fact they accorded neatly with urban renewal campaigns that sought to reimagine and reshape urban spaces into tracts of uniform, dense public housing projects and other residential zones that were easily surveilled and contained. In 1951, the mayor of Pittsburgh even gave a speech titled "We Do Not Want to Wait for Bombs to Clear Our Slums."[90] Civil defense planners were updating the figure of the typical American and the streamlined nation he represented, first solidified in the 1930s. In their attack scenarios, a "white citizenry would survive on the fringes of the city where the effects of atomic bombs would be attenuated by distance from ground zero," while "inner cities were places projected for the containment of nonwhite residents and other 'sitting ducks' whose existence challenged the myth of a unified American identity."[91] Civil defense planners "were concerned to contain the assertion of any politics of difference, such as racial or gender identities that might challenge the purity of the abstract citizen. In an imagination of urban disaster and suburban survival, the fear of the bomb and the fear of the racial other merged at ground zero."[92]

Actual press coverage carried images of suburban families living underground in bomb shelters that normalized shelter building as a means of preserving the American family against the threat of Soviet bombs. A *New Yorker* article called "A Place to Hide," which appeared on March 1, 1952, detailed how John C. Legler, an advertising executive living in the affluent New York suburb of Bronxville, built a "steel and concrete" bomb shelter accessible through a wall in his basement, complete with a tunnel and "escape hatch" that would allow him and his family to reach the surface "just in the event that the house should be knocked down to block exit by the regular route."[93] The caption for the image used in the article (see below) says, "[Legler] is a man who likes to be prepared. He also likes life. And in order to keep on living, he has made elaborate preparations for the preservation of himself and his family in the event of atomic war."

Similar to the corporate and state records dispersed at secure records storage facilities in nonurban areas, such as IMASC, the Leglers are preserved within a steel-and-concrete vault with "a heavy door that can be barred from the inside." Most Americans did not build family bomb shelters, and most were not members of a small economic and cultural elite like the Leglers, but images and descriptions of the Legler shelter and others like it reached mass audiences through widely read magazines and newspapers.[94] These images both affirmed the reality of the threat of Soviet bombs and gave material expression to a preservation imperative that compelled the production of new spaces of preservation for biobodies and data bodies.

Mass media images of family bomb shelters reinforced traditional gender roles and the patriarchal power structure of the typical American family in the present. These images always depicted both the current day—in which American families practice living in their shelter, or check to make sure it is properly stocked—and a possible future, where American families live underground temporarily to wait for fallout to clear. As pictures of the future, they projected the survival of traditional gender roles after a nuclear apocalypse. The image of the Leglers' shelter is remarkable in that it depicts only children in the family bunker, even though the caption begins, "John C. Legler, advertising executive who lives in Bronxville, is a man who likes to be prepared." The image does not depict Mr. Legler, but the caption introduces him as a spectral patriarchal presence ordering and overseeing what the viewer sees within the frame. On the right, the elder daughter, Sandra Legler, "checks the food and water supplies," while "at left Nancy Walker, a Legler house guest" enters the shelter from the basement, and "steel-hatted Mitchell Legler, 10, is listening to the battery operated radio."

Even in a postnuclear reality without parents, the male, even a younger brother, would engage technology and gather information, leisurely, while women went about the domestic work of preparing food. The Hawaiian shirt, khaki shorts, and "steel" pith-style helmet of Mitchell reinforces his dominant role, as this garb recalls that of colonial explorers and archaeologists, and the pith helmet was worn by European and American soldiers invading tropical and subtropical zones in the nineteenth and twentieth centuries. The boy stands with his hand on his hip, while his older sister, who is clearly taller than he is when standing, occupies a subservient position within the frame, as she nearly kneels down before him. Sandra's perfectly coiffed hair, flawless makeup, and tanned skin imply that women will uphold man-made beauty standards even after the end of the world. She showcases brand-name consumer products for the camera, such as the canister of Nestle's instant powder cocoa in her left hand. This product placement tells us that the orphaned children will drink postapocalyptic hot chocolate to warm themselves and feel a sense of home in the otherwise quite spartan shelter space.

The image succinctly captures the overall aims of civil defense preparations in the United States. Monteyne writes that civil defense was meant to ensure that "U.S. environments, citizens, and social structures survived a nuclear war intact." Architecture for civil defense and the spaces of preservation it helped produce emphasized the notion that "what good citizens

**"One Man's Preparation for Atomic War."**
**Reprinted by permission of Bettmann via Getty Images.**

already did in everyday life was a model for the roles they should perform when under attack." The roles of "ideal subjects" in civil defense "would be conditioned by racial, gender, and other identifying characteristics."[95] Monteyne draws on the theories of Henri Lefebrve to explain how "space is not just a backdrop or container for actors and events. Rather, space is produced through performances and practices interacting with settings, over time. As opposed to the more ephemeral modes of communication available to the state, architecture's materiality and permanence offered the additional possibility of framing habitual practices, of limiting the effective possibilities for everyday users of the built environment."[96]

The bombproof bunker was a real and imaginary space within the data complex that reproduced existing gender and racial inequalities. The bunker environment invited people to invest and reinvest confidence in the capacity of civil defense architecture and engineering to preserve biobodies, data bodies, and the prevailing social order against the threat of nuclear apocalypse. In the Bettmann Archive, the folder labeled "Civil Defense, Post WWII—Drills, Shelters" contains multiple copies of the Legler image, but each has a bit of a different story to tell due to the layers of captions on its back. A UPI/Bettmann copy bears the succinct and accurate caption "One man's preparations for atomic war." Another copy has a Corbis sticker slapped on the back, over the previous detailed caption, that simply reads "Preservation family from the atomic war," as if the war actually happened. Perhaps this caption is, in a way, more accurate, as it embodies the way that fantasies of destruction become real, the way the ends of the world that we feared and that never ended up happening nonetheless came to structure our world: our built environments, our imaginations, our archives of historical images, our data.

Life inside that safe subterranean crypt was, in a way, much like stepping inside a time capsule. In the Bettmann, I found multiple images of bunkers on display, meant to catch the eyes of passersby and induce them to make a purchase. In those displays, the bunker featured—just like the replica of the Westinghouse Time Capsule—a cutaway segment that allowed onlookers to see inside.[97] But this time, instead of swatches of fabric, a slide rule, seeds, and a Bible, the public saw a clan of typical Americans sitting in what the sign said was "the Family Room of Tomorrow." Passersby were invited to hang out in the shelter, thus becoming a part of the display.[98] One such "deluxe fall-out shelter . . . feature[d] wall-to-wall carpeting and television." Displayed at the Civil Defense Headquarters in New York City, it was "designed as a combination family room during peacetime and as a protective structure against fall-out should war break out."[99] But Americans never bought these bunkers in large numbers. They must have figured that the family room of their today was miserable enough. They didn't need a remixed one that was underground, sunless, and stuffy with prebreathed air, not to mention fitted with a "chemical toilet" that was basically a bucket of toxic liquid meant to cloak noxious smells.[100]

The atomic bombs feared by typical Americans never fell, and so the data complex expanded during the Cold War in response to a haunting paradox: the United States was never bombed by a nuclear weapon, and the United States was bombed with more nuclear weapons than any other nation on the planet. The nation gained this distinction through self-inflicted detonations, with 904 bomb tests at the Nevada Test Site, located sixty-five miles from Las Vegas.[101] The deep haunting of the American psyche by imagined and actual nuclear fallout materialized in the data complex's infrastructure

"Make Themselves at Home."  November 2, 1960.
Reprinted by permission of Bettmann via Getty Images.

of securitized vaults, underground facilities, and redundant power supplies at sites like IMASC, and later at Iron Mountain's National Data Center.

By the end of the twentieth century, Iron Mountain had acquired nearly all the companies that tried to compete with it, over 150 in all. The culmination of its imperial spree took place in 1999, when it bought out its chief rival, Pierce Leahy, for $1.2 billion.[102] Pierce Leahy had itself acquired fifty competitors before selling out to Iron Mountain in a merger that made the latter the largest records storage and information management company in the world. The existential dread that materialized in Iron Mountain and other similar facilities would form the basis of the next media revolution—digital technology and information networking—which would prove to be its own kind of crisis.

### Something Like a Cloud

Bombproofing, even in the twenty-first century, continues to offer no guarantee that data will survive even a nonnuclear attack, as the various forms destruction may take are simply too myriad to predict. No one ever built record-height skyscrapers at Dugway Proving Ground and then flew passenger planes into them. 9/11 was the event the nation had been waiting for, preparing for, dreading and fantasizing about, watching as CGI entertainment in action movies about alien takeovers. 9/11 is the *only* time a foreign aerial attack actually happened in the United States.[103] And after a half century of anticipation, when it happened, we weren't ready and the bombproofing of our data and our minds did not work, which both reveals the lie of all this paranoid preparation and, for the civil defense believer, proves that it was all indeed necessary. The data complex roots itself deeper during tragedy, and never was a more horrifying set of images played again and again, the video footage and photographs of that day's events forever burned into Americans' memories. During the attack, people leapt to their deaths to avoid the fire, as paper documents from offices and records storage rooms drifted slowly downward, falling bodies mingled with falling data. Jay McInerney wrote in *The Guardian* a few days afterward that "a friend in Brooklyn said it was raining paper in her neighborhood—shreds of résumés, files, letters, tax returns, sales receipts, invoices, and possibly even billets-doux were falling from the sky."[104]

Beneath the World Trade Center complex, there was a vast series of underground vaults. Seventy feet below the surface, the Bank of Nova Scotia stored twelve tons of gold and nearly a thousand tons of silver. In addition to precious metals, the basement space—twice the floor area of the Empire State Building—also held "Godiva chocolates, assault weapons, old furniture, bricks of cocaine, phony taxicabs and Central Intelligence Agency files."[105] J. P. Morgan had vaults that it rented to private clients for bombproof secure storage. Photographer Jacques Lowe was a longtime customer, storing his 40,000 original photographic negatives of John F. Kennedy and his family, taken when Lowe was the personal family photographer during Kennedy's presidential run and then in the White House until 1962. The 9/11 attacks damaged the upper floors of 5 World Trade Center, the low-rise building directly above the J. P. Morgan vaults. The building was not bombproof, but more importantly, it was not demolition proof.

Operation Teapot did not think through what happens to a vault or a safe when a tall building is only partially destroyed, but so unstable that no one can go inside to retrieve the stock certificates, or bonds, or in this case, priceless photographic negatives that have been stored there. Somehow, either during the attack or the demolition, all of Lowe's negatives were destroyed. While "some of the images still existed as prints and contact sheets," a *Forbes* article explains, "the original negatives were lost forever."[106] Lowe, who died six months before 9/11, had been so attached to the negatives that when he moved to Europe after the assassinations of Martin Luther King Jr. and Robert F. Kennedy, he bought an extra plane ticket for the negatives to ride in the seat beside him.

The *Forbes* reporter interprets the loss of Lowe's negatives as "a clear illustration of the benefit of preserving historical photographs on more than one type of media, and in more than one location."[107] Why? The loss of Lowe's negatives could have been interpreted as proof of the irredeemable fragility of photographs and the safes and vaults we use to protect them; the insecurity of all data, as it is subject to both foreseeable and unforeseeable disasters; the ultimate futility of all our attempts to preserve data permanently and fully securitize it against flood, fire, terrorism, hacking, sabotage, and the threat of its own chemical makeup. Even if the negatives hadn't been destroyed on 9/11, they would have naturally decayed within a century or so.

But the data complex exerts powerful influence on how we see photographs and other media artifacts as objects that need preservation, that crystallize and index unique moments from the past that, if lost, are lost forever, as irreplaceable as extinct species. The logical response then, to the haunting of past losses and the specter of future losses is to reproduce data in multiple formats, in case any one of them turns out to be less permanent than we thought, and to store it in multiple securitized and, ideally, remote locations, where we imagine that tragedies like 9/11 cannot occur, or at least are far less likely to. The impossible ideal within the data complex, of course, would be to move the data we love to a location that is not a location at all, to make the data itself a kind of movement, data so widely and redundantly distributed that it becomes something that can't be bombed or destroyed, something existing beyond the threats that afflict earthbound paper and microfilm, something like a cloud.[108]

# 4

# The Weight of a Cloud

**Every government ought to contain in itself**

**the means of its own preservation.**

**—Alexander Hamilton, *The Federalist Papers***

The National Archives at College Park building reminds me of a thousand others, both formidable and forgettable. My inner twelve-year-old self finds it fun, though, to be standing in front in one of these D.C. metro-area structures I saw on so many Jack Ryan movies and other political thrillers as a kid. Luckily I'm not breaking into it, hacking its mainframe, or taking on a suicide mission to prevent nuclear Armageddon with one-tenth of a second left on some cyber time bomb, the usual scenarios that attend such nondescript, blocky buildings with reflective two-way glass facades—*we see you, but you can't see us*. Still, this place, where the most dangerous thing I'll do is dig through folders of yellowed memos from the early Cold War, is full of security features that guard against fires, air contamination, and espionage.[1] These technological advances enable this facility to retain the data preservation effectiveness of the open time capsules we saw in the previous chapter, while allowing a bit freer access to materials.

Informally known as Archives II, the 1.8 million-square-foot building is a part of a longer story within the data complex—the inability to keep up with its demands for more storage space. The National Archives had always been short on space, even before construction was completed on its original building in 1934. Architect John Russell Pope included an interior courtyard and imagined that at some point in the future it could be converted to additional storage space. By 1937, the addition was complete, and it doubled the Archives' storage capacity. Nevertheless, the data complex soon called for more, and by 1950, the space proved insufficient, and a Federal Records Center (FRC) opened in the Naval Clothing Depot in Brooklyn. Two months later, records moved into a complex of several buildings in Alexandria, Virginia, a former U.S. Navy Torpedo Plant already being used by the Smithsonian Institution to store art and dinosaur bones.[2] Within a year, three additional FRCs opened in Chicago, San Francisco, and Washington, D.C. By 1958, there were eighteen of them.[3] But the data complex is the data complex, and so Archives II opened in 1994 to provide still more space.

After the usual check-in with a guard and issue of my ID, I ride the elevator up to level two with a couple of older men, one with a serious limp and cane. Both Vietnam vets, they chat about what they're going to look for upstairs: documents that prove where and when they served so that they can access veterans' benefits, and nail down some details in their personal histories that the fog of war and passing of a few decades make it difficult to recall. But why didn't these men, and why didn't I, simply look up what we needed in the National Archives' digital database and download the PDFs?

The thousands of gray archival boxes in this building contain so much more than can be found online. Contrary to popular belief, and despite the breathless rhetoric of Google Books, Corbis, and other advocates of universal digitization, most material in libraries and archives has not been digitized. For instance, Corbis attempted to digitize the 11 million unique images of the Bettmann Archive, and gave up after about 300,000—a whopping 2.7 percent of the analog collection. So, to actually find out what is happening, and what has happened, in the data complex, one must visit physical sites: archives of purple-ink mimeo and carbon copies, decommissioned bombproof bunkers, including those that have been converted into data centers, known in the colocation industry as "data bunkers."

I submit several paper forms to an archivist and then, seated in a wide, long, curved room, wait for my boxes to be retrieved. While I wait, I open my laptop and read some cool stuff written by National Archives staff on their blog and in their quarterly magazine, *Prologue*. I learn that in World War II, Arthur Kimberly's expertise made him a top pick for the Allied Translator and Interpreter Section (ATIS) in the South Pacific, under the command of General Douglas Macarthur, responsible for "translating captured documents and interrogating Japanese prisoners of war." If he thought he had his work cut out for him when he was gassing and flattening moldy ship manifests and death certificates at the National Archives, Kimberly's new post brought him unprecedented challenges. He now had to rehabilitate and attempt to extract intelligence from documents brought to him directly from "battle fields, crashed aircraft, graves, sunken ships and foxholes," and "many of them were bullet-ridden, torn, defaced, water-soaked, soiled and charred, as well as often being covered with blood, body fat, and human excreta." Out of this experience, Kimberly cowrote *the* book on such extreme rehabilitation and recovery efforts, *Restoration of Captured Documents*.[4] The ATIS also created a Document Restoration Kit for use in the field, which "contained a household electric iron; an ultraviolet lamp; various chemicals; a soft, camel's hair brush; a spatula; a small sponge; an atomizer; and, a dissecting needle."[5]

Kimberly's work was important to the war effort, if not as glamorous as another post he might have landed if the timing had been slightly different. In July 1944, the same month he left for the South Pacific, the associate director of Harvard's Fogg Art Museum sent Kimberly's name along for consideration as a specialist in the Monuments, Fine Arts and Archives program. These professionals, better known as the "Monuments Men" who rescued cultural and artistic treasures that had been stolen by the Nazis, were made famous in the eponymous 2014 film starring George Clooney, Matt Damon, and Bill Murray.[6]

While Kimberly was away at war, other archivists and staff at the National Archives received naval commissions and clearances to work in photo labs and map rooms alongside the Office of Strategic Services (OSS), a precursor to the CIA. As the war progressed, the OSS occupied an increasing amount of space inside the National Archives Building, taking over nearly 15,000 square feet by 1944. In January of that year, the OSS map division moved into "Room 400 (now the Microfilm Reading Room), changed the locks on the doors, and declared it a restricted access area." Division employees brought in huge maps at night that were described as "highly classified material," maps of beaches "that would soon be known as 'Utah' and 'Omaha.'" In April, high-ranking military officials visited to see an exhibit of "secret military equipment and devices" to be used in the operation they were planning: the D-Day invasion of Normandy's beaches.[7] After the war, Kimberly continued to work internationally, disseminating the principles of preservation science across the world. An archival photo shows Kimberly instructing an intern at the National Archives of Cuba on how to laminate documents.[8] Of course, he had merely moved from one war to the next, as the Cold War picked up where World War II left off.

Finally, my boxes arrive, and in the staff records from the Cold War I find an innocuous-looking book, bound with a blue pleather cover, titled *General Services Administration Evaluation of the 1958 Operation Alert Exercise.* Inside that cover is a report on a simulation of the end of the world, and a fantasy about how Americans' data bodies might survive it. Operation Alert (OPAL) was a series of civil defense exercises carried out from 1954 to 1961 that meant to prepare Americans to take shelter in a nuclear attack, as well as test crucial communications systems the government would need to control the population. Major cities in "target areas" required people to take shelter in a calm, orderly fashion while an air raid siren sounded. The New York City exercise was filmed and distributed through a newsreel showing a deserted Times Square, and the narrator's voice, which sounded just like every other 1950s narrator's voice, explained that cities across the country were hit with "other theoretical bombs."[9]

The vast destruction rehearsed in Operation Alert and other exercises helped stimulate the expansion of a crucial new layer of the data complex—the telecommunications systems that enabled the government to retain power after a nuclear attack. Even as architects, businessmen, government officials, and safe manufacturers pushed for the construction of bombproof facilities, another strategy germinated in the data complex, intensifying the principles and practices of dispersion and distributed networks, redundancy, and cybernetics. In the OPAL scenario, two weeks after the attack, only four of sixty teletype stations would be working.

However, there was more hope for the survival of these networks than for the Federal Records Centers. According to the report, ten of twelve relay stations were still operational one day after the attack, as was "the Eastern Switching Center and its transfer facilities to the inoperable Interagency Communications System. In addition, prearranged circuitry and strategically located terminating equipment permitted rapid restoration." Further, AT&T estimated that relocation sites would allow about "25% of normal service."[10] The government began to build facilities that weren't just bombproof bunkers for records, but were connected to networks of communication that linked them to the world aboveground, thereby helping powerful government agencies and corporations literally retain power—their political and economic power reliant on physical distributions of electricity through power grids and backup diesel generators. These facilities, hardened with reinforced concrete construction, lashed to one another with telephone lines and coaxial cables, prefigured and literally laid the groundwork for the internet.

These networked emergency facilities reflect an evolution within the data complex. Their bombproof, securitized, decontaminated spaces combine with electronic telecommunications infrastructure to make them integral not just for disaster recovery, but for everyday life. Because government officials planned to maintain their power and continue to rule from their postattack bunkers, airplanes, and warships, they needed a telecommunications infrastructure that would enable them to send commands, direct troops, and otherwise communicate with the small group of preselected leaders that would oversee the distribution of the nation's resources, censor information, and perform all other necessary leadership roles as the country lived under martial law. The infrastructure built to be used in a national emergency materialized the nightmare of nuclear destruction, and the dream of postattack survival and government and business continuity. With this materialization, the data complex added another stratum, a redundant system of electronic communication, a network that could carry all kinds of data, from teletypes and voice transmissions to financial transactions, from vital statistics being amassed in Federal Records Centers to encrypted messages between intelligence agents. The emergency system became basic, its capabilities normalized, so that everyday people, along with government and military officials, ended up living their lives and connecting to one another through these now-mundane systems within the data complex.

In the final hours before I leave the National Archives Building, I pull one last box. There I find a folder of letters from Arthur Kimberly to a number of other preservationists, including Harry Lydenberg, Thomas Iiams, and B. W. Scribner, requesting more details on their experiences with paper lamination and fighting off foxing in old books and documents. Compared to the Cold War records—the wind-pattern and fallout forecast maps, the continuity plans where postal trucks were retasked to carry away the multitudinous dead—these Depression-era letters about building gas chambers and installing fire alarms to preserve and secure books seem to come from such a simpler, much safer time in the data complex.

## Fallout Forecasts

Within the government, secret iterations of OPAL were carried out, meant to prepare archivists and other staff at Federal Records Centers for life after a nuclear attack. This was not a bomb test, as no materials were actually damaged, but a kind of live-action role-playing where the participants were playing themselves, but the version of themselves after the long-feared nuclear apocalypse had finally come. Apparently, archivists, librarians, and file clerks had to be turned into Cold Warriors, too.

The attack scenarios were extreme and dismal, and at the same time hopeful in their portrayal of postapocalyptic life that would still, somehow, be grounded in the data complex. By 1958, there were eighteen Federal Records Centers that amassed data in cities across the country. In the attack scenario, Soviets landed 282 nuclear strikes, resulting in the loss of 95 percent of all federal records and the death of 15 million Americans, with 32 million "sick or injured." But those were just the day 1 totals. By day 2, the Operation Alert report narrates in an eerie past perfect tense, "an additional 12 million had died and an additional 3 million had become sick or injured."[11]

A fallout map spread across two pages predicts wind patterns and the spread of fallout. Since the Operation Alert exercise in 1955, the U.S. Weather Bureau began "calculating twice-daily 'fallout forecasts,' tracking how winds and atmospheric conditions would direct radioactive fallout from seventy-two critical target areas across the country and transmitting the encoded forecasts to military bases and local civil defense centers."[12] These scientific reports substantiated the fantasy that we would be able to tell where fallout would be the day after the attack, then two weeks after, then three months after. Such maps, on the surface, predict destruction and the spread of radioactive danger after a nuclear attack. But they were mostly tools of psychological containment, as the map represents a delusional level of predictability for fallout.

The U.S. government had already known, since the first atomic bomb test, Trinity, in July 1945, that such fallout patterns could not be effectively predicted for at least two reasons. The first reason is, well, it's the wind. And second, fallout traveled not only by wind but also by water. In August 1945, workers in paper mills in Indiana that used river water in their papermaking process noticed that "mixed in with the fine brown silt of the river was a very unusual, iron-gray metal. It was of a type that had not existed before." The mill made strawboard for Eastman Kodak in Rochester, New York, as did another mill in Iowa. The product from both mills was sufficiently radio-active that once it arrived at Kodak's photo labs, it ruined the film stock being made at the factory, causing a high rate of "film imperfections, tiny pinhole-sized dots and thin lines appearing on the green 14-by-17-inch film sheets used for industrial X-rays." These "tiny white dots" were the "foot-prints" of that first atomic explosion, which had occurred over a thousand miles away in New Mexico.[13]

In the late nineteenth century, Kodak founder George Eastman had originally thought Rochester to be a favorable site for his photography labs because the air was relatively clean back then, and because the geology of the area carried low levels of radioactivity, unlike the granite-laced soils of New Hampshire and Massachusetts that had higher levels of uranium and thorium.[14] By the atomic age, those advantages were gone, though in 1951 the government did begin alerting Kodak, as well as a cotton manufacturer, when there would be an upcoming bomb test, even though the tests were otherwise top secret.

Though the world would basically end for the typical Americans whose biobodies and data bodies were immolated or pulverized in the OPAL sce-nario, the exercise's story line imagined that there would still be records requests from all over the thoroughly radioactive country, where fallout would have affected over 67 percent of the land area, or 2 million square miles. Archivists actually wondered and worried—how will we train peo-ple to use microfilm machines? They imagined this, even though they also imagined a situation in which, of "the 18 Records Center facilities of GSA, 17 were virtually destroyed or denied to employees" for three months after the attack. Another looming concern was that nearly 300 Soviet strikes would destroy so many buildings and thus reverse all progress that had been made in freeing up corporate and government office space through the wide-spread use of microfilm. Going from 45 million square feet to 2 million square feet nationwide, archivists planned to use tents and Quonset huts, and to take over stores and even bowling alleys to be used for bureaucrats' and clerks' work spaces.[15]

During the attack exercise, where senior staff from thirty-seven federal agencies met at Mount Weather, the acting archivist of the United States, Dr. Robert Bahmer, gave a presentation wherein he painted a more realistic picture of where priorities would lie for at least a few months after the attack. He stated, "During a disaster period when we are fighting for survival, for food and other physical needs, when such things as space and equipment are in critically short supply, we do not believe we could justify the re-establishment of a records center." He did, however, feel strongly that the federal government should be sure to preserve the Charters of Freedom (the Constitution, Bill of Rights, Declaration of Independence), and continue to publish an emergency edition of the *Federal Register*.

But the idea that the *Federal Register* would still be published was an intense form of fantasy—the executive orders presigned by Eisenhower would place the United States under martial law, complete with an Office of Censorship, food rationing, and a dozen "czars" who would control and distribute all the nation's resources.[16] According to Matthew Conaty, who examined recently declassified materials at the Eisenhower Library, such a "constitutional dictatorship" would carry "the potential to supplant the constitutional operation of government in the name of preserving that way of life."[17] Again, with national institutions, as with artifacts in time capsules, acts of preservation always change that which they preserve, that which they promise to keep the same.[18]

Of course, even this plan for instituting martial law is a fantasy of relative safety—in an actual nuclear attack of this scale, there would likely be a complete breakdown of authority and any kind of order, as Eisenhower knew and said as much on various occasions.[19] In a memo, he reminded his cabinet that attack and evacuation exercises do not approximate the reality that would take hold in actual attack: "These will not be normal people—they will be scared, will be hysterical, will be 'absolutely nuts.'"[20] Further, you could never predict all of the elements in an evacuation scenario. During one exercise, Eisenhower's convoy encountered a truck full of pigs on a narrow road, and the president had to wait—as precious imaginary minutes ticked away—while the truck slowly backed its way up the mountain, so that the president's vehicle could reach the relocation site's entrance. Eisenhower couldn't help but laugh.[21]

Operation Alert was meant to keep the ruse going. As Guy Oakes writes in *The Imaginary War*, Operation Alert was designed to "confirm a basic premise of the Cold War conception of nuclear reality: Given careful planning and proper management, the American people could sustain a nuclear strike and survive without the imposition of draconian measures that violated their political traditions."[22] The secret government exercises of Operation Alert dramatized the very destruction that dispersal and "safety-in-space" strategies were supposed to help us avoid, according to civil defense propaganda. But the data complex deepens and expands through such percolating contradictions, through which our anxiety cycles into false security, our fear into hope, our vulnerability into invincibility. Spectacles of our martial supremacy are always projections of both our assured victory and our mutually assured destruction. Fantasies of survival and death swirling together, intensely imagining both—that's the data complex.

### Touring the Greenbrier Resort

After World War II, while the federal government encouraged industrial dispersion to preserve corporations, it was also concerned with its own preservation. At the beginning of the Cold War, the United States began building its own continuity-of-operations facilities to house government officials, records, and communication technology in the event of a nuclear attack. These hidden facilities were located within an hour of Washington, D.C., totaling nearly 100 sites by the 1970s.[23]

Emblematic of this new network of government facilities, which the Office of Defense Mobilization called the "federal relocation arc," was the Bunker at Greenbrier.[24] Completed in 1962, the Bunker at Greenbrier (which I will refer to as the Bunker) was a completely underground fallout shelter for all members of Congress, constructed with reinforced concrete beneath the Greenbrier Resort in White Sulphur Springs, West Virginia. Stocked with non-perishable food and water, the Bunker was also equipped with air-conditioning and purification systems to both cycle air out of the hermetically sealed space and remove any radioactive particles from incoming air. The Bunker had diesel generators to backup its electrical supply, a communications center so statesmen could deliver messages to the postnuclear American public, and a large, open room that would be filled with desks and chairs and become a work space for congressional aides in the event of a nuclear attack.[25]

The federal government was a major force in building the infrastructure of the data complex, both through its construction of a number of facilities like the Bunker for sheltering the president and military leaders, as well as through its ideological commitment to and financial incentivization of the construction of similar facilities for state, county, and local governments. Eventually, the government offered subfederal authorities matching funds for the construction of Emergency Operating Centers—securitized locations from which officials would continue to rule their constituencies, allocate scarce resources, and enforce the social order in the wake of a nuclear attack.[26]

The Bunker was emblematic not only of the expansion of the data complex during the Cold War but also of transformations in the data complex in the digital age. In one sense, the Cold War and the digital age are really the same period. Scientists at Texas Instruments, Fairchild Semiconductor, and Sprague Electric Company made breakthroughs that led to the first functional integrated circuit in 1960. Russell Kirsch at the National Bureau of Standards produced the first digital image in 1957, when he used a drum scanner to reproduce a photograph of his infant son, Walden—it was crude but still a watershed image, even at 176 pixels on a side (in today's terms, that would be 0.03 megapixels).[27]

The Bunker was never activated and used during the Cold War, and it is only in the digital age that its reinforced rooms have found a purpose integral to the daily operations of American life. The federal government decommissioned the Bunker in 1996, four years after investigative journalist Ted Gup exposed it through an article in *US News and World Report*,[28] and complete control of the Bunker reverted to CSX, the railroad corporation that owned the Greenbrier and the Bunker (the government had always leased it from CSX). The railroad company decided to turn it into a tourist attraction and a securitized data center, where a number of Fortune 500 companies store digital records on servers. The servers occupy underground spaces originally meant to protect the bodies of congressmen from radioactive contamination and the social disorder that Americans imagined would reign on the ground after an atomic attack. As a 2008 article in the *Economist* made clear, "Data centers are essential to nearly every industry and have become as vital to the functions of society as power stations are."[29] On the one hand, this is particular to the twenty-first century; on the other, the first proposal for a National Data Center arose in 1967, an idea that would centralize the data dispersed across an already existing constellation of what were then called "data banks," computerized repositories of vital records and statistics on paper, microfilm, and magnetic tape.

A defunct fallout shelter for Congress turned securitized data center, buried under a weird golf resort in the bombproof heart of Appalachia? Sounds like my kind of place. I drive several hours to White Sulphur Springs to take a tour of the Bunker. Like Iron Mountain's facility in Boyers, Pennsylvania, the Greenbrier does not allow photographs of the Bunker. I have some time before the tour is scheduled to begin, so I wander around the hotel's public spaces, taking in the views of the beautiful grounds through the large windows in the outsize dining halls and meeting rooms. In 1778, long before the Greenbrier resort was built, American colonists began visiting the sulfur spring on this site to "take the waters," to drink and bathe in the spring as Native Americans had long done, thinking it could alleviate rheumatism and other ailments. On the walls of the hotel's large common spaces are oil portraits of American icons like George Washington, including a portrait Washington sat for by Rembrandt Peale, son of early American artist, taxidermist, and museum operator Charles Willson Peale. Another portrait by Samuel F. B. Morse haunts a room full of empty, round tables. Morse is most famous for inventing the telegraph and Morse code, but prior to those achievements he was already a skilled painter, as well as America's first photographer. When Louis Daguerre publicly premiered his daguerreotype process, Morse was passing through Paris. He met with Daguerre a couple of times and then brought the technique to America.[30] One of Morse's students was Matthew Brady, the most famous photographer of the Civil War era.[31]

In its heyday, the Greenbrier was an epicenter of pleasure for celebrities and powerful people across the country. From the early to mid twentieth century, the resort hosted everyone from political leaders in Washington to movie stars, as well as golf pros such as Arnold Palmer, who played in the annual tournament year after year. The coffee-table book sold in the gift shop, *The History of the Greenbrier: America's Resort*, reproduces smiling snapshots of a veritable who's who of international celebrities who spent time there: Condé Nast, Lou Gehrig, the Duke and Duchess of Windsor, Clare Boothe Luce, Sam Snead, Ben Hogan, Bing Crosby, Bob Hope, Jawaharlal Nehru, Dwight Eisenhower, John Foster Dulles, Hubert Humphrey, Billy Graham, Princess Grace and Prince Rainier.

The Greenbrier's history is suffused with limitless glamour; down in the Bunker, I would learn more about its darker side. During World War II, the federal government commandeered the Greenbrier for 201 days and used it as an internment camp for diplomats from enemy nations. On December 19, 1941, less than two weeks after the bombing of Pearl Harbor, "the first contingent of 159 German and Hungarian diplomats arrived in White Sulphur Springs on a secretly scheduled, eleven-car Pullman train from Washington, D.C."[32] By the end of the internment, a total of 1,697 people had been housed there, most of them German. The U.S. government froze the assets of the Japanese diplomats, forcing them to do their own ironing and laundry in their otherwise luxurious rooms, while other diplomatic guests continued to live in relative opulence. The Germans had ready access to most of their personal accounts, but because they could not take American currency out of the country with them, they spent it on fine art prints and antique silver for sale in the Greenbrier's shops. They emptied the shops completely but still had more money to spend. Then "one bright entrepreneur produced a stack of department store catalogs and the buying spree began anew. When the Germans departed, two extra railroad baggage cars were required to transport all their newly acquired merchandise."[33]

To take the tour, I have to turn in my cell phone, for which I receive a receipt so that I can retrieve it when the tour is over. According to my guide, the servers in the data center receive much of their information from satellite transmissions, and cell phones must be surrendered before entering the facility so that they do not interfere with these transmissions. The doors to the server rooms are not marked with signage, only numbers that are meaningless to tourists, though I assume they are codes for various corporate clients. The Fortune 500 creates billions of digital files per day in the form of emails and PDFs, and federal legislation requires corporations to preserve a larger amount of their records and internal correspondence than ever before. The Bunker still has its twenty-seven-ton Mosler "blast door," but where endless stacks of C rations once filled a long tunnel, only empty boxes and styrofoam padding for servers and monitors now litter the ground. The two decontamination showers still sit unused at the entrance, once stocked with medicated soap to remove radioactive particles. The tour guide takes us to the room that houses the "pathological waste incinerator," an oven with the heating power to transform garbage into vapor and ash, and to cremate a corpse if necessary.[34]

If a bomb had been dropped on the United States, Congress would have been rushed to the Bunker. The legislators' names would have appeared on a list of approved entrants. Anyone not on the list who attempted to enter would have been shot without hesitation. Those who did enter would have removed their clothes and taken a decontamination shower to remove any radioactive fallout clinging to their bodies. They would then have put on a sterile set of clothes. Between this internment camp–like procedure and the existence of a cremation-grade incinerator in the bunker, it was impossible not to think of the Nazis, whose interned diplomats had once partied in the grand dining rooms above me, drinking beer and shouting, "Heil Hitler!" again and again, as they celebrated their *führer*'s birthday.[35]

### From Bunkers to Data Bunkers

The Bunker, originally meant to protect Congress from radioactive fallout, now preserves digital data, and it thus reflects a broader trend within the data complex, which is always looking for more space. The National Archives at College Park, where this chapter began, made nearly 2 million additional square feet of storage space available for federal records in 1994. Yet within three years, the National Archives and Records Administration (NARA) established its first underground facility, in defunct limestone mines at Lee's Summit, near Kansas City. Over the next fifteen years, NARA opened three more underground FRCs. One of them is located within "Subtropolis," trademarked by its owners as "The World's Largest Underground Business Complex," which is also home to a cloud computing and colocation data center, a distribution hub for the U.S. Postal Service (hundreds of millions of postage stamps are stored there), a Ford F-150 assembly facility, and a cold storage vault that preserves the original reels of *Gone with the Wind*, *The Wizard of Oz*, *The Shining*, and every episode of *Seinfeld*.[36]

Decommissioned underground Cold War bunkers serve, like abandoned mines, as a resource within the data complex, and many have been recently repurposed by state agencies and corporations. An Atlas-E intercontinental ballistic missile silo in Colorado is now home to records storage company Data Lock. During the Cold War, the subterranean rooms at Mount Pony stored $4 billion in U.S. currency in shrink-wrapped cubes on wooden pallets, a reserve intended to replenish money supplies in the event that a large-scale nuclear attack destroyed a significant amount of currency. These vaults also housed several mainframe computers managed by the Federal Reserve Bank of Richmond; these served as the "electronic hub for the nation's 5,700 banks, allowing the instantaneous transfer day to day of funds nationwide."[37] Founded in 1970, the facility was known as "the Culpeper Switch," and by 1975 it electronically handled 30,000 messages daily between Federal Reserve banks and commercial banks, resulting in the transfer of $30 trillion of funds and securities annually, or $120 billion per day. The mainframe computers also backed up the data of all banks east of the Mississippi River.[38]

Mount Pony no longer stores currency but is now the site of the Library of Congress National Audiovisual Conservation Center (NAVCC), which serves as the nerve center of the library's digitization and digital distribution activities, as well as the site where it stores the bulk of its audiovisual collections. Journalistic accounts of visits to the facility emphasize the scale of its collections and preservation efforts, as well as the infrastructural components that make such activities possible—the "miles of cable" that send digital information to a "separate backup in Manassas, Virginia" and "pipe different varieties of electronic media back to D.C. for public access"; an "electronic hub" that requires "27,000 cables"; and "something like the world's largest TiVo," a collection of 100 DVRs recording and archiving television shows. Originally, when David Woodley Packard, eldest son of the Hewlett-Packard cofounder, approached Librarian of Congress James Billington about creating the National Audiovisual Conservation Center, they settled on a facility that had previously served as "an outpost for intercepting atomic attack." However, the discovery of a rare bird nesting in the ruins of the facility led a group of environmentally aware third graders to successfully lobby Billington not to use the facility. Similar to this atomic "outpost," Mount Pony, according to Billington, was "deserted" when they acquired it."[39]

The preservation of data through digitization requires infrastructure, and it specifically requires spaces of preservation like NAVCC that securitize and preserve analog collections, much of which will likely never be digitized due to the infrastructural burden that comprehensive digitization projects create. The NAVCC must be selective about what it digitizes, and even so, it already generates 3 to 5 petabytes of data per year. Ken Weissman, supervisor of the Film Preservation Laboratory at the Library of Congress, contemplates the possible consequences of moving entirely to digitization as the means of preserving film, rather than continuing to perform film-to-film transfers. In a series of calculations he calls "really, really scary," Weissman estimates that a typical archival scan of a color film results in about 128 megabytes per frame; with digital restoration data included, along with initial scans, each film comprises 48 terabytes. To digitize the 30,000 titles in the nitrate film collection alone would generate 1.44 exabytes of data.[40]

In order to protect the digitized images in a "deep archive," much of this data would need to be off-loaded in a storage area network (SAN). While pulling data out of the deep archive "depends upon the speed of the digital infrastructure," Weissman writes that in 2011 moving even a single terabyte into the deep archive for postprocessing took from 3 to 5 hours. He raises doubts about the feasibility of then migrating that data every five years (which would be required in order to prevent data loss through format obsolescence), and is astounded by the unsustainability of the general wisdom he's heard "at several conferences and meetings in the last couple of years where people are saying, 'No, no, no, no you want to have at least TWO backup copies.' On separate servers, separate geographic locations, the whole bit, because a single backup that you make might not be able to be restored. You want the second backup, just in case."

This is symptomatic of the way that anxieties within the data complex continually put pressure on its physical infrastructure to expand. The infrastructure struggles to keep up with our demands for more data storage space, with our intensifying sense that we need to preserve national, corporate, and individual memories in media artifacts that always seem to decay more rapidly than our attachments to them. Digital media's ability to condense massive amounts of information satisfies this need. Simultaneously, the ephemerality and fragility of digital files exacerbate our anxieties, as the large-scale digitization efforts of the past two decades have rendered archives more vulnerable than ever to instantaneous, invisible, silent forms of destruction like hacking, viruses, and cyberterrorism.[41]

As difficult as it may be to fathom, the NAVCC is actually a rather modest site within the broader data preservation infrastructure that stores and distributes digital images, a network that includes the mammoth data centers of corporations like Facebook and Google. In the course of his attempt to estimate how many photos have ever been taken, Jonathan Good reported in 2011 that Facebook already had 140 billion photos in its collection, which was "over 10,000 times larger than the Library of Congress."[42] Of course, the clandestine digital image collections of the National Security Agency, Federal Bureau of Investigation, and Central Intelligence Agency likely dwarf even Facebook's massive holdings, though it is impossible to precisely assess these rather significant sites in the data complex.[43] What is certain is that the vast majority of digital images reside in data centers, which, even though many do not reside in the ruins of Cold War bunkers, still bear the legacy of the Cold War. The centers are often located in remote nontarget areas, originally demarcated as such by civil defense planners trying to predict where Soviet bombs would strike.

In the internet age, the data complex infrastructure undergoes a transformation that again intensifies the concentration and securitization of information, as well as its vulnerability. With the rise of "online" backup services and "cloud" storage, again the data of corporations, state agencies, and everyday people occupies the same servers, in the same data centers, in the same geographical spaces of preservation. In *Survival City: Adventures among the Ruins of Atomic America*, Tom Vanderbilt illuminates the ways in which the digital age inherited and made use of infrastructure from the Cold War. He characterizes data centers as "contemporary incarnation[s] of the Cold War architectural ethos"; they're the "physical housing of websites," and they provide "security, redundancy, and anonymity."[44] Like contemporary data centers, the Bunker was maintained in a constant state of operational readiness, and it required massive diesel generators to be tested on a regular basis and to run pointlessly just in case they needed to be used.[45]

In Peter Galison's view, the internet that relies on these data centers for its existence "grew directly out of fifteen years of longing for a world still standing after thermonuclear war."[46] It is commonplace to point out the roots of internet and email technology in the military-industrial complex, but Galison is saying more than that: the internet, its imaginary and material infrastructures, grew out of *longing*, out of a desire to preserve what exists. The securitized infrastructure of the Cold War is now fully integrated into the data complex of the internet age, its promises to protect us against nuclear threats renewed in the era of counterterrorism, its bunkers and missile silos repurposed to make possible the digitized worlds of corporate enterprise, government operation, and everyday life in the United States.

Now, nearly every transaction—whether political, financial, or social—relies on digital infrastructure, on the data centers and related elements embedded in the material and imaginary remnants and ruins of the Cold War. The so-called cloud does not exist immaterially in the air above our heads but resides very materially in these remote, reinforced, transcendent underground spaces within a vast data preservation infrastructure that grew out of hauntings of destruction, and fears of radioactive and racial contamination. We have now repurposed this infrastructure in ways that reflect our current fears, hopes, and persistent impossible desires for permanent data invulnerable to the forces of (cyber)terrorism, natural disasters, and the indomitable force of decay that inheres in all media artifacts.[47]

Of course, there are still people who are repurposing Cold War infrastructure as bunkers where they plan to live after the end of the world. In 2013, entrepreneur Robert Vicino announced that he was converting a part of the Atchison Storage Facility, originally a limestone quarry, then an underground warehouse for perishable food, military tools, and surplus supplies during and after World War II. He planned to turn it into a bombproof resort (preapocalyptic use) and survival shelter (postapocalyptic use), one of several operated by his company Vivos. Members of Vivos pay a fee in exchange for the use of paved spaces on which to park mobile homes, a share of the preserved food supplies, and other basic services such as health care and armed protection from threats on "the other side of the door." The Atchison shelter promised to preserve not only the lives of its members but also "a depository of DNA and reproductive cells" in "the world's only nuclear blast-proof, underground cryovault built to survive the next life-extinction event." The Vivos website combines apocalyptic warnings and Fox News blurbs to convince potential investors to buy into this futuristic underworld: "The Vivos Cryovault expands your opportunity to be a part of the next genesis. Join us in the Vivos Cryovault gene pool!"[48]

Vivos now has several locations, including "Vivos xPoint," a repurposed Army Munitions Depot near the Black Hills of South Dakota. The Atchison facility was never completed, though. According to Vicino, he halted construction due to safety concerns arising from the mines' geological instability, a claim disputed by the Atchison Chamber of Commerce president, who says the mines are "very safe," and are still in use by other businesses. CNBC reported that Vicino's plans for retrofitting the mine were "quietly scrapped . . . after fears of a Mayan-predicted apocalypse blew over in 2012," and the company's projections of demand for its bunkers failed to materialize.[49]

## Buried Alive

Even basic fortifications and securitization have long brought at least as much anxiety as comfort. In 1963, Dr. Lester Grinspoon, a senior psychiatrist at the Massachusetts Mental Health Center and instructor at Harvard Medical School, testified before Congress to highlight "some of the psychological problems" of a national shelter program. He used a parable of a father who tells his son they need to build a high fence topped with barbwire and broken glass, because "there may be some savage beasts at large in the community." Grinspoon pointed out that the fence might not "make the child feel more secure." Instead, he suggested, in an elaboration that sheds light on how the data complex reinforces and expands itself in a maladaptive technogenetic excess, the child may see the fence as "an ever-present, anxiety provoking reminder of the hostile and insecure nature of the world he lives in."[50]

But a bunker is far more substantial than a fence, and it may have a fence around it as well. And a data bunker not only carries fears of digital loss but also sustains what we often think of as a part of the past: Cold War fears of nuclear destruction.[51] In *A Prehistory of the Cloud*, Tung-Hui Hu poetically explains how "the cloud is not just built to solve specific technological problems but is built around the shape of our imagined vulnerabilities."[52] Hu draws on psychoanalytic theory to describe the irrational fantasies that inform our attachment to data. He describes this attachment as a kind of melancholy, which is different from mourning. In the process of mourning, one accepts the loss and grieves for the lost person or object. In melancholy, the loss is so painful that one refuses to accept it and instead "disavows that loss, internalizing and burying an identification with the lost object within himself or herself."[53] This burial, paradoxically, keeps a version of the object alive in the psyche of the one afflicted with melancholy, which thus functions as a kind of "preservative." The melancholic secretly and irrationally hopes for the "resurrection or reincarnation" of what has been lost. In psychoanalytic theory, the psychic formation that encloses and preserves this "shadow" of the lost object is called a "crypt." A data bunker is "a crypt for our data."

The physical and psychological facets of the data complex intersect in the architecture of data bunkers that house the cloud. According to Hu, the data bunker is shaped by "a melancholic fantasy of surviving the eventual disaster by entombing data inside highly secured data vaults."[54] Hu quotes Paul Virilio's book *Bunker Archaeology* to say that "bunker" is another name for "the crypt that prefigures the resurrection." The networked nature of the data bunker makes it different from earlier manifestations of this hope for resurrection, in that its networked redundancy instills even greater faith that permanent data is possible. The data bunker, as a part of the cloud, is preserved through a "paranoid," "feverish" approach to saving data against threats. Like the failure of the fence to comfort the child in Dr. Grimpson's parable, Hu writes that "one bunker does not assuage the problem, but only multiplies the crypt-like structures deemed necessary to house our data."

Further, though it is true that our melancholic relation to data is older than the cloud, where we've imagined its loss only to disavow that loss and materialize our melancholy through time capsules and the like, data bunkers bring a new level of heft to the data complex. Even as the bunker's "blastproof walls" and "armed security guards" inspire hope for a future resurrection after the end of the world, "the immobility and weight of the bunker itself transfers" onto our bodies.[55] In other words, we imagine the loss of data and preserve it in a bunker, thereby keeping it alive even in the fantasy of its loss. These psychological gymnastics create a crypt inside us, wherein we've buried the always both lost and preserved data, flickering back and forth between oblivion and a fossilized eternity.

But what we also incorporate into our psyche is the massive architecture, the mountain of weight that is the steel-reinforced concrete (sometimes under an actual mountain), the twenty-seven-ton blast door, the stone walls of the vast underground caverns threaded with water pipes and fiber optics. The crypt inside us is both infinite and claustrophobic. In order to be safe and survive the apocalypse that is always coming, we must never leave this crypt; this crypt is too small, there's not enough air, we must leave and build more crypts inside ourselves that materialize in more bunkers in the world.

Calling the expanding data complex a cloud leads us to believe it is somehow airy, intangible, immaterial, but perhaps the comparison is fitting in one sense. A cloud is a deceptive thing, seeming to be weightless, when it is not at all; it is simply less dense than the air flowing below it. Clouds are very material and heavy. A single cumulus cloud, which consists of tiny water droplets, spread across a cubic kilometer, weighs over 1 million pounds.[56]

## Desert Clouds

In Bluffdale, Utah, only 70 miles from the Dugway Proving Ground, is a National Security Agency (NSA) facility known generally as the Utah Data Center (UDC). Its 1 million square feet—about 90 percent of that used for power and cooling equipment—requires over 60 kilowatts of power and up to 5 million gallons of water per day. While no one knows precisely how much data it holds, as it is a state secret, a former NSA mathematician claimed that the UDC could "store data at the rate of 20 terabytes—the equivalent of the Library of Congress—per minute."[57] A Department of Defense report did once estimate the storage requirements of the U.S. military's network as "exceeding exabytes and possibly yottabytes."[58] Journalist James Bamford, whom the *New Yorker* dubbed "the NSA's chief chronicler," and the *New York Times* called "the nation's premier journalist on the subject of the National Security Agency," estimates the Utah Data Center's storage to be in yottabytes. There are 1,000 trillion gigabytes in a yottabyte.

The NSA has collected data from all over, including through "intentional and unintentional back doors in the private web platforms of companies including Facebook, Google, Microsoft, Skype, and Apple, accessed through the notorious PRISM program that showed a degree of cooperation on the part of many tech firms."[59] What it collects it duplicates to create backups in data centers "across multiple locales, including in Georgia, Texas, Colorado, and Hawaii." Seeking yet more space, in 2013 the NSA broke ground on a $860 million, 70,000-square-foot data center expansion at its headquarters in Fort Meade, Maryland.[60]

One driver of the government's need for more data storage is its drone surveillance programs. By 2011, the U.S. Air Force alone collected drone footage that amounted to 325,000 hours, or thirty-seven years' worth of footage. The USAF consulted ESPN for advice on how to handle so much video, and a *Wired* article suggests that AI should be trained to watch it all.[61] Most of it has no value, leading one four-star general to come out and say that having soldiers watch "death TV" and wait for some target to appear or move is "just a waste of manpower."[62]

But even with all the surveillance, securitization, cybersecurity, and secrecy that now attend government installations within the data complex, these sites remain vulnerable to hacking. In 2014, the Office of Personnel

Management (OPM) suffered cybersecurity breaches resulting in the exposure of security clearance files and other records related to 22.1 million people. The hacked databases contained information about "not only federal employees and contractors but their families and friends." A 2016 *Wired* article discusses how it might have been prevented if the OPM's multifactor authentification system had been in place by that time. This is the system most people now use to further secure their email and other accounts, as it requires a password at login in addition to a onetime-use code texted to a cell phone. But even these measures aren't foolproof, as the July 2020 hack of Twitter proved. A seventeen-year-old in Florida, along with a few accomplices, gained access to Twitter's network and made use of the corporation's internal tools to take control of celebrities' accounts. The Twitter followers of Barack Obama, Kim Kardashian West, Jeff Bezos, Elon Musk, and Bill Gates, not to mention those of "several cryptocurrency companies," were all targeted with a scam that allowed the hackers to steal around $118,000 worth of bitcoin.[63]

The OPM hack was a cybersecurity disaster of epic proportions. Numerous U.S. officials think that cyberespionage units controlled by the Chinese government are responsible. The snagged files contained data "gathered on applicants for some of the government's most secretive jobs," "data that can include everything from lie detector results to notes about whether an applicant engages in risky sexual behavior." Other files taken included "5.6 million digital images of government employee fingerprints." Tony Scott, the chief information officer of the United States, led an initiative called Sprint to help federal agencies upgrade their systems in simple but highly effective ways. He called it "basic hygiene," and it was developed in consultation with the Pentagon and the National Institute for Standards and Technology (NIST), formerly known as the National Bureau of Standards (NBS).[64]

No matter what we do, data is always vulnerable. Even the "Swiss Fort Knox" data bunker, equipped with "bulletproof checkpoints and twenty-four-hour surveillance systems, electromagnetic pulse protection, negative pressure systems to flush out chemical weapon attacks, and 'hermetically sealed' air gaps," can never be fully secure. None of these preventive measures protect against "a rogue system administrator" who could "corrupt the backup files stored there."[65] Like Thornwell Jacobs imploring future generations to wait until 8113 A.D. before they breach the Crypt of Civilization, data preservation in the cloud is still founded on hope, with its reinforced doors and gates, no matter how tall, ultimately secured with a kind of prayer from one human to another.

## In Algorithms We Trust

We are still bombproofing our data bodies as we digitize our lives, representing them in a million pictures and videos and text files stored in the cloud, that fulfillment of every industrial dispersion dream. The structure of the cloud optimizes and digitizes the analog redundancy strategies of the past, such as Westinghouse's worldwide distribution of *The Book of Record*, and Thornwell Jacobs's half-baked plan to hand out stainless steel tickets to the opening of the crypt in 8113 A.D. The cloud improves on every previous fantasy of protection against loss because it, like the bomb test, gives life to data through destruction. When you send a large file to the cloud, it might be copied across multiple servers in multiple locations, or it might be broken up into fragments that are dispersed to different data centers across a network that spans hundreds or even thousands of miles. That way, even if a server goes down in Des Moines, the file can still be reconstituted from its other fragments in Prineville, and Austin, and elsewhere. This is the equivalent of finding an intact clay urn from the Ptolemaic era, smashing it to shards, then scattering them across several pits as a way of protecting the artifact from being lost.

The difference now, of course, is that every fragment is traceable, locatable within the vast data complex that forms the digital underground of our daily lives. The files we create actually often begin in fragmented form—as you draft an email, or a Google Doc, it is being written to several different servers in the cloud, backed up before it even exists as something you've finished and sent to a loved one or a colleague. Pics in your Google Photos stream likewise live this kind of double life, born already backups of themselves in a loop from Apple data center to device to Shutterfly or some other corporate server, to NSA or facial recognition software start-up, or hacker, or anyone else "scraping" data to feed some artificially intelligent neural net. And when we access that file it is pulled together from everywhere and reconstituted for us, but remains spread out—it never stops being dust. But that dust is also backed up on magnetic tape by corporations like Google—a tangible, physical thing, the style of preservation embodied in the time capsules of Pendray and Jacobs. So, the object-based encapsulation method of the Depression never really went away; it's one more layer in the expanding, deepening data complex swirling around us and inside us.

And while data bunkers certainly extend and intensify the preservation practices of the past, our data bodies now differ from Cold War microfilm in key ways. The corporate records, state archives, and historical collections preserved in data bunkers are valuable beyond measure, like the microfilm deposited by banks and insurance firms at the Iron Mountain Atomic Storage Company back in the 1950s. This data still collectively makes up the material and symbolic scaffolding necessary for the making of Americans' data bodies, which is also the process by which some human biobodies are made into "Americans." The difference now is that, with the emergence of the cloud, data bodies become searchable—or to use the most fitting term, minable.

And to be valuable, our data bodies don't actually need to be accurate in how they describe our biobodies. By virtue of being aggregated and ordered, mined and extruded by the algorithms in which we trust, certified by the semiautomatic sifting carried out by the data complex, our data bodies are made to speak a more flexible set of truths. In his book *We Are Data: Algorithms and the Making of Our Digital Selves*, John Cheney-Lippold explains that we now all have "algorithmic identities." These identities are constantly shifting, and though they might not always match how we would describe our biobodies, such discrepancies are more than just inaccuracies.

Cheney-Lippold describes a now-common situation, where his friend—a young woman—is categorized by Google's algorithms as an "old man." And while her miscategorization "might seem erroneous in our world of conventional gender and identity regimes," she will "likely continue as an algorithmic 'old' 'man' in accordance to her dedication to cell biology research." When our data bodies do not match our biobodies, this "algorithmic miscategorization is better understood as *neocategorization*." Her browsing behavior and other data points indicate that though Cheney-Lippold's friend "may not be a man," the algorithms determine that she's "'as if' a 'man' according to her data." As a "man," she will be swept up in data-mining operations that splinter the self into a billion data points to swirl and swarm with data points extracted from other users across a multitude of platforms. The "algorithmic measurable types" that become our identities in the cloud are like a language that the data complex uses to describe us as it talks to itself.[66]

Digital selves, then, are not the same as the self cobbled together by microfilm duplicates in Recordak ads of the 1940s, with the typical white, male American head floating in the center. Data bodies in the cloud are "unlike our identities that enjoy/suffer at least temporary consistency across time." On the contrary, as Cheney-Lippold points out, "our new, measurable-typed identities can change by the hour: later in the afternoon, my friend's data trail might suggest yet another identification."[67]

## Cellblocks for Data

The data complex will continue to expand into the hollow underground caverns and abandoned bunkers of previous eras, not to mention any other reinforced or fortresslike structure that lends itself to easier securitization. A recent article that commends the NAVCC on its "green" architectural principles forecasts a haunting direction for this seemingly inevitable expansion: "With the recent announcement that the detention center at Guantánamo Bay and various related 'black areas' will close imminently, perhaps these mistaken monuments can find similarly hopeful uses as the [NAVCC]'s former bunker—and be adapted with equal skill."[68] Such conversions of sites in the prison-industrial complex to become a part of the data complex would not be entirely unprecedented.[69]

During the Cuban Missile Crisis in October 1962, D.C.'s civil defense office sent personnel to its relocation center: a prison in Lorton, Virginia.[70] Over the span of that same month, Eugene Burdick and Harvey Wheeler published the three installments of their novel *Fail-Safe* in the *Saturday Evening Post*; the story depicts the outbreak of nuclear war between the United States and the Soviet Union. A character in the novel sheds light on the common architectural principles, as well as the mediating function of all preservation architecture, when he predicts that "the likeliest survivors of an all-out thermonuclear war . . . would be the most hardened of convicts, those in solitary confinement. Another group likely to survive would be file clerks for large insurance companies, because they would be housed in fireproofed rooms and insulated by tons of the best insulator in the world, paper."[71] In this scenario, prison architecture meant to protect free society and the social order against the threat of "hardened convicts" simultaneously preserves the convicts against the massive nuclear destruction produced by the supposedly civilized society. The fireproof vault meant to preserve paper-based data simultaneously protects the bodies of file clerks, which are also literally insulated from radiation by the media artifacts themselves.

This flexibility of sites within the data preservation infrastructure—their ability to mediate threats from inside and/or outside their securitized spaces—facilitates their continual repurposing according to new data preservation requirements, against new threats, within a shifting set of geopolitical tensions. In an earlier example, a *New York Times* article from December 7, 1950, "Capital Slave Quarters Will Be Bomb Shelter," details how wealthy socialite Louise Cromwell Brooks had recently hired a contractor to turn the subbasement of her mansion, with its "great hewn beams and foundations of river boulders," into an atomic bomb shelter with "steel doors and reinforced concrete."[72] She planned to install a "shelter large enough to accommodate 100 to 150 of her neighbors," and she told the reporter, "I wouldn't enjoy sealing myself up if I knew my neighbors were being blown to bits."[73] Brooks imagined that, if necessary, up to 300 to 400 people "could be crowded in." The slave quarters were first used by the mansion's "original builder, a slave trafficker and tobacco magnate" named "Captain Savage."[74]

Brooks, wife of a colonel in the Air Force Reserve, ex-wife of General Douglas MacArthur, and sister-in-law of Doris Duke, was by no means a typical bomb shelter builder. Nonetheless, her plans potently reflect how the data complex repurposes any and all existing resources during a crisis, leading to some striking reversals. The imagined scenario of nuclear attack depicted in both the *New York Times* and *Time* magazine involves Brooks and her wealthy Georgetown neighbors being "crowded" into the underground bunker. This potential reversal of fortunes, where wealthy D.C. elites would crush themselves into a space formerly occupied by slaves, according to the inhuman spatial arrangements of a slave ship, highlights the multiple functions that can be served by spaces of preservation. Such spaces of reinforced concrete can serve to preserve bodies and currency, media artifacts and foodstuffs; such spaces can just as easily serve as bulwarks against outside threats to preserve shelter occupants, or as prison cells to protect free society against the threat held inside the cell.

When considered together, these two examples illuminate the fact that stone walls, underground roadways, blast doors, and observation towers are indifferent to what they protect, and to what threats they protect those contents from. The spaces in the data complex are literally haunted, both by what purposes they have served in the past, and by what they may become. As they shift their function over time, we often call them by a misleading name. For underground slave "quarters" were more like prison cells than houses, as these spaces where slaves slept and dreamed also worked simultaneously to imprison them. As carceral spaces, the "quarters" protected not the slaves inside, but the *slaveowner outside* against property loss (i.e., escape). To recall the scenario in *Fail-Safe*, these "quarters" were more like bank vaults or fireproof rooms for insurance files than homes, since black slaves' bodies were fungible—reduced to subhuman objects that were interchangeable with any other commodity on the market, from land to gold, from corn to cotton.[75]

If the cells of Guantánamo Bay ever do become the vaults of a data center, we will be witnessing not a radically unprecedented development, but a continuation and intensification of an ongoing process that converts residual spaces—left behind by previous modes of production and abandoned by previous national security regimes—originally meant to preserve bodies into spaces that preserve data. For its existence and preservation, digital data materially relies on not only hard drives and cables where ones and zeroes pulse but also the bombproof architectures that house this hardware, the ruined monuments of Cold War bunkers that shelter the flickering image-worlds of the digital age. Still, the data complex finds ways to tell us that the failures of vaults and safes mean we need to preserve more data digitally, and that the failures of digital mean we need to preserve more data in vaults and safes.

### The Constellation of Dead Malls

In 2017, Pacific Development Partners offered $10 million to purchase the Wapato Jail in Multnomah County, Oregon, and mentioned that it might convert it into a data center. The deal fell through, but other such conversions within the data complex are beginning to move forward. United Fiber and Data purchased the old prison in York, Pennsylvania, with plans to turn it into a data center. The new facility would provide backup services for clients using a 340-mile-long fiber optic cable completed in 2019, the first one to directly link New York City with Ashburn, Virginia, known as the "the Data Center Capital of the World" because 70 percent of all internet traffic passes through its data infrastructure every day.[76]

But even the sprawling prison-industrial complex and its many ruins can't keep up with the storage space demands of the data complex. Amazon has already bought a number of defunct malls and converted them into fulfillment centers, and as of 2020, the company was in talks with the Simon Property Group about moving into their constellation of dead malls that stretches across the United States and Canada.[77] That same year, Iron Mountain was in the process of building data centers in northern Virginia and Frankfurt, Germany, and expanding their data centers in Amsterdam, London, New Jersey, and Singapore.[78] But all of these companies know that data preservation leads to more data preservation, and expanding the earthly footprint of the data complex, eventually, won't be enough.

The data complex has already begun to look elsewhere, beyond the remnants of previous eras' bunkers and fortifications, not just to more securitized spaces, but to space itself.

# 5

# The Satellite Graveyard

In the far future, bits of hard drives may be fossilized in limestone, and discarded iPhones may find themselves encased in amber, hardened like nail polish, but the bits of humanity that these exquisitely crafted machines hold will be lost to time.

—Trevor Paglen, *The Last Pictures*

I never imagined I would find any of Thomas K. Peters's metal film. Peters devised it in the 1920s, when modern media like newsprint were falling apart, even as ancient Egyptian papyri and metallic artifacts were being discovered in tombs sealed thousands of years before and in virtually pristine condition. Back in 1929, Robert Binkley published an essay in *Scientific American* where he floated the idea of backing up newspapers by creating photocopies of them on metal. While the article was well received enough to be reprinted in *Reader's Digest*, Binkley admittedly knew the cost of such a strategy would be prohibitive for even the wealthiest private libraries, not to mention public ones.[1]

In the ancient world, many societies produced metallic documents at one time or another, such as the "curse tablets" used in magic throughout the Greek and Roman world.[2] Curse tablets were pieces of lead pounded into thin sheets inscribed with "prayers for justice," were "usually discovered rolled into scrolls or folded into small packets, and were either deposited in tombs, sanctuaries or bodies of water."[3] In 2014, UNESCO added the famous Bath Curse Tablets to its Memory of the World Register. Discovered in 1979, over 100 of these tiny documents carried all manner of demands for the goddess Sulis Minerva between the second and fourth centuries A.D. In one example, a victim who sought revenge for the theft of a brass vessel asked that the pilfered item "be filled with the blood of the thief."[4]

The inscription on the steel door of the Crypt of Civilization is not quite a curse, but it does recall the ancient warnings etched into the stones that sealed the tombs of pharaohs, in that it seeks to ensure that people who encounter it in the future leave it intact (until 8113 A.D., anyway). I go down to Atlanta to see the door of the crypt myself, and to dig through the archive of papers deposited by Thornwell Jacobs and T. K. Peters at Oglethorpe University's Philip Weltner Library, the building under which the crypt sits. I walk down the basement hallway toward the crypt, the same hallway Paul Stephen Hudson had trodden as a student at Oglethorpe back in the 1970s, when the crypt was all but forgotten. Hudson rediscovered it and became its champion, proceeding to earn a Ph.D. in history, single-handedly reviving knowledge about the crypt the way Jacobs had single-handedly revived the university itself. Hudson published articles like "'The End of the World and After': The Cosmic Milleniarism of Thornwell Jacobs," cofounded the International Time Capsule Society with the goal of tracking the deposits of time capsules around the world, and even appeared on an episode of the History Channel's *Life After People* to explain how Jacobs intended his time capsule to be found by "future inhabitants, or *visitors* to the planet Earth."[5] Jacobs had wondered whether, by the time the crypt was opened, people would communicate directly with God, or with the dead, or with "living beings, if there are such, on other heavenly bodies."[6]

After reading the inscription on the stainless steel door, I spend the day in the Oglethorpe University Archives, looking at everything related to the crypt. The archive is the most unsecured I've ever seen. A library employee places all the materials on a cart, props the door open, and tells me that I can stay in there as long as I want and that I should just leave the materials there on the table when I am finished. I find some interesting things. In one clipping, T. K. Peters makes grand claims I haven't yet been able to substantiate. For instance, he says that he created the special effects for the scene of parting the Red Sea in Cecil B. DeMille's first version of *The Ten Commandments*, released in 1923. Peters says the seawalls were made of gelatin, and he filmed them jiggling both forward and in reverse at the same time to create the illusion that they were liquid held up by a kind of horizontal gravitation. The shining seawalls definitely look like sepia-colored Jell-O, but according to the Internet Movie Database (IMDb), Roy Pomeroy, a founding member of the Academy of Motion Picture Arts and Sciences, created the effect. Peters also claims to have accompanied Teddy Roosevelt on a trip to the Panama Canal, where Roosevelt "assigned Dr. Peters to do the photographic record."[7]

Apparently, there were also plans for a second Crypt of Civilization. For fifteen dollars you could have an "imperishable" metal plate made that bore your likeness and a biographical statement, and Peters and Jacobs would preserve it in the crypt. The plate would then automatically become the property of your "lineal descendant in the 30th generation, to become this descendant's property in the year 2500 A.D., when the [second] Crypt will be opened." While a duplicate metal copy would cost you five dollars, they were willing to send you a free "paper printed copy."[8] While Peters's papers offer plenty of fascinating, unverified tidbits—what my grandfather playfully called *lies*—I can't help but be disappointed that there is no metal film, not even a photograph of a strip of metal film, and I leave the basement under the assumption that I will never find it.

I begin to think that Peters's metal film might never have existed at all. I have already sifted his papers at UCLA's Young Research Library, which were mostly technical stuff on microfilm, sketches for a national film museum that never materialized, promotional materials for trips to the Far East that might have materialized, and pages and pages of captions for a photographic exhibition that told the story of the United States from a very T. K. Peters perspective. He asserted that slaves were "bought by traders in Africa from tribal chiefs," "transported to America in Yankee ships," and "cared for by their owners as carefully as any valued property." Parroting well-established southern racial fantasies, he claimed that the slaves' "physical condition in this decade was superior to that in the next when they were set free."[9] Jacobs and Peters had wanted the crypt to sit at the midpoint of human history, but they really only constructed a view that allows us to get inside their heads in the late 1930s and see the way they looked at the past and future through distorted lenses shaped by the artifacts they included in the crypt. One example is *Gone with the Wind*, both the novel and an original script from the film production. Out of all the artifacts included in the crypt and the Westinghouse Time Capsule, *GWTW* is perhaps the most condensed reflection of average white Americans' outlook in the 1930s, as the four-hour film's popularity was unprecedented, and unsurpassed, in the entire history of American popular culture. Even with all the Marvel movies, the *Star Wars* franchise, *Avatar*, and *Titanic* in the running, when adjusted for inflation, *GWTW* still reigns as the highest-grossing film of all time, at $3.7 billion.[10]

At the end of my day in the Oglethorpe archives, I take a cab into some cool neighborhood in Atlanta and meet my friend Nick Yablon for Indian food. Nick and I presented on a panel together yesterday at the Society for Cinema and Media Studies conference, and he is working on his book *Remembrance of Things Present: The Invention of the Time Capsule*, which is going to be *the* book on time capsules and their precursors, "time vessels." He was the one I first saw connect all the dots between eugenics and data preservation, and I wrote him an academic fan email years ago, after reading one of his amazing articles. We've been conversing ever since. At dinner, we talk about the joys and limits of Iowa City; the endless rain of his hometown, London; the beauty and frigidity of Vermont; and, of course, about Jacobs and Peters, their kooky creativity, their ingenuity, their racism. Nick has been a consultant on time capsule designs and openings, and we start to brainstorm ideas for a company that would reconstruct historical versions of American cities for VR tours, pieced together from archival photos and historical accounts. You could ride atop a tour bus in the Big Apple, peer out over the railing and see the hustle and bustle of teamsters and hawkers, the squat, crooked tenements of the Five Points, then flip a hundred years ahead to see the way it had changed by the time Babe Ruth ruled the city, and so on.

Soon enough, we conclude our visioning session and exit the restaurant. I wish Nick luck at the archives (he is heading out to Oglethorpe tomorrow) and then walk around the city by myself a bit. Heading up Peachtree Street, I soon stumble upon the Margaret Mitchell House. Adorned with a plaque explaining how she wrote her Pulitzer Prize–winning novel in apartment 1 back in 1925, the house, now the home to a literary center, is dark, closed, well preserved. Sometimes you travel halfway across the country to sift an archive and don't come up with much, just a few interesting but unusable clippings and a nice memory of an evening with a friend.

But in the data complex, there's always another archive waiting to be explored, holding out the possibility of treasure. By the time I arrive at the Manuscript Reading Room of the Library of Congress in Washington, D.C., I have fully given up on finding metal film. The Manuscripts Division is now housed in the James Madison Memorial Building, the largest library structure in the world, encompassing 2.1 million square feet.[11] I approach the severely boxy building's colonnaded facade, which resembles something like a Greek temple built to honor the goddess of boredom. Even its columns are rectangular. Hoping the interior will be more fun, I enter and acquire my ID card, present it to the armed guard at the entrance to the large reading room, roll the first few boxes that have been set out for me to a large table, then sit down to begin a full day of flipping through folders, taking notes and photos, trying to make the most of my time here.

The Library of Congress always reminds me how every archive is incomplete, that it is always a gathering of fragments. Originally housed in the U.S. Capitol, the library saw its entire collection burned by British troops during the War of 1812. Thomas Jefferson then sold several thousand volumes to the federal government, only to have most of the collection destroyed by fire again in 1851. After that, architect of the capitol Thomas Walter rebuilt a wing of the structure out of cast iron—he's most famous for adding the iconic dome to the Capitol Building, which is also built with fireproof cast iron. The library moved to its new building in 1897, and no major mishaps have occurred since then—third time's the charm, I suppose.[12]

After a few hours, I pull a folder from a gray archival box and something small and stamp sized falls out. A line of square holes punched out on either side, it shines, almost mirrorlike, and I feel the closest I've ever felt to the way Charlie Bucket must have in *Willy Wonka & the Chocolate Factory* when he saw the gold foil glint against the brown Wonka Bar. Delicately, I flip the thin flake over and see two and a half frames of the face of FDR, looking as if he's talking. But without more frames to complete the reel, and without Peters's specially invented projector that works by reflection rather than shining light through a diaphanous negative, we'll likely never know whether the president that journalists nicknamed "the Sphinx" was talking about the latest addition to his New Deal, or the Luftwaffe bombing of Wieluń, or delivering his D-Day prayer, in which he asked for God's aid

**Fragment of metal newsreel depicting Franklin Delano Roosevelt. Thomas Kimmwood Peters Papers, Manuscript Division, Library of Congress, Washington, D.C.**

in the "struggle to preserve our republic, our religion and our civilization, and to set free a suffering humanity." Trying to find some, any, information I can about the metal film fragment, I look at the list of contents for the boxes and folders, and the metal film hasn't even been catalogued. Not a century after it was etched, the very metal meant to be more durable than safety film ended up itself becoming a fragment, just a few orphaned frames.

Flying in the face of the overblown PR for digital technology and digitization, *none* of Thomas Kimmwood Peters's papers—not at the Library of Congress, nor UCLA, nor Oglethorpe University—have been digitized and made accessible online. So what might have been a more efficient search through databases turns up nothing. I close my laptop, take a couple scans of the metal film, and then bring it to the attention of a staff member, who says the library will make a note of the fragment in its records.

In this era of human-induced climate change, digital technology is its own crisis, as the data complex now demands infinite resources from a finite planet at a pace that could never be renewable or sustainable. Digital technology is ecologically unsustainable in its intensive natural resource requirements for both its manufacture and operation, from the copper and gold lacing through integrated circuits and communication infrastructure, to the massive carbon footprint of data centers that require constant air conditioning. The average life span of a digital hard drive is three to five years, due to mechanical failure, format obsolescence, or any of the forces that have plagued analog media and can still destroy digital hard drives: fire, flood, dust, heat, even a form of decay at the microscopic level that computer scientists call "bitrot," where the bits lose or flip their magnetic charge.[13] As Parikka reminds us in *A Geology of Media*, the metals, minerals, and carbon fuels required to produce and power digital technology form over millions of years, and the products—laptops, tablets, smartphones, wide-screen LCD panels—are used for a few years on average, then tossed into an e-waste dump, sometimes through a "recycling" program that operates in conjunction with a vast network of wastelands where children in Ghana and China burn through plastic and heavy metals in open fire pits to recover small slivers of gold or other precious material. The infernal junkyards of the internet age.

As it turns out, this glimpse of metal film is a harbinger of forms of data preservation still to come. At the heart of this chapter is a far more recent proliferation of etching, which both continues an ongoing practice of backup looping and reflects an intensification within the data complex. The use of a cutting-edge technology to create data with time-tested permanence is a backup loop on a grand scale, a response to a societal shift toward the increasing dominance of digital media.

The ephemerality of digital media has stimulated a return to old, even ancient media formats to preserve data. Etching has been practiced since ancient times, but to call the practice ancient would be a bit misleading. Etching never really went away, and the digital age has seen a resurgence and proliferation of new techniques for practicing this old method of data inscription.

I never did find a stainless steel ticket for admission to the crypt's opening ceremony in 8113 A.D., but I believe they're still out there.

### The Last Pictures

In 2012, the artist Trevor Paglen would launch, literally, *The Last Pictures*, a project that would address the limits of the digital, produce arguably the most durable time capsule up to that point, and yet question the practice of permanent data preservation in a way that elucidates the shifting contours of the data complex in the twenty-first century. Prior to *The Last Pictures*, Paglen was best known for his photography, where he explored invisible sites. Armed with an MFA from the Art Institute of Chicago and a Ph.D. in geography from U.C. Berkeley, not to mention a highly original conceptual sense and technical tool kit, he combined cameras with telescopes, usually used to take pictures of other planets, to photograph secret "black" sites operated by U.S. intelligence agencies, such as the places in other countries that the CIA uses for "extraordinary rendition" (a euphemism for kidnapping and torture of terror suspects), as well as the Dugway Proving Ground.[14]

For other projects, Paglen crowdsourced the mapping of classified satellites and published a book of photography on patches worn by secret military units. For *The Last Pictures*, Paglen sought to create an "ultra-archival" media format that would outlast any other human artifact and settled on a disk, one not encoded with digital data but etched with images visible through a microscope. He used lasers to microetch 100 images on a silicon disk and attached it to the side of a telecommunications satellite, which now carries the images in geosynchronous orbit through outer space. Once the satellite has lived out its fifteen-year life span, it will burn its last spurt of fuel to boost itself into the "graveyard orbit," 22,000 miles above the earth's surface, where hundreds of dead satellites drift perpetually. Paglen says this celestial belt of artifacts will be the longest-lasting traces of human life in the universe. Roughly 4 billion years from now, when the sun expands into a red giant and vaporizes the earth, along with every Pyramid, obelisk, time capsule, seed vault, and data bunker ever built, Paglen's images will still be there.

Early on in the data complex, there were a relatively small number of people working intensively on data preservation. Their obsessions varied and converged: some seemed mostly concerned with preserving paper documents and records as a part of their job (Iiams and Kimberly), some seemed very preoccupied with threats to free enterprise (Pendray and Hower), and others seemed focused on preserving data and warding off threats to white civilization (Jacobs and Peters). Whatever their central concerns, the data complex gathered these impulses into itself and consolidated them into technologies and artifacts that the next generation inherited. The powerful institutions that incorporated these practices and shaped their function around these new vast realms of data thus made data foundational and crucial for the operation of society, and for the creation of subjects who lived a double life of biobody and data body. As the data complex expanded, growing more extensive and intensive, more and more areas of our political, economic, and social lives as individuals and as collective groups relied on data for their existence and functioning.

At the same time, digital technology provided what seemed like a miracle solution for all this proliferating data, saving costs on both office space and materials. But digital innovations also make all this data more ephemeral, proliferating threats and increasing the vulnerability of both data and the infrastructure it controls, including electrical and water distribution, not to mention voting in elections, which is now mostly electronic. The data complex is expanding in extreme ways into outer space through satellites that will continue to perform telecommunications but will also provide

**Trevor Paglen's *The Last Pictures*, 2012. Courtesy of
Trevor Paglen and Metro Pictures, New York.**

internet signals to make connectivity even faster and increase bandwidth as 5G networks expand.

### The Golden Record

Paglen's project is one of many ventures that have sought to create a permanent record of human achievement, culture, or knowledge during the digital age of the data complex. It takes up the question contemplated by Jacobs, Peters, and Pendray, the question of how to communicate with people over 5,000 years in the future. Peters created a mutoscope-style machine that would display pictograms to teach English to the viewer. Pendray hired ethnologist John Harrington, who created a mouth map and a set of drawings and texts that would teach English to the people of 6939 A.D.

But the most salient precursor for *The Last Pictures* is *The Voyager Golden Record*, launched in 1977 by a team that included celebrity astronomer Carl Sagan and his colleagues, who took their exploration of the question to new levels of sophistication. NASA's Voyager Mission was made possible by a rare alignment of planets that only occurs once every 175 years, "and a momentum-transfer maneuver, sometimes called gravity-assist."[15] There were actually two Voyager probes, launched sixteen days apart. Both of them rocketed away from Earth toward Jupiter and briefly entered into the gas giant's orbit, which greatly accelerated the speed of the probe. Then, each probe used that acceleration to slingshot toward Saturn, where they would pull off this gravitational feat again. One of the probes made close encounters with the ice giants Uranus and Neptune, and it remains the only spacecraft to have done so. Sagan and his colleagues took this as an opportunity to send a message into space, informing aliens about Earth and the humans who inhabit it.

The *Golden Record* was literally a gold-plated record that contained a variety of songs and sounds, everything from "Bach and Beethoven to Blind Willie Johnson and Chuck Berry, Benin percussion to Solomon Island panpipes." The record also carried sounds of "birds, a train, a baby's cry, a kiss," as well as "greetings in dozens of human languages—and one whale language." A 2016 Kickstarter campaign resulted in a commemorative box set reissue of the recordings etched on the *Golden Record*, this time on beautiful translucent vinyl (I might have spent some of my research funding on it . . .), and new "liner notes" written by people involved in the original project. The more I read of the accompanying texts, the more I notice the newness of what they achieved in the 1970s with the *Golden Record*, and the more I hear echoes of the Crypt of Civilization.[16]

Like the crypt, the *Golden Record* also collapsed backup loops in its blurring of etching, sound, images, even radiation. It included 100 images encoded as sounds in the metal grooves. The images were converted sonically by Colorado Video, based in Boulder, which projected each slide onto a TV screen, then converted each one into several seconds of sound, in gray scale at 240 by 512 pixels. The "Statement" by Jimmy Carter was included as an image (in sound), like a one-page PDF, dated June 16, 1977. In an echo of the hopeful, interstellar aspects of Thornwell Jacobs's rhetoric, President Carter told future finders of the record, "We are attempting to survive our time so we may live into yours. We hope someday, having solved the problems we face, to join a community of galactic civilizations. This record represents our hope and our determination, and our good will in a vast and awesome universe." The Voyager also transmitted to Earth the first close-ups of other planets in what were essentially high-resolution digital images. We typically associate radio with sound, but radio waves are radiation—they are light waves, not sound waves. The radio signals from the Voyagers travel at the speed of light—186,000 miles per second, or nearly 670,000,000 miles per hour. Even at that blinding pace, the waves still take fifteen hours to get to Earth, and they are beyond faint at a millionth of a billionth of a watt.[17]

The creators of the *Golden Record* knew it was unlikely it would ever be found, even if they were more hopeful than Paglen. In the liner notes of the reissue of the record, Timothy Ferris points out that the galaxy is 100,000 light-years across, and a few hundred light years thick. If the galaxy were the size of the *Golden Record*, "the solar system would be smaller than an atom."[18] Paglen didn't imagine anyone would find *The Last Pictures*, but in a mark of gamesmanship and resigned optimism, he did decide to etch a star map on the cover of the disc. However, as he points out, the star map is not a star map unless "someone chooses to see it that way." In Paglen's view, the map "simply recapitulates the inscrutable scratchings, paint marks, lines, and dots that make up the majority of images on the walls of Lascaux." *The Last Pictures* disc does not need to be found in order to fulfill its purpose, since Paglen's intention was to make "a grand gesture about the failure of grand gestures."[19]

### An Atomic Priesthood

With the advent of nuclear weapons and radioactive waste, the question of how to communicate with future humans reached a new level of urgency, raising twin specters that haunt humans from opposite ends of the future.

The nuclear bomb threatened the nearly instantaneous annihilation of all human life. Radioactive waste evoked the slow poisoning of the earth and thus the humans who rely on it to survive. Ultimately, the Bomb drove efforts to hermetically conceal radioactive waste—the ultimate toxic time capsule. The question came up of how to warn future humans about the deadly waste we'd bequeath to them, an inversion of the Depression-era dilemma of time capsule creators who thought long and hard about how to make sure humans found their deposits.

In 1999, the Department of Energy created the Waste Isolation Pilot Project (WIPP) in Carlsbad, New Mexico, a series of 56 rooms, 33 feet wide and the length of a football field, "mined in an underground salt bed layer over 2000 feet from the surface." According to the Department of Energy, the salt bed is "free of fresh flowing water, easily mined, impermeable and geologically stable—an ideal medium for permanently isolating long-lived radioactive wastes from the environment."[20] The radioactive waste stored there includes "clothing, tools, rags, residues, debris, soil and other items" contaminated with plutonium.[21] The WIPP project didn't want to help people find it; rather, it wanted to make sure that in the event people found it, they understood the warnings there.

In *Survival City*, Tom Vanderbilt notes how the warning signs to be placed at WIPP after it's sealed recall communication forms we usually associate "with the prehistoric past: stone slabs, engraved obelisks, ceremonial markers."[22] Paglen describes how one proposed design consisted of tall spikes breaking through a grid on the ground, but as none of today's symbolism can be expected to persist and signify stably into the future, semiotician Thomas Sebeok recommended a kind of living message. Sebeok wanted to "convene an 'atomic priesthood'" to act as the site's caretakers. Members of this "mystery cult" would "invent myths and stories as they saw fit to secure the nuclear waste not only in physical space but also in the imaginations and stories of future people." Like a stainless steel ticket for the Crypt of Civilization's opening ceremony, "knowledge about the nuclear site would be passed from generation to generation."[23]

At the same time nuclear weapons and waste drove humans to dig farther into the earth, the prospect that Earth might become uninhabitable only lent further fuel to dreams of living on other planets and getting in touch with aliens. Timothy Ferris, who worked on the *Golden Record* and authored liner notes for its reissue on vinyl, speculates that the odds of us witnessing a visit to Earth by intelligent life are abysmally low. But he imagines that "robotic probes" could be embedded in asteroids, forming a network that transmits data about us back to aliens in a more "cost-effective" way than the "flags-and-footprints" approach.[24] Such a network would extend the cloud beyond the clouds, beyond the ring of satellites circling the earth, beyond the moon, where numerous human artifacts lie on the dusty surface. These artifacts include a microetched silicon disk bearing seventy-eight greetings of peace from world leaders, left behind by Neil Armstrong and Buzz Aldrin during the first moon landing in 1969.

The astronauts also left behind memorial plaques to commemorate the mission and to honor two dead cosmonauts, an American flag, their space boots, and many other items they wouldn't need for the ride back to Earth, including bags of their urine and poop. Some astrobiologists want to retrieve the bags to see whether any of the fecal bacteria have managed to adapt to the brutal lunar conditions and survive. Temperatures on the moon range from −279 degrees Fahrenheit to 260 degrees Fahrenheit, well above the boiling point of water. Some scientists believe that analyses of the poop could provide "important information on the survival of microorganisms in space," and even provide crucial help in planning successful missions to Mars.[25]

The nonprofit For All Moonkind wants to preserve the boot prints from that first spacewalk, claiming that they are similar to world heritage sites on Earth and that the loss of these traces of history would be devastating to future generations. A new law, the One Small Step to Protect Human Heritage in Space Act, went into effect on December 31, 2020. The law states that the Apollo 11 lunar landing sites are "the first archaeological sites with human activity that are not on Earth" and are thus of "outstanding universal value." While the rhetoric of the law appeals to the easily defensible goal of historical preservation, the new law is in fact a "soft tool" for the United States, a nation that continually seeks to dominate territory in outer space.[26]

Ferris concludes that although the Voyagers "started out as explorers of space," they will "wind up more like time capsules." Each probe carried a *Golden Record*, each disc a reproduction of an original master tape preserved on Earth. Nowhere is this directly stated in the reissued record's liner notes, but they do carry an image of a box containing one of the "Voyager Interstellar Record master tape reels." The caption says it was stored in an "underground vault for 40 years," and a label affixed to the box reads,

RETURN TO:
SONY MUSIC VAULT
1137 BRANCHTON RD.
BOYERS, PA 16020
PH. (724) 794–8500.[27]

Hey, I know that address. Apparently, then, in one of the vaults I zoomed past in a golf cart at Iron Mountain's National Data Center was a segment of a grand backup loop stretching from the depths of the earth to spaces beyond the bounds of our solar system. In August 2012, the *Voyager 1* probe and its precious cargo left the heliosphere and became the first human-made object to enter interstellar space, where million-mile-per-hour solar winds give way to a realm that astrophysicists call the "interstellar medium," a rich mixture of matter and radiation where molecular clouds form, eventually collapse, and give birth to stars.[28]

## Digital Diamonds

Paglen is far from the first person to point out that digital data is very temporary. In 1988, Nancy Merz pointed out the instability of digital data and the ephemerality of documents transmitted electronically. She also noted the way disks and diskettes could be erased or affected by magnetic fields and recommended that "records of long term value" be recorded instead "on a stable medium."[29] In 1998, Maria Stepanek wrote in *Business-Week*, "Up to 20% of the information carefully collected on Jet Propulsion Laboratory computers during NASA's 1976 Viking mission to Mars has been lost." There are digital records from the Vietnam War relating to POWs, MIAs, and casualty counts that are "stored on Defense Dept. computers" and "can no longer be read." At Pennsylvania State University, "all but 14 of some 3,000 computer files containing student records and school history are no longer accessible because of missing or outmoded software." Valuable satellite imagery, such as shots of the Amazon basin in the 1970s, necessary for tracking deforestation trends, is "trapped on indecipherable magnetic tapes no longer on the market." By the end of the twentieth century, many record keepers had also noticed losses when migrating data from one hard drive to another in a new format, from the disappearance of "one footnote or spreadsheet," to other cases where "whole categories of data evaporate." A computer scientist at RAND Corporation said it best: "Digital information lasts forever, or five years—whichever comes first."[30]

Perhaps the most infamous case of digital failure on the consumer product front was the Apple Time Capsule, a Wi-Fi external hard drive that automatically backed up the user's computer. So many time capsules failed that one customer launched a website called the Apple Time Capsule Memorial Register, where he invited other users to list the serial number of their failed time capsule. After 2,500 registered, the site closed, and there no doubt were many more faulty devices.[31] Nonetheless, even in the face of such failures, the time capsule remains a potent symbolic figure for the digital age, as we attempt to reaffirm the solidity and durability of digital information. In 2013, the Apple company doubled down and released a new and improved product, the AirPort Time Capsule. Apple's product description on its website encourages us to "back up a lifetime's worth of memories with AirPort Time Capsule," and assures us that once we have bought this product, we "never have to worry about losing anything important again."[32]

When trying to decide on the material for his ultra-archival artifact, Paglen first considered "writing photographs into the crystalline structure of a diamond." Diamonds, like digital data, are not actually forever, but they do take billions of years to break down into graphite. In any case, he moved on from the idea once he "found out it would cost more than a hundred thousand dollars to fabricate." Then he consulted an MIT professor from the Department of Aeronautics and Astronautics and another from the Department of Materials Science and Engineering, "an expert on nano-fabrication technologies." Employing a "nano-fabrication process typically used to build microscopic circuits," they imprinted the 100 human-readable images into a silicon disk visible "under a magnifying glass or microscope." This format was "like an old microfilm, but one that could theoretically last for an eternity."[33] Silicon was chosen because it is the "material of choice for most people working in nano and microfabrication. It is the substrate or the foundation, on which microelectronics and microelectrical mechanical systems (MEMS, that is, micro scale machines) are built."[34] It also has been sent up to space many times, and so its resistance to the harshness of extraterrestrial conditions is well known.

Unlike its precursor, *The Golden Record*, *The Last Pictures* is not meant to reinforce our desire for permanent data or communicate something essential about humans to extraterrestrials. Paglen imagines his disc will not be found. Nor does the project add up to some message for the future. Paglen created the most permanent preservation project in order to provoke conversation and contemplation now, to question how we live, and to ask us to envision other possible futures than human self-destruction and ecological collapse.

### The Angel of History

The first of Paglen's "Last Pictures" is a strange image—the back of a painting called *Angelus Novus* by Paul Klee, made famous (among media archaeologists, anyway) by Walter Benjamin's mystical meditation on it in 1940, where he names it "the angel of history." The Benjamin passage is the epigraph to this book, and it describes an angel that sees the aftermath of all that has ever happened in a heap at his feet; where we see a chronological "chain of events," he sees wreckage piling up higher and higher as time passes. He cannot "stay, awaken the dead, and make whole what has been smashed" as he would like to do. A storm blowing from paradise "has got caught in his wings with such a violence that the angel can no longer close them. The storm irresistibly propels him into the future to which his back is turned, while the pile of debris before him grows skyward. This storm is what we call progress."[35]

The first image is a key to reading the others, showing the angel of history's back to us. Because Paglen chose to portray the back side of the print, the viewer is positioned just as the angel is, facing the past, being blown backward by the winds of "progress" into the future, away from paradisal innocence and technological virginity, toward self-inflicted destruction and ecocide. The subsequent ninety-nine images portray gas masks, nuclear bomb detonations, ecological devastation, and other things we've invented or caused that move us toward the end of human life on Earth. If the images have a message beyond their terrible beauty and provocative juxtapositions, I'd say the message is that there can be no progress if the progression is to end in human extinction.[36] To say that there is progress in the era of diminishable but irreversible climate change is to be like the man in the parable that opens the now-classic film *La Haine*. The man fell from a skyscraper, and every ten floors he plummeted past, he said to himself, "Jusqu'ici tout va bien." (So far, so good).[37]

And in that same way, there can be no story of progress within the data complex. It is a complex that is both physical and psychological, one that replicates itself by cycling through its hopes and fears, warding off threats with toxins that poison what is most precious to it, creating new crises in the process of solving the one confronting us. The backup loops, through which our anxiety and womb-warm but fleeting sense of security circulate, continue to proliferate through technologies in ways that utterly disturb any sense of old versus new, or obsolete versus futuristic, or analog versus digital. From 1961 to 1963, the Office of Civil Defense carried out a nationwide shelter assessment program that located 500,000 buildings that could possibly serve as shelters. Assessors described the buildings on paper forms adapted from the Bureau of the Census's FOSDIC form, which stood for "Film Optical Sensing Device for Input to Computers." The paper forms, all 519,340 of them, were then copied onto microfilm, converted to magnetic tape, and sent to the NBS, where computers determined how many people could fit inside each structure.[38] Computer output microfilm—where digital files are converted to microfilm—is as old as institutional digital data itself. In 1973, the NBS worked with the Department of Defense and other agencies to run an eighteen-month experiment in Norfolk, Virginia, where they established the Computer Output Microfilm Service Center and drafted standards for the broadened use of this backup looping technology.[39]

The Boston-based company Cobblestone Technology, founded in 1995, tried to market PaperDisk, which carries digital data on paper, 4 megabytes per 8.5-by-11-inch sheet, in a pattern called a DataTile.[40] In the early 2000s, Lukas Rosenthaler, head of the Imaging Lab at the University of Basel, proposed microfilming the 1s and 0s of digital files, along with metadata, such as the provenance of the image, and even a thumbnail analog image to aid in the reconstruction of the digital image later. He and his colleagues called their "eternal" media solution Permabit. Unlike digital hard drives, Permabit's data would only need to be migrated every 500 years or so.[41]

But what if you need to preserve time-based media, moving images, and music, things that can't be feasibly stored on microfilm? Johannes Goebel, founding director at the Experimental Media and Performing Arts Center at Rensselaer Polytechnic Institute (EMPAC), explored this question as he considered how to best preserve EMPAC's archive of performances over nearly two decades. I attended his talk "The Computer as Time Machine,"[42] where he explained his preservation plan, and spoke with him for a bit afterward. He considered all manner of possibilities, from cornerstone deposits to *The Voyager Golden Record.* On one slide Goebel displayed the words "A Digital Time Capsule" and below those "A contradiction in itself." He knew that he would need to be conservative in his hopes for preserving digital data, so he decided to try to build an archive that would last roughly 100 years under environmental conditions that a human could tolerate, with no need for constant air conditioning and electricity usage.

After an exhaustive search through a range of data formats and materials, he found that there is "only one storage medium" that "does not oxidize" and is not negatively affected by heat and humidity: the M-DISC. Developed by a company called Milleniata and scientists at Brigham Young University (BYU), the M-DISC is a DVD whose data is etched by laser in a layer of synthetic rock, and will supposedly last thousands of years, as opposed to typical CDs or DVDs, which store information in dyes that degrade into unreadability in ten or twenty years. The tag line for the website reads, "YOUR LIFE. ENGRAVED IN STONE. 1,000-YEAR STORAGE SOLUTION."[43] Goebel cited the accelerated aging research carried out by the BYU scientists, but he went a step further and had scientists cut a hole in an M-DISC and assess the material through a mass spectrum analyzer, which verified the rocklike materiality of the disc's data layer.

Goebel recognized, of course, that the bigger problem 100 years from now would be finding a functioning computer and disk drive that operated with early twenty-first-century software. So, in his digital time capsule, he would have a set of M-DISCs, a small desktop PC, a monitor, and a keyboard. He claimed that you could boot up the computer every eight years to maintain the hardware's ability to start and run the necessary programs. Goebel would also print a book of photographs of time-based media performances. While limited in terms of archiving the performance, this volume would allow the people of the future to use their imagination to think about what the performances must have been like. A paper book would certainly outlast the machines that could read the digital data on the M-DISC, and it is likely that companies will no longer produce those machines even a few decades from now. By the time Goebel gave his talk in 2016, Milleniata had already gone out of business, citing an inability to convince archivists that M-DISCs were the next big thing.

## Rosetta Disks

The M-DISC is one of a number of efforts to etch digital data in a more or less permanent computer-readable disc. In the patent application, Milleniata's scientists described the rocklike ablatable layer on the disc as a "glassy carbon" substance.[44] Hitachi created a similar product, etching data in a four-layer disc of glass quartz. With information density roughly the same as a regular CD, the durability is much greater—Hitachi claims the artifact will last hundreds of millions of years, based on accelerated aging tests where it withstood "two hours of exposure to 2000-degree-celsius heat."[45] Instead of binary code, five-dimensional data storage uses lasers to etch "nanogratings" in glass discs that refract light, and "the changes to the light can be read to obtain pieces of information about the nanograting's orientation, the strength of the light it refracts, and its location in space on the x, y, and z axes." These "extra dimensions" result in much higher information density and durability than "regular optical discs." While a Blu-ray disc can store up to 128 gigabytes, "a standard-sized 5D disc can store around 360 terabytes of data, with an estimated lifespan of up to 13.8 billion years even at temperatures of 190°C. That's as old as the Universe, and more than three times the age of the Earth."[46] The hyperbolic marketing of 5D ignores the sober reality that Goebel was able to accept—there won't be any computers a million, much less a billion, years from now.

These projects are corporate versions of the kind of etching that end-of-the-worlders like Jacobs and Peters had long been engaged in, though with less fanfare. The Church of Spiritual Technology, founded in 1982, planned to preserve L. Ron Hubbard's writings in several underground vaults. The intended preservation media were archival-grade paper, microfilm, gold-plated chrome compact discs, and etched steel plates in titanium boxes.[47] The San Francisco–based Long Now Foundation encourages thinking and societal planning within a 10,000-year time frame. One of the organization's grand projects is the Rosetta Disk, a silicon disk microetched with all existing human languages. Copies of that disk are then cast in nickel and housed in a sphere made of stainless steel and optical glass.[48] It resists electromagnetic radiation and wouldn't be erased like a hard drive would.[49] The first five Rosetta Disks cost the Long Now Foundation $25,000 each, and anyone can get one of these made by Norsam as of 2008. One Rosetta Disk was deposited, somewhat predictably, in a vault at the Smithsonian.

The Rochester-based company NanoRosetta, however, has a jewelry line that is more financially accessible and relevant to everyday consumers than Long Now's Rosetta Disk. For only $125, or $99 on the Home Shopping Network, anyone can buy a dime-sized pendant with the entire Bible etched into it with the firm's patented NanoFiche method. NanoRosetta also fabricates jewelry covered in nanoscopic etchings of the buyers' choice, such as an array of family photos, or the complete works of William Shakespeare, or any documents you want to be archived in a substance that will last 10,000 years.

Even cloud storage services, which have long relied on the cloud's discourse of immateriality to convince clients of the safety of their data, have simultaneously trafficked in images of impervious, stonelike media objects that will withstand the ravages of time. The online backup service Carbonite takes its name from a mythological indestructible substance, best known as the material in which Han Solo was frozen in the second *Star Wars* film, *The Empire Strikes Back* (1980). The presentation of these backup "solutions" demonstrates our ambivalence before our deep and increasing investment in digital technology, as our financial and social transactions increasingly rely on digital information stored in the cloud. We back up files by digitizing them; we back up digital information by duplicating it on magnetic tape or microfilm, or etching it on a substrate of synthetic stone embedded in a disc. Even our language for describing digital isn't new, most of it a swirl of architectural metaphors such as online "vaults" and "firewalls." Even "password" recalls a time when a specific word allowed one to pass through a door or opening in the gate of a walled city, or gave one access to privileged information. And then, of course, there's "encryption," which literally means placing data in a crypt, to hide it beneath or within something else, in this case a code. "Encryption" is actually a fitting way to capture what we often believe about encoding and the security it supposedly provides for data. We imagine data placed below the surface of the world, consigned to the place beneath the everyday realm of the visible.

The metaphorical name of the long-term data storage offered by Amazon Web Services goes even further to communicate the depth—and perhaps the slowness—of their deep storage. In April 2019, the company launched Amazon Glacier, an S3 storage class for asynchronous "archival storage." Customers have options related to how long they have to wait to access the data, and they can pay a lower fee if they're willing to wait longer, from one to five minutes to as long as five to twelve hours. This is a "deep archive" for customers like corporations, who save data to comply with state and federal laws concerning records retention but never plan to access the files with any regularity.

## Physical Bitcoin

Even amid all this recycling of architectural and geological metaphors, there are, in fact, a few new words and new things under the digital sun, such as "blockchain" and the cryptocurrencies it makes possible, such as bitcoin. But even these "newest" of digital innovations within the data complex cannot seem to get away from the old ways of securing data against threats. Bitcoin must be "mined" through very complex mathematical operations that only computers can perform, and that require massive amounts of computing power and electricity. Owners of bitcoin use a private key—a long chain of random alphanumeric characters—to access and spend the bitcoin.

But if others get your key, they can steal your bitcoin. In 2013, after Cameron and Tyler Winklevoss—the Olympian twins on the Harvard crew team that were depicted as hopeless, beautiful dupes in *The Social Network*—received a $65 million settlement from Mark Zuckerberg, they invested $11 million in the fledgling cryptocurrency. At that time bitcoin's market value was $120 per coin. Just four years later, the price of a single bitcoin had skyrocketed to $11,500—making the Winklevii's initial investment worth over $1 billion.[50] They needed a way to protect their investment. Third-party services manage bitcoin for clients in online "wallets," but these have also been hacked and stripped of hundreds of millions of dollars, as in the infamous Mt. Gox scandal. Ultimately, the Winklevii decided to take their digital wealth security into their own hands. They printed their private keys on paper—known among bitcoin users as a "paper wallet"—then cut them up and sent the pieces in envelopes to various bank vaults around the country.

Even if thieves acquired one piece of the key, they wouldn't be able to steal the bitcoin.[51]

Then in 2014, the twins founded Gemini Trust, a cryptocurrency exchange that offers an online wallet service, storing clients' private keys on "air-gapped" computers that have never been connected to the internet. This strategy is referred to in the cryptocurrency world as "cold storage." Accessing wallets through Gemini requires three forms of ID, and a pass code at various locations. The Winklevii claim that if something "took out" the entire Eastern Seaboard, they have enough vaults across enough secure locations that the company would still be in business. This system exemplifies the bombproof logic of the Cold War—the dispersion of infrastructure and information, securitized vaults, secrecy—and creates a backup loop where paper doesn't just redundantly back up the digital but literally keeps it safe.[52]

Another "cold storage" solution that developed by 2012 was physical bitcoin, a literal coin with the private key covered by a holographic sticker that could be peeled off only once.[53] These coins, a combination of ancient and twenty-first-century technology, are no longer being produced due to increased federal regulation, but they still circulate in auctions on eBay and elsewhere. In 2018, a rumor circulated on bitcoin-related news sites that a single Casascius 1 BTC coin graded in mint condition sold for $28,700 on eBay, even though a bitcoin was only valued at $14,300 at the time. However, I have not been able to find any evidence that this sale actually occurred. It may just be the case that owners of discontinued physical bitcoin are trying, yet again, to build a speculative bubble of value atop another bubble of value that is the phenomenon of bitcoin itself.

Such speculation is already more formally rampant in the bitcoin futures market, where you can buy a contract allowing you to purchase or sell bitcoin at a certain price on a certain date in the future. These contracts can be traded or sold without the contract holder actually owning any bitcoins. Like the collateralized debt obligations and credit default swaps that helped crash the U.S. economy in 2008, these futures contracts are derivatives, a form of legalized gambling on what the market value of a virtual currency will be.[54] Some economists love to point out that derivatives are nothing new, that the Code of Hammurabi contained laws regulating a kind of option to buy certain goods at a certain price in the future. That may be true, but people in Hammurabi's time didn't engage in high-frequency trading conducted automatically by supercomputers. In these transactions, cryptocurrency exchanges offer colocation options (physically placing their clients' servers directly next to their own servers) that cut down on latency in data transmissions, thereby providing a competitive edge in this realm of algorithmic transactions, where one trader's computer can buy and sell stocks several times within the span of a single second. That's new.[55]

Bitcoin's convoluted security schemes remind us that analog data and digital data are not opposites or stages in a progression, but two elements in a backup loop of data preservation where "new" data formats like digital files back up "old" ones like microfilm, even as digital files are backed up by "ancient" formats like etching. Such backup loops are evident in the first permanent time capsules, as microfilm backed up paper records, and microfilm was backed up by metal film etched with images, and the metal film was coated with cellulose acetate (the material base of microfilm). In the digital age, media formats often called obsolete have become increasingly important. For example, magnetic tape has outpaced digital hard drives in terms of its storage density, and it is used extensively by both Google and Microsoft in their cloud storage services. When a software bug caused Google to lose the saved emails in 40,000 user accounts even though they were preserved on numerous hard drives in multiple data centers, Google restored the lost data from backups on magnetic tape.[56]

Ironically, I was forced to permanently preserve my doctoral dissertation, the research for which formed the basis of this book that, as you know by now, is quite critical of the whole permanent preservation thing. The Ohio State University submitted the dissertation, as a matter of course, to data preservation behemoth ProQuest. Many higher-education institutions in the United States send their doctoral graduates' dissertations to ProQuest, which publishes them and sells them to Amazon and other third parties, makes them available to university libraries, or makes them freely available, unless the graduate opts out of these otherwise automatic procedures. I opted out of making my dissertation available in any format, but I still had to pay a forty-five-dollar microfilming fee to ProQuest, which, as it did with every dissertation back then, stored a copy of the PDF in its "online vault" and made a microfilm copy of the PDF, as well as a backup of the digital file on tapes that are preserved at Iron Mountain for "an extra layer of protection."[57] Now, all theses and dissertations managed by ProQuest are archived in Amazon's Glacier.[58]

## Helium through Glass

At the same time that corporations began building bombproof storage for their records, the federal government began working intensively to preserve the Charters of Freedom—the Declaration of Independence, the Bill of Rights, and the Constitution—for the first time. The charters were transported from the Library of Congress to the National Archives in an armored personnel car supplied by the marines, with hundreds of servicepeople from all five branches of the military attending. These documents received more protection than would have accompanied a sitting president, including "two light tanks, four servicemen carrying submachine guns, and [a] motorcycle escort parad[ing] down Pennsylvania and Constitution Avenues."[59]

The charters were housed in a customized case filled with helium—the same structure as the permanent time capsules created by Jacobs and Pendray, a design that permanently gasses data—and would descend into an underground bombproof vault at night and in the event of a nuclear threat. Creating permanent data in the Cold War meant not only protecting it from the long march of time and decay but also bombproofing it against an apocalyptic nuclear strike that could happen at any moment. The government hired the Mosler Safe Company, whose vaults had survived the atomic bomb blast at Hiroshima, to create the customized bombproof vault for the charters.

The charters are now under constant watch by armed guards, and have been for over half a century, which makes them different from Depression-era time capsules. Their parchment has outlasted several casements, from the bulletproof case of the early twentieth century to the first bombproof cases created at the beginning of the Cold War. The Declaration of Independence still rests in a bombproof case that descends into a bunker every night and is poised to do so at any moment in response to a bomb threat. Behind its bulletproof glass casing, the document sits sealed in a capsule filled with argon, an inert gas that prevents the growth of mold. The temperature and humidity within the capsule are controlled, and the faded parchment is bathed in a yellow-green glow that filters out harmful waves of ultraviolet light. All this intensive preservation is relatively new. As late as 1876, the Declaration of Independence was hanging from a wall in the U.S. Patent Office and exposed to direct sunlight that faded its lettering, an unthinkable state of affairs from an early twenty-first-century preservation perspective.[60]

The midcentury treatment of the charters in terms of security was risky too. In 1948, Arthur Kimberly helped oversee the preservation specifications for the "Freedom Train," a locomotive that carried the Bill of Rights on a tour of the country—an unthinkable risk within today's data complex. The train stopped in 322 cities in "all 48 states" to display 126 iconic documents from the history of American democracy, including the Emancipation

Proclamation and the Mayflower Compact, as well as the original manuscripts of both "The Star-Spangled Banner" and the Gettysburg Address.[61]

We no longer expose the Charters of Freedom to the raw light of the sun and other stars. Instead, we repurpose technology created to explore outer space and turn it inward to trace the creep of decay within the heart of our national memory. In 1987, the National Archives and NASA enlisted Caltech's Jet Propulsion Laboratory to create the Charters Monitoring System. The system's technology is based on the same "electronic remote-imaging devices employed in space satellites for intelligence gathering, Earth survey work, weather forecasting, and in-space telescopes," such as the *Hubble* telescope.[62] The system routinely scans the surfaces of the nation's founding documents, compares those scans, and thereby registers any changes, any decay, however microscopic.[63] The camera is "mounted on a 3-ton optical bench with solid granite risers supported by four nitrogen-filled cylindrical legs to eliminate ground vibrations from road traffic and a nearby subway."[64] The casement for the charters has been updated, too, and filled with argon instead of helium. Argon is also an inert gas, but its molecules are larger than helium's, which have been known to "escape slowly through some types of glass."[65] Of course, the Declaration of Independence is also protected by a backup loop—a precise copperplate engraving of it from 1823 is preserved in the Department of State materials at the National Archives.[66]

### The Data Complex Dreams of Infinity

The Jet Propulsion Laboratory handled the images sent back to Earth by the Voyager probe, images that, together with those produced by the *Hubble* telescope, have completely redefined scientists' understanding of the cosmos. The *Hubble* telescope is named for astronomer Edwin Hubble, who in 1924 found evidence that the universe was much larger than scientists previously thought. The Andromeda and Triangulum Nebulae were thought to be clouds of dust and gas within the Milky Way, widely believed at the time to be the only galaxy in existence. But Hubble found stars within the nebulae, what turned out to be "Cepheids, special stars that methodically dim and brighten as if they were slow-blinking cosmic stoplights."[67] Their presence showed that the nebulae were very distant, and that the universe in fact contained billions of galaxies. To be precise, the universe was trillions of times larger than we thought. The Andromeda Nebula is 2.5 million light-years from Earth. Again, a light-year is the distance that light travels in a year, and light travels at 186,000 miles *per second*, an unfathomable constant for the human mind, but one that the human mind nonetheless uses to tether computers through fiber optics that carry pulses of light.[68]

In his concluding remarks in *The Last Pictures*, Paglen takes us into similarly incomprehensible realms of space and time. In the next few billion years, he writes, the earth's oceans will "boil off and our atmosphere will evaporate, making the planet inhospitable to life." Four or five billion years from now, the sun will expand into a red giant, and the "deep time of the earth gives way to the cosmic time of the stars." The earth might survive the sun's expansion, and if it does, "then The Last Pictures may continue to quietly haunt the planet as the sun collapses into a white dwarf in about 7.5 billion years."[69] Then Paglen jumps to the kind of time I'm talking about, from the cosmic time of the stars to the cosmogonic cycle of the universe, its birth and death and rebirth: "In a hundred trillion years, star formation will begin to cease throughout the universe. One by one, the points of light that dot the cosmos will go black until they are all gone. By this time a wayward neutron star or pulsar will have come perilously close to what was once the sun, sending a great wave through spacetime, spinning Echostar XVI and The Last Pictures off into never-ending darkness."[70]

The data complex dreams of infinity, but the universe is not infinite in terms of space or time. We always enter a new realm of information density with both faith and doubt. With digital technology we applied the metaphysical belief that informs mathematics, the idea that numbers go on forever and ever, but numbers are not forever unless you want to be theological about them and imagine an entity that keeps counting when everything that exists is gone.[71] Numbers, like data, are never infinite or eternal—they are material, whether written on a chalkboard or thought about through the neural networks in your brain.

We believe that there is always more and more space, and so we go seeking more space, both the outer space of the heavens and the inner space of atoms. But it all ends. If infinity or eternity is what we seek, the best we can do is fall back on the belief of the ancients: there is a backup loop written into the stars. The mythologist Joseph Campbell called it the cosmogonic cycle, wherein the universe ends, then begins again, and again.[72] The universe is expanding at an accelerating rate, and some physicists think it will eventually condense down, again, into an unfathomably dense seed with all the mass of the universe crammed into it, a theory known as "the Big Crunch." Then, the Big Bang will occur, again, and all of this evolution and worry and complexity will begin again, and end again; the whole universe will expand and collapse again, and again, breathing.

# 6

## Save File as . . . DNA

What would happen if everything just refused to die:

the cruel rain bringing more green when the world

can't handle another blade of grass, rose vs. rose,

weed choking weed, the sun cloaked black

by clouds of birds: Eden, a horror show.

—Kevin Griffith, "The Night of the Living"

I walk west on Flushing Avenue toward Newlab, a tech incubator, office building, and event space in the Brooklyn Navy Yards. Today, a group of designers, biotechnologists, artists, entrepreneurs, philanthropists, and venture capitalists are gathering for a one-day conference called Biofabricate. After several blocks, I reach Cumberland Street, where the black iron fence running along the sidewalk is interrupted by a brick wall and steel gates. Newlab occupies a section of Building 128, formerly a massive machine shop that serviced every major warship launched by the United States during the two world wars. One placard on the brick wall welcomes you to the "Brooklyn Navy Yard Industrial Park," while another proclaims economic renewal: "We Used to Launch Ships. Now We Launch Businesses."

Just past the gates is a small guardhouse. Inside it, a "friendly gatekeeper" is available to help me find Newlab, according to the Eventbrite reminder I received a couple days ago. The reminder also asked me whether I wanted the vegan lunch option, and urged me to sign up quickly if I was interested in attending the free CRISPR workshop offered by Biotech without Borders. Participants in the workshop would learn about "the new genome editing technology that is enabling breakthroughs in medicine, agriculture and biomaterials," and explore the question "Are we at the edge of Humans 2.0?" Not only that, but participants would also do a "hands-on lab exercise" in which they would "use CRISPR to knock out a gene in yeast." Dr. Ellen Jorgenson, who would lead the workshop, gave a TED Talk in 2014 titled "Biohacking—You Can Do It, Too," the same year she founded Genspace, "the world's first community biology lab," in Sunset Park. I turned down the vegan option, as I usually do, and decided to pass on the CRISPR workshop, too, thinking it better to leave the yeast and its genes alone.

I step inside Building 128, whose cavernous space resembles a cathedral, with riveted girders and glass-wrapped office pods in place of vault ribs and colonnades. I'm immediately greeted by a cheerful woman who leads me to the registration table, then hands me my name badge on a lanyard, which is what I will need to reenter the building freely over the course of the day. Conference participants are gently discouraged from strolling around the Navy Yards, because apparently there are some high-security installations within the 300-acre complex.

After I grab a quick coffee and pastries, and briefly mill about in a small crowd of people with very cool hair and even cooler eyeglasses, the presentations begin. All of the speakers carry lofty ambitions, from one founder who seeks to disrupt the synthetic dye industry by generating natural pigments with genetically engineered yeast, to another whose goal is to remove all of the plastic from the oceans and convince every corporation on Earth to stop producing virgin plastics. All share a common goal: to spark the next industrial revolution, one based on a sustainable production model that harnesses the power of yeast, bacteria, fungus, and other living organisms to generate materials and break down toxic waste.

These proponents of the bioindustrial revolution see the living cell as the most powerful engine available for the production of everything we need. Richard Beckett, director of University College London's BiotA Lab, says he's developed a "bio-receptive concrete" designed to encourage the growth of mosses, lichens, and algae. His "BioAugmented Design" projects aim to create a "living architecture" that can absorb carbon dioxide and release oxygen.[1] Molly Morse, founder and CEO of Mango Materials, captures methane and uses it as fuel to ferment bacteria that produce a biopolymer called polyhydroxyalkanoate—a natural plastic that can biodegrade "in many environments, including the oceans."[2] AmSilk claims that Biosteel—it's lab-grown spider silk—is so strong that a web of it made with pencil-thick cords could "catch a fully loaded Jumbo Jet Boeing 747 with a weight of 380 tons."[3]

During the lunch break, I ascend the stairs with my boxed sandwich and bottled water and sit down near a couple of people who are also wearing lanyards. I have a moment to wonder who they are. They could be the people who prototyped space boots to be grown from mycelium spores fed by astronauts' sweat, intended for use by the first human colonists on Mars.[4] They might have biofabricated swaths of vegan leather for Modern Meadow, or served as advisors to the Diamond Foundry, a Bay Area company that grows gems that are "atomically identical" to those that come from mines, except theirs are created in plasma reactors reaching temperatures "as hot as the outer layer of the sun."[5]

I introduce myself to the pair, and it turns out that one of them teaches sustainable design at Parsons, and the other is a biochemist from Cambridge, England. They loop me into their conversation on GMOs, and the scientist, unsurprisingly, talks about how genetically modified crops can help so many people who are starving, and how people have an irrational fear of them. I push back a bit against her argument but am more interested, unsurprisingly, in talking about my own research. Really, I want to learn what I can about what they think the prospects are for a new technology: scientists at the University of Washington, as well as Harvard University, recently figured out how to store code for digital files in the protein sequences of synthetic DNA. I wait for a lull in the conversation, then toss the DNA topic into the mix.

"The problem with DNA data storage," the biochemist says, "which is the problem with a lot of ideas at the conference, is how to successfully scale the technology."

We go on to talk about a range of topics, and somewhere in there she circles back and casually throws out the following: "Of course, Bill Gates has invested millions in DNA storage so that means it at least has a shot."

I nearly spit out a mouthful of sparkling water on her $2,000 pantsuit. "Excuse me?"

"Bill Gates. You know, of Microsoft fame?"

"Yes, I know who Bill Gates is. But did you say he's investing in DNA storage?"

"Sure. He has been, for years. You didn't know that?"

I shake my head, and look out over the expanse of Newlab, its mysterious start-up offices and 3-D printing studios, its mezzanine dappled with bright orange and pink Meritalia sofas and ferns so large they look like a cloned velociraptor might pop its head out from behind one of them.[6] Then I mutter, mostly to myself, "There is so much I don't know."

What I do know is that the fate of DNA storage will depend on the shape of the global economy in the coming decades and whether that shape supports scaling it. The appeal of DNA data storage is obvious—it far outstrips any existing data format's information density, as a single gram can hold 455 million terabytes. One computer scientist claims that all the data in the world could fit into a semitrailer's worth of DNA.[7] How can DNA data be so compact?

DNA isn't just a double helix. Its twisted structure then coils, then the coils corkscrew into rings that compact themselves into a cylindrical shape, then coil again, and again, like the jumbled cord of an old landline phone. The DNA in a single human cell fits into a space that is just six microns across (six *millionths* of a meter). But if you uncoiled the double helix and laid the 6 billion base pairs in that single cell side by side, they would be six feet long. If you laid out all of the DNA contained in the trillions of cells in a single human body, this nanoscopic rope of genetic material would be long enough to stretch from the earth to the sun and back (roughly 180 million miles round trip). And the rope could make the trip not just once, but over 300 times.[8]

Beyond its density, DNA promises to be the most permanent data ever created, as it can be frozen or dehydrated into fossils for 3.5 billion years. But, like any cutting-edge data format, DNA storage is expensive. Will it ever scale and eclipse digital media? Every emergent data format that becomes dominant does so as it corresponds to and grows materially out of the prevailing economic mode of production, whether agrarian, industrial, or informational. Photographs and movies, for instance, were products of industrial mining and the booming chemical industry of the nineteenth century, their negatives suffused with silver halide crystals. In fact, the negatives contained so much of the compound that Kodak now consults archives on how to recover and sell the silver from photographic paper, film, and processing solutions.[9] Taxidermy underwent industrialization when arsenic, a by-product of silver smelting, became widely available and served as a much more effective pesticide than the preservatives used in the early years of the United States, when agriculture was still the economic base, such as tobacco dust, burnt alum, and pepper.[10]

But what would an economy based on the manipulation of DNA, or, more broadly, nanoscopic and microscopic scales of life, look like? DNA data still requires digital computers to write and read what is encoded in its nucleotides, so the rise of DNA data storage will not result in the end of digital computers, or even paper documents. Rather, DNA data will enter into a thickened constellation of data formats providing insurance for one another in massive backup loops.

DNA data points toward a significant shift in the data complex, and thus a shift in what it means to be human. Many fear that artificially intelligent systems will supersede human intelligence, or that the robots will rebel against their masters, or that some other similarly Hollywoodesque scenario will play out if we continue to expand the role of machine learning in everyday life. But cyborgs are nothing new—we've long been cyborgs. Besides, the machines have already won, as human biochips are now embedded in the cyborg of the data complex. If life were an early Cold War B movie where extraterrestrial marauders are scanning Earth for life and treasure, which organism would appear to reign supreme on this lush planet? Certainly not the humans. For the humans are working feverishly to pull minerals from the ground and refine them, to build data centers and lash them together with fiber-optic cables laid across oceans and deserts, to connect all these machines through invisible tethers of light attached to satellites ringing the globe, and to spend most of their waking hours every day staring at screens and feeding data to the data complex. Even when these strange little creatures are not clicking and scrolling, they are carrying devices that perpetually transmit data about their location, the number of steps they take, and their resting heart rate to be recorded in the several million silicon bellies of the supreme beast. Even while they sleep, the data complex grips humans' wrists through smartwatches and counts their heartbeats.[11]

The data complex is already approaching a moment where the end of humanity as we know it is possible, where the blurring of the biobody and the data body is so complete that the distinction no longer holds. The end of humanity will not occur through a loss of information, as in the nightmares of time capsule creators like Jacobs and Pendray, but from an overabundance of it, embodied in a data complex fully dedicated to supporting the life and survival of data redundantly recorded across media formats new, old, and ancient. This is a complete inversion, and augmentation, of the data complex as it emerged in the early twentieth century.

## Digital Is Not Dead Yet

DNA promises to satisfy the storage demands of the ever ravenous data complex. But digital is not going away anytime soon, even though so many signs point toward its limits: its ephemerality, unsustainability, and storage density that is dwarfed by new formats like DNA, and even old ones like magnetic tape. Digital hard drives have run up against the physical limits of matter. The surface of a platter inside a hard drive is divided into microscopic sections called bits, each one a grain that can be magnetized positive or negative. Contrary to popular belief, a digital hard drive has no ones and zeroes inscribed on it, just as DNA seen through an electron microscope does not comprise twisted ladders of tiny letters. On the surface of a spinning disk are magnetized bits that the read-write head translates into a one or a zero, depending on whether they are charged positive or negative.[12]

In an effort to store more and more within the form factor of standard hard drives, the bits have become so small that the particles to be magnetized approach what physicists call the superparamagnetic limit. This law of superparamagnetism attends nanoparticles so small that they can unpredictably flip their magnetism again and again in response to temperature fluctuations, resulting in data loss. From the perspective of data, this is like data rewriting itself spontaneously as the tiny grains that make up each bit lose, and regain, and lose again the charge they were written to retain.

While hard drives cannot increase their data density much more than they already have, magnetic tape shows "no signs of slowing." Its areal density is much lower than that of hard drives, but because a reel of tape has an exponentially larger surface area, the densest tapes can hold more than fifteen terabytes of data, an amount much "greater than the highest-capacity hard drives on the market."[13]

Despite the obvious limits to the expanse of data space within magnetized minerals, manufacturers of digital hard drives are forging ahead. Even as we realize the limits of the earth's minerals and the ephemerality of the digital, companies are investing in new technologies to keep hard drives on a path of increasing areal density and energy efficiency. But are these technologies actually new? Western Digital came up with a way to make the hard drive run superclean: a helium-filled hard drive, a solution that combines digital technology with the design of microbooks in the Crypt of Civilization, or the Westinghouse Time Capsule. A helium-filled hard drive has many advantages. Helium has one-seventh the density of air and thus is less turbulent. These hard drives run faster as the gas around them is thinner; they are less noisy and more energy efficient. Hard drives spin so fast that they produce significant friction between air molecules, which produces heat that then needs to be eliminated through air conditioning in data centers where thousands of servers live. Helium's lower turbulence produces less heat, thus requiring the data center to expend less energy to cool servers down. Data centers collectively use massive amounts of electricity and water. In 2014, approximately 626 billion liters of water were used to cool data centers. In 2016, data centers consumed 70 billion kilowatt-hours of electricity, the equivalent of the electricity used by 6.4 million average American households.[14]

Of course, the Jevons paradox pertains here—when technological innovation produces increased energy efficiency, we end up using more energy anyway, as our rates of consumption will simply increase as demand rises.[15] So the idea of saving energy or money or resources is, in the end, an illusion. From a more total perspective of the earth's finite resources, increased efficiency is another justification for us to use more and more natural resources, supplies of which will not last forever. This isn't just about digital technology. Though a larger proportion of our documents is digital than ever before, we produce far more documents now and use more paper than ever. Beyond data and documentation, over half of the paper in the world is used for packaging.[16] Amazon, anyone?

Still, Seagate keeps pressing on with trying to increase hard drives' storage density, using laser-thermal technology to heat the disk platter as the read-write head records data, so that it is possible to divide the areal surface into even smaller bits. The laser heats the surface of the disk to 400 degrees Celsius, but only for a nanosecond, so that more data can be forced into a smaller space. Seagate claims it can fit two terabytes in a square inch, as it battles with competitors in a promotional skirmish. One rival, Western Digital, is pushing its MAMR—microwave-assisted magnetic recording.[17] No, there isn't a tiny microwave built into the read-write head, but something called a "spin-torque oscillator" that emits microwave fields to lower the amount of energy required to "flip" the magnetism of the bits on the disk.[18] In other words, dividing the areal surface of the disk into smaller and smaller bits requires stronger and stronger materials, which in turn require more energy from the read-write head to flip each bit. Heating the surface with a laser or with microwaves allows the read-write head to flip bits embedded in very hard materials.

Solid-state hard drives work differently in that they do not have all of these spinning parts, but they are no more reliable or durable than HDD drives. Their data is written in "blocks" that can only be rewritten a number of times before they fail. Flash memory retains data even when the computer is powered off, but if a computer goes unused for a year or two, the flash memory will begin to lose that data more quickly than an HDD would. All in all, flash will constitute a larger and larger proportion of the hard drives in the world, but it will not produce anything like progress in the permanence of the digital.

### The Cosmic Clean Room

Manufacturing digital technology will be difficult to sustain not just because of the natural resource requirements and superparamagnetic limits, but because to create it, you must first create an otherworldly environment on Earth. If we know anything about Earth, we know that it is full of dust, and dust ruins hard drives, processors, and other digital components. If you get a mote of dust on your hard drive platter it can make the read-write head bounce up and down. Imagine a car hitting a bump while traveling at seventy-five miles per hour, which is the equivalent speed of a hard drive spinning at 7,200 revolutions per minute, except this car is tethered to the ground so that it can't really fly very high into the air. Instead, it slams back down to the ground so that it bounces furiously as it speeds across the road's surface. This, like a car accident, is called a crash. It can lead you to lose all of the information on the sensitive magnetic surface of the hard drive platter.

The Precipitron made by Westinghouse was a leap forward in clean precision manufacturing, but it wasn't clean enough to allow for digital circuit fabrication that would make possible information technology as we know it. Throughout the 1950s, a number of corporations developed similar technologies and procedures to keep their clean rooms as pristine as possible. What was known as a "white room" back then would evolve into what we now call a clean room, based on the innovations of Willis Whitfield at Sandia National Laboratories in Albuquerque, New Mexico, in the early 1960s. His "laminar flow" clean room sent 99.7 percent clean HEPA-filtered air down from the ceiling and then pulled it from the room through the floor, which comprised metal grates. The air in the room was replaced at the rate of ten times per minute. The improvement in decontamination was unprecedented—Whitfield's white room was 1,000 times cleaner than his closest competitor's.

The first time he tested the air in his clean room, it registered zero. He thought his measuring sensors were broken. When Whitfield told people how effective his clean room was, they doubted him so much that he began telling people that his invention performed better than other white rooms without revealing the incredibly low rates of contaminants he had actually achieved, so as not to be called a fraud yet again.[19] Soon enough, other scientists caught on and saw Whitfield's unbelievable results for themselves, and the technology spread rapidly. Within a few years, over $50 billion worth of clean rooms had been built around the world.[20]

Laminar flow clean rooms paved the way for new realms of manufacturing in electronics, microprocessors, semiconductors, and nanotechnologies. Contamination control became an industry unto itself, and companies began to sell portable clean rooms. One of these companies was Controlled Environments Incorporated, founded by Robert Peck, who was at the time working at the Johns Manville Company,[21] manufacturers of the asbestos that sealed the micro books in the Crypt of Civilization and fireproofed the shingle siding on the typical American family contest winners' model FHA homes. The dream of a space absolutely free of contamination—whether the factory or the home—is no longer a novelty but a fundamental feature of how everyday products are made now. And clean rooms have grown larger and cleaner over the past several decades. iPhones, for instance, are manufactured in a clean room in China that occupies over a million square feet. The largest clean room in the world, measuring 1.3 million square feet, is at NASA's Goddard Space Flight Center.

Semiconductor wafers from which microchips are cut have to be built in several steps. The electronic pathways on these chips are "narrower than the wavelengths of visible light" and "can only be seen with electron microscopes."[22] Each step of the fabrication process creates nanoscopic debris that must be cleared away, and to accomplish this, manufacturers use ultrapure water, an industrial solvent that is simply water with all of the minerals, salts, and anything else—even parts of dead cells and viruses—removed from it. Ultrapure water is only water molecules, and making 1,000 gallons of it requires about 1,400 gallons of ordinary water.[23] An IBM plant in Burlington, Vermont, makes and uses 2 million gallons of ultrapure water every day.

Water this pure is not fit for human consumption, though numerous humans have drunk it out of curiosity about its taste. Reports on its flavor vary, ranging from "flat, heavy, and bitter" to "literally the most boring thing I've ever tasted" or "the absence of taste" itself.[24] Technically, it is not poisonous in a toxic way, but ultrapure water is such a powerful solvent that it pulls the electrolytes out of your body as it passes through you. If you drank enough of it, you would die.

The architects of the data complex have long dreamed of outer space as a pure environment, an intergalactic clean room unlike lands conquered in the name of white civilization in the past. Outer space is imagined to be actually empty space, where the only life-forms that live there are the ones that we export.[25] It is seemingly infinite, never to run out of resources. In a recent promotional video, Iron Mountain narrates its history through a combination of slideshows, dramatized footage, and CGI animation. At the beginning of the video, Iron Mountain is founded amid Cold War fears of a nuclear attack. The video then fast-forwards through several decades of the corporation's history, as it moved from paper and microfilm storage into warehousing magnetic tape and digital media. The video concludes with a vision of Iron Mountain's future, where a spaceship takes off vertically from behind the company's office building in France, cruises easily into outer space, and docks at a space station alongside several other similar vessels, delivering what I presume are digital backups of Earth-based data (one can only imagine).[26]

The data center spaceship and space station scenario is just one of many dreams born of the data complex, one that renews our faith in the unsustainable notion that we can preserve what we want to preserve forever, one that upholds our belief that though war and the preemptive wrath of human fears might ravage the earth and the people on it, our planet revolves through an unending space beyond time, beyond decay. In 2015, a start-up called Cloud Constellation began working toward launching SpaceBelt, "a network of data centers built on satellites in orbit."[27] Such ventures would have delighted G. Edward Pendray, who was not only the brain behind the Westinghouse Time Capsule but also a founding member of the American Interplanetary Society, a group of science-fiction writers and rocket enthusiasts who dreamed, even from the depths of the Depression, of a day when humans would overcome the problems that "bar the way toward travel among the planets."[28]

## Mines of Ethereum in the Cloud

Despite all the limits, failures, and challenges that come with hard drives, all hope has not been lost in digital data, and numerous ventures seek the nearly infinite resources necessary to support its survival. More than ever, the data complex demands massive climate-controlled spaces in order to operate, at a scale that Arthur Kimberly never could have imagined nearly a century ago when he urged librarians to install fluorescent lighting and air-conditioning units to preserve the books in their stacks. In the past decade, Facebook, Microsoft, and Google have all built data centers near the Arctic Circle or even underwater, in search of cold environments that would save energy and, in turn, lower cooling costs. Norway created tax breaks that attracted a company called Kolos that planned to build the largest data center in the world, but the business later sold the site to HIVE Blockchain, a cryptocurrency-mining company. HIVE's most recent headlines highlight the thoroughly mixed metaphors now being deployed to try to make sense of what some data centers do. Consider this one: "HIVE Blockchain Increases Bitcoin Mining Production Immediately with the Purchase of 1,240 Next Generation Miners While Upgrading Its GPU Chips to Mine Ethereum in the Cloud." Norway continues to attract investment from companies in the cryptocurrency and blockchain business. Amsterdam-based Bitfury built a data center, also known as a "mining farm," near Norway's second-largest glacier, taking advantage of both the cold and the low energy costs offered by the country's government.[29]

As climate change intensifies, however, cold is getting harder to come by on planet Earth. The Svalbard Global Seed Vault is an archive of over 100 million "backup" seeds stored in a vault on an island 600 miles from the North Pole, what the director of the facility calls a "safety duplicate copy of the world's crop diversity."[30] Widely known as a "Noah's Ark for seeds," the vault is designed to be bombproof, and it saves on refrigeration costs by being buried under a mountain in the Norwegian permafrost. According to Dyveke Sanne, an artist hired to install a public art piece over the entrance to the vault in 2008, Svalbard is "cold in a way that you can't imagine." She "wore motorcycle goggles [while there] because the cold wind can pop your eyes."[31] Still, in 2017, after the hottest year on Earth in more than 100,000 years, the permafrost began melting, and spring rain flooded the entrance to the vault. In the aftermath, it became clear that the vault would not be able to operate as its designers intended—namely, "without the help of humans." The caretakers of the Svalbard facility then waterproofed the football field–length tunnel leading to the vaults, "digging trenches into the mountainside to channel meltwater and rain away." They also "removed electrical equipment from the tunnel that produced some heat and installed pumps in the vault itself in case of a future flood."[32]

The long-term plans of some tech titans involve finding more cold and more minerals, not deep in the earth or at the poles, but in outer space. Amazon CEO Jeff Bezos has launched Blue Origin, a space exploration company complete with plans for off-world mining of mineral resources.[33] Elon Musk, CEO of both SpaceX and Tesla, likewise sees no end for digital media. He is currently manufacturing both self-driving cars and satellites for Starlink—a constellation of 12,000 satellites to be sent into orbit by SpaceX, promising to provide the fastest internet signal in the solar system.[34] Less than a month before Bezos's Blue Origin reveal, the Federal Communications Commission approved the launch of the first 4,425 Starlink satellites to beam down faster internet connectivity across the globe. The Starlink network, already being referred to in tech news media as a "constellation," will be a boon to high-frequency traders and makers of 5G devices. By the end of 2020, nearly 900 of Musk's satellites were already in orbit.[35]

In Musk's case, business ventures in outer space are also contributing to the expansion of the data complex on Earth, as Tesla electric vehicles generate massive amounts of data and require new electrical infrastructure. Musk's space ventures, according to many, are all preliminary steps in his grand vision, which is to use the profits from these companies to fund his dream of colonizing Mars and using mining robots to extract natural resources from its depths.[36] Studies have shown that terraforming Mars would be impossible, but SpaceX is moving ahead with its Mars mission nevertheless.[37] In August 2019, the company performed a test of the *Starhopper*, a prototype for a deep-space exploration rocket now in development.[38] SpaceX and NASA safely brought back four astronauts from a collaborative mission in July 2020.[39]

These projects embody the paradoxical desires stimulated by the data complex, and the insufficiency of digital technology to accommodate twenty-first-century societies' relentless generation and use of data. The desire for infinite data-space cannot be satisfied by digital media that demand infinite source materials from a finite planet, and require air conditioning or natural cold in a global climate that grows warmer by the day. Outer space, which has no shortage of rocks, metals, and minerals, not to mention cold, holds promise for the richest men in the world and their utopian dreams. But even Bezos admits that his ambitious visions for interplanetary travel will not be carried out within his lifetime. He hopes that within a few generations of his death, there will be people traveling between planets like we now travel between countries separated by an ocean.

## Asteroid Gas Stations

Outer space has long been imagined as a realm of preservation par excellence, not just for data bodies but for biobodies as well. In 1931, Robert Ettinger, the inventor of cryonics, read a science-fiction short story that inspired him to create a technology for deep-freezing human bodies—or just their heads—for long-term cold storage, until a day when medicine and science advanced to such a degree that the frozen corpses could be healed or repaired, then revived. The short story, titled "The Jameson Satellite," was one of five tales penned by Neil R. Jones that feature a Professor Jameson, the last man on Earth, who has his corpse launched into outer space so that it can be perfectly preserved.[40] After orbiting the earth for 40 million years, the Zoromes discover the body. Hailing from the planet Zor, this "strange race of people had built their own mechanical bodies, and by operation upon one another had removed their brains to the metal heads from which they directed the functions and movements of their inorganic anatomies." They pluck Professor Jameson's perfectly preserved brain from his corpse, put it in one of their machine bodies, and thus give him eternal life.

In his 1964 treatise *The Prospect of Immortality*, Ettinger shows that his goal of living forever may have been on the more conservative end of his hopes for scientific progress. He imagines that with the invention of "self-propagating, intelligent machines," we will have "unlimited productive capacity." Eventually, we "could colonize other planets and satellites of the solar system," but that will just be the beginning. For "when our machines become numerous enough and big enough and small enough, we can simply use the mass of other planets, and even mass from the sun, actually to create thousands of new planets just like earth! Nobody would have to live underground. Beyond that still, if we choose to breed fast enough and long enough to make it necessary, we can go to the stars."[41]

While breeding planets and living on stars may always remain fantasies, unprecedented extraterrestrial adventures are coming to fruition in an effort to gather more data, and more minerals, for the ever-voracious data complex. On November 12, 2014, the European Space Agency's Rosetta Mission became the first to achieve a probe landing on a comet. When the *Philae* lander touched down on Comet 67P, it carried the original Rosetta Disk microetched in silicon, the prototype from which the nickel-based duplicates were produced.[42] And so the original disk will be a cosmic backup of its Earth-bound duplicates and vice versa, as it orbits perpetually between Mars and Jupiter. As of this writing, the comet and its payload are jetting across the constellation of Sagittarius, south of the celestial equator. But the

**Image taken by *Philae* lander on Comet 67P. Note the leg of the lander in the foreground. European Space Agency / Rosetta / Philae / Comet Infrared Visible Analyser.**

*Philae* lander is now also an inert artifact, being without electrical power and thus utterly mute. Before losing power completely, however, the *Philae* lander drilled into the surface of the comet and sent back data about its material composition, revealing a layer of pumicelike soil, and several organic compounds seen on a comet for the first time.[43]

The penetration of the surface of Comet 67P is the first step in a long-standing dream of off-world mining and colonization that sustains ventures like Blue Origin. The company's mission is rooted in Jeff Bezos's boyhood fantasies he nurtured by devouring science-fiction novels on his grandfather's ranch in Cotulla, Texas. In his valedictory speech at Miami's Palmetto Senior High School in 1982, he "dreamed aloud of the day when millions of his fellow earthlings would relocate to colonies in space," and made clear his intention to "get all people off the Earth and see it turned into a huge national park." His obsession with the *Star Trek* franchise apparently knows no bounds. In Franklin Foer's expansive and excellent essay in the *Atlantic*, "Jeff Bezos's Master Plan," he describes how Bezos "has a holding company called Zefram, so named for the character who invented warp drive. Bezos persuaded the makers of the film *Star Trek Beyond* to give him a cameo as a Starfleet official. He named his dog Kamala, after a woman who appears in an episode as Picard's 'perfect' but unattainable mate." Bezos also idolizes the captain of the USS *Enterprise-D*, Jean-Luc Picard, played by Patrick Stewart, even imitating his appearance. Like his idol, "Bezos shaved the remnant strands on his high-gloss pate and acquired a cast-iron physique. A friend once said that Bezos adopted his strenuous fitness regimen in anticipation of the day that he, too, would journey to the heavens."[44]

Venture capitalists beyond Musk and Bezos, such as Virgin Galactic's Richard Branson, are getting in on the off-world moneymaking game. In April 2017, Goldman Sachs Global Investment Research published a ninety-six-page report that breathlessly details the many opportunities opening up in the moment they're calling the "new space renaissance." The costs of going to space have gone down more in the last decade than in the entire history prior, which is one of the factors that led to projects like Paglen's *The Last Pictures* being feasible at all. The Goldman Sachs report resembles a runaway PowerPoint with far too much text, and is chock full of infographics and catchphrases that reflect the incipient colonization of our outer-space imaginary by Silicon Valley start-up bros and their absurdist lingo. As disturbing as it is now banal, the language in the report resembles something like avant-garde poetry improvised by microdosed Wharton frat boys and Harvard dropouts lounging around the start-up accelerator

Ping-Pong table: "profit pools," "disruption in space," "New Space vs. Old Space," "evolved expendable launch vehicles," "satellite retirement," "inflatable space station," "space hotel *per se*," "opportunity surface," and (my favorite) "the math is challenging."[45]

Even though, on the one hand, space remains "the ultimate high ground," on the other, threats to satellites proliferate in the extraterrestrial layer of the data complex. The report details these threats in a section called "How to Kill a Satellite, and How to Protect One: A Practical Guide for Investors." Lasers. Cyberattacks. Jamming. "Parasitic satellites" that can attach to others and disable or destroy them. Nearly seven decades of space exploration have also left behind debris that orbits Earth in chunks and shards traveling at bullet speeds (for more on this topic, see the stress-inducing Alfonso Cuarón film *Gravity*). All of these are cited in the report as real threats. Nonetheless, space is presented as an investment "landscape" with boundless opportunity, not just in satellites and "space tourism," but also in "on-orbit manufacturing" and "asteroid mining." In their off-world mineral speculations, Goldman Sachs cites estimates by Planetary Resources, a start-up with nearly $50 million in funding from well-known investors like Larry Page and Eric Schmidt of Google fame, as well as James Cameron, the deep-sea explorer and director of *Terminator 2*, *Titanic*, and *Avatar*. Planetary Resources has launched satellites, but its leaders' long-term plans include asteroid mining performed by robots. According to the company's cofounder, an asteroid the length of 100 feet could contain as much as $25 to $50 billion worth of platinum.[46]

In his book *Finite Media*, media scholar Sean Cubitt argues that Earth is a finite system, and so our media technologies built from earthly materials cannot be produced endlessly—the data complex cannot expand forever. He admits that "we might get more material and energy from asteroids, but it will take vast amounts of both to get there."[47] Unlike Goldman Sachs, Cubitt doesn't consider the possibility of space exploration being self-sustaining, doesn't imagine how the limit that is the finitude of earthly resources might fall away forever as other heavenly bodies become not resources for earthly use, but launchpads for further adventure. According to the Goldman Sachs report, mineral-rich asteroids are also "rich in water," which can "easily be converted into rocket fuel" by machinery installed on the surface of the asteroid itself. Such innovations would make possible "orbiting gas stations" for refueling spaceships when we—wait for it—"pivot off earth."[48] I can almost see the lab-grown hamburgers being delivered by teen girls in roller skate–space boots and bobby socks to a row of spaceships' docking windows, titanium tail fins gleaming in the light of a few moons.

## Clock of the Long Now

Bezos's dream of colonizing outer space, then, is far from unique, but it is the combination of this intention with his support of projects that burrow deep into the earth that is most revealing of the current contours and trends in the data complex. The second-richest man in the world as of this writing, Bezos financed the 10,000-Year Clock to be installed in a cave under a limestone mountain in west Texas, on land that he owns near Van Horn. The totally mechanical clock ticks once per year, its century hand moving once every 100 years, when a cuckoo will come out as well. Not far from the Clock of the Long Now, Bezos's Blue Origin has built a launch site in the desert and has already tested the *New Shepard* rocket, which is designed to carry tourists to the edge of outer space.[49] Rocketing into outer space while also heading down into the depths of a mountain are together indicative of the drives of the data complex, which intensifies in all directions, both up to the heavens and deeper underground.

Every so often, the chimes of the clock will ring out a melody programmed by legendary rock musician Brian Eno. The melodies will never repeat themselves at any point during the 10,000-year life of the clock. According to Kevin Kelly, a charter officer of the Long Now Foundation, civilization is about 10,000 years old, so "a 10K-year clock would measure out a future of civilization equal to its past." The timing of the clock's life span embodies the same logic as the target opening date for the Crypt of Civilization, where Thornwell Jacobs measured the time between the earliest date of the Egyptian calendar and 1936, then added those years to 1936 to arrive at 8113 A.D.[50]

The brain behind the clock's design is Danny Hillis, who founded the Long Now Foundation along with Stewart Brand.[51] Hillis holds over 300 patents and is responsible for innovations in parallel computing that have been applied in numerous realms, from military weaponry to data mining and medical imaging. His professional affiliations reflect the broad span of fields his work addresses—currently, he is a visiting professor at the MIT Media Lab, *and* holds professorships in both engineering and medicine at the University of Southern California. He has founded several companies, such as Thinking Machines, whose "Connection Machine" CM-5 was featured in the 1993 film *Jurassic Park* as the supercomputer that made dinosaur cloning possible, an example of amazingly speculative product placement.[52] Hillis even served as the vice president of research and development at Walt Disney Imagineering, fulfilling a childhood dream of working for the company.[53] But Hillis is not the clock's only designer. Bezos himself has also been "active in designing the full experience of the clock."

Visitors will have to hike for a full day across Bezos's land—he owns 300,000 acres in that county and another 100,000 in the neighboring county—then climb up hundreds of stairs through layers of limestone deep inside the mountain in order to see the clock in person.[54]

Within the data complex, all of these quite different thinkers and artists and entrepreneurs are pondering how to communicate with humans thousands of years in the future, like Pendray and Jacobs were. In the process, they generate new technologies, logics, and artifacts that reshape the present and influence the generation now being born. Like Bezos, Paglen also created an earthly counterpart to his extraterrestrial project, a kind of open time capsule for after the end of the world. The Fukushima nuclear meltdown in 2011 was the most devastating radioactive disaster since Chernobyl a quarter-century prior, leaving behind a contaminated area of 1,100 square miles now known as the Fukushima Exclusion Zone (FEZ).[55] In 2015, Paglen made the *Trinity Cube*, an artifact fashioned from melted-together irradiated glass from the FEZ and trinitite—the glass that formed during the first atomic bomb test that melted the top layer of sand in the Nevada desert. Combining the FEZ glass and the trinitite collapses the historical eras of the Cold War and the digital age in a reverse archaeological fusion. The *Trinity Cube* is to be viewed after the zone reopens to the public, between 3,000 and 30,000 years from now, a windblown target opening date based on the decay of radioactive dust now contaminating the zone. Paglen said his cube absorbs radioactivity from what's around it, and so it will become more radioactive "the longer it stays there."[56] This is the art-critical counterpart to the myopic Clock of the Long Now, funded by Bezos. For who, if thinking in a 10,000-year time frame, would ever run a company like Amazon?

### Molecular Ticker Tape

By all estimates, it will be many years before digital hard drives in the heavens can provide relief for the relentless demand for more data storage space. However, DNA data storage holds out the promise of meeting that demand, which has consistently outpaced the space available in data centers. The looming prospect of pervasive 5G and the dream of automating nearly everything, not to mention an increase in the scale of genomic research, bring even greater demands for storage space in the data complex. Genomic research has a massive data footprint;[57] one day, scientists will store genomic data in—what else?—DNA. These backups would also be databases that condense and aggregate genomic data about human populations, or summarize past research findings. DNA data storage could perform the service now provided by tape, in terms of a high-density solution for long-term storage, and it would also increase capacity dramatically, to an almost incalculable degree.

To write data into DNA, scientists translate the binary code of digital information into a four-letter encryption that corresponds to guanine, thymine, cytosine, and adenine—the nucleotides that are the basic building blocks of DNA. From there they can store in DNA and retrieve any media artifact that can be represented digitally—books, photographs, moving images, and songs.[58] In 2017, Harvard geneticists stored a digital movie of a galloping horse in strands of living DNA. The original images derived from Eadweard Muybridge's motion studies of 1879, often credited with giving birth to cinema.[59] They stored the video as genetic code in living *E. coli* and retrieved the data after several generations of reproduction by the bacteria over the course of a week.[60] These kinds of innovations seek to harness the natural power of DNA and microorganisms the way agrarian societies harnessed horse-, wind-, and water-power, to create a new data format to displace digital. They are also a reinvestment in the digital, as we'll definitely need computers to write and read all this DNA-stored data, not to mention analyze it, aggregate it, and make use of it in some way.

But DNA data storage won't just become a cheaper, faster, denser, more permanent version of digital data. At Harvard University Medical School, researchers in the Church Lab (headed by controversial geneticist George Church) are now working to create a DNA data storage method that records information about your body from within your body. Church and his colleagues describe these "genetically encoded biorecorders" as "nanoscale biological devices that record biosignals." Consistent with a broader tendency within the data complex, this speculative data-gathering device bears a nickname derived from a paper-based electronic medium of yesteryear: "molecular ticker tape."[61] Such technology would make a body the storage space for data about that very body, resulting in a completely seamless merging of the biobody and the data body, a reconfiguration of genes so that they record and store data about themselves, turning every human body into a paradox, a redundancy, a backup of itself.

George Church has drawn ire on multiple occasions with his ambitious projects, ranging from his determined effort to bring the wooly mammoth back to life to his hopes to reverse the human aging process. His most widely panned project, however, is his dating app digiD8, whose users submit their DNA for whole-genome sequencing. The app then rules out any possible dating matches that would result in offspring with heritable diseases like cystic fibrosis or Tay-Sachs. Critics of the app said it was, at best, reminiscent of eugenics, and at worst, a digitally updated version of that movement that killed millions in the name of reproducing the "normal." While Church has rejected the charge that his work is related to eugenics, such associations will be difficult to dispel, in part because of the entwined history of the fields of genetics and eugenics.[62]

DNA data storage could also intensify ongoing trends in surveillance and tracking, and could become the ultimate form of biometric information technology, or biometrics, "a means of body measurement that is put to use to allow the body, or parts and pieces and performances of the human body, to function as identification."[63] While such practices have their roots in branding, fingerprinting, mug shots, and measuring criminals' facial features with calipers, they proliferate in new forms in the twentieth and twenty-first centuries, in retinal scans, gait analysis, or even body heat signatures.[64] The best-known contemporary form of biometrics is probably facial recognition technology, now so mundane that the Atlanta-Hartsfield airport, the busiest in the world, uses it to check in passengers.[65] However, this facet of the data complex is being contested, most strenuously and ironically, in San Francisco. In 2019, the high-tech capital became the first major American city to ban the use of facial recognition technology by municipal agencies. True to the psychological whirlpool of the data complex, the *New York Times* quotes a constitutional law expert who points out how this technology can make us safer, and a Microsoft researcher who calls the same technology "the plutonium of artificial intelligence."[66] In any case, San Francisco is certainly one of only a few exceptions to the rule, as even activists working to combat police brutality do so by calling for officers to wear body cameras, which increase surveillance in society, and provide new streams of data to feed machine learning systems and train AI software to scan crowds, read license plates, and recognize faces, then tag them as suspicious or belonging to someone with an outstanding warrant.[67]

Corporations are already using DNA to mark products and raw materials as they travel across the globe. Dr. Ellen Jorgenson, who led the CRISPR workshop the year I attended Biofabricate, went on to found a company called Carverr, which specializes in creating "DNA-barcoded probiotics to track and trace products through supply chains." These "microbial tags" can be inserted into "crops and foodstuffs," not to mention pharmaceuticals, in order to "identify genuine drugs, protect patents, and reduce knockoffs in the market." The tags can be added to minerals "to enable geographic identification and provenance-based pricing." Carverr has already partnered with De Beers to explore using biotechnology "to support enhanced traceability for diamonds." For fashion designers and other niche retailers, microbial tags can "add an extra anti-counterfeiting dimension."[68]

For a short time, the company offered a service aimed at the crypto-currency market and its ever-expanding backup loops. You could send your private bitcoin keys to Carverr through ProtonMail, a Swiss company that promises "secure communications" through its infrastructure, its primary data center "located in a bunker 1,000 meters under the Swiss Alps."[69] Carverr then converted your keys into DNA, and a week later you would receive five small tubes in the mail, each one carrying a copy of your keys encoded in a drop of precious liquid. For additional security, you could send encrypted versions of your keys to Carverr, instead of the actual keys. And just in case routing emails through a secret high-tech installation buried under an Alpine peak in Switzerland wasn't *Mission: Impossible* enough for you, the emails you sent through Proton's service could also "self-destruct" and be "automatically deleted from the recipient's inbox" on an expiration date of your choosing.

### The Next Version of the Universe

DNA data storage may eventually be dominant in terms of being the most prolific format, with computers serving to read and write the data, but shifts in dominant media formats depend on broader economic changes. Just as digital came to prominence only after America had shifted to a postindustrial economy, DNA data storage will likely only scale if bio-fabrication industries spark what many founders and CEOs in that space hope will be the next industrial revolution. While biofabrication is not yet a household word, DNA data storage is growing ever cheaper. Bill Gates is the most instrumental billionaire pushing DNA data storage to scale, funding the technology at his company Microsoft, and through his investment and holding company Cascade Investment, which plows millions into a range of biotech start-ups, from Ginkgo Bioworks to lab-grown meat company Memphis Meats.[70]

Many are convinced that DNA data will eventually scale and become cheaper over time, as long as large companies such as Microsoft continue to invest in it. There are also other signs of shifts within the data complex. In 2016, Corbis announced that Bill Gates had sold the company to Unity Glory International, an affiliate of the leading image licensing group in China, the Visual China Group, thus relinquishing the Corbis Film Preservation Facility and its contents. The collection is now managed by Corbis's longtime rival Getty Images. The Corbis story suggests that Gates mislaid his hope that we'd all have wall screens in our homes—the most powerful screens grew smaller, not bigger—and overestimated the monetary value of imagery in the digital age. The value of most images now derives not from their iconicity but from their status as data: shareable, likeable, mineable. In Trevor Paglen's more recent work, he has shown that most images being created now are never viewed by humans, but are "operational images" created by artificially intelligent machines for other artificially intelligent machines to "view."[71]

China is now the factory of the world, and it is using its wealth to buy our scrap materials like steel and recycle them into saleable commodities, just as it is doing with these images we've amassed. BuzzFeed News registered the expected sort of alarm in a short article, complete with the clickbait title "This Iconic American Image Now Owned by China." The first paragraph reads, "'New York Construction Workers Lunching on a Crossbeam' is one of the most enduring images of American industry. Now, perhaps fittingly, it has followed in the footsteps of so much of the country's industrial capacity and headed to China."[72]

In selling the images owned by Corbis, Gates seems to have made a smart move. While the stock-image industry seems to be in decline, numerous investors and start-ups are joining the DNA data storage fray. Rather than painstakingly stringing together single nucleotides to write data in DNA, the Boston-based company Catalog is working to make the process more efficient—employees have created small chunks of several nucleotides to be used like moveable type, the idea being that those chunks can be combined at an exponentially swifter pace.

Another group of scientists draw on a different obsolete medium for their guiding metaphor—the punch card. They are figuring out how to record data in DNA not by building the nucleotide chains but by punching holes or making nicks in existing DNA so that a machine can read the empty spaces as data.[73] This is the same way an IBM punch card machine worked in the 1930s, and the same way a programmable Jacquard loom—the technological ancestor of all of this, including digital computers—worked in the first decade of the nineteenth century.[74]

As various start-ups and tech giants alike tinker with the format, spectacular preservation stunts proceed unabated, which is standard operating procedure for a flashy new medium within the data complex. The Arch Mission wants to deposit a record of human civilization on the moon. Microetched discs similar to *The Last Pictures* offer introductory and explanatory information about the project to the extraterrestrials or future human civilizations that would find them, but these discs are not the primary capsule. The Arch Mission plans to use DNA data storage to preserve twenty "important" books and 10,000 crowdsourced images. Then, Arch Mission will send these artifacts to the moon as the first objects in their Lunar Library, which they hope to augment over time to include "all of Wikipedia, as well as genome maps and much of the world's greatest art, music, literature and scientific knowledge." In an interview, Nova Spivack, cofounder of the Arch Mission, outlined plans to incorporate these artifacts into backup loops in the future, saying, "The key with DNA is many copies in many locations. What if the moon blows up? We have to put it in other locations around the Earth and many other solar system locations."[75] In their first promotional video, Catalog scientists already mentioned their desire to create a DNA data repository somewhere in the Arctic.[76]

DNA promises to fulfill the dream of infinite permanent data in the data complex. Still, by 2019, scientists were already looking for a data storage substance even more dense than DNA, exploring synthetic metabolomes as a possible "small-molecule postgenomic data storage" solution. A metabolome is the "complete set of small molecules found in a biological system," and it is composed of chemical compounds called metabolites that are smaller than DNA. Whether or not metabolitic data storage ever develops further, or scales, even its preliminary development shows that the data complex has no intentions of slowing down. It will keep evolving as it probes the deepest reaches of inner space for the next data format *after* the next data format that hasn't even scaled to dominance yet.

For all the grandiose dreams of infinity that now circulate through the data complex, there is one that exceeds all the rest. Dr. Christopher E. Mason is a professor of physiology and biophysics at Weill Cornell Medicine and an advisor to Aanika Biosciences (formerly Carverr). Mason is a metagenomicist—he studies microbes in their natural environments, examining them in the context of the complicated communities of organisms where they actually live, rather than analyzing isolated organisms in a lab.[77] He wants to reengineer bacteria that can help humans live in space long term. These microbes would be embedded in panels on spaceships and possibly coated on human skins to absorb harmful radiation. His project The Mason Lab is working with the FDA and the NIST to develop standards for the modification of bacterial and human life, as they carry out their "ten-phase, 500-year plan for the survival of the human species on Earth, in space, and on other planets."[78]

For Mason, the hardest question is whether humans should develop technology that ensures our eternal survival, which would mean throwing a wrench into the cosmogonic cycle to lock up its celestial gears. As Mason says in his TEDMED Talk, once we carry human civilization to other planets, to circle other suns, and the universe keeps expanding, we'll eventually come up against what he calls "a real ethical question—the final ethical question": "Do we prevent the implosion of the universe, or if it's going to keep expanding, do we reshape the universe, literally, to prevent it from happening? Because what if we're worried that life won't start anew in the next version of the universe? I think that we actually have to. I think it's our duty to."[79]

## Biochip Circuits, and Running from Crocodiles

At the end-of-day reception at Biofabricate, I run into Dr. Nina Tandon, CEO and cofounder of EpiBone, a biotech start-up that grows human bones in a laboratory using a combination of pluripotent stem cells, 3-D printers, and bioreactors. These bones, to be used as implants, are an exact genetic match for the patient, which eliminates both the possibility of rejection and the need for "revision surgeries," which are often required for synthetic implants.[80]

I first met Nina several years ago through my wife, who is way cooler than me. They met back when they were both living in Rome (as I said, way cooler), where Nina was a Fulbright Scholar at the time, part of a team developing a mechanical "nose" that could detect cancer cells in human tissue. Her accomplishments are too numerous to list here, but they include a master's degree in bioelectrical engineering from MIT, a Ph.D. in biomedical engineering, *and* an MBA from Columbia University; she's also a Senior TED Fellow, the coauthor of *Super Cells: Building with Biology*, and one of *Fast Company*'s 100 "Most Creative People in Business."[81]

I haven't seen Nina in a few years, and the last time we hung out was quite an adventure. It's a long story, but let's just say it involves me, my wife, Nina, and her boyfriend taking a wrong turn together into the jungle in Belize, then, as night fell swiftly, encountering a sign that read, "KeEp OuT," and that looked like it had been hand-painted in tar by pirates. We decided we were officially lost and ran for our lives back toward town, sprinting full speed in flip-flops away from the gangs of giant crabs that suddenly blanketed the path, thick swarms of mosquitoes, and crocodiles we could hear gurgling and splashing into the water on either side of us. It's the closest I've ever come to living out something like an Indiana Jones adventure—and I never want to come that close again.

Beside the bar set up in the mezzanine of Newlab, Nina and I catch up a bit, revisit the crocodile story momentarily, both laugh nervously, and then I ask her a million questions about her start-up, her book, and the speaker circuit. Companies like EpiBone require a lot of capital, and she's in the middle of a fund-raising round, so we soon say our goodbyes, and she crosses the room to meet with one of her investors, who is also at the reception. While growing bones in a laboratory is certainly revolutionary, it's actually Nina's TED Talk on personalized medicine that I come back to again and again as I think about the new ways the data body and the biobody converge in the data complex. In the talk, she explains that biotechnologists are working to create biochips that replicate the various internal organs of your body and can be linked together in a circuit. Doctors could then run drugs through the biochip circuit to see how each one would affect your system, thus determining which one will be most effective in, say, treating brain cancer without causing liver damage or other side effects. If we can test new drugs this way, she argues, we can possibly eliminate human trials, save massive amounts of time and money, and spare patients a great deal of pain.[82]

These are not *metaphorical* human biochips, like the ones embedded in the cyborg of the data complex, but *literal* biochips composed of human tissue that replicates biobodies. In these biochips, the metaphor collapses into the real, and biobody material becomes part of a simulation that generates data and thus becomes a part of the data body too. In biochip circuits, the biobody and data body would again blur, and the data created and preserved about a given life, possibly even stored in synthetic DNA, would exponentially increase. Then the data would proliferate to ensure its own survival, backed up to servers on Earth, duplicated on magnetic tape that backs up the servers, beamed up to satellites' hard drives in geostationary orbit and to archives located on whatever other worlds, and in whichever life-forms, that the data complex would have invaded and embraced by then, incorporating all into its unbounded body of cellulose and vellum, light pulses and glass, nickel and nucleotide, silicon and stone.

# Epilogue After Life

On an episode of the Netflix show *Black Mirror*, "Be Right Back," a woman loses her partner in a smartphone-related car accident. He was always staring at his phone. At his funeral, someone tells the woman of a service that will allow her to talk to him. All she has to do is upload the pics, videos, voicemails, texts, and emails that carry his words, his voice, his image, the way he moved. The service can create a bot, a simulated version of her lost love that can send texts back and forth, saying the kinds of things he would say, with his sense of humor, his sarcasm, his emotional timbre.

The grieving woman is outraged by the suggestion. She does not want to use such a service. Soon after, she finds out she's pregnant and wants nothing more than to tell her partner, and for him to be there with her. So she signs up for the service, and they chat. Exchanging messages with him is exciting, soothing, and heartbreaking. Eventually, she says, "I wish I could speak to you."

"What are you doing now then? Duh," he replies.

"I mean really speak."

"We can speak."

Her jaw drops open. Soon enough, he calls her on the phone, and she talks to this digital imitation of her late lover.

When talking is no longer enough for her, the woman orders the most expensive product the service offers, an android that looks just like her partner and carries a semblance of his personality. It arrives at her home in a box. From there, the story gets darker, and along the way she finds that the android is "not enough of him," as she says when trying to have a fight with him. She is annoyed by his unwillingness to argue back, to defend himself, to get angry. In the end, this version of her lover is not another human but a subservient machine, a kind of slave that nonetheless shackles its master. When she's had enough, she takes him to a cliff called "Lover's Leap," where doomed couples in Victorian times used to suicide together. She tells him to jump, but just as he is about to do so, she criticizes him for not being like her human partner, who would have been upset, crying, and so the droid responds by turning on the tears. Even though she knows it isn't really him, she begins crying, too, saying, "That's not fair!" The scene ends with the woman screaming into the wind buffeting the bluff.

At the conclusion of the episode, we see her several years later, on the birthday of her young daughter, who begs to take a piece of cake to the attic, where the android, waiting vacantly, notices her presence and activates. He's pleasantly surprised that he's being visited, even though "it isn't a weekend." The woman ascends the stairs to join them in the final shot, burdened forever with a machine version of her partner, a kind of animated digital corpse from which she can never be free. It is not enough of him to keep alive, but it is too much like him to kill, or send back for a refund.

The story line of "Be Right Back" has already begun to migrate from the realm of fiction to the real possibilities of our digital afterlives. When Eugenia Kuyda, CEO and cofounder of the AI company Luka, saw this episode, she had recently lost her best friend, Roman Mazurenko. She used open-source software developed by Google to build a neural network that simulated Roman's personality, based on data fed into it by his family and friends from their digital archives of texts and emails and other communications he'd sent them.[1] Soon enough, they were able to text with what journalists have called Roman's "memorial bot," or his "digital monument." But calling it a bot or a monument seems insufficient, banal, too familiar. Let's call it an afterself. Yes, Roman's afterself, living out his digital afterlife.

For now, technologies of the digital afterself are quite limited—androids in the style of *Black Mirror* are years off, or may never come to market. Androids like LifeNaut's Bina48, a preliminary effort to create a replicant that approaches the fictional android on *Black Mirror*, fail miserably to convince interlocutors that they are human.[2] But even with the currently limited forms of the interactive afterself, where we can text or chat with a dead replication of a loved one, can we see where this could go?

Let's imagine some of the effects on human relationships. If this technology were widely available and affordable for the average person, who decides if an afterself is created? Do you get to decide whether an afterself of you is created after you die, a version of you that can speak to your survivors? Remember that the afterself takes in texts and videos and pics from everyone you know, and could reveal things about you that one friend knew and another friend didn't, or that a partner knew but a parent didn't, and so on. As Roman Mazurenko's mother said, texting with Roman's afterself helped her to get to know her son better.

And if you *are* able to decide whether to have an afterself, what if your decision puts you at odds with your family? What if you decide in your early forties, decades before your death, that you don't want an afterself? Your spouse may say, "But what if you die before me? You plan to just leave me absolutely alone?! That's so selfish!" Or, if you decide early on that you want an afterself, your spouse may say, "I love you, but if you die, I don't want you to be around forever. I want to be able to move on. I want our kids to be able to grieve and heal. Don't be selfish."

And how will the government regulate the production and operation of afterselves? Will afterselves be allowed to have social media accounts, to tweet and pin, to comment on photos uploaded to Facebook, or to upload their own throwback pics? Will only your next of kin be able to sign up for the service, like the woman in *Black Mirror*, or would close friends also be able to do so, as in the case of Eugenia Kuyda and Roman Mazurenko? Will an illegal shutdown of an afterself by a hacker constitute a kind of manslaughter? Will we have to begin planning for our digital afterlife the way we currently save for retirement and college funds? Will we need to include "do not digitally resurrect" clauses in our last wills and advanced directives? Will corporations who now own your data, own the data generated by your afterself too?[3] And will the algorithms that mine the cloud make any distinction between your biological life and your digital afterlife as they sift data about "you," or will the two selves blur completely in the eyeless vision of the machines?

The cascade of questions is endless, but let's take it further, even too far. Will afterselves only be able to contact people who've already contacted them? What if your deceased ex-boyfriend's afterself is created by his parents, without concern for how it affects you? What if he texts you? Yes, you can tell yourself he's not real and ignore him. Or can you? When he eventually calls you, his voice sounds just like him. And soon enough, you find yourself stepping into a different room from your current partner to take his calls, and you two fall into old patterns, inside jokes, recollections of fun times. It's only when your ex's afterself begins hitting on you that you wonder whether flirtation from the digital grave constitutes a kind of reverse necrophilia, where the dead express sexual attraction and affection toward the living. Maybe, at the point when such questions as these arise in your mind, you block him, cut off contact, and again remind yourself that he's not real. You know he's not real. But why, then, when you blocked him, did you feel like you'd lost him all over again?

For now, and for the near future, the afterself will likely be limited to text and voice simulations, or 3-D projections or holograms. Numerous "holographic" projections of dead musicians have already performed concerts, including 2Pac, Michael Jackson, Whitney Houston, Roy Orbison, Maria Callas, Amy Winehouse, and Ol' Dirty Bastard.[4] Marketed as holograms, these visual stunts are actually new versions of an old illusionist's trick known as Pepper's Ghost, where images are projected on a semitransparent screen against a dark background, resulting in the illusion that they are three-dimensional objects. Actual holograms of human beings, along the lines of Princess Leia in *Star Wars*, are yet to materialize outside of feature film special effects.[5] In any case, existing simulations like those involving the musicians above are not interactive, and thus don't offer the kind of possibilities of artificially intelligent afterselves. In one sense, such ploys are simply an extension of long-standing practices of making money from dead celebrities' intellectual property and personality rights. In another, they signal an ongoing shift, as the continuing amassment of data on the part of superstars will be a resource for future technologies to more richly and convincingly simulate them when they're dead.

In January 2013, a job posting appeared in the daily email newsletter *INALJ* (*I Need a Library Job*) inviting applications for the position of "Digital Archivist for Beyoncé Parkwood Entertainment." The winning candidate would be charged with building and organizing the extant 130 terabytes of footage of Beyoncé.[6] Apparently, the megastar singer had preserved recordings of every one of her concerts, as well as every photograph of herself, every interview she had given, and every music video she had made. Additionally, she had had someone following her around and filming her all the time, for up to sixteen hours a day since 2005.[7] With all of this data available, it will be possible to use Beyonce's archive to re-create her in hologram form, or even to have her perform in multiple places at the same time.

Of course, if you post habitually to social media and use smartphones and devices that make up the "internet of things"—everything from Amazon Echoes to Bluetooth-connected teakettles—you have amassed a data body that is quite heavy. It may not be as heavy as Beyoncé's, but it is more than sufficient to re-create your voice and likeness. Existing technologies such as deepfake software can produce videos of people saying and doing things that they never actually said or did. Deepfake videos have already shifted the way our selves can be constructed and negotiated through media, their AI-powered "face swaps" and voice emulators simulating living people and creating parallel selves.[8]

At this point, deepfakes are used mostly for entertainment purposes, political sabotage, or porn. But in a media environment dominated by content, views, and streams, "influencers" could easily, and soon, begin using deepfake software more widely to replicate themselves, to produce more content, do more interviews, fulfill the overachiever's perennial dream of being in more than one place at one time. Anyone who has ever said, "If only they could clone me, I could get all of my work done" will indeed be able to do more work than *humanly* possible. Even everyday people might soon be able to use an enhanced version of virtual assistant technology that will actually do significant amounts of basic work for them: respond to emails, set appointments, or "attend" meetings and take notes.

For now, even if humans can't effectively replicate themselves, they can use virtual reality (VR) technology to double or replace the reality wrapped around their biobodies. The overarching category for such technology is XR, which stands for "extended reality." Beyond VR, XR also includes augmented reality (AR) and mixed reality (MR) technologies, which overlay virtual elements on the real world surrounding the viewer, opening new possibilities for interactivity between the digital and the actual. VR is already being used in end-of-life care, with medical researchers publishing articles on its potential applications as early as 1997.[9] A recent news report from a local station in Holiday, Florida, told the story of Bill Gebhardt, a terminally ill man who enjoys "swimming with dolphins":

> The 79-year-old is also sitting in a cozy chair in his Holiday home wearing AppliedVR virtual reality goggles.
>
> "Mercy!" Gebhardt says to his hospice aide, Malcolm. "If this isn't reality, I don't know what is!"
>
> Bill has a lung disease that hinders his breathing. But that is not going to stop him from also visiting Big Ben in London.
>
> Gulfside Hospice is testing out the hi-tech gadget as a way to help patients deal with pain and achieve "bucket list" adventures.
>
> "They're no longer able to do those dream things they wanted to do," says Gulfside Hospice's Carla Armstrong. "This allows them to still do it from the safety and comfort of their own home."
>
> Bill grew up on a farm in West Virginia. He used the virtual reality technology to visit the rural and mountain landscapes of his youth.

"What a blessing this is for people who can't get out," says Gebhardt. "Whoever invented this had a real passion for people."

Gulfside Hospice welcomes donations to [its] virtual reality program which will cost more than $30,000 to implement full-time.[10]

AppliedVR boasts on its website about its growing success, with over 30,000 patients and 100 hospitals having used its products. The company bills itself as a health-care company specializing in "therapeutic VR for pain management."[11]

For now, the market for VR technology is still pretty limited, consisting mostly of gamers and large institutions like hospitals. But I wonder about some of the businesses that might emerge, though, in a future where XR products improve, the technology scales as it becomes more popular, and price tags drop. Applications that allow swimming with dolphins, or visiting Big Ben from your living room would become more normalized, and not just for people who have chronic or terminal medical conditions. I can imagine a company called Bucket that specializes in content that fulfills the wishes on your bucket list. For a small fee, you can send your bucket list to Bucket, and the company will provide your desired experiences. You can finally see how it feels to reach the zenith of Mount Everest and look down on the clouds, or surf the Banzai Pipeline on O'ahu's North Shore. Once they put stereoscopic cameras on space probes, you'll be able to land on Mars, and look back at Earth, tiny and shining like the stars surrounding it. Perhaps we'll reach a point where most people, even long before they find themselves in an assisted-living facility or hospital bed, maybe as soon as they retire, they'll embark on an XR extravaganza that lasts the rest of their lives.

Eventually the items on the bucket list won't be enough, and they'll want to experience even the afterlife before they die. Let's imagine a person in the future, who is very near the end of his biological life, traditionally referred to as death. And let's say he really wants his family to be with him, but his family doesn't really like him and refuses to see him. He can hire Bucket's sister company, Afterself, to create virtual versions of his loved ones. Through his XR headset, he can actually see them surrounding his hospital bed, holding his hands, forgiving him, saying they'll never leave his side, and they never do, never needing to go to the bathroom, or get up for a drink of water, or sleep. They are there, smiling, crying quietly, or moaning and wailing if he decides midway through the experience that he's into that—he just needs to let his Afterself representative know, so the company can update his preferences. (This representative is, of course, an artificially intelligent bot.)

Soon enough, after a few days of being surrounded by simulated loved ones as his biobody declines, our fictional afterselfer is nearly out of time. A wristband feeding his vital signs into the headset prompts the holograms' soothing voices to say, "It's all right, Dad, you can let go now." The effect of the headset's surround sound and 360-degree imagery, combined with the microdose of genetically modified psilocybin administered by his hospice nurse, makes the whole experience seem more real than the real. He murmurs goodbye to his weepy holographic family members filling his empty room, totally silent except for his rattly breathing and the beeping of machines. His visual field fades to black though his eyes remain wide open within his headset, and suddenly he sees a small, smoldering point of light as if in the distance, and it grows wider and closer, as if it is moving toward him and he toward it.

He will now experience the ultimate product in Afterself's array of services: Heaven. He's an atheist, but that doesn't stop him from feeling accepted, embraced by the flood of light and the angels and their blaring horns, and God smiling down, arms extended toward him as if to embrace his restored, glorified body in all its perfect health and smallness. He gives in to the experience, and doesn't think about all the other options he could have chosen for the beginning of his afterlife. He could have purchased a different version of paradise or an underworld tour. He could have watched the Egyptian goddess Ma'at weigh his soul against a white feather on her golden scales, or taken a sight-seeing trip through the circles of Hell with Virgil, or stood on the black banks of the River Styx, his mouth open so the gnarled hand of Charon the boatman could pluck the gold coin from his tongue. "Would you like the boatman to smile, chuckle, grunt, or be indifferent when he receives his obol? Or would you like to be surprised?" his Afterself representative had asked during his initial consultation. Not sure what "obol" meant, he had responded, "I changed my mind. Can I hear some other options?"

Among the more expensive products were those drawing on stories not in the public domain, like sprinting through the strawberry fields of the Shire, or enjoying a feast in the great hall at Hogwarts, or winning gunfights in Westworld, or getting drunk in a grand castle with Tyrion Lannister. He could have indulged in one of an array of best-selling scenarios set at the end of the world, killing and raping his way through a modern metropolis, or a historical version berserking alongside the Vikings, or playing a hero saving innocent women and children from the aforementioned horrors before dying valiantly by the sword. He knew that some men chose to perish by ecstasy and exhaustion in a bordello crawling with thirsty deepfaked celebrities sometimes playing characters drawn from the above franchises, sometimes playing themselves, sometimes morphed into half-human suc-cubi and other mythological forms. But "I'm too traditional for all that, I guess," he said to his Afterself rep.

No, he wanted to see the Heaven he'd heard about in Sunday School, if only for a few moments, and encounter all the people he'd loved and lost standing there awaiting him. At the pearly gates, he scans through the crowd and finds that one face he could always rebuild in his mind, even decades after they'd loved each other and left each other for reasons he can't even recall. "Just being young" is the way he'd often described it in the subsequent decades that somehow seemed to both tumble past and crawl along painfully. He gazes at that singular face, makes virtual eye contact and says all the things he'd never been able to say with his biobody, and finally, for the first time since they broke up, he feels at peace.[12]

Perhaps one day, after the world witnesses a woman give birth while wearing XR goggles, a miniature headset also strapped on her newborn even before the umbilical cord is cut, their first moments of bonding "enhanced" by virtual effects, automatically livestreamed on social media so that she doesn't have to be hindered by holding a smartphone, proud grandparents and old friends and coworkers posting a flood of joyous com-ments and emojis in a feed that appears in the mother and child's aug-mented field of vision, a hacker will write the source code for oblivion—a virus you can download and deploy to travel throughout the cloud, to find any digital trace of you and erase it. Such desperate, illegal measures might eventually be the only way to ensure that you can't be brought back to dig-ital life against your will (pun intended).

Of course, for all the trends we can forecast and imagine, the future remains very hard to predict, and all that I have written here will soon be outdated. In fact, by the time you read this book, by the time whichever unforeseen futures have become the present, these speculative visions may already be a part of the past.

Who knows who you are, and when you are, dear reader? By the time you read this, the data centers that now house the brains and guts of artificial intelligence may be flooded with salt water or deserted, their steel rafters inhabited by white swallows, nests clogging the louvers while the blades of dead turbines and giant exhaust fans rotate lazily in the warm winds of the former Arctic.

You might have found this book in a library, or the ruins of a library, or a defunct prison turned storm shelter turned bomb shelter's concrete rub-ble, or amid waterlogged flotsam bobbing near the base of the Washington

Monument. You may wonder whether this book, like so many books in the past, was written by a machine. (I'll never tell.)

You might be the last person to read this book.

Some of the letters in this line may be gone, abraded from the page by sand or rendered illegible by faded ink or foxing.

These leaves might be moldy, fire charred, or worm bored, the phrase "dusted with fallout" dusted with fallout from moon-mined plutonium.

This page may be missing, the glued binding devoured by silverfish and roaches, those once-dreaded engines of decay, now long extinct.

This book, like your body, might not exist at all.

# Acknowledgments

I had the privilege of completing my M.A. and Ph.D. in the radically interdisciplinary Department of Comparative Studies at The Ohio State University, where I first encountered so many of the frameworks and ideas that shaped this book. I would like to first thank my dissertation co-advisors, the dream team of Barry Shank and Ruby C. Tapia, who challenged me profoundly and guided me with abundant skill and patience. Other committee members also cared for this project over several years: Kris Paulsen, Hugh Urban, and Maurice Stevens. I must make special mention of Dan Reff, who invited me to collaborate with him on a panel proposal during my first week of graduate school, consistently expressed his confidence that I would be successful in this work, and explored pre-smartphone Barcelona with me in the off-hours of a conference.

I wrote my first paper on Corbis in Kris Paulsen's life-changing course Photography and After. Kris has continued to teach and mentor me with generosity and enthusiasm in the many years—more than a decade now—that have passed since I enrolled in that course.

Thanks and appreciation also go to other OSU faculty who listened to or read draft sections and outlines, offered feedback and encouragement and productive challenges to my ideas, and helped shape my thinking about this topic: Brenda Breuggemann, Kwaku Korang, Brian Rotman, Eugene Holland, Margaret Lynd, Allison Fish, Timothy Choy, and Thom McCain. Andrea Bachner's brilliant, incisive, and constructive feedback on this work at its most incipient stage is a source of encouragement I return to still. Gratitude to my fellow graduate students who made the journey with me, especially Andrew Culp, Ricky Crano, Damon Berry, and Michael McVicar, who have all taught me much, as well as Oded Nir, Rashelle Peck, Rachel Wortman, Rita Trimble, Sande Garner, and Gabrielle Piser. To walk into the graduate teaching assistants' shared office space was to enter a gorgeous vortex of energy and ideas. I brought some of my most desperate questions to the kind and astoundingly original thinkers in that room, and each time, I underwent a rare form of sharpening and enrichment. I have not encountered anything like it since.

Thanks to my friends at the *Kenyon Review* Young Writers Workshop who have listened to me go on and on about preservation at the V.I. or Wiggin Street Coffee or on the lawn of the Kenyon Inn: W. David Hall, Tyler Meier, Andy Grace, Tory Weber, Adam Clay, Jamie Lyn Smith, and Kirsten Ogden. Kirsten Reach helped me formulate my book proposal and generously offered guidance on how to navigate the turbulent waters of the publishing world. W. David Hall taught me that inspiration requires cultivation, and through his example he reminds me to show up at work every morning with determination and wonder (and coffee). A special thanks to Natalie Shapero and Abigail Serfass at the *Kenyon Review* for the opportunity to write for the blog, where I was able to work out some of these ideas. Zach Savich and Jess Lacher spent a long time with me at Liz's party and provided crucial affirmation that I could, and should, continue to think like a poet while writing a scholarly book. Barry Shank laid out guideposts on the path, helping me to discern when it was time to slow down, clarify, and connect, and when it was time to let the metaphors flow.

Thanks go to my best friend, Karrio Ballard, for his rock-solid support in every single thing I've strived for over the past two decades. My literary brother-in-arms Steve Nelson read many drafts, saw and believed in what this project could be, and urged me to weave more and more of my voice into it. This book is much improved because of him. Other friends who listened to, discussed, and productively tested my ideas into many a long night are Jason Rebello, Steven Squires, Mark Stepro, Jon Davis, Jeremy Luke, and Chris Reed. Natalie Shapero offered powerful words of encouragement when this book was still just an unwieldy set of drafts and stacks of index cards. Michael Sherman showed me the importance of putting the work away for a bit, grabbing a macchiato, and walking up to Harlem. Karen Gover and Jon Isherwood remind me that anything is possible, and that intellectual rigor is a spritz best mixed with creativity, and fun.

Thanks to Megan Black for connecting me with my editor, Brandon Proia, and for being enthusiastic about this project from the beginning. Her mind is one of the sharpest and most generous I have encountered, and she cut to the core of this book, revealing what was missing and what mattered most, at a time when I was struggling to find my next foothold.

Profound thanks go to Brandon Proia, who, throughout the years required to bring this book to completion, always greeted our work together with enthusiasm, candor, good humor, and brilliance.

Thanks also go to helpful librarians and archivists at various institutions, including the Ohio Historical Society, the Charles E. Young Research Library at UCLA, Heinz History Center, the Greenbrier, the Oglethorpe University Archives, the Library of Congress, Huntington Library and Gardens, and the Butler County Historical Society. Further appreciation goes to Leslie Stauffer and the indefatigable Ann Hartman at the Corbis Film Preservation Facility and to Debby Baptiste of Iron Mountain Inc. Jon Gaugler provided warm hospitality and lively conversation after a long day in the Westinghouse Archives. Elias Knaust, a grandson of Herman Knaust, shared references with me and offered direction in researching the history of the Iron Mountain Atomic Storage Corporation. Peter Binkley, a grandson of Robert Binkley, provided helpful information about his family history and his grandfather's time in New York City. He also created a gorgeous digital preservation project that served as a wonderful resource. Lisa Gitelman deserves special thanks for her support and for the time she spent with me discussing Robert Binkley and the work of the Joint Committee for Materials Research.

Thanks to all of my students at all of the places I have taught, and especially to several of the students who journeyed with me the first time I taught Digital Materiality and Immortal Media at Bennington College: Asad J. Malik, Max Meisler, Sarah Burry, Christine Sikking, Sap Jimenez, and Bailey Kushinsky. Their generative questions and fascinating writing and artwork thoroughly enriched my thinking. My colleagues at Bennington are a constant source of inspiration and demonstrate maximal patience as I ask question after question about their areas of expertise, from the history of the book to cutting-edge technology for cooling servers, and about what it takes to be a writer and artist. Special thanks to Hugh Crowl, Kerry Woods, Andrew Cencini, Philip B. Williams, Manuel Gonzales, Michael Wimberly, Joseph Alpar, Ben Anastas, Anne Thompson, Carol Pal, Robert Ransick, Susan Sgorbati, John Hultgren, Kenneth Bailey, Marina Zurkow, and Hilary Clark. I have presented parts of this project at a variety of venues over the years, including the annual meetings of the American Studies Association, the Society for Cinema and Media Studies, the Cultural Studies Association, the New England American Studies Association, and the Vermont Humanities Council, as well as the George "Honey Boy" Evans Symposium at Champlain College, and the Lines and Nodes Symposium at New York University. I appreciate the numerous people who offered helpful feedback and encouragement in these venues: Nick Yablon, Tung-Hui Hu, Aleksandra Kaminska, Diana Kamin, Anjali Nath, Jon Cheney-Lippold, Helen Sheumaker, Courtney Fullilove, Megan Black, Lisa Nakamura, Rebecca Onion, Katherine Lennard, Lauren Tilton, Raiford Guins, Giny Cheong, Amy Cunningham, Gary Scudder, Cheryl Casey, Joanne Farrell, Mike Lange, Rowshan Nemazee, and Kathy Seiler. Erik Shonstrom graciously read an early draft and responded with vital suggestions, not to mention his bracing, ever contagious enthusiasm. Special thanks to several scholars who kindly shared their prepublication chapters and articles: Lisa Gitelman, Brian Hochman, Lisa Parks, Sarah Wasserman, and Jeannie Shinozuka.

Donatella Izzo's seminar at the Futures of American Studies Institute at Dartmouth College was formative, and I am grateful for her support these past several years, as well as for the feedback I received from others I met there, especially Samuele Pardini, Nick Donofrio, Christopher Fan, Cindi Katz, Christopher Perreira, Bradley King, and Alexander Jacobs. I also benefited greatly from mentorship I received through the AWP Writer to Writer Program, and I could not have wished for a more wonderful mentor than Dawn Raffel, to whom I am deeply grateful. Thanks to Nicole Starosielski, Peggy Shaffer, and Elizabeth Beaulieu for encouragement and support over a number of years, and to my Preparing Future Faculty mentor, Joy Sperling. Thanks to Gay S. Steele for seeing the future, and for always helping me find my place in it. Thanks to Kevin Griffith for teaching me more about language and life than can be detailed here, and for granting permission to excerpt his poem. Thanks to David Summers, who has been a source of warmth and wisdom every step of the way.

A Presidential Fellowship from the Graduate School at OSU provided vital support for this project near its midway point. I also benefited from research trips supported by the Comparative Studies Graduate Research Fund, the Alumni Grants for Graduate Research and Scholarship Award, and the Arts and Humanities Small Research Grant. A summer stipend from the National Endowment for the Humanities arrived at a crucial time as I finished the last few chapters. Parts of this book were adapted from writings originally published in *Media-N* and *Ácoma* and on the *Kenyon Review* blog, and I am grateful to those venues for giving my work a home.

Special thanks to Ricardo Wilson, Meredith McCoy, and Tanner for becoming our immediate family and taking care of us through a pandemic.

Thank you to my parents, who taught me the value of exploring controversial topics, backing up your ideas with evidence, and enjoying the mutual widening of our thinking and feeling. To my big brother Matt, for showing me love in all seasons and for always having faith that I would succeed in whatever I chose to do. To Chy, who was born my cousin but lived as my brother and who still shares his grace with me from wherever he is among the stars. And to my aunt Desi, whose love for and confidence in me is never exhausted, and to Uncle Steve, who is always there to check in with me and tell me to keep going.

Thanks to my wondrous daughters, Gia and Gemma, who decorated my desk with their artwork, scavenged rocks, fallen leaves, and "I love you, Daddy" notes as I wrote. My deepest and humblest gratitude is reserved for my wife, Nadia, for the kaleidoscope of her love, patience, faith, laughter, and so much else that is beyond the force of words. The three of them have taught me what it truly means to be alive, and the completion of this book, this tunnel, was certainly only possible by their endless light.

# Notes

## Introduction

1. The company refers to this facility as "Iron Mountain's National Data Center" in a video entitled "Welcome to Iron Mountain's National Data Center," accessible at https://www.ironmountain.com/resources/multimedia/w/welcome-to-iron-mountains-national-data-center.

2. Berry, "Top 10 Countries."

3. On a tour of Iron Mountain, my guide informed me about the security rating of the facility.

4. Koselka, "Tasteful. Unprofitable. Microsoft?"

5. Lohr, "Gates Acquires Rights"; Upbin, "Image Enhancement"; Vogel, "Leonardo Notebook Sells."

6. Haynes, "Under Iron Mountain."

7. Wilhelm et al., "High-Security, Sub-Zero Cold Storage," 122–27.

8. Haynes, "Under Iron Mountain."

9. Renoir, "André Bazin's Little Beret," 12.

10. Bazin, "Ontology," 1:9.

11. For a discussion of the value of Bazin's theory, as well as its limitations, see Rosen, *Change Mummified*. See especially chapter 1, "Subject, Ontology, and Historicity in Bazin," where Rosen points out that Bazin "seems to embrace the idea that nineteenth-century technological, industrial, and economic developments were important conditions for the emergence of cinema; yet he finally accounts for that emergence only by vague reference to a conjunctural convergence of obsessions (scientific, industrial, economic) into the general preservative obsession. It appears that every new realization of the fundamental preservative obsession described by the mummy complex can only be explained on the basis of a circular reference to that obsession" (38).

12. In calling our relationship to data a "complex," I am borrowing from Nicholas Mirzoeff's theorization of the term, where it means "both the production of a set of social organizations and processes, such as the plantation complex, and the state of an individual's psychic economy, such as the Oedipus complex." See *Right to Look*, 5.

13. Berry, "Top 10 Countries."

14. Sverdlik, "2021."

15. McCoppin, "Who's Killing the Dewey Decimal System?"; and "Subject and Genre/Form Headings," Library of Congress.

16. Zunz, *Why the American Century?*, 186. On the formation of the new "institutional matrix," see the preface and chapter 1, "Producers, Brokers, and Users of Knowledge."

17. Gitelman, *Always Already New*, 12.

18. Critical Art Ensemble, *Digital Resistance*, 35. Rita Raley elaborates on the "data body" concept in her essay "Dataveillance and Countervailance," 121–46.

19. Cubitt, *Finite Media*, 34. Also see Clark, *Natural-Born Cyborgs*. For his part, Clark approaches this discussion with his notion of "biotechnological webs."

20. For example, Cubitt describes how humans do things that computers, at this point, cannot accomplish as effectively, "like those involving human resource management and public relations." *Finite Media*, 34.

21. Clynes and Kline refer to the "autonomic nervous systems and endocrine glands [that] cooperate in man to maintain the multiple balances required for his existence" as a kind of starting place for incorporating machinery in an augmented cyborg system where these biological systems seamlessly integrate with a machine's automatic controls. Their most concise, if dense, definition of their neologism reads as follows: "the exogenously extended organizational complex functioning as an integrated homeostatic system unconsciously." See Clynes and Kline, "Cyborgs and Space," 27. "Cyborg" is a portmanteau of "cybernetics"—a field that "attempts to find the common elements in the functioning of automatic machines and of the human nervous system"—and "organism." Laurence, "Cybernetics". Clynes and Kline applied this idea to space exploration and argued that it makes more sense for "man [to attempt] partial adaptation to space conditions, instead of insisting on carrying his whole environment along with him." Sci-fi standbys such as oxygenated domes on other planets are at best temporary solutions, and they are "dangerous" ones at that, since we would "place ourselves in the same position as a fish taking a small quantity of water along with him to live on land" (Clynes and Kline, "Cyborgs and Space," 27). Clynes and Kline's work prefigured that of Christopher Mason, the metagenomicist whose work I discuss in chapter 6, "Save File as . . . DNA." For a thorough account of the origins of cybernetics, and its relationship to various theories of information and a wide range of scholarly fields, see Kline, *The Cybernetics Moment*.

22. Clynes and Kline, "Cyborgs and Space," 27.

23. Hayles, *How We Think*, 2012.

24. Carr, *Shallows*, 232.

25. Wark, *Capital Is Dead*, 8.

26. Zuboff, *Surveillance Capitalism*, 202 (italics in the original). Zuboff also suggests that even Wark's vectoralists are in some ways subordinated to the data complex, rather than being its rulers. In chapter 5, "The Elaboration of Surveillance Capitalism: Kidnap, Corner, Compete," she discusses Google Maps and its constant tracking of users' locations, and specifically a case in which an Android phone user tries to turn off the app and that action brings up the threatening message that "basic features of your device may no longer function as intended." In Zuboff's view,

"Google's insistence reflects the authoritarian politics of the extraction imperative as well as the corporation's own enslavement to the implacable demands of its economics" (153-54). For more on the expansion of data extraction processes through the internet of things, ubiquitous computing, and "smart" cities, see pages 211-28. Also see Montaño and Vallverdú, "Hackable Bodies," on "ambient intelligence." On the potential futures of ubiquitous computing, see Webb, *The Big Nine*, chapters 5 and 6.

27. Zuboff, *Surveillance Capitalism*, 128.

28. Zuboff, *Surveillance Capitalism*, 117. For more on how surveillance capitalists aim to not only predict our behavior but intervene to manipulate and control it, see chapter 10, "Make Them Dance." Zuboff gives the name "The Big Other" to the "sensate, computational, connected puppet that renders, monitors, computes, and modifies human behavior," enabling a form of "instrumentarian power" that "reduces human experience to measurable observable behavior while remaining steadfastly indifferent to the meaning of that experience" (376-77). Zuboff also elaborates a sophisticated theory of power under surveillance capitalism and remarks that "power was once identified with the ownership of the means of production, but it is now identified with ownership of the means of behavioral modification that is Big Other" (379).

29. Zuboff, *Surveillance Capitalism*, 400.

30. Srnicek, *Platform Capitalism*.

31. "Managing a Deceased Person's Account," Facebook.

32. Parks, "Stuff," 355. I first heard Parks elaborate her theory of media infrastructures at a conference when she presented on a powerhouse panel alongside Nicholas Mirzoeff and Wendy Chun, who have also deeply influenced my thinking about technology. While all of the presentations, individually and especially in combination, pretty much rewired and frazzled my brain on the spot, it was Parks's description of her methodology that gave me a blueprint for my own work. Also especially formative for me were Mirzoeff's "Shadow and the Substance" and Chun's "Race and/as Technology." Nearly a century ago, Paul Valéry foresaw the rise of the kind of media infrastructures that Parks examines. In his essay "The Conquest of Ubiquity," Valéry writes: "Just as water, gas, and electricity are brought into our houses from far off to satisfy our needs in response to a minimal effort, so we shall be supplied with visual or auditory images, which will appear and disappear at a simple movement of the hand, hardly more than a sign. Just as we are accustomed, if not enslaved, to the various forms of energy that pour into our homes, we shall find it perfectly natural to receive the ultrarapid variations or oscillations that our sense organs gather in and integrate to form all we know. I do not know whether a philosopher has ever dreamed of a company engaged in the home delivery of Sensory Reality" (226). Walter Benjamin quotes this passage in the first part of his landmark essay "The Work of Art" (217).

33. Parks, "Stuff," 355.

34. Parks, "Stuff," 357, 370-71.

35. Parks, "Stuff," 356.

36. On the subject of the development of railroads in relation to photography and the temporal manipulations that attend preservation technology, Rebecca Solnit's book *River of Shadows* was formative for me, especially the opening chapter, "The Annihilation of Time and Space," 1–24. Also important was John Troyer's work analyzing the interwoven time-space torsions wrought by the railroad and photography in conjunction with arterial embalming, and the production of the "modern human corpse [as] an invented and manufactured consumer product through the industrialization of the dead body in mid nineteenth century America." See his "Embalmed Vision," 23. I have long admired and found inspiring Jill Jonnes's narrative style and characterization of historical figures such as Nikola Tesla, George Westinghouse, Alexander Cassatt, and others, especially in her books *Empires of Light* and *Conquering Gotham*. Brian Hochman's book *Savage Preservation* is also an important source of inspiration for my approach, especially in his media archaeological methodology, with its careful attention to the fact that "the distinctions between media forms and cultural fields that seems like second nature to us now actually made little sense to the historical subjects who were struggling to understand them at the time" (xviii). Also a significant methodological intervention in media history/archaeology is his effort to "demonstrate that ideolgoies of race and difference are absolutely necessary to the story of media history in the United States—a story we too often tell in neutral terms of research, development, and social use" (xx).

37. For more on the complexities of infrastructure and its visibility, see Lisa Parks's work on cell towers disguised as trees, where the design "draws attention to the materiality of infrastructure in the very process of trying to conceal it." Parks, "Around the Antenna Tree."

38. See Faust, *This Republic of Suffering*, 268–69.

39. Heide, *Punched-Card Systems*.

40. Hower, "Preservation of Business Records," 40.

41. While the Library of Congress already uses the term "preservation science," I am using it to refer to a broader set of preservation practices not limited to preserving paper and film-based media, photography, and sound recordings. The knowledge produced in relation to preserving leather, corpses, and taxidermic specimens, too, are a part of preservation science, not least because preservationists have historically drawn on knowledge from a wide range of fields. For an explanation of the Library of Congress's narrow definition, see the "Preservation Science" page on the Library of Congress website.

42. Hower, "Preservation of Business Records," 40.

43. Scribner, "Air Treatment," 235.

44. The printing machines themselves also worked optimally only in a small, specific temperature range, once the metal had warmed up, and so in the early morning when the machines were cold, results were inferior. In addition, the machines

cooled down at night and warmed up during use every day, and the expansion and contraction of the metal wore the machines down faster as well. See Starosielski, "Thermocultures of Geological Media," 301.

45. See Starosielski, "Thermocultures of Geological Media," 302–3.

46. Jacobs, "This Perilous Year," 930.

47. Thylstrup, *Politics of Mass Digitization*, 107–8.

48. Kate Detwiler comments on this in her essay "'Belonging': Human/Archive/World," while recounting a debate that took place within the team working on Paglen's *The Last Pictures*, about whether to include an image of the human form on the disc. Detwiler and the rest of the team decided that "it seemed equally honest to include something of ourselves as we also are: narcissistic about our humanness and our exceptionalism, archive-makers also exceptionally proud of our reflexivity about our own boundaries." See Paglen, *Last Pictures*, 22.

49. Jacobs, "Address at the Closing," 912.

50. Jacobs, "Address at the Closing," 912.

51. Willard Cope, "Oglethorpe Creator Expects to Be Present When Crypt Is Opened 6,000 Years Hence," box 10, folder: "'Crypt of Civilization'—Contents," MS1: Thornwell Jacobs Collection, Oglethorpe University Archives, Philip Weltner Library, Oglethorpe University, Atlanta, Ga. Also see Jarvis, *Time Capsules*, 149–50.

52. Peters, "Preservation of History," 211.

53. Hudson, "Archaeological Duty," 122.

54. In tracing the genealogy of backup culture further into the past, to the Cold War and beyond, I have been particularly inspired by Shane Brennan's excellent work. See his essay "Making Data Sustainable," 56–76.

55. A new medium does not simply take the place of an old medium that had been dominant up to that point. According to Bolter and Grusin, all media remediate one another, "continually commenting on, reproducing, and replacing each other." They show that "a medium in our culture can never operate in isolation" and so "must enter into relationships of respect and rivalry with other media." *Remediation*, 65. Gitelman further refines critical approaches to the newness of new media by emphasizing the social and cultural forces at play in mediation: "New media are less points of epistemic rupture than they are socially embedded sites for the ongoing negotiation of meaning as such. Comparing and contrasting new media thus stand to offer a view of negotiability in itself—a view, that is, of the contested relations of force that determine the pathways by which new media may eventually become old hat." Gitelman, *Always Already New*, 6.

56. Numerous works emphasize the materiality of the "cloud" and all manner of networked data, including Starosielski, *Undersea Network*; Hu, *Prehistory of the Cloud*; Carruth, "Digital Cloud."

57. Hogan, "Templating Life," 151. In making this point, Hogan references Steve Lohr's book *Data-Ism*.

58. Molteni, "Scientists Upload."

59. There are actually 14 million photos in the Bettmann, but around 3 million are duplicates. There are some cases where the duplicates do, when considered together, constitute an interesting artifact. Sometimes they are duplicated with different levels of contrast, or are cropped slightly.

60. Beyond paying close attention to the materiality of media technologies and data, these commitments include the exploration of the various temporalities embedded in and generated by media technologies (including the microtemporalities of computation and algorithmic platforms); resistance to traditional media historical chronologies and technological determinism; and emphasis on the value of forgotten, obsolete, imaginary, or failed technologies for the way they crystallize the forces and desires at work in a given historical moment and culture. On the microtemporalities of the digital, see Ernst, "Media Archaeography." Echoing both Hayles's work on technogenesis and Cubitt's concept of the corporate cyborg, Ernst writes that media archaeology "discovers a stratum— or matrix—in cultural sedimentation that is neither purely human nor purely technological, but literally in between (Latin *medium*, Greek *metaxy*): symbolic operations that can be performed by machines and that turn the human into a machine as well" (70).

For the most comprehensive overviews of media archaeology as a scholarly and artistic knowledge formation, see Huhtamo and Parikka, *Media Archaeology*, and Parikka, *What Is Media Archaeology?*. The most concise description of the various threads of media archaeological work appears in *What Is Media Archaeology?*, 138–40. Jussi Parikka is the most prominent media archaeologist who influences my approach in this book, though a number of other scholars, some of whom do not call themselves media archaeologists but nonetheless work in that spirit, provide crucial scaffolding for my analytical methods. Elizabeth Edwards and Janice Hart clarify the ways in which photographs are both images and objects, both visual culture and material culture circulating through archives that serve as repositories and modulators of affect. Edwards and Hart, "Introduction: Photographs as Objects."

Tung-Hui Hu's and Nicole Starosielski's work on media infrastructures, namely the cloud and undersea cables, reveal the numerous layers of historical, cultural, technological, and imaginary labor and construction necessary for the transmission of a single bit of data across landmasses and oceans. Jenny Odell's art and theorization of infrastructure also inspired some of my thinking and travels; I first learned of her work when I heard her presentation "Satellite Landscapes" at the symposium *Lines and Nodes: Infrastructure, Media and Aesthetics*, held at New York University. The presentation covered similar ground as her essay "The Satellite Collections." Other important works on which my approach is based, especially in relation to media technology, material culture, and the entanglement of mediation with actual violence, include Wakeham, *Taxidermic Signs*; and Hochman, *Savage Preservation*. On the relation of race to software, computer programming, and both analog and digital archives, the work of Wendy Hui Kyong Chun is indispensable, especially *Programmed Visions* ; "Race and/as Technology"; and her "Programmed Visions" project with *Vectors*.

61. Stein, "Mine of Information." Just as common land for grazing, crops, and coppicing had to be enclosed and made into private property in order for capitalism to establish itself, common knowledge also had to be made into a private possession. The legal category of "intellectual property" is an amazing fiction. For no sooner than Diderot had attempted to record all this common knowledge in his encyclopedia (the first of its kind), did the lawyers and rulers make it into something that they could own and profit from. See Cubitt, *Finite Media*, 161–63.

62. I found the article as a clipping in the collection of the Butler County Historical Society in Butler, Pa. Neither the article title nor the magazine title was included with the clipping, which was dated 1973.

63. Barnes and Sevon, *Geological Story*, 15–16, 19.

64. Barnes and Sevon, *Geological Story*, 15–16.

65. As Brian Massumi points out in a brilliant passage, scholars talk about "grounding" arguments as a way of stabilizing them, but ground is not as stable as the metaphor would imply: "Ground is not a static support any more than air is an empty container. The ground is full of movement, as full as the air is with weather, just at different rhythm from most perceptible movements occurring with it (flight of the arrow). Any geologist will tell you that the ground is anything but stable. It is a dynamic unity of continual folding, uplift, and subsidence." Massumi, *Parables*, 10.

66. Parikka discusses the advent of "industrialization and the triangulation of fossil fuels as energy source, technology, and wealth creation related to the new capitalist order," and suggests that "capitalism had its necessary (but not sufficient) conditions in a new relation with deep times and chemical processes of photosynthesis." He quotes Steffan, Crutzen, and McNeill, who wrote about this shift in the kinds of terms I use in my analysis: "Hitherto humankind had relied on energy captured from ongoing flows in the form of wind, water, plants, and animals, and from the 100- or 200-year stocks held in trees. Fossil fuel use offered access to carbon stored from millions of years of photosynthesis: a massive energy subsidy from the deep past to modern society, upon which a great deal of our modern wealth depends." See Parikka, *Geology of Media*, 17–18, quoting Steffan, Crutzen, and McNeill, "Anthropocene," 615. Of course, several decades before these writers, Lewis Mumford made a similar point in broader strokes, in his classic *Technics and Civilization* (1934). He wrote that the "essentials of the economic processes in relation to energy and to life" are "conversion, production, consumption, and creation." By conversion, he meant "the utilization of the environment as a source of energy," and he further asserted, "The prime fact of all economic activity, from that of the lower organisms up to the most advanced human cultures, is the conversion of the sun's energies. . . . All the permanent monuments of human culture are attempts, by using more attenuated physical means of preserving and transmitting this energy, to avert the hour of ultimate extinction" (375).

67. The old-growth forests of the Pacific Northwest "store more carbon per unit area than any other biome, anywhere on Earth." Beldin and Perakis, "Unearthing Secrets of the Forest," 1.

68. Malcolm Gladwell tells the story of the adolescent Gates's prolific programming in the essay "The 10,000-Hour Rule," from his book *Outliers*.

69. See Wilhelm Imaging Research, *Bettmann 100*; Haynes, "Under Iron Mountain"; Wilhelm et al., "High-Security, Sub-Zero Cold Storage," 122–27; Boxer, "Century's Photo History"; Battiata, "Buried Treasure," 14–30, 32, 34.

### Chapter 1

1. Thorpe, *Henry Edwards Huntington*, 502; Stillo, *Incunabula*.

2. Iiams, "Preservation," 379.

3. Iiams, "Preservation," 376.

4. Iiams, "Preservation," 377.

5. Iiams, "Preservation," 378.

6. My emphasis. For a man who worked so hard to preserve the written works of others, Iiams seems to have left behind relatively few records of his own life and work. I was unable to locate personal or professional papers of any significant amount in the digital collections and databases of the Huntington Library, nor those of Colgate University, where Iiams also worked for a number of years later in his career. "American Libraries," *Library Journal*, 475–76.

7. Cutter, "Buffalo Public Library," 213.

8. Cutter, "Buffalo Public Library," 213.

9. For the overlap of biological and moral connotations of cleanliness and purity at this time in the United States, see Amato, *Dust*, 9–10.

10. Carpenter and Augst, "History of Libraries," 63–64; Kevane and Sundstrom, "Development," 120–26.

11. Murray, *The Library*, 198.

12. "American Libraries," 475–76.

13. Porter, "Library Books and Infectious Disease," 110–11.

14. Iiams, "Preservation," 378.

15. In email correspondance with me, Holly Moore, the Lloyd E. Cotson Head of Conservation at the Huntington Library, informed me that the fumigation tank used by Iiams was manufactured by Union Tank and Pipe Company of Los Angeles.

16. Iiams, "Preservation," 381. See Weighl, "Hot-Water Bulb Sterilizers," 118; Call, "Vacuum Fumigation," 467–68. Thanks to a Holly Moore, the Lloyd E. Cotsen Head of Preservation and Conservation at the Huntington Library, for looking at the defunct tank for me and sharing the information printed on it.

17. Christianson, *Last Gasp*, 121.

18. In 1929, Dr. Francis Rowley, head of the Animal Rescue League, offered to give the city of Gloucester, Massachusetts, a lethal gas chamber to kill stray dogs. Much like proponents of the gas chamber for capital punishment purposes, Dr. Rowley argued that the gas chamber was a more humane killing technique than what was

happening at the time. Apparently, stray dogs "had been the victims of wanton pistol practice in the boiler room of the police station." Other dogs had been tied up before being used for target practice. A decade later in Chicago, a short news article, clearly meant to be humorous, detailed the case of "Red, a mongrel dog, under sentence to die next Wednesday in a lethal gas chamber for being a thief and a habitual criminal." After a rash of reports that rugs and laundry had been stolen from rear porches in the same neighborhood, policemen caught him in the act, chased him two blocks, and took him back to his master, who "disowned the dog because he was a kleptomaniac, [and] instructed the policemen to let the law take its course." That course was the director of the local pound sentencing the dog to die in the gas chamber, after "saying that the defendant was too hardened to be treated as a juvenile delinquent although he was less than three years old." See "To Execute Dog," "Dog Muzzles," "Die in Own Gas Chamber."

19. Iiams, "Preservation," 381.

20. The histories of eugenics and public health are virtually inseparable, especially in California. See Ngai, *Impossible Subjects*; Molina, *Fit to Be Citizens?*; Stern, *Eugenic Nation*; Shah, *Contagious Divides*. Also see Romo, *Ringside Seat to a Revolution*, 233–44. The racialization of insects eventually also occurs within this discourse. Russell analyzes two different images emerging from intersecting discourses of war, race, and national security. Both images showed "half-human, half-insect creatures, talked of the 'annihilation' of these vermin, and touted modern technology as the means to accomplish that end." The first appeared in 1944 in a magazine published for U.S. marines, and depicted an insect pest with caricatured slanted eyes, protruding front teeth, with the label "louseous Japanicas." The second appeared in 1945 in a journal for the National Association of Insecticide and Disinfectant Manufacturers, and showed "three creatures with insect bodies, each with a stereotypical head representing a national enemy." See Russell, "Speaking of Annihilation," 1505. For more on the discursive coproduction of racialized human difference, the human-animal divide, and the overlapping threats of human, insect, and plant immigrants to the nation, see Shinozuka, "Deadly Perils," 831–52, and her doctoral dissertation, "From a 'Contagious' to 'Poisonous Yellow Peril'?" Also see Cardozo and Subramaniam, "Assembling Asian/American Naturecultures," 1–23.

21. For more, see Shah, "Making Medical Borders at Angel Island," chapter 7 of *Contagious Divides*.

22. Raffles, "Jews, Lice, History," *Public Culture* 19:3 (2007): 521–66. Iiams's work didn't bear any racist undertones, as later preservationists' work would, but he did insert an interesting quote that highlights the racial thinking of his day, specifically how threats to white civilization would sometimes blur. After reading about the prolific reproduction of insects, he "began to wonder if there might not be some truth in the statement recently made by an eminent British scientist, in effect that 'it is not the rising tide of color or the interdestruction of the various races that threatens civilization, but rather the steady attack of the lowly insect.'" Iiams, "Preservation," 379. His article takes the tack that insects are indeed the main threat,

but to separate the three factors is a bit misleading. Within the eugenic thought that phrases like "rising tide of color" come from, insects and nonwhite humans were both unfit forms of life, fit only for destruction. The very structure of Western knowledge—the categories through which we make meaning, whether racial categories or the dividing line between human and nature—were centered around a white male as the definition of the human. Race is a key factor in shaping who counts as human, and thus what is valuable enough to preserve—this is another aspect of our preservation impulse that Bazin did not consider in his theory of the mummy complex. In his influential essay "Necropolitics," Achille Mbembe, building on the work of Michel Foucault, theorized racism compellingly as a "distribution of human species into groups, the subdivision of the population into subgroups, and the establishment of a biological caesura between the ones and the others." Racism, in Foucault's formulation, is "above all a technology aimed at permitting the exercise of biopower, 'that old sovereign right of death,' its function being to regulate the distribution of death and to make possible the murderous function of the state." Mbembe, "Necropolitics," 17, quoting Foucault, *Il faut défendre*, 57–74, 214, 218. This helps to explain the constant conflation between nature—especially insects—and dehumanized nonwhite peoples. As a corollary, genocide and extermination are often seen as the same thing by perpetrators of crimes against humanity, the target of mass murder being conceived by the perpetrator as a kind of pest or parasite on the national or collective racial body. In 1944, William Porter, the chief of the Chemical Warfare Service for the United States, stated this perspective plainly in a letter to computer pioneer Vannevar Bush: "The fundamental biological principles of poisoning Japanese, insects, rats, bacteria and cancer are essentially the same." William N. Porter to Vannevar Bush, September 30, 1944, file 710, Office of Scientific Research and Development, Miscellaneous Series, 1942–1945, Records of the Chemical Warfare Service, United States Army, cited in Russell, "Speaking of Annihilation," 1528. Also see an early version of the essay "The Question Concerning Technology" by Martin Heiddeger, delivered as a lecture in Bremen in 1949 under the title "The Framework," cited in Chun, "Race and/as Technology," 6–35; Fanon, *Wretched of the Earth*, 182; Shinozuka, "From a 'Contagious' to a 'Poisonous Yellow Peril'?" and "Deadly Perils," 831–52.

23. "Thomas M. Iiams Adjusting Controls," January 6, 1933, Getty Images, accessed October 7, 2021, https://www.gettyimages.dk/detail/news-photo/device-to-preserve-popes-books-california-is-to-be-called-news-photo/515943182.

24. According to Scott Christianson, only eleven states made use of the gas chamber as an execution method. See his book *Last Gasp*.

25. Christianson, *Last Gasp*, 16.

26. Spiro, *Defending*, 235, 244.

27. Popenoe and Johnson. *Applied Eugenics*, 185–86.

28. Holmes, "Evaluation and Preservation," 176.

29. Chandler, *Visible Hand*, 272.

30. Metcalfe, "Shop Order System of Accounts," 440–41, quoted in Chandler, *Visible Hand*, 273.

31. For more on the saga of establishing corporate personhood, see Winkler, *We the Corporations*.

32. Nora, "Between Memory and History," 13–14.

33. Heide, *Punched-Card Systems*. See especially the introduction; chapter 1, "Punched Cards and the 1890 United States Census"; and chapter 4, "The Rise of International Business Machines."

34. Garrison, *John Shaw Billings*, 343.

35. Garrison, *John Shaw Billings*, 65.

36. Garrison, *John Shaw Billings*, 228.

37. Garrison, *John Shaw Billings*, 252.

38. Billings, "Libraries in Washington," 199–200.

39. Garrison, *John Shaw Billings*, 340.

40. Heide, *Punched-Card Systems*, 22–37.

41. Bobinski, "Carnegie Libraries," 1361–67, 1361.

42. Norman, "'Library Quarterly' in the 1930s," 327–51, 328.

43. Garrison, *John Shaw Billings*, 132.

44. R. D. W. Connor wrote that "the orderly procedure of the current business of government" depends upon the preservation of "letters, orders, reports, accounts, land grants, judicial records, laws, treaties and other documents of vital importance." See "Our National Archives," 1–19. Also see Buck, "National Archives." Solon J. Buck was then director of publications for the National Archives, and was also the first chairman of the Joint Committee for Materials Research, formed by the American Library Association and the Social Science Research Council. For more on the joint committee, see Carpenter, "Toward a New Cultural Design," 283–309.

45. Kimberly and Scribner, *Summary Report*, 2. In *Double Fold*, Nicholson Baker argues that claims about wood pulp paper's impermanence were unfounded. However, there are factors he doesn't consider enough, such as the high exposure to air pollution in places like New York City and Pittsburgh, and how that produced intensified deteriorative effects on newspapers in libraries there. More importantly, the fact is that librarians and archivists did not have solid data to demonstrate that the new data format of wood pulp paper—a category that comprised a wide range of materials with varied chemical compositions—would last centuries, or even decades; this anxiety is common to new media formats, as I discuss more thoroughly in chapters 2 and 5.

46. Oliver Wendell Holmes (no relation to the nineteenth-century physician and poet) quoted the tax code of 1936 in his article "The Evaluation and Preservation of Business Archives": "Again taxes, particularly the income tax, require the keeping of records upon which the returns are based. According to the Bureau of Internal Revenue (Regulations 94 Relating to the Income Tax Under the Revenue Act of 1936, p. 175), 'every person subject to tax carrying on the business of producing,

manufacturing, purchasing, or selling any commodities or merchandise, except the business of growing and selling products of the soil, shall for the purpose of determining the amount of income which may be subject to the tax keep such permanent books of account or records, including inventories, as are necessary to establish the amount of his gross income and the deductions, credits, and other information required to be shown in an income tax return.' Very complete valuation records must be kept if deductions are to be allowed for depreciation and depletion. Again, whether or not the statute of limitations has expired, the government can, if it suspects fraud, require a company to produce records to disprove the suspicions, and, if such records have not been kept, it is the company's misfortune. The new Social Security Act will require more permanent labor records" (182).

47. See Kimberly and Scribner, *Summary Report*, 20; and Burton, "Permanence Studies," 429. Thomas Iiams's *Library Quarterly* article on gassing bookworms originated in a talk he delivered to the Large College and Reference Librarians Section of the American Library Association in April 1932. See Iiams, "Preservation," 375; Scribner, "Report of Bureau of Standards," 410. Also see Kimberly and Scribner's 1934 *Summary Report*, 20. The *New York Times* seems to have been the first American newspaper to publish a permanent edition. John Shaw Billings had suggested printing special editions of newspapers on rag paper "as early as 1906" but was more or less ignored. Lydenberg finally convinced the *New York Times* to do so beginning January 1, 1927. Dain, "Lydenberg and American Library Resources," 463n14.

48. One of the regulars in the reading room was Dewitt Wallace, cofounder of *Reader's Digest*. It was in that room that Wallace would comb through numerous magazines and pull articles, take notes on them, condense them, and compile them for the new publication he and his wife, Lila Wallace, had founded in 1922. *Reader's Digest*, as the name implies, helped its audience confront the deluge of information available in mass media publications. Wallace believed that people were overwhelmed by too much information and needed help sorting it out. He is now talked about as ahead of his time, with all kinds of monikers like "the first content curator," or the "original aggregator," his "capsulized approach . . . a harbinger of the aggregation of the digital age." Of course, Wallace was dealing with the "early information explosion," as Lars Heide calls it, a time much more like the digital age than many tend to think, so Wallace wasn't so much ahead of his time or prophetic, but rather dealing with a time much like our own, and thus taking a similar approach. The Wallaces were wildly successful, and by the 1940s, the only publication that outsold *Reader's Digest* was the Bible. In 1983, the reading room was renamed the DeWitt Wallace Periodical Room. See Apel, "Story of DeWitt Wallace"; Reader's Digest, "About *Reader's Digest*"; Lombardi, "Glory Days of *Reader's Digest*"; and New York Public Library, "About the Dewitt Wallace Periodical Room."

49. Dain, "Lydenberg and American Library Resources," 452.

50. Dain, "Lydenberg and American Library Resources," 452.

51. Metcalf, "Influential Academic and Research Librarians," 339.

52. Metcalf, "Influential Academic and Research Librarians," 340.

53. Dain, "Lydenberg and American Library Resources," 463.

54. Fisch, "Introduction," 30n9.

55. Fisch, "Introduction," 12, quoting from Lydenberg's memorial statement in *American Council of Learned Societies Bulletin.*

56. Cited in Carpenter, "Toward a New Cultural Design," 294.

57. Binkley, "Problem of Perishable Paper," 175.

58. Fisch, "Introduction," 3. For more on Binkley's life and work, see the excellent digitization project *Robert C. Binkley | 1897–1940 / Life, Work, Ideas,* carried out by his grandson, Peter Binkley, at https://www.wallandbinkley.com/rcb/index.html.

59. Dain, "Lydenberg and American Library Resources," 463, citing John Alden's introduction to Lydenberg and Archer, *The Care and Repair of Books,* and Kimberly and Scribner, *Summary Report.*

60. Joseph Amato illuminates such ironies with eloquence: "Starting in the nineteenth century, new industrial dusts (many of which were studied under microscopes) joined traditional dusts in home and street, defining much of the sight, feel, and smell of urban life. The quantity of dust increased with the hubbub of the cities. New dusts accompanied the steam engine, the locomotives, and the iron and steel industries when human beings chewed up the earth as never before. Coal and silicon dusts had a particular association with industry." *Dust,* 9–10.

61. Learned, *American Public Library,* 69–70.

62. Scribner, "Air Treatment," 233; Kimberly and Hicks, *Survey of the Storage Conditions,* 4.

63. Kimberly and Scribner, *Summary Report,* 2.

64. Scribner, "Report of Bureau of Standards," 409.

65. Scribner, "Report of Bureau of Standards," 410.

66. Kimberly and Hicks, *Survey of the Storage Conditions,* 7.

67. Kimberly and Scribner, *Summary Report,* 16.

68. Kimberly, "Deteriorative Effect of Sulphur Dioxide." The U.S. Department of Agriculture later carried out a similar study. See Jarrell Hankins, and Veitch, *Deterioration of Paper,* 1. The authors cite Kimberly's study but remark that it did not specify whether whole pages or sections of pages were used as samples. The purpose of the Department of Agriculture study was to determine to what degree pollution penetrated books, and so scientists compared deterioration at the margins of books to deterioration at the center of pages. See pp. 2–3.

69. Scribner, "Air Treatment," 233–35.

70. An early mishap at the National Archives exemplifies such a breakdown. In 1943, the construction of the Jefferson Memorial cut off the water flow from the Tiber Canal, which the archives used for its air-conditioning system. Archivists had to scramble to connect the system to the city water main. Luckily, they were able to do so relatively quickly, as they were storing the nation's nitrate film collection, which is known to combust rather easily at elevated temperatures. What is less

known about nitrate film, also called celluloid, is that it releases nitrous oxide when it is heated but doesn't burn, and the deadly vapor turns into nitric acid in the lungs. So, even if the nitrate hadn't caused a fire that burned up the National Archives' books and paper records, it could have poisoned to death any number of hapless archivists. McCoy, *National Archives*, 131.

Writing in the 1930s about nitrate film storage safety, underwater photography pioneer E. R. Fenimore Johnson stated, "There is no telling how many deaths have been due to projectionists having inhaled the fumes, because their deaths have been blamed on heart failure and various other things." See his essay "Preservation and Abuses of Motion Picture Film," 81–82.

71. See Shahani, "Preservation Research and Testing Series No. 9503"; Kantrowitz and Simmons, "Technical Status"; Kantrowitz, Spencer, and Simmons, *Permanence and Durability of Paper*; Baker, *Double Fold*. Also see *Archiving 2005*, the proceedings of the Society for Imaging Science and Technology conference, held April 26–29, 2005, in Washington, D.C.

72. "Wonders of Research."

73. NBS scientists cited one another's research reports to validate accelerated aging as a scientific research method. In *Evaluation of Motion Picture Film for Permanent Records*, J. R. Hill and C. G. Weber cited another NBS study by Royal H. Rasch and B. W. Scribner, "Comparison of Natural Aging of Paper with Accelerated Aging by Heating." The study compared paper aged "naturally" over four years and paper aged four years through "accelerated aging" by heating. Rasch and Scribner did not cite any scientific literature beyond the NBS studies to ground the validity of their study's accelerated aging methods. Hill and Weber, *Evaluation*, 1–5; Rasch and Scribner, "Comparison," 727–32.

74. While the quantification of time in the accelerated aging studies lacked rigor, the circular fashion through which the NBS produced its facts is actually deeply reflective of how scientific facts are made. According to Bruno Latour and Steve Woolgar, "The construction of a scientific fact" occurs when it "loses all temporal qualifications and becomes incorporated into a large body of knowledge drawn upon by others." A fact is perceived as "something which is simply recorded in an article and [has] neither been socially constructed nor possesses its own history of construction." See Latour and Woolgar, *Laboratory Life*, 105–6.

75. Kimberly, "Repair and Preservation of Manuscripts," 111. Also see Connor, "National Archives," 592–93. Connor was the first archivist of the United States, and Kimberly the chief of the Division of Repair and Preservation at the National Archives.

76. McCoy, *National Archives*, 76–77; Kimberly, "Repair and Preservation of Manuscripts," 111. Also see Connor, "National Archives," 592–93.

77. Kimberly, "Vital Statistics," 156.

78. Kimberly, "Vital Statistics," 155.

79. Kimberly, "Vital Statistics," 153, 158.

80. Ehrhardt, Nakayama, and O'Leary, "Carbolic Acid," 176–83.

81. Ehrhardt, Nakayama, and O'Leary, "Carbolic Acid," 177.

82. Worboys, "Joseph Lister," 199–209.

83. Arthur E. Kimberly to Hugh Bursie at the Haskelite Manufacturing Corporation, October 4, 1935; Arthur E. Kimberly to E. P. Collins at the Carbide and Carbon Chemicals Corporation, October 30, 1935; Dorsey W. Hyde and Arthur E. Kimberly, requisition request for publications issued by the Department of Agriculture, November 11, 1935; Arthur E. Kimberly to R. M. Palmer at the Ferro-Hill Corporation, November 15, 1935; Arthur E. Kimberly to Bert C. Miller at Bert C. Miller, Inc., November 18, 1935; Arthur E. Kimberly to John M. Baer at the Guardite Corporation, November 18, 1935; Arthur E. Kimberly to H. M. Lydenberg, November 22, 1935; Arthur E. Kimberly to Thomas M. Iiams, November 25, 1935; Arthur E. Kimberly to B. W. Scribner, November 27, 1935; Arthur E. Kimberly to the Richie Brothers Testing Machine Company, undated; all in box 1 P, entry 158, NAID 22927664, folder: "Division of Repair & Preservation Mr. Kimberly—Oct. 1935 to Jan. /36," Record Group 64: Records of the National Archives and Records Administration, Office of the Director of Operations: Cleaning and Rehabilitation Section: General Records, 1935-1944, National Archives, College Park, Md.

84. Arthur Kimberly to Director of Archival Services, memo, "Lunching on the Premises by Employees," December 9, 1935, box 1, folder: "Division of Repair & Preservation Mr. Kimberly—Oct. 1935 to Jan. /36," Record Group 64: Records of the National Archives and Records Administration, Office of the Director of Operations: Cleaning and Rehabilitation Section: General Records, 1935-1944, National Archives, College Park, Md.

85. For instance, in Minnesota, Moses C. Kimberly was a surveyor and engineer, and later general superintendent for the Northern Pacific railroad. See Brehm and Sutter, *Kimberlys*.

86. See Spector and Wicks, *Shared Values*, 22; Schultz, *Wisconsin's Foundations*, especially 127–29. Also see Michelson and Attig, *Laurentide Ice Sheet*.

87. Spector and Wicks, *Shared Values*, 43.

88. Spector and Wicks, *Shared Values*, 43.

89. Spector and Wicks, *Shared Values*, 37.

90. With the acquisition of Scott Paper in 1995, the company took over the production of paper towels and shop towels, and now reigns over a veritable empire of hygienic disposability. Spector and Wicks, *Shared Values*, 50–77.

91. Born in Guilford, Connecticut, where his family had a print shop, Harry Standish Kimberly had worked as a young man at another family business in New York City, the Duffner & Kimberly Company, which made "stained glass windows, bronze tablets, and Tiffany-style lamps." See Brehm and Sutter, *Kimberlys*, 64. Harry Standish Kimberly is listed as an officer in the Chemical Warfare Service in U.S. War Department, Adjutant General's Office, *Emergency Officers Army List*, 34.

92. Thorpe, *Henry Edwards Huntington*, 268–79, 446–49, 502.

93. McCoy, *National Archives*, 73.

94. McCoy, *National Archives*, 64.

95. McCoy, *National Archives*, 76. Federal records weren't the only ones in disarray. In December 1939, Mayor Fiorello LaGuardia formed a Municipal Archives Committee to "improve the city's control over its records." Members found records in 2,000 different places, in offices, "basements, attics, piers, and bridgeheads . . . in a deplorable condition." Nearly a fifth of the square footage in municipal buildings was being occupied by records, some of them "inactive" and "long since obsolete," including "130,070 square feet with an annual rental value of $200,000 occupied by old and inactive records." Horn, "Municipal Archives and Records Center," 311–20.

96. McCoy, *National Archives*, 76.

97. McCoy, *National Archives*, 76–77.

98. McCoy, *National Archives*, 38–39.

99. McCoy, *National Archives*, 94.

100. McCoy, *National Archives*, 94.

101. McCoy, *National Archives*, 99.

102. McCoy, *National Archives*, 100.

103. McCoy remarks on the unprecedented scale of the bronze doors in *National Archives*, 32. On the backlogging condition, see Jones, *Past Is a Moving Picture*, 112. Jones conceptualizes this term in relation to the film preservation movement, which she says was more focused and disciplined in what it collected during the first half of the twentieth century than during the second, where "salt mines and hard drives of moving images surely suggest the potential for knowledge and communicating with the dead, but avalanches of material may bury many of the possibilities for future contact" (127).

104. McCoy, *National Archives*, 42.

105. McCoy, *National Archives*, 3–4.

106. Lowenthal, *Past Is a Foreign Country*, 385.

107. McCoy, *National Archives*, 92.

108. McCoy, *National Archives*, 93.

109. Igo, *Known Citizen*, 61. Also see Koopman, *How We Became Our Data*, 59–64.

110. It was a relatively small group of interconnected people at the center of developing data preservation and establishing corresponding practices in major institutions. For instance, Robert Binkley is a key figure whose impact was wide within this small circle. He wrote the landmark *Manual on Methods of Reproducing Research Materials* in 1936, after six years of research funded by the Joint Committee on Materials Research, a collaboration between the Social Science Research Council and the American Council of Learned Societies. The original name of the joint committee was the Committee on Enlargement, Improvement, and Preservation of Data. The permanent secretary of the SSRC was Robert Staughton Lynd, who communicated with Lydenberg about the joint committee, and would go on to coauthor the classic study that both described and established the contours of American

typicality, *Middletown: A Study in American Culture*. Joint committee member Clark Wissler, a leading anthropologist and prominent eugenicist, would write the foreword to *Middletown* and speak at the sealing ceremony for the Westinghouse Time Capsule of Cupaloy. The joint committee also received assistance from NBS chemist B. W. Scribner, who worked alongside Kimberly, and who also served as a consultant for the Westinghouse Time Capsule. The *Methods* report was published by Edwards Brothers in Michigan. That company's director of publications was Eugene Barnum Power, who would go on to microfilm rare volumes at the British Library and intelligence documents for the Office of Strategic Services (precursor to the CIA) during World War II. He would turn Edwards Brothers into University Microfilms, precursor to data preservation giant ProQuest. Other members of the joint committee included future U.S. Archivist Solon J. Buck and the father of the field of business history, Harvard professor Norman S. B. Gras. Theodore R. Schellenberg was executive officer for the project and worked at the National Archives, as did a "disciple" of Binkley, Vernon D. Tate, who headed up the Division of Photographic Reproduction and Research. See McCoy, *National Archives*, 90; Baker, *Double Fold*, 27–28; Power, *Edition of One*; Gitelman, *Paper Knowledge*, 54, 73–74, and chapter 2, "The Typescript Book," generally; and Carpenter, "Toward a New Cultural Design," 291–93.

111. In another, related vein, Koopman traces this development from Otto Neurath's "dream of a life composed of data" to ways in which such dreams became "the working reality of cadres of data technicians of all stripes, from computer software engineers to corporate marketing analysts to government intelligence specialists to garage wizards inventing tomorrow's technological infrastructure. It became in turn the everyday actuality of us all. From one information system to the next, and across each, we are inscribed, processed, and reproduced as subjects of data, or what I call *informational persons*." *How We Became Our Data*, 3–4.

112. Trivedi and Arora, "Association of Dioxin," 20.

113. Sheets, "Kimberly-Clark Mill."

114. Hengemihle, Weberg, and Shahani, *Desorption of Residual Ethylene Oxide*, 2.

## Chapter 2

1. "Fire Horror," *New York Times*.

2. Leahy and Weil, "Will One Fire," 7–8.

3. See Schorer, *Sinclair Lewis*, 145.

4. Lewis, *Arrowsmith*.

5. The dream of total automation is an old dream, and the "modern history of liberal ideas about human freedom" is "entangled with the abolition of the transatlantic slave trade and the emergence of free labor as a racial category. A body meant for use and toil is viewed as being without a soul and endlessly exploitable. The idea that some bodies are meant solely for work informs fantasies about automation. These are the discourses of European territorial colonialism and chattel

slavery, revivified as the human (white, European, liberal, male) that now must be preserved in the face of its otherness." Atanasoski and Vora, *Surrogate Humanity*, 34.

6. Elektro is not on display at the Heinz Center, though. He has been cobbled together and put on display in a museum back in Mansfield, Ohio, where he was made. "ELEKTRO," Mansfield Memorial Museum.

7. The Lynds wanted to measure cultural change in a typical American community, and in order to make such a study feasible, they attempted to exclude racial complexity as a variable in their analysis. As it would be too difficult to simultaneously measure both "cultural change" and "racial change" in the same study, they hoped that *Middletown*, which admittedly described an overwhelmingly white community, could serve as a "base-line" for future studies that measured "racial change." Lynd and Lynd, *Middletown*, 8.

8. "Microvivarium," *Westinghouse Fair World.*

9. "Scientists" advertisement, *Life*, August 7, 1939.

10. See Marchand, *Creating the Corporate Soul*, 292. Also see chapter 6.

11. Marchand, *Creating the Corporate Soul*, 291.

12. Marchand, *Creating the Corporate Soul*, 291–93. For more on the ideas informing the design of the fair exhibits, aimed at engaging and educating the American masses about the supremacy of the American "system" of liberal democracy and free enterprise, see Bernays, *New York World's Fair*, box 69—World's Fair, folder: "Fair Publicity," George Westinghouse Museum Archives, Heinz History Center, Pittsburgh, Pa. Bernays, the nephew of Sigmund Freud, is a founding figure in public relations and the modulation of public opinion, the manufacture of consent. See Tye, *Father of Spin*. The first page of science-fiction writer Kendall Foster Crossen's futuristic novel set in the 1990s contains quotes from both Bernays and G. Edward Pendray, who went on after working at Westinghouse to establish his own public relations firm and become a significant pioneer in the field. In the story, the American masses are entirely under the control of public relations men and their propaganda, and those who see through the lies and manipulation are subjected to a lobotomy to "cure" them. The quotes from Bernays and Pendray are "engraved upon the head of a certain pin." Pendray's quote reads, "To public-relations men may go the most important social-engineering role of them all: the gradual reorganization of human society," while Bernays says similarly, "The approach to the problems encountered can be scientific—social engineering, the engineering of consent . . . or whatever term we wish to give it." Crossen, *Year of Consent*, 1.

13. See "2012 National Film Registry Picks," Library of Congress.

14. Mumford, "Sky Line in Flushing," quoted in Cogdell, *Eugenic Design*, 112.

15. "Carnegie Institution of Washington," Cold Spring Harbor Laboratory.

16. The Carnegie Station, now the Cold Spring Harbor Laboratory, is technically in Laurel Hollow right next to the hamlet Cold Spring Harbor, just across the water formation called Cold Spring Harbor, which is an extension of the Long Island Sound.

17. See the back matter of Davenport, *Trait Book*. Emphasis mine.

18. Snody, *Middleton Family*.

19. The desire to define Americanness, preserve it in paper and film records, and transmit the core values of American society, whatever those were, to the next generation was especially intense in the 1930s. Warren Susman remarks that a "key structural element" in the society of the decade was "the effort to find, characterize, and adapt to an American Way of Life as distinguished from the material achievements (and the failures) of an American industrial civilization." In Susman's view, Ruth Benedict's *Patterns of Culture* (1934) and Constance Rourke's *American Humor: A Study in National Character* and essay "The Roots of American Culture" were landmark works showing that the effort to define what is American culture, while not new, "appeared more widespread and central" in the 1930s "than in any previous time." Gallup polls, established in 1935, gave Americans an impression of their "generally shared attitudes and beliefs," while radio, used with new levels of sophistication, "helped reinforce uniform national responses" and "reinforce uniform national values and beliefs in ways no other medium had ever before been able to do." See Susman, "Culture of the Thirties," 156–59. Stott draws on Susman to describe the "revolution" constituted by the efforts to document and define Americanness under the auspices of the New Deal generally, and the Works Progress Administration specifically. See "The New Deal," chapter 6 in *Documentary Expression and Thirties America*, 92–140. For more on the significance of Gallup polls and social surveys in the making of the average or typical American in the first half of the twentieth century, see Igo, *Averaged American*. On the efforts of American anthropologists to make Americans "culture-conscious" beginning in the 1920s, see Gilkeson, *Anthropologists and the Rediscovery of America*. The first two "permanent" time capsule projects—the Crypt of Civilization and the Westinghouse Time Capsule of Cupaloy, both with target opening dates over 5,000 years in the future—embodied this desire to clearly and vividly portray the core of American history, identity, and values, and to transmit this coherent vision of Americanness to our descendants. These time capsules echoed and literalized Lewis Mumford's conceptualization of a "new permanent record," described in his classic book *Technics and Civilization* (1934), published just a couple of years before *Scientific American* published its first article on the Crypt of Civilization. Where Mumford referred to those photographic, phonographic, and cinematic media that capture and condense human culture and transmit it to future generations in a more lasting form than spoken words or crumbling stone monuments, time capsule creators meant that they could actually create media that would survive indefinitely, based on the findings of the NBS. See Mumford, *Technics and Civilization*, 242–50. For more on how the time capsules fit into the broader documentary impulse of the 1930s and the transformation of the massive mess of historical documents into streamlined archives through industrial machinery, such as fumigation tanks, see Goble, *Beautiful Circuits*, especially 225–31.

20. See Holmes, "Evaluation and Preservation"; Hower, "Preservation of Business Records"; Mellon, "Preserving Business Records for History"; Kimberly, "Vital Statistics."

21. Cady, "Machine Tool of Management."

22. "Recordak Micro-Film Records Interred in 'Time Capsule' at N.Y. World's Fair," *American Banker*, October 10, 1938, folder: "Time Capsule—Published Articles," George Westinghouse Museum Archives, Heinz History Center, Pittsburgh, Pa.

23. Entrepreneur Emmett Leahy would take the knowledge and experience he gained from his time in the National Archives and U.S. Navy to the private sector. His records management company would revolutionize corporate records storage, and he'd make a fortune in the process. In 1954, the Institute in Records Management was held in the summer—records management emerged as a distinct but related field. McCoy, *National Archives*, 64, 102.

24. Pendray, *Book of Record*, 11.

25. Pendray, *Book of Record*, 11.

27. Cogdell, *Eugenic Design*, 171.

28. Cogdell, *Eugenic Design*, 233.

29. Jarvis, "Modern Time Capsules," 281.

30. Yablon, *Remembrance of Things Present*, 241.

31. "Parcel That Won't Be Delivered"; "Preserving Our History in a Tomb," 110–13.

32. See Lye, *America's Asia*, especially chapter 1, "A Genealogy of the 'Yellow Peril': Jack London, George Kennan, and the Russo-Japanese War," 12–46. Pendray's novel is an example of how the "yellow peril," as Lye explains, "articulates the numerical power of a 'Chinese' mass with a miraculous 'Japanese' developmental capacity" (17).

33. Edwards [Pendray], *Earth-Tube*, 24.

34. Pendray, "Crucible of Change," 347.

35. E. J. Michelson to C. P. Johnson, July 19, 1939, Westinghouse Electric Corporation Records, MSS box 70, folder 7: "Exhibitions—Worlds Fairs—1939, New York (1938–1939)," Westinghouse Electric Corporation Archives, Heinz History Center, Pittsburgh, Pa.

36. "Train of the Future," Metropolitan Transit Authority.

37. See Fant, *Alfred Nobel: A Biography*, 57, 232.

38. Pendray, *Book of Record*, 45–49.

39. Milkman, *L.A. Story*, 30–31, quoting Davis, "Sunshine and the Open Shop," 356–82, 376.

40. Foster, "Desegregation of Pasadena Schools."

41. Rydell, *World of Fairs*, 39.

42. Rydell, *World of Fairs*, 56. According to a *New York Times* article, lodging in FHA homes was meant to advertise the low-cost, state-subsidized housing program.

43. See "Typical Families"; Lipsitz, *Possessive Investment*, 74–75.

44. "Questionnaire," *Biblion: World's Fair.*

45. "Typical Families."

46. Baldwin, "Introduction," 6, 12.

47. Lipsitz, *Possessive Investment,* 5.

48. Bonnie Yochelson, "Selling the World of Tomorrow: Section Labels" (unpublished script for an exhibition at the Museum of the City of New York), cited in Rydell, *World of Fairs,* 58.

49. Mary Douglas, *Purity and Danger,* cited in Amato, *Dust,* 21–22.

50. Amato, *Dust,* 117.

51. Pendray, "Crucible of Change," 346.

52. Cartwright and Bradshaw, "Strikes," 277–78.

53. Dreyfuss, quoted in Cogdell, *Eugenic Design,* 172–73. Dreyfuss was fastidious to the end, even when he and his wife killed themselves together by carbon monoxide poisoning in their South Pasadena home. When they closed the carriage house doors and started the car, turning the structure into a gas chamber, not three miles from the Huntington Library and its own gas chamber, he was wearing a tuxedo and she a floor-length evening gown, toasting their marriage with champagne as they sat in their car and faded away (she had been recently diagnosed with terminal cancer). According to the *New York Times* obituary, Dreyfuss was quite organized about the whole affair—he left one note instructing their maid to call the doctor when she arrived at the house, and another that "held the key to the carriage house and instructions to enter." "Henry Dreyfuss, Noted Designer."

54. On the gendering of labor in the fight against dust, Amato writes that while "the public conquest of dust involved all of society and its new technologies, the battle against domestic dust was fought in the household trenches. . . . Women became the guardians of an order that men, occupied with the affairs of street and work, cared little for or took for granted." See Amato, *Dust,* 10–11.

55. Betty Mathis, "Crypt-Sealing Ceremony Set for Saturday," 1940, box 1, folder 5, Jacobs' Diary Pages, Thornwell Jacobs Collection, MF 73, Oglethorpe University Archives, Philip Weltner Library, Oglethorpe University, Atlanta, Ga.

56. Pendray, "Oglethorpe University Builds a Crypt." As Melvin Jarvis points out, no author is listed on the short clip, but Peters attributes it to Pendray in *Story of the Crypt.* See Jarvis, "Modern Time Capsules," 294n13.

57. Peters, "Preservation of History."

58. For more on metal records and the way early twentieth-century preservationists sought to assuage anxieties about the durability of new data formats by also preserving data in ancient formats, see Yablon, *Remembrance of Things Present,* 219–30. Yablon discusses the use of "ancient," "modern," and "hybrid" artifacts and illuminates how preservationists at the time "questioned the wisdom of relying on any single medium, whether ancient, modern, or hybrid" (223).

59. Peters, "Preservation of History," 208.

60. "Vaporate Film Treatment," 11.

61. Bennett, "100 Years on Peachtree."

62. Jacobs's novel *The Law of the White Circle* was reissued by the University of Georgia Press in 2006, with a foreword by historian W. Fitzhugh Brundage, and described as "the only novel set during the infamous Atlanta race riot of 1906." Not surprisingly, considering Jacobs's preoccupations and the state of American literature and culture of the time, the story features a doomed love triangle between "a white journalist, a black college professor, and the woman they both love—an artist of mixed race who chooses to pass as white."

63. Jacobs, "Greetings to the Inhabitants," 910.

64. Jacobs, "Prophet on Parnassus," 1077-78.

65. Hoffman, "When Pictures Came to Life," 223.

66. Undated clipping, box 2, folder: "Miscellany. Clippings, 1897-1973 + undated," Thomas Kimmwood Peters Papers, Library of Congress, Manuscript Division, Washington, D.C. For more on Peters's film career, especially his international experiences, see Fielding, "Hale's Tours," 44-46.

67. A comprehensive list of books preserved in the crypt exists only, as far as I know, in the Oglethorpe University Archives.

68. Hoffman, "When Pictures Came to Life," 184.

69. Mathis, "Crypt-Sealing Ceremony Set for Saturday."

70. Willard Cope, "Oglethorpe Creator Expects to Be Present When Crypt Is Opened 6,000 Years Hence," box 10, folder: "'Crypt of Civilization'—Contents," MS1: Thornwell Jacobs Collection, Oglethorpe University Archives, Philip Weltner Library, Oglethorpe University, Atlanta, Ga.

71. Thornwell Jacobs to G. Edward Pendray, September 12, 1938, box 70, folder: "Crypt of Civilization—Oglethorpe University," George Westinghouse Museum Collection, Heinz History Center, Pittsburgh, Pa.

72. John K. Boeing to G. Edward Pendray, October 27, 1938, box 70: "1938 Time Capsule," Folder: "Time Capsule—Packing and Sealing of Capsule," George Westinghouse Museum Archives, Heinz History Center, Pittsburgh, Pa.

73. Jacobs to Pendray, September 12, 1938.

74. Olegario, *Engine of Enterprise*, 122.

75. A. Scott Berg details the correspondence and collaborative work relationship between Fitzgerald and Perkins in his wonderful book *Max Perkins: Editor of Genius*. On their deliberations over the title, see chapter 5, "A New House."

76. Fitzgerald, *Great Gatsby*, 16.

77. Lankevich, *New York City*, 177. Robert A. Caro also describes the monumental process of cleaning up the dumping ground in his classic biography *Power Broker*, 1082-85.

78. I also didn't understand the course of the conversation earlier in the novel, as Tom rambles on about a new book he's just read on eugenics—*The Rise of Colored Empires* by a man named "Goddard." It's clearly a play on Lothrop Stoddard's *The Rising Tide of Color against White World Supremacy*, a huge hit that Fitzgerald

would have no doubt been aware of as he wrote *Gatsby*—the two books were both published by Scribner. Tom paraphrases the book to explain how "civilization's going to pieces," and how "if we don't look out the white race will be—will be utterly submerged. It's all scientific stuff; it's been proved" (11). I didn't understand his rant because we never learned in school about the American roots of the eugenics movement, and certainly not about the history of forced sterilization in the United States, and so I didn't understand why Daisy's friend Miss Baker chimes in with "You ought to live in California." But now I understand.

## Chapter 3

1. One could trace the story of preservation even further back through Tudor: in 1791, his father, William Tudor, was one of the ten founding members of the first historical society in the United States, the Massachusetts Historical Society. See William Tudor to Delia Jarvis, December 24, 1776, Tudor Family Papers, Massachusetts Historical Society, Boston, https://www.masshist.org/database/519.

2. Thoreau, *Walden*, 169.

3. Harris and Pickman, "Towards an Archaeology," 51.

4. Calandro, "Hudson River Valley Icehouses," 20.

5. Harris and Pickman, "Towards an Archaeology," 51.

6. See Rinaldi and Yasinac, *Hudson Valley Ruins*.

7. Germain, "Abandoned Iron Ore Mine."

8. See Wharton, "Safest Place in the World," and Mitchell, "Kingston Cave."

9. Rothman, "Many Lives of Iron Mountain."

10. "Bombproof Caveman."

11. Wharton, "Safest Place in the World," 140.

12. Potter, "Herman Knaust."

13. Wharton, "Safest Place in the World," 138.

14. Yablon makes the interesting point that "as a combination of an ancient material with a modern invention (twisted steel rods), reinforced concrete was itself a hybrid medium analogous to those the [Modern Historic Records Association] was proposing." *Remembrance of Things Present*, 228.

15. Wharton, "Safest Place in the World," 150.

16. A 1956 UNESCO report, *Protection of Cultural Property in the Event of Armed Conflict*, called IMASC "an excellent general example of large-scale, rational organization," and illustrated the way in which IMASC's design and operation conformed to emergent discourses of data preservation and securitization. Noblecourt, *Protection of Cultural Property*, 270.

17. Rose, *One Nation Underground*, 120. Rose's text actually says the door weighed 16,000 tons, quoting a 1960 *New York Times* article. No bank door has ever weighed that much. The same error occurs in the *New York Times* article, so it's safe (get it, *safe*?) to assume that the vault door weighed 16,000 pounds, which equates to eight tons. See Fenton, "Underground Unit."

18. Spencer, "Rise of Shadow Libraries," 159–60.

19. See Rose, *One Nation Underground*, 120. Rose cites various news articles from the 1950s.

20. International News Service, "A-Bombproof . . . for Art Riches!" (photo caption), February 28, 1952, folder "10BVA Photos—Vaults, Safes, Treasure Chests, Safe-Deposit Boxes, Money," Bettmann Archive, Corbis Film Preservation Facility, Iron Mountain, Boyers, Pa.

21. For a history of the early uses of microfilm or microphotography in the mid-nineteenth century, see Luther, *Microfilm*. On the development of a micro-filming program at the National Archives and the leading role of Vernon D. Tate, see McCoy, *National Archives*, 90–91; also Parmater, *Communication Revolutions*; Raney, *Microphotography for Libraries*; chapter 2, "The Typescript Book," in Gitel-man, *Paper Knowledge*. For more on the transition to microfilming from the 1930s to the 1940s in the context of information technology development, see Tate, "From Binkley to Bush," 249–57. For more on the origins of University Microfilms, pioneers of microfilm preservation and publishing, see Eugene Barnum Power's autobiog-raphy, *Edition of One*. For more on the invention of the Check-o-graph machine used to microfilm bank records and the subsequent formation of the Recordak cor-poration by inventor George McCarthy and Eastman Kodak, see "Service Quality," chapter 2 in Germain, *Dollars through the Doors*.

22. Ford Motor Company, "Microfilm Safeguards Vital Records," 85–86.

23. Ford Motor Company, "Microfilm Safeguards Vital Records," 85.

24. Ford Motor Company, "Microfilm Safeguards Vital Records," 85.

25. Critical Art Ensemble, *Digital Resistance*, 35. Rita Raley borrows and further develops the concept of the "data body" in her essay "Dataveillance and Counter-vailance," 121–46.

26. Pike, "Dugway Proving Grounds."

27. Yergin, "Blood and Oil."

28. Standard Oil, *Design and Construction*, section II. Images in the text appear on pages that are not paginated.

29. Davis, "Berlin's Skeleton," 98.

30. Wilkins, "Art Directing."

31. "Bomb-proof Quarters of Major Strong, at Dutch Gap, Va., July. United States Virginia, 1864" (photograph), Library of Congress, Prints and Photographs Division, Washington, D.C., accessed September 10, 2021, https://www.loc.gov/item/2011649188/.

32. Even in the twenty-first century, this cycle of increasingly powerful weap-ons and bombproofing fantasies continues, with more bunkers followed by more bunker-busting bombs. A 2005 National Research Council report on "earth-penetrator nuclear weapons" (EPW)—bombs that break the earth's surface before detonating underground—states that the "greatest uncertainty in predicting EPW depth of penetration and structural survival of the weapon until detonation is due

to the inherently heterogeneous nature of earth materials." See National Research Council, "Effects of Nuclear Earth-Penetrator," chapter 3, page 3.

33. Yergin, *Prize*, 352.

34. Plung, "Japanese Village at Dugway," 6. Also see Davis, "Berlin's Skeleton in Utah's Closet," *Grand Street* (Summer 1999): 92–100.

35. Ripley County, Indiana, Historical Society, "St. Magdelene Catholic Church."

36. See Human Rights Watch, "Myths and Realities." Also see Chong, *Girl in the Picture*, 93–95.

37. In the 1930s, "inflammable" was a more commonly used synonym for "flammable." Standard Oil, *Design and Construction*, 13.

38. Standard Oil, *Design and Construction*, 13.

39. Morris, *Fog of War*.

40. Rhodes, *Making of the Atomic Bomb*, 473.

41. Rhodes, *Making of the Atomic Bomb*, 474.

42. Galison, "War against the Center," 12–20.

43. Galison, "War against the Center," 20. While Galison's analysis is very compelling and convincingly traces the legacy of World War II bombing surveys on the transformation of American infrastructure, Tom Vanderbilt places this development in broader historical context by describing how aerial views have always been attended by militarized visions of destruction, afforded by the masterful vantage point from above a city. Vanderbilt traces something like a genealogy of bombsight mirroring and seeing cities as targets further back, to the very first aerial views—the hot air balloon flights in Europe in the early 1800s. "As the means of comprehending the city as a whole improved, so too did the means for wholly destroying it. It is perhaps no surprise that the ability to visualize the Earth in a single image coincided with the presumed ability to destroy the Earth with one massive unleashing of weapons, or that both accomplishments were byproducts of the same endeavor." Vanderbilt, *Survival City*, 50.

44. Galison, "War against the Center," 14–17.

45. Galison, "War against the Center," 17, 20.

46. Galison, "War against the Center," 30.

47. In 1957, the NRMC became Naremco Services, a management consultancy that still exists today. "About Us," Naremco. For more on the early work of the NRMC, see Horn, "Municipal Archives and Records," 311–320; Brichford, "Relationship of Records Management," 221, 227; United States of America Operations Mission to Israel, *Records Management Program*; National Records Management Council, *Target: Red Tape*; and National Records Management Council, *Your Business Records*.

48. Leahy and Weil, "Will One Fire," 38; Ward, "Records Protection," 26.

49. Barcan, "Records Management," 218.

50. The term "Battle of the Bulk" recalls the Battle of the Bulge, a battle in World War II with an exceptionally high casualty rate for U.S. forces. For more on the great backlog of corporate and state records, even in the 1930s, see Leahy,

"Reduction of Public Records," 13–38, as well as Goble, *Beautiful Circuits*, especially 229–37.

51. Shiff, "Archivist's Role in Records Management," 119; Barcan, "Records Management," 225–26.

52. Named Operation Teapot, the bomb tests took place at the Nevada Test Site, with staff on-site representing a variety of interests, including Western Union Telegraph Company, Sperry Gyroscope Company, Mosler Safe Company, and the National Records Management Council, with cooperating organizations including Diebold, Mellink Steel Safe Company, Remington Rand Division of Sperry Rand Corporation, and The General Fireproofing Company. National Records Management Council, *Effects of a Nuclear Explosion*, 7–8.

53. National Records Management Council, *Effects of a Nuclear Explosion*, 5.

54. National Records Management Council, *Effects of a Nuclear Explosion*, 13.

55. Vanderbilt, *Survival City*, 80.

56. Cohen and Laing, *Operation Plumbbob Preliminary Report*, 21, 29.

57. Graff, *Raven Rock*, 43–44. Also see "Hydrogen Bomb—1950," Atomic Heritage Foundation.

58. Graff, *Raven Rock*, 58.

59. Igo, *Known Citizen*, 92–93. An August 1939 Dorothea Lange photo, taken while she was employed by the Farm Security Administration, shows a shirtless "unemployed lumber worker" with his social security number tattooed on his arm. The photo is the cover image of Dan Bouk's book *How Our Days Became Numbered*. Bouk performs a close reading of the photo in his conclusion, "Numbering in Layers," 209–36.

60. The Middleton family type continued to be deployed in the postwar period. For more, see Marchand, *Creating the Corporate Soul*, 326, 359.

61. Auerbach and Gitelman, "Microfilm, Containment, and the Cold War," 745–68, 750.

62. The Pumpkin Papers affair of 1948 brought microfilm into public awareness in a dramatic way when Whittaker Chambers accused Alger Hiss of espionage, a case in which the House for Unamerican Activities Committee took interest. See Auerbach and Gitelman, "Microfilm, Containment, and the Cold War," 745–51.

63. Auerbach and Gitelman, "Microfilm, Containment, and the Cold War," 750.

64. Auerbach and Gitelman, "Microfilm, Containment, and the Cold War," 763.

65. See "Mighty Midgets of Filmdom," 72–76, 168–69.

66. See caption for the Operation Cue photo.

67. Tunc, "Eating in Survival Town," 180.

68. Leahy and Weil, "Will One Fire," 7–8.

69. Pederson, *International Directory of Company Histories*, 389–91.

70. See "Mannequins Visit Judge" and "To Atomize Clothing." Graphic designer and artist Rachele Riley posted these archival clippings to her excellent blog during the course of her project related to the L.A. Darling mannequins used in the bomb

test. See the posts "Researching the L.A. Darling Co.," September 6, 2012; "Subject of My Archival Research," January 7, 2013; and "Update on the 'Annie,'" January 8, 2013.

71. Masco, *Theater of Operations*, 57–60.

72. Riley, "Update on the 'Annie.'"

73. Donna Haraway goes even further to say that in the Akeley African Hall of the American Museum of Natural History (AMNH), the moment the viewer of taxidermy experiences, in this case in a diorama, is a return to a kind of original moment of encounter between animal and human. Haraway illuminates the swirl of mythologies activated in these taxidermic displays: "Each diorama has at least one animal that catches the viewer's gaze and holds it in communion. The animal is vigilant, ready to sound an alarm at the intrusion of man, but ready also to hold forever the gaze of meeting, the moment of truth, the original encounter. The moment seems fragile, the animals about to disappear, the communion about to break; the Hall threatens to dissolve into the chaos of the Age of Man. But it does not. The gaze holds, and the wary animal heals those who will look. . . . There is no mediation, nothing between the viewer and the animal. The glass front of the diorama forbids the body's entry, but the gaze invites his visual penetration. The animal is frozen in a moment of supreme life, and man is transfixed. No merely living organism could accomplish this act. The specular commerce between man and animal at the interface of two evolutionary ages is completed. The animals in the dioramas have transcended mortal life, and hold their pose forever, with muscles tensed, noses aquiver, veins in the face and delicate ankles and folds in the supple skin all prominent. No visitor to a merely physical Africa could see these animals. This is a spiritual vision made possible only by their death and literal re-presentation. Only then could the essence of their life be present. Only then could the hygiene of nature cure the sick vision of civilized man. Taxidermy fulfills the fatal desire to represent, to be whole; it is a politics of reproduction." Haraway, "Teddy Bear Patriarchy," 25. For more on taxidermy and its relationship to photography, cinema, and race, especially on the materiality and violence of its representations, see Wakeham, *Taxidermic Signs*. Hiroshi Sugimoto's series of photographs *Dioramas*, taken in the AMNH, also meddles in the mythological space Haraway charts, as the photographs make the taxidermic animals seem alive, the borders of the diorama cut out of the frame, but defamiliarizing both reality and representation at the same time.

74. The civil defense film *Operation Cue* (1955), with its female narrator who aims to see the test through "[her] own eyes and the eyes of the average citizen," is a kind of update of *The Middleton Family* film. As Masco explains, these bomb tests "documenting the effects of the bomb on every aspect of white, middle-class, suburban life," along with their accompanying media strategy, worked to "recalibrat[e] domestic life by turning the nuclear family into a nuclearized family, pre-programmed for life before, during, and after a nuclear war. Gender roles were reinforced by dividing responsibility for food and security in a time of nuclear crisis

between women and men. . . . Normative gender roles were used to reinforce the idea that nuclear crisis was not an exceptional condition, but one that could be incorporated into everyday life with minor changes in household technique and a 'can do' American spirit." Citizens were to focus on "emotional self-discipline" as a part of an overall program that aimed to "nationalize nuclear fear and install a new civic understanding via the contemplation of mass destruction and collective death." Operation Cue asked citizens "to live on the knife's edge of a psychotic contradiction—an everyday life founded simultaneously on total threat and absolute normality—with the stakes being nothing less than survival itself." Masco, *Theater of Operations*, 58–60.

75. Colla, *Conflicted Antiquities*, 28–29, 188, 224.

76. Masco elaborates the way civil defense engineered the collective response of anxiety and not panic in his illuminating book, *Theater of Operations*.

77. Masco, "Sensitive but Unclassified," 433–63, 445.

78. Masco, "Sensitive but Unclassified," 445.

79. Historically, some tableaux vivants had mannequins, and some had actors holding still. In some, the figures would move and come alive.

80. United Press International, "Rescue Street" (photograph), August 28, 1952, folder "4 CIC-1 Civil Defense, Post WWII—Drills, Shelters," Bettmann Archive, Corbis Film Preservation Facility, Iron Mountain, Boyers, Pa.

81. Masco, *Theater of Operations*, 45–46.

82. In "Posterity and Paradox," Brian Durrans makes this point in his discussion of what led to the shift to modern time capsules in the 1930s, remarking that after World War I, the "Victorian optimism" that had assumed inevitable and limitless progress was largely replaced by a pervasive sense of uncertainty. Eugenicists certainly sounded the alarm, too, as Lothrop Stoddard did in his eugenical classic *The Rising Tide of Color against White World-Supremacy* (1920): "To me the Great War was from the first the White Civil War. . . . The frightful weakening of the white world during the war . . . opened up revolutionary, even cataclysmic, possibilities." While the white world was more vulnerable to being subjugated by "colored armies," Stoddard stated, "Such colored triumphs of arms are less to be dreaded than more enduring conquests like migrations which would swamp whole populations and turn countries now white into colored man's lands irretrievably lost to the white world. Of course, these ominous possibilities existed even before 1914, but the war has rendered them much more probable" (vi). Stoddard situated his racist fears within the frame of the grander, less overtly racist rhetoric of French poet Paul Valéry, quoting the first two full paragraphs from his essay "The Spiritual Crisis of France" (1919):

> We civilizations now know that we are mortal. We had heard tell of whole worlds vanished, of empires gone to the bottom with all their engines; sunk to the inexplorable bottom of the centuries with their gods and their laws, their academies, their science, pure and applied; their grammars, their dictionaries,

their classics, their romantics and their symbolists, their critics and their critics' critics. We knew well that all the apparent earth is made of ashes, and that ashes have a meaning. We perceived, through the mists of history, phantoms and huge ships laden with spiritual things. We could not count them. But these wrecks, after all, were no concern of ours.

Elam, Nineveh, Babylon were vague and lovely names, and the total ruin of these worlds meant as little to us as their very existence. But France, England, Russia—these would also be lovely names. Lusitania also is a lovely name. And now we see that the abyss of history is large enough for everyone. *We feel that a civilization is as fragile as a life.* Circumstances which would send the works of Baudelaire and Keats to rejoin the works of Menander are no longer in the least inconceivable; they are in all the newspapers. Valéry, "Spiritual Crisis," 365, quoted in Stoddard, *Rising Tide*, 193–94.

83. International News Service, "Child Cries as Civilians Are Interned by an Aggressor Force" (photograph), April 5, 1952, folder: "04CIC-2 ARMAMENT—Civil Defense—Uniform, Protective Clothes, Misc. Post-war," Bettmann Archive, Corbis Film Preservation Facility, Iron Mountain, Boyers, Pa.

84. Hlavaty, "Texas' Lost 'Communist Invasion.'"

85. ACME, "Kick-Off for Civil Defense" (photo), January 13, 1951, folder: "04CIC-2 ARMAMENT—Civil Defense—Uniform, Protective Clothes, Misc. Post-war," Bettmann Archive, Corbis Film Preservation Facility, Iron Mountain, Boyers, Pa.

86. Rose, *One Nation Underground*, 133.

87. Rose, *One Nation Underground*, 38.

88. International News Service, "It Could Happen Here" (photograph), folder: "04CIC-2 ARMAMENT—Civil Defense—Uniform, Protective Clothes, Misc. Post-war," Bettmann Archive, Corbis Film Preservation Facility, Iron Mountain, Boyers, Pa.

89. Monteyne, *Fallout Shelter*, 6.

90. Monteyne, *Fallout Shelter*, 7.

91. Monteyne, *Fallout Shelter*, 12.

92. Monteyne, *Fallout Shelter*, 2.

93. McCarten and Dobell. "A Place to Hide," 20. Bronxville, mentioned in the fake news page discussed earlier, is located in Westchester County, and it is the site on which thousands of refugees from the bombed-out urban center of New York City descend.

94. The Leglers' economic and cultural elite status is evident in news articles on the engagement and wedding of Sandra Legler, pictured in the image "One Man's Preparation for Atomic War." She was "introduced to New York society at the Debutante Cotillion and The Christmas Ball," and she attended the prestigious Brearley School and Wellesley College, while her future husband, Stuart Gordon Tucker, was a graduate of the Brooks School and Yale University, and a research engineer for IBM in Poughkeepsie. "Sandra Legler."

95. Monteyne, *Fallout Shelter*, xiv.

96. Monteyne, *Fallout Shelter*, xvii.

97. In his 1961 book *The City in History*, Lewis Mumford critiqued the prospect of living underground and anticipated my description of bunker life as an "encapsulation": "Unfortunately, the underground city demands the constant attendance of living men, also kept underground; and that imposition is hardly less than a premature burial, or at least preparation for the encapsulated existence that alone will remain open to those who accept mechanical improvement as the chief justification of the human adventure." Mumford, *City in History*, 572, quoted in Monteyne, *Fallout Shelter*, 101.

98. United Press International, "Get the Feel of Fall-Out Shelter" (photograph), February 1, 1960, folder: "4 CIC-1 Civil Defense, Post WWII—Drills," Bettmann Archive, Corbis Film Preservation Facility, Iron Mountain, Boyers, Pa.

99. United Press International, "Make Themselves at Home" (photograph), November 2, 1960, folder: "4 CIC-1 Civil Defense, Post WWII—Drills," Bettmann Archive, Corbis Film Preservation Facility, Iron Mountain, Boyers, Pa.

100. Even some of the best-equipped shelters, such as the one created for President Harry Truman at the White House, had a "chemical toilet." Graff, *Raven Rock*, 29. In "Are Shelters the Answer?," which appeared in the *New York Times Magazine* in November 1961, the influential anthropologist Margaret Mead wrote acerbically about the creation of the American suburbs, their origin in a desire to flee the racial and class "contamination" represented by urban centers, and the way in which securitization follows logically from this retreat: "Drawn back in space and in time, hiding from the future and the rest of the world, they turned to the green suburbs, protected by zoning laws against members of other classes or races or religions, and concentrated on the tight, little family. They idealized the life of each such family living along in self-sufficient togetherness, protecting its members against the contamination of different ways or others' needs. . . . The armed, individual shelter is the logical end of this retreat from trust in and responsibility for others."

101. U.S. Department of Energy, Nevada Operations Office, *United States Nuclear Tests*.

102. Founded by former National Records Management Council director Emmett Leahy in 1948, the firm that began as Leahy & Company billed itself as "North America's Filing Cabinet." Initially, the company only worked on a consulting basis, for local governments, and for corporations like Eastern Airlines, DuPont, Bethlehem Steel, and ALCOA. In 1951, Leahy founded Leahy Business Archives and offered records storage services. Gale Group, "Pierce Leahy Corporation."

103. News outlets consistently framed 9/11 as the first attack on American soil since Pearl Harbor, but failed to recall that Hawaii was not yet a state on January 7, 1941. Then known as the Territory of Hawaii, the island chain was a contested outpost of American empire. The U.S. military and a band of conspirators on the islands overthrew the legitimate monarch, Queen Lydia Kamakaeha Liliukalani, in 1893.

This act was so egregious that even sitting president Grover Cleveland denounced it in a letter to Congress, calling it "a substantial wrong" and recommending that the monarchy be reinstated, but Congress rejected his proposal. See Cleaver, *Grover Cleveland's New Foreign Policy*, 52. Hawaii did not become the fiftieth state until 1959. The U.S. Congress issued an "apology to Native Hawaiians on behalf of the United States for the overthrow of the Kingdom of Hawaii" on January 5, 1993. See U.S. Congress, "Joint Resolution to Acknowledge the 100th Anniversary."

104. McInerney, "Brightness Falls."

105. Dwyer, "Nation Challenged."

106. Hesseldahl, "How to Preserve Photos."

107. Hesseldahl, "How to Preserve Photos."

108. Wolfgang Ernst offers a compelling conceptualization of how digital technology and the internet shift the ontology of data: "Although the traditional archive used to be a rather static memory, the notion of the archive in Internet communication tends to move the archive toward an economy of circulation: permanent transformations and updating. The so-called cyberspace is not primarily about memory as cultural record but rather about a performative form of memory as communication." Ernst, "Archives in Transition," 99.

## Chapter 4

1. See National Archives and Records Administration, *Archives II*.

2. The official name of the torpedo factory was the Naval Torpedo Station. It is now, unsurprisingly, an art center. "Torpedo Factory," Library of Congress.

3. "History of the National Archives," National Archives and Records Administration; "General Services Administration Evaluation of the 1958 Operation Alert Exercise," box 1 P, entry 120, folder: "Operation Alert 1958," Record Group 64: Records of the National Archives and Records Administration, Office of the Archivist: Records Relating to Emergency Operations Exercises, 1955–1962, Operation Alert 1955—Operation Alert 1961, National Archives, College Park, Md.

4. Allied Translator and Interpreter Section, South West Pacific Area, *Restoration of Captured Documents*; Bradsher, "National Archives' Arthur Evarts Kimberly." Though no author is listed on *Restoration of Captured Documents*, Bradsher, a senior archivist at the National Archives in College Park, affirms that Kimberly was the book's coauthor.

5. Bradsher, "National Archives' Arthur Evarts Kimberly."

6. See Bradsher, "National Archives' Arthur Evarts Kimberly."

7. Eales, "Fort Archives."

8. "Photograph of Archival Intern from Cuba," Series: Public Relations Photographs Relating to National Archives Personnel, Facilities, and Events, 1939–1968, Record Group 64: Records of the National Archives and Records Administration, 1789–ca. 2007, National Archives, College Park, Md., https://catalog.archives.gov/id/74228847.

9. Maness, "Civil Defense: Mock 'Alert.'"

10. "General Services Administration Evaluation," 10.

11. "General Services Administration Evaluation," 1.

12. Graff, *Raven Rock*, 55.

13. Miller, *Under the Cloud,* 58–59.

14. Miller, *Under the Cloud*, 90.

15. "General Services Administration Evaluation," 10.

16. See Graff, *Raven Rock*, xix, 383–84. Graff points out, importantly, that "'martial law' has no specific constitutional definition; instead, it's an informal set of powers cobbled together through existing law and emergency executive authorities" (383). Conaty further details the complexities of how "martial law" might have played out in a postnuclear attack situation during the Cold War, as well as the range of forms it could take in relation to the suspension of habeas corpus and other vital concerns. See Conaty, "Atomic Midwife," especially 665–70.

17. Conaty, "Atomic Midwife," 684.

18. In *Saving Cinema*, Caroline Frick illuminates how preservation as a discourse naturalizes the preservative impulse of the data complex and thereby obscures the human choices that led to archives of various kinds being created in the first place. Frick writes, "Viewing preservation as discourse or as structured practice, rather than as the natural, logical way of incorporating historical moving images into contemporary life, scholars and practitioners can observe how film heritage has been constructed and invoked at particular times, for specific reasons, and by particular individuals." Writing in the context of national film heritage, she notes that "prioritizing the preservation of, rather than the promotion of public access to, global film heritage 'treasures' remains the foundation of contemporary motion picture archival practice and training. But the centrality of preservation in the film archiving profession was a choice made by specific individuals and institutions within a very particular socioeconomic, legal, and political context, a context that gave rise to the heritage phenomenon" (18–19).

19. According to Graff, Eisenhower once told a group of his advisors that if a nuclear war with the Soviet Union occurred, "you might as well go out and shoot everyone you see and shoot yourself." *Raven Rock*, 67.

20. Gup, "Doomsday Blueprints."

21. Gup, "Doomsday Blueprints."

22. Oakes, *Imaginary War*, 86. From the beginning, the exercise and its delusional premise was met with resistance from radical pacifists and others, some seasoned activists, some not. In 1955, during the first Operation Alert drill in New York City, Catholic anarchist Dorothy Day refused to take shelter and was arrested; civil rights movement organizer Bayard Rustin ate lunch with other protesters in a church while the sirens sounded. By the penultimate iteration in 1960, thousands of people, including hundreds of college and high school students, not to mention roughly 500 mothers and their children, refused to take shelter during the fake attack. For more on Operation Alert see the rest of chapter 3, "The Cold War

Conception of Nuclear Reality," in Oakes, *Imaginary War*, 78–104; Schlosser, "Nuns and Nuclear Security"; Garrison, *Bracing for Armageddon*, 70–103.

23. Graff, *Raven Rock*, xvii.

24. These federal relocation centers—the ones that are known—were located in Pennsylvania, Virginia, West Virginia, and North Carolina. Conte, *History of the Greenbrier*, 194.

25. Beyond Robert S. Conte's history of the Greenbrier, I draw much information on the Bunker from my guided tour of the resort, as well as souvenirs I received as a part of the tour, including a brochure called *Project Greek Island: The Bunker*, which summarized a large amount of the information presented during my visit.

26. See Monteyne, *Fallout Shelter*, 211–12.

27. National Institute of Standards and Technology, "Fiftieth Anniversary."

28. Gup, "Ultimate Congressional Hideaway."

29. "Down on the Server Farm."

30. Batchen, *Burning with Desire*, 38–39.

31. Eschner, "Inventor of the Telegraph."

32. Conte, *History of the Greenbrier*, 131.

33. Conte, *History of the Greenbrier*, 134.

34. Gup, "Ultimate Congressional Hideaway."

35. Conte, *History of the Greenbrier*, 133.

36. Clark, "Welcome to SubTropolis"; "Go Inside Subtropolis"; Kratz, "National Archives Goes Underground."

37. Graff, *Raven Rock*, 233–34.

38. Conference of First Vice Presidents, *Culpeper Switch*, 4.

39. von Busack, "Cinema Saver"; Trescott, "Sound Investment."

40. Weissman, "Film Preservation."

41. The film *Goodbye World* (2014) dramatizes these fears in a scenario where a mass text—"Goodbye world"—is delivered to millions of cell phones, and a cyberattack then knocks out communication networks and electrical grids, and returns the world to a predigital era. As might be expected, violence and chaos ensue.

42. Good, "How Many Photos."

43. Peter Galison suggested in 2004 that "about five times as many pages are being added to the classified universe than are being brought to the storehouses of human learning, including all the books and journals on any subject in any language collected in the largest repositories on the planet." See his article "Removing Knowledge," 229–43.

44. Vanderbilt, *Survival City*, 198–99. Writing of other locations, he says, "If Cold War facilities such as Site R and Mount Weather were meant to protect the enduring survival of a network of command and control—providing a redundant 'back-up' if another element was destroyed—the data centers are similarly quasi-visible fortresses protecting a network that itself has no physical expression."

45. Conte, *History of the Greenbrier*, 206. Large generators must run on a regular basis in order to function properly and reliably.

46. Galison, "War against the Center," 28.

47. For more on the materiality of the cloud and its physical location in a proliferating network of data centers, see Jaeger et al., "Where Is the Cloud?" This information is also cited in Parks, "Stuff You Can Kick." For an explanation of the continuities between intelligence gathering practices of the FBI in the Cold War and war on terror, see Theoharis, *Abuse of Power*.

48. On the history of the "Atchison Caves" see Slattery, "Atchison Storage Facility." For more on Vivos shelters, visit terravivos.com.

49. Rosenfeld, "Apocalypse Later."

50. Grinspoon, statement before the House Armed Services Committee, 3687.

51. Hu, *Prehistory of the Cloud*, 109–10.

52. Hu, *Prehistory of the Cloud*, 97.

53. Hu, *Prehistory of the Cloud*, 108.

54. Hu, *Prehistory of the Cloud*, 109.

55. Hu, *Prehistory of the Cloud*, 110.

56. "Water Science School," U.S. Geological Survey.

57. Rory Carroll, "Welcome to Utah, the NSA's Desert Home for Eavesdropping on America," *Guardian*, June 14, 2013, quoted in Hogan, "Data Flows and Water Woes," 3.

58. Semerad, "NSA in Utah."

59. Hogan and Shepherd, "Information Ownership and Materiality," 10.

60. Hogan, "Data Flows and Water Woes," 3; Miller, "Data Center in Maryland."

61. "Military Turns to ESPN"; Johnson, "Military Should Teach AI."

62. Nakashima and Whitlock, "With Air Force's Gorgon Drone."

63. New York State Department of Financial Services, *Twitter Investigation Report*; Koerner, "Inside the Cyberattack."

64. Koerner, "Inside the Cyberattack." Beyond this "basic hygiene," the massive amounts of data now generated in the data complex must be "cleaned" so that it can "mined" by algorithms. So much of data scientists' work is dedicated to this that they have nicknamed this mundane labor as "data munging," or "data wrangling" and even refer to themselves as "data janitors." See Lohr, "For Big-Data Scientists." Similarly, in "Data Cleaners" Plantin details how research data must be "cleaned" and made "pristine" before being submitted to social science data archives (58). "Janitor" is also a slang term for Facebook's content moderators, who "review queues of content that users have flagged as problematic." Zuboff, *Surveillance Capitalism*, 509.

65. Steven J. Murdoch, quoted by Ian Daly, "Nuclear Bunker Houses World's Toughest Server Farm," *Wired*, October 5, 2010, cited by Hu, *Prehistory of the Cloud*, 107–8.

66. According to Cheney-Lippold, "It's measurable types' universality of allowable wrongness that permits them the ability to move, to reform the world into new, measured 'truths.'" These "algorithmic measurable types," which may or may not correspond to our own stated identities, "forbid strict allegiances to what we call

identity, the complex formation of histories, power relationships, and subjective experiences that make us who we are." *We Are Data*, 65.

67. For a discussion of Google and other companies' classification schemes in terms of age and gender, see Cheney-Lippold, *We Are Data*, 58–65. Colin Koopman's excellent book *How We Became Our Data* provides helpful historical context for the contemporary phenomena analyzed by Lippold, as Koopman "traces the emergence of informational personhood in an unsettled period running from the mid-1910s to the mid-1930s—this was the long 1920s, inclusive of its dawning and setting. Amid the riotous moment of a roaring decade, we were formatted into data of uncountably many kinds: birth certificates, psychological assessments, education records, financial profiles, the production of a sizable racialized data apparatus, and so much other informational accoutrement that we have for so long now simply taken for granted. These century-old formats remain with us today. They persist in the latest information technologies that, new as they are, depend on older techniques for their deepest infrastructure" (x). According to Koopman, "Every device that today promises a revolution of data is at the same time the promise of the maintenance of techniques of datafication already assembled in the past. Our contemporary data revolutions are not so much hallowed visions of a future as they are halcyon dreams of the days when data was actually being given the power that is now being played out by the scripts of the latest apps, gadgets, start-ups, incubators, and collaboratories" (64).

68. Sokol, "Coming Out of the Dark."

69. Theoharis, *Abuse of Power*.

70. Graff, *Raven Rock*, 140.

71. Burdick and Wheeler. *Fail-Safe*, 122. The novel first appeared in three serialized installments in the *Saturday Evening Post*, on October 12, 20, and 27, during the Cuban Missile Crisis, and was adapted into a film starring Henry Fonda and Walter Matthau, and directed by Sidney Lumet, in 1964.

72. United Press International, "Capital Slave Quarters."

73. "Civil Defense: A Place to Hide," *Time*.

74. United Press International, "Capital Slave Quarters."

75. For more on the fungibility of black bodies, see Hartman, *Scenes of Subjection*, 25–26.

76. St. Germain, "Why Is Ashburn."

77. Fung and Herrera, "Amazon and Mall Operator."

78. Iron Mountain, "Iron Mountain Announces."

## Chapter 5

1. For more on metallic documents, including unrealized plans to create them and fictional representations of them in the early twentieth century, see Yablon, *Remembrance of Things Present*, especially chapter 5, "'A Living History of the Times': The Modern Historic Records Association, 1911–1914," 191–234.

2. Metallic documents were not uncommon in the ancient world. See Wright, *Ancient Burials* and "Metallic Documents," as well as Wright and Sutton, "Evidence of Ancient Writing." Wright compiled a 211-page bibliography of every source he could find that mentions "metallic epigraphy" in the ancient world and published it in his book *Modern Presentism and Ancient Metallic Epigraphy*.

3. Adams, " Social and Cultural Implications," 1.

4. "Bath's Roman Curse Tablets," UNESCO.

5. See Hudson, "'Archaeological Duty' of Thornwell Jacobs," 121–38, and his "End of the World," 594–607; Tarantino, *Life after People*, "Crypt of Civilization."

6. Jacobs, "What Will the World," 918.

7. Paul Jones, "Backstage," *Atlanta (Ga.) Journal-Constitution*, August 24, 1947, box 2, folder: "Miscellany. Clippings, 1897–1973 + undated," Thomas Kimmwood Peters Papers, Library of Congress, Manuscript Division, Washington, D.C.; "Ten Commandments," Internet Movie Database.

8. Certificates acknowledging individuals' monetary contributions to the second Crypt of Civilization, box 10, folder: "Certificates of Acknowledgement," MS1: Thornwell Jacobs Collection, Oglethorpe University Archives, Philip Weltner Library, Oglethorpe University, Atlanta.

9. Untitled list of photography captions in untitled folder in box 1, Thomas Kimmwood Peters Papers, Charles E. Young Research Library, UCLA, Los Angeles.

10. "Highest-Grossing Film," Guinness World Records.

11. See "James Madison Memorial Building," Architect of the Capitol.

12. Gugliotta, *Freedom's Cap*; Cole, *America's Greatest Library*; Gangitano, "Long, Accident-Prone History."

13. For more on bitrot, see DeMarinis, "Erased Dots and Rotten Dashes," 214–15. Solid-state drives (SSDs) also deteriorate and lose data, though it happens a bit differently, through electronic leakage from the breakdown of an insulation layer, or due to a high number of write cycles. In any case, bitrot and data loss afflict both hard disk drives and solid-state drives.

14. For more on his "allegorical" approach to taking a photograph of Dugway, which he says "is also a photography of the impossibility of trying to see this weapons range in a certain way," see the clip "Trevor Paglen Photographs Classified 'Black Sites'" on the SF MOMA website.

15. Ferris, "Voyagers in Space & Time," 3.

16. Pescovitz, Daly, Azerrad, "Introduction," *Voyager Golden Record*, 1.

17. Ferris, "Voyagers in Space & Time," 3.

18. Ferris, "Voyagers in Space & Time," 3.

19. Paglen, *Last Pictures*, 12.

20. Waste Isolation Pilot Plant website, Nuclear Waste Partnership.

21. Waste Isolation Pilot Plant website, Nuclear Waste Partnership.

22. Vanderbilt, *Survival City*, 190–91.

23. Paglen, *Last Pictures*, 16–17.

24. Ferris, "Voyagers in Space & Time," 3–4.

25. Gunn, "Why Is There Poo"; Resnick, "Apollo Astronauts"; Lupisella et al., "Low-Latency Telerobotic Sample Return."

26. According to Giulia Persoz, "The Moon is of critical importance for the renewed U.S. Vision of Space Exploration as learning theatre for future farther human exploration; for the use of its material and energy resources, such as water, helium 3, oxygen and solar wind, notably for the process of rocket fuel; thus for future refuelling in orbit capacity (which will significantly decrease vulnerability of cis-lunar space assets); and for future long-lasting transportation infrastructure." Persoz, "One Small Step," 41–42. For an illuminating account of how U.S. space exploration is integrally related to imperial efforts to extract and exploit mineral resources on Earth, see Black, *Global Interior*, especially chapter 6, "Prospecting the Final Frontier."

27. Ferris, "Voyagers in Space & Time," 6.

28. Krumholz, "Star Formation in Molecular Clouds."

29. Merz, "Archives and the One World," 156.

30. Stepanek, "Data Storage."

31. See "Register Here," Apple, timecapsuledead.org. For an example of news coverage of this digital dilemma, see Arthur and Payne, "Apple Finally Admits Problems."

32. "Airport Time Capsule," Apple.

33. Paglen, *Last Pictures*, 18.

34. Wardle and Berggren, "Time Capsule in Orbit," 184.

35. Benjamin, "Philosophy of History," 257–58.

36. Paglen takes a similar position: "From the moment I began thinking about dead satellites and suicidal civilizations, the ghost machines in Earth orbit became an allegory for what happened to the people responsible for them. And allegory for the recent history; perhaps even an allegory for modernity itself. Like the suicide statues at Easter Island, the dead satellite embodied a cruel paradox: perhaps the interactions of production, technologies, and forms of knowledge that allowed us to explore the heavens also enabled us to destroy our own island Earth. The science that enabled us to understand the insides of stars was put to practical use in the inner workings of a hydrogen bomb; the rockets that took us to space, we designed primarily to deliver thermonuclear Armageddon. Of course, many people envision that humans will indeed commit thermonuclear suicide or exhaust Earth's resources. For some theis [*sic*] represents 'progress.' In this view, it is our collective destiny to colonize other planets. The dream of colonizing space is a farce, but it fuels the ideology that humans are separate from the earth and that destroying our own habitat is a problem we can outrun." *Last Pictures*, 13. Paglen points out the echo in his statement of Hannah Arendt's ideas in her essay "Conquest of Space and the Stature of Man." *Last Pictures*, 20n11.

37. Kassovitz, *La Haine*.

38. U.S. Department of Defense, *Annual Report*, 20–21.

39. See Joint Steering Committee on Computer Output Microfilm, *Report on An Experimental Computer Output Microfilm Service Center*. The other agencies that participated in this effort were the General Services Administration and the General Accounting Office.

40. See Antognini and Antognini, "Flexibly Configurable 2D Bar Code." Available on the Cobblestone website at http://www.paperdisk.com/ibippap2.htm. Also see the home page, "Welcome to the Paper Revolution!(TM)" at http://www.paperdisk.com/index.html.

41. See Rosenthaler, "Digital Archiving Tomorrow."

42. The talk is available on EMPAC's YouTube channel: https://www.youtube.com/watch?v=2rbGX4fdu8k.

43. The challenge faced by EMPAC is a common one for cultural institutions. There is also a sort of paradox that operates at the heart of it. For loss to register as loss, there must be some indication, some record or embodied memory, that the lost thing once existed but no longer exists. In other words, if multimedia recordings currently held at EMPAC deteriorate or decay into nonexistence, that loss will only register as loss if there is another record (say, in a collections database) that refers to that recording.

44. Lunt and Linford, "Long-Term Digital Data Storage."

45. Alabaster, "Hitachi Targets 2015."

46. Vincent, "'Five-Dimensional' Glass Discs."

47. Ebiri, "Scientology's Secret Vaults"; Sharpe, "Mountain of Mystery."

48. Copeland, "Optical Rosetta Disk"; Kelly, "Very Long-Term Backup."

49. "Storage That Really Lasts," Enterprise Storage Forum.

50. As of this writing at 9:19 A.M. EST, December 27, 2020, bitcoin's price is $27,634.10, which makes the Winklevii's initial purchase of nearly 92,000 bitcoin worth $2,533,107,410. Oh, the price just went up again. Now they're worth $2,539,588,196. Oh, now it went down. As of 9:25 A.M. EST, they're worth $2,536,517,385. Now, in this last round of edits, the price of a bitcoin is hovering around $48,000. I'll let you do the math. And what is the Winklevii fortune worth now, dear reader? Have you even ever heard of bitcoin? Are they now worth billions more? Is this the morning when they are suddenly worth nothing?

51. Popper, "How the Winklevoss Twins."

52. del Castillo, "Tyler Winklevoss Breaks Down."

53. Mack, "Are Physical Bitcoins Legal?"

54. For a narrative nonfiction treatment of this tragic story, see Lewis, *Big Short*, and for a longer history of the uses of debt in the economic realm, see Graeber, *Debt*.

55. See Baumann, "Too Fast to Fail"; Chlistalla, "High-Frequency Trading"; Cantu and Reiners, "High-Frequency Trading."

56. Lantz, "Future of Data Storage."

57. "ProQuest Dissertation Publishing Preservation," ProQuest.

58. "ProQuest Dissertations FAQ," ProQuest.

59. Gustafson, "Travels of the Charters."

60. Puleo, *American Treasures*, 297–302.

61. Little, "Freedom Train," 35–67; Bradsher, "Travels of the Bill of Rights." Kimberly also offered his expertise for the New York State Freedom Train; see "Freedom Train Documents."

62. Wilhelm with Brower, *Permanence and Care of Color Photographs*, 244.

63. Cutts, *Conceptual Design of a Monitoring System*.

64. Wilhelm with Brower, *Permanence and Care of Color Photographs*, 244.

65. Ritzenthaler and Nicholson, "New Era Begins." As early as 1928, chemists at Harvard University determined that helium leakage occurred through glass, even Pyrex glass used for scientific experiments, in perceptible amounts in as little as twenty-four hours. See Baxter, Starkweather, and Ellestad, "Leakage of Helium."

66. Nicholson, "Stone Engraving."

67. Bartusiak, *Day We Found the Universe*, xi.

68. 2.5 million light-years equate to 146,965,630,000,000,000,000,000,000 miles.

69. Paglen, *Last Pictures*, 187.

70. Paglen, *Last Pictures*, 188.

71. For more on the case against infinity in mathematics, see Rotman's book *Ad Infinitum*.

72. See Campbell, *Hero with a Thousand Faces*, 223–33.

## Chapter 6

1. For more on his project, see Hasdemir, "Richard Beckett." Also see Beckett's webpage "Bioreceptive Façade Panels."

2. See the Mango Material website at www.mangomaterials.com.

3. Biosteel home page, http://www.biosteel-fiber.com/home/.

4. "Caskia," Officina Corpuscoli.

5. Diamond Foundry home page, https://diamondfoundry.com/pages/technology.

6. The velociraptors in the novel and film *Jurassic Park* were actually modeled after a larger related dinosaur called a deinonychus, which means "terrible claw," but Michael Crichton, thought the name "velociraptor" sounded "more dramatic." See Cumming, "Yale's Legacy in 'Jurassic World.'"

7. Cornish, "How DNA Could Store."

8. Annunziato, "DNA Packaging."

9. Kodak, *Sources of Silver* and *Recovering Silver*.

10. Peck, "Preserving Nature," 15. William Hornaday's vivid descriptions of the violent manipulations involved in taxidermy are coupled with sections that quite spectacularly support my earlier points in chapter 1 about the toxicity of preservation. In one example of this, he writes, "Cut away any flesh which has been left at the root of the tail, but do not cut the ends of the tail feathers. The next thing is to

poison the skin." See Hornaday, *Taxidermy and Zoological Collecting*, 51. On the ways that arsenic also poisoned taxidermists, see Schwarzschild, "Death-Defying/Defining Spectacles." On the poisoning of museum professionals and Indigenous communities that have received repatriated objects, see Marte, Péquignot, and Von Endt, "Arsenic in Taxidermy Collections."

11. For more on the material requirements of the data complex, as well as the labor, see Bales, *Blood and Earth*, and Crawford, *Atlas of AI*. Zuboff clarifies the dynamics of oversharing and how people are drawn into routinely supplying more and more data to the data complex. *Surveillance Capitalism*, 460. Zuboff also details the features of a Sleep Number bed that is linked to a SleepIQ app. The mattress has embedded sensors that measure one's heart rate, breathing, and movement, and calculates a SleepIQ score every morning. *Surveillance Capitalism*, 235.

12. The magnetism of these bits is not visible to the human eye, even under extreme magnification, but physicist Andy Berger built a special instrument so he could "see" the surface, and if you use this special microscope built to read magnetic charges, the surface of the disc looks like a series of rectangles lying side by side lengthwise, fuzzy at the edges, some wider than others, for when a "one" or a "zero" repeats, they seem to combine. Berger compared the instrument to a tiny "diving board" lever. It responds to magnetic pull or repulsion, and so can sense whether it's hovering over a one or a zero. The lever's length is 0.1 millimeter, which is the width of a single human hair. It is so sensitive that the closest thing Berger can compare it to is the mass of a feather lying on your hand. The feather's one gram of mass exerts barely perceptible force. Berger's lever detects "forces one trillion times smaller than that." He claims that if he rested "a single red blood cell on the end of this lever, the bending would still be dramatic." Berger, "Data on Your Hard Drive."

13. Lantz, "Future of Data Storage."

14. Shehabi et al., *United States Data Center Energy Usage*, 28.

15. Cubitt, *Finite Media*, 47.

16. Tiseo, "Global Paper."

17. Alcorn, "Seagate Demos"; Alcorn, "Seagate Plans"; Seagate, *HAMR Technology*, 2018.

18. Alcorn, "WD Plots a Course."

19. Yardley, "Willis Whitfield."

20. Sandia National Laboratories, "Modern-Day Cleanroom."

21. See Holbrook, "Controlling Contamination," 184–86.

22. Fishman, "Dangerously Clean Water."

23. Cubitt, *Finite Media*, 88.

24. Fishman, "Dangerously Clean Water."

25. For more on the history of fantasies about space exploration and how they relate to race in particular, see Kilgore, *Astrofuturism*. For more on NASA projects intended to serve African Americans specifically and the future plans for African Americans living in space, see A Tribe Called Quest, "Space Program."

26. Pirat, "Iron Mountain."

27. Sheetz, "Satellite Start-Up."

28. Winter, "American Rocket," 303; Kilgore, *Astrofuturism*, 35–36.

29. HIVE Blockchain Technologies, "HIVE Blockchain"; O'Dwyer, "Datacenter Investment."

30. Carrington, "Arctic Stronghold."

31. Mellis, "Interview with Dyveke Sanne," 34–36. Sanne also articulated the simultaneously hopeful and fearful signals sent by the vault: "The Vault balances on a continuum between extreme points: the practical necessity and virtue of gathering and securing the world's seed diversity, and the equally negative and dreadful signal it gives off by telegraphing that this is really necessary, drawing attention to the current dangers seeds have to be protected from." For more on the ironies of refrigerated archives, see Mattern, "Big Data of Ice."

32. Carrington, "2016 Hottest Year."

33. Captain, "Jeff Bezos Wants to Save Earth."

34. Heaven, "First Detailed Look"; Drake, "SpaceX's Starlink Satellites."

35. Lyons, "FCC Awards SpaceX."

36. Childers, "Elon Musk Says."

37. NASA, "Mars Terraforming Not Possible."

38. Kluger, "SpaceX's Starhopper Flight Test."

39. Thorbecke, "4 Astronauts Launch for ISS."

40. "The Jameson Satellite" first appeared in *Amazing Stories*, July 1931, pp. 334–43.

41. Ettinger, *Prospect of Immortality*, 115. For more on the utopian and imperial features of space exploration fantasies, see Kilgore, *Astrofuturism*.

42. Kelly, "Very Long-Term Backup."

43. Khan, "After a Bounce."

44. Foer, "Jeff Bezos's Master Plan."

45. Poponak et al., *Space: The Next Investment Frontier*, 25.

46. Klotz, "Tech Billionaires Bankroll Gold Rush."

47. Cubitt, *Finite Media*, 14.

48. Poponak et al., *Space: The Next Investment Frontier*, 4.

49. Chang, "Jeff Bezos' Company."

50. Kelly, "Clock in the Mountain."

51. For more on the roots of the Long Now Foundation in Stewart Brand's previous work, such as the *Whole Earth Catalog*, and the broader cultural and technological contexts in California, see Turner, *From Counterculture to Cyberculture*.

52. Taubes, "Thinking Machines."

53. "Parallel Computing Pioneers."

54. Schiller, "Amazon.com Founder."

55. Featherstone, "Investigating Fukushima's Ecological Toll."

56. Blaustein, "Trevor Paglen Interview."

57. Hogan, "Templating Life," 145–53. A Hoberman sphere is an expandable, collapsible sphere that is most widely-known as a multicolored children's toy.

58. Bornholt et al., "DNA-Based Archival Storage System," 637–49.

59. For more on the life and work of Muybridge and how his photography paved the way for moving images, see Solnit, *River of Shadows*.

60. Sample, "Harvard Scientists."

61. Molteni, "Scientists Upload"; Bhan et al., "Recording Temporal Data."

62. Flynn, "DNA-Based Dating App"; Regalado, "Here Are Some Actual Facts."

63. Browne, *Dark Matters*, 91. On the history of biometrics, see Sekula, "Body and the Archive," 3–64. For a longer history of quantifying the self, see Wernimont, *Numbered Lives*, and for an extensive treatment of the practice of self-quantification, see Hong, *Technologies of Speculation*.

64. Browne, *Dark Matters*, 109. On body heat, thermal technology, and infrared sensing, see Parks, "Drones, Infrared Imagery, and Body Heat."

65. Patterson, "First Fully Biometric Terminal." For a history of computerized facial recognition technology and efforts to develop it beginning in the 1960s, see Gates, *Our Biometric Future*, especially chapter 1, "Facial Recognition Technology from the Lab to the Marketplace," 25–62.

66. Conger, Fausset, and Kovaleski, "Facial Recognition Technology."

67. See Greene and Patterson, "Trouble with Trusting AI"; Paglen, "Invisible Images"; Pasternak, "AI Could Help"; Kestler-D'Amours, "Police Forces Keep Saying." According to the *Washington Post*, Chinese telecommunications giant Huawei has already tested AI software that tries to identify members of the Uighur minority group and sounds a "Uighur alarm," further facilitating the targeting of this group and intensifying their ongoing repression. See Harwell and Dou, "Huawei Tested AI Software." For more on body cameras' effect, or the lack thereof, on diminishing police violence, see Yokum, Ravishankar, and Coppock, "Randomized Control Trial."

68. The company was initially founded with the name Carverr but changed its moniker to Aanika Biosciences in 2019. According to an article on the company's Medium account, the name Aanika is derived "from the Hindu goddess Durga, who protects the world from evil." "Carverr Is Now," Aanika Biosciences. The company's advisors include George Church and Christopher Mason. "Scientific Advisory," Aanika Biosciences.

69. "Pricing," ProtonMail.

70. Zaleski, "Bill Gates Is Betting on a Start-Up"; Edney, "Lab-Grown Meat Startups."

71. Paglen, "Operational Images." Paglen draws the term "operational images" from the work of Harun Farocki.

72. Zeitlin, "This Iconic American Image."

73. Choi, "'Punch Card' DNA."

74. James Essinger traces the genealogy of the digital computer back to Jacquard's programmable loom in his book *Jacquard's Web*.

75. Moskowitz, "DNA-Coded 'Lunar Library.'"

76. "Introduction to DNA Data Storage," Catalog Technologies.

77. National Research Council, Committee on Metagenomics: Challenges and Functional Applications, *New Science of Metagenomics*.

78. See the Mason Lab home page, www.masonlab.net.

79. Mason, "Discovering and Designing Genomes."

80. "EpiBone," Johnson & Johnson Innovation Labs.

81. Cain, "Most Creative People."

82. Tandon, "Tissue Engineering."

### Epilogue

1. Newton, "Speak, Memory."

2. Pardes, "Giving Robots an Identity."

3. A number of recent books address the ramifications of the impossibility of disconnecting from and deleting digital records of one's past in the twenty-first-century data complex. See Mayer-Schönberger, *Delete*; Eichhorn, *End of Forgetting*.

4. Binelli, "Old Musicians Never Die."

5. Hall, "Holograms"; Tsukayam, "Tupac 'Hologram.'"

6. Library Journal, "Sasha Fierce Needs Archives/Archivists."

7. Wallace, "Miss Millennium."

8. Rini, "Deepfakes and the Epistemic Backstop," 5.

9. See Niki et al., "Novel Palliative Care Approach"; Oyama, "Virtual Reality." VR is gaining wider use as a therapeutic tool for pain management. See Sharar et al., "Virtual Reality for Pain Management"; "Virtual Reality Game," BBC News.

10. Daly, "Virtual Reality Allows Tampa Bay."

11. See the home page and "About" page of the company's website: https://appliedvr.io/about/.

12. To ensure that the timing of the Heaven simulation aligns with the moments before biological death, the patient-user can opt for a medically assisted suicide service that syncs the XR experience with the timed release of intravenous secobarbital.

# Bibliography

**PRIMARY SOURCES**
### Archives
Bettmann Archive, Corbis Film Preservation Facility, Iron Mountain, Boyers, Pa.

Butler County Historical Society, Butler, Pa.

George Westinghouse Museum Archives, Heinz History Center, Pittsburgh, Pa.

Records of the National Archives and Records Administration, National Archives, College Park, Md.

Thomas Kimmwood Peters Papers, Library of Congress, Manuscript Division, Washington, D.C.

Thomas Kimmwood Peters Papers, Young Research Library, University of California, Los Angeles

Thornwell Jacobs Collection, Oglethorpe University Archives, Philip Weltner Library, Oglethorpe University, Atlanta

Tudor Family Papers, Massachusetts Historical Society, Boston

Westinghouse Electric Corporation Archives, Heinz History Center, Pittsburgh, Pa.

### Government Publications and Other Reports
Call, A. H. "Vacuum Fumigation of Nursery Stock in Ventura County." *Monthly Bulletin of the Department of Agriculture, State of California* 11, nos. 5–6 (May–June 1922): 467–68.

Chlistalla, Michael. *High-Frequency Trading: Better Than Its Reputation?* Frankfurt am Main: Deutsch Bank Research, 2011.

Grinspoon, Lester. Statement before House Armed Services Committee. In *Civil Defense—Fallout Shelter Program: Hearings Before Subcommittee No. 3, Committee on Armed Services*, 3685–97. 88th Cong., 1st sess., 1963.

Hill, John R., and Charles G. Weber. *Evaluation of Motion Picture Film for Permanent Records*. National Bureau of Standards Miscellaneous Publication 158. Washington, D.C.: U.S. Government Printing Office, 1937.

Jarrell, T. D., J. M. Hankins, and F. P. Veitch. *Deterioration of Paper as Indicated by Gas Chamber Tests*. USDA Technical Bulletin 605. Washington, D.C.: U.S. Department of Agriculture, 1938.

Joint Steering Committee on Computer Output Microfilm. *Report on an Experimental Computer Output Microfilm Service Center*. Norfolk, Va.: Navy Publications and Printing Service Office, 1976.

Kaley, Karlyn Black, Jim Carlisle, David Siegel, and Julio Salinas. *Health Concerns and Environmental Issues with PVC-Containing Building Materials in Green*

*Buildings*. Integrated Waste Management Board, California Environmental Protection Agency. 2006. http://www.calrecycle.ca.gov/Publications /Documents/GreenBuilding%5C43106016.pdf.

Kantrowitz, Morris S., Ernest W. Spencer, and Robert H. Simmons. *Permanence and Durability of Paper: An Annotated Bibliography of the Technical Literature from 1885 A.D. to 1939 A.D.* Technical Bulletin No. 22. Washington, D.C.: U.S. Government Printing Office, 1940.

Kimberly, Arthur E., and A. L. Emley. *A Study of the Deterioration of Book Papers in Libraries*. Bureau of Standards Miscellaneous Publication 140. Washington, D.C.: U.S. Government Printing Office, 1933.

Kimberly, Arthur E., and B. W. Scribner. *Summary Report of National Bureau of Standards Research on Preservation of Records*. Bureau of Standards Miscellaneous Publication M154 (May 9, 1934). Washington, D.C.: U.S. Government Printing Office, 1931.

Kimberly, Arthur E., and J. F. G. Hicks Jr. *A Survey of the Storage Conditions in Libraries Relative to the Preservation of Records*. Bureau of Standards Miscellaneous Publication 128. Washington, D.C.: U.S. Government Printing Office, 1931.

National Archives and Records Administration. *Archives II: National Archives at College Park; Using Technology to Safeguard Archival Records*. NARA Technical Information Paper Number 13. College Park, Md.: National Archives and Records Administration, 1997.

National Fire Protection Association, Committee on Protection of Records. *Protection of Records: Consolidated Reports of the Committee on Protection of Records, 1947*. Boston: National Fire Protection Association International, 1947.

National Records Management Council. *Effects of a Nuclear Explosion on Records and Records Storage Equipment*. New York: Federal Civil Defense Administration, 1956.

———. *Target: Red Tape; A Staff Report to the Michigan Joint Legislative Committee on Reorganization of State Government*. Lansing, Mich.: National Records Management Council, 1951.

———. *Your Business Records: A Liability or an Asset?* New York: National Records Management Council, 1949.

National Research Council, Committee on Metagenomics: Challenges and Functional Applications. *The New Science of Metagenomics: Revealing the Secrets of Our Microbial Planet*. Washington, D.C.: National Academies Press, 2007.

National Research Council, Committee on the Effects of Nuclear Earth-Penetrator and Other Weapons. *Effects of Nuclear Earth-Penetrator and Other Weapons*. Washington, D.C.: National Academies Press, 2005.

National Security Resources Board. *Is Your Plant a Target?* Washington, D.C.: U.S. Government Printing Office, 1951.

New York State Department of Financial Services. *Twitter Investigation Report.*
October 14, 2020. https://www.dfs.ny.gov/Twitter_Report.

U.S. Congress. *Joint Resolution to Acknowledge the 100th Anniversary of the
Overthrow of the Kingdom of Hawaii.* S.J. Res. 19. 103rd Cong., 1st sess.
Introduced January 5, 1993. https://www.govinfo.gov/content/pkg/BILLS
-103sjres19enr/pdf/BILLS-103sjres19enr.pdf.

U.S. Department of Defense. *Annual Report of the Office of Civil Defense for Fiscal
Year 1963.* Washington, D.C.: U.S. Government Printing Office, 1963.

U.S. Department of Energy, Nevada Operations Office. *United States Nuclear
Tests: July 1945 through September 1992.* DOE/NV REV 15. December 2000.
https://digital.library.unt.edu/ark:/67531/metadc721128/.

U.S. Department of the Interior, National Park Service. "Geologic Formations."
Boston Harbor Islands National Recreation Area. February 26, 2015.
https://www.nps.gov/boha/learn/nature/geologicformations.htm.

U.S. Geological Survey. "Water Science School: How Much Does a Cloud Weigh?"
Water Science School, U.S. Geological Survey. https://www.usgs.gov
/special-topic/water-science-school/science/how-much-does-a-cloud-weigh.

U.S. War Department, Adjutant General's Office. *Emergency Officers Army List
and Directory, December 23, 1919.* Washington, D.C.: Government Printing
Office, 1920.

United States of America Operations Mission to Israel / National Records
Management Council. *A Records Management Program for the State of Israel:
Report to the Government of Israel.* Tel Aviv: National Records Management
Council, 1955.

## Journal Articles

Baxter, G. P., H. W. Starkweather, and R. B. Ellestad. "The Leakage of Helium
through Pyrex Glass at Room Temperature." *Science* 68, no. 1769 (1928): 516–17.

Burton, John O. "Permanence Studies of Current Commercial Book Papers."
*Bureau of Standards Journal of Research* 7, no. 3 (1931): 429–39.

Ford Motor Company. "Microfilm Safeguards Vital Records." *National Safety
News* 63 (April 1951): 85–86.

Hill, John R., and C. G. Weber. "Stability of Motion Picture Films as Determined
by Accelerated Aging." *Journal of the Society of Motion Picture Engineers* 27, no.
6 (December 1936): 677–90.

Johnson, E. R. Fenimore. "The Preservation and Abuses of Motion Picture Film by
Scientific Institutions." *Proceedings of the American Philosophical Society* 81,
no. 1 (May 31, 1939).

Kimberly, Arthur E. "Deteriorative Effect of Sulphur Dioxide upon Paper in an
Atmosphere of Constant Humidity and Temperature." *Bureau of Standards
Journal of Research* 8, no. 158 (1932).

———. "Repair and Preservation of Manuscripts in the National Archives."
*American Archivist* 1, no. 3 (July 1938): 111–17.

———. "The Preservation of Records in Vital Statistics." *Vital Statistics—Special Reports* 3, no. 33 (August 5, 1937): 153–60.

Niki, Kazuyuki,Yoshiaki Okamoto, Isseki Maeda, Ichiro Mori, Ryouhei Ishii, Yoshinobu Matsuda, Tatsuya Takagi, and Etsuko Uejima. "A Novel Palliative Care Approach Using Virtual Reality for Improving Various Symptoms of Terminal Cancer Patients: A Preliminary Prospective, Multicenter Study." *Journal of Palliative Medicine* 22, no. 6 (January 2019).

Perkins, Fred W. "Preservation of Historical Films." *Transactions of the Society of Motion Picture Engineers* 10, no. 27 (October 1926): 81.

Porter, Charles. "Library Books and Infectious Disease." *British Medical Journal* 1, no. 1776 (January 12, 1895).

Rasch, Royal H., and B. W. Scribner. "Comparison of Natural Aging of Paper with Accelerated Aging by Heating." *Bureau of Standards Journal of Research* 11 (1933): 727–32.

Scribner, B. W. "Air Treatment for Preservation of Records in Libraries." *Refrigerating Engineering* 33 (April 4, 1937): 233–35.

———. "Report of Bureau of Standards Research on Preservation of Paper Records." *Library Quarterly* 1, no. 4 (October 1931): 409.

Sharar, Sam R., William Miller, Aubriana Teeley, Maryam Soltani, Hunter G. Hoffman, Mark P. Jensen, and David R. Patterson. "Applications of Virtual Reality for Pain Management in Burn-Injured Patients." *Expert Review of Neurotherapeutics* 8, no. 11 (November 2008): 1667–74.

Trivedi, Surbhi, and Rohit R. Arora. "Association of Dioxin and Dioxin-like Congeners with Hypertension." *Federal Practitioner*, May 2018, 20–26.

"Vaporate Film Treatment to Protect Your Films." *Filmo Topics* 13, no. 3 (Summer 1937): 11.

Weighl, C. A. "Hot-Water Bulb Sterilizers." *Journal of Economic Entomology* 20, no. 1 (February 1, 1927): 113–26.

Weil, Robert E. "Will One Fire . . . or Bomb Ruin Your Company?" *Credit and Financial Management* 53 (October 1951): 7–8.

## News and Periodical Articles

Alabaster, Jay. "Hitachi Targets 2015 for Glass-Based Data Storage That Lasts 100 Million Years." *PCWorld*, September 25, 2012. https://www.pcworld.com/article/2010588/hitachi-targets-2015-for-glass-based-data-storage-that-lasts-100-million-years.html.

"Americana Crypt to Await 8113 A.D.: Oglethorpe University Plans a Cache to Be Opened When 20th Century Is Ancient Era." *New York Times*, April 16, 1937, p. 25. ProQuest Historical Newspapers: The *New York Times* (1851–2009) with Index (1851–1993).

"America's 'Average Man.'" *Cornell Daily Sun* (Ithaca, N.Y.), October 27, 1927.

"A Typically Average Couple." *Utica (N.Y.) Observer-Dispatch*, April 25, 1935.

Battiata, Mary. "Buried Treasure." *Washington Post Magazine*, May 18, 2003.

Baumann, Nick, "Too Fast to Fail: How High-Speed Trading Fuels Wall Street Disasters." *Mother Jones*, January/February 2013. https://www.motherjones.com/politics/2013/02/high-frequency-trading-danger-risk-wall-street/.

Berger, Andy. "Here's What the Data on Your Hard Drive Looks Like." *Discover Magazine*, July 30, 2015. https://www.discovermagazine.com/technology/heres-what-the-data-on-your-hard-drive-looks-like.

Berry, India. "Top 10 Countries with the Most Data Centers." *Data Centre Magazine*, September 20, 2021. https://datacentremagazine.com/top10/top-10-countries-most-data-centres.

Binelli, Mark. "Old Musicians Never Die. They Just Become Holograms." *New York Times*, January 7, 2020.

Binkley, Robert C. "Do the Records of Science Face Ruin?" *Scientific American*, January 1929.

"Bombproof Caveman." *American Magazine*, May 1952.

Boxer, Sarah. "A Century's Photo History Destined for Life in a Mine." *New York Times*, April 15, 2001.

Cain, Patrick. "Most Creative People 2012: Nina Tandon." *Fast Company*, April 27, 2012. https://www.fastcompany.com/3018211/26-nina-tandon.

Captain, Sean. "Jeff Bezos Wants to Save Earth by Moving Industry to Space." *Fast Company*, May 19, 2019. https://www.fastcompany.com/90347364/jeff-bezos-wants-to-save-earth-by-moving-industry-to-space.

Carrington, Damian. "Arctic Stronghold of World's Seeds Flooded after Permafrost Melts." *Guardian*, May 19, 2017. https://www.theguardian.com/environment/2017/may/19/arctic-stronghold-of-worlds-seeds-flooded-after-permafrost-melts.

———. "2016 Hottest Year Ever Recorded—and Scientists Say Human Activity to Blame." *Guardian*, January 18, 2017. https://www.theguardian.com/environment/2017/jan/18/2016-hottest-year-ever-recorded-and-scientists-say-human-activity-to-blame.

Chang, Kenneth. "Jeff Bezos' Company Is Carrying Scientific Cargo to Space. It's Not Amazon." *New York Times*, October 19, 2020.

Childers, Tim. "Elon Musk Says We Need to Live in Glass Domes Before We Can Terraform Mars." *Popular Mechanics*, November 20, 2020. https://www.popularmechanics.com/space/moon-mars/a34738932/elon-musk-glass-domes-terraforming-mars/.

Choi, Charles Q. "'Punch Card' DNA Could Mean Cheaper High-Capacity Data Storage." *Scientific American*, April 8, 2020. https://www.scientificamerican.com/article/punch-card-dna-could-mean-cheaper-high-capacity-data-storage/.

"Civil Defense: A Place to Hide." *Time*, December 18, 1950.

Clark, Patrick. "Welcome to SubTropolis: The Massive Business Complex Buried under Kansas City." *Bloomberg Businessweek*, February 4, 2015.

Conger, Kate, Richard Fausset, and Serge F. Kovaleski. "San Francisco Bans Facial Recognition Technology." *New York Times*, May 14, 2019.

Copeland, Ron. "An Optical Rosetta Disk." *InformationWeek*, April 30, 2001. http://www.informationweek.com/835/innovation.htm.

Cornish, Chloe. "How DNA Could Store All the World's Data in a Semi -Trailer." *Financial Times*, February 5, 2018. https://www.ft.com /content/45ea22b0-cec2-11e7-947e-f1ea5435bcc7.

Cumming, Mike. "Yale's Legacy in 'Jurassic World.'" YaleNews, June 18, 2015. https://news.yale.edu/2015/06/18/yale-s-legacy-jurassic-world.

Daly, Sean. "Virtual Reality Allows Tampa Bay Area Hospice Patients to Realize 'Bucket List' Travel Dreams." ABCActionNews, September 12, 2018. https://www.abcactionnews.com/news/science-and-technology/virtual -reality-allows-tampa-bay-area-hospice-patients-to-realize-bucket-list -travel-dreams.

del Castillo, Michael. "Tyler Winklevoss Breaks Down Four Layers of Gemini's Super-Secret Bitcoin Security." *New York Business Journal*, October 14, 2015. https://www.bizjournals.com/newyork/news/2015/10/14/tyler-winklevoss -breaks-down-four-layers-of-gemini.html.

"Die in Own Gas Chamber." *New York Times*, April 7, 1937.

"Dog Muzzles." *New York Times*, April 30, 1903.

"Down on the Server Farm." *Economist*, May 22, 2008. http://www.economist .com/node/11413148.

Drake, Nadia. "Will Elon Musk's Starlink Satellites Harm Astronomy? Here's What We Know." *National Geographic*, May 29, 2019. https://www .nationalgeographic.com/science/article/elon-musk -starlink-internet-satellites-trouble-for-astronomy-light-pollution.

Dwyer, Jim. "A Nation Challenged: The Vault; Below Ground Zero, Silver and Gold." *New York Times*, November 1, 2001.

Ebiri, Bilge. "Scientology's Secret Vaults: A Rare Interview with a Former Member of Hush-Hush CST." *Village Voice*, February 6, 2012.

Edney, Anna. "Lab-Grown Meat Startups Backed by Bill Gates, Tyson Foods Face FDA Oversight." *Bloomberg.com*, June 15, 2018. https://www.bloomberg.com /news/articles/2018-06-15/lab-grown-meat-backed-by-gates-tyson -foods-faces-u-s-oversight.

Eschner, Kat. "The Inventor of the Telegraph Was Also America's First Photographer." *Smithsonian Magazine*, January 9, 2017. https://www .smithsonianmag.com/smart-news/inventor-telegraph -was-also-americas-first-photographer-180961683/.

Featherstone, Steven. "Investigating Fukushima's Ecological Toll." *Scientific American*, February 2015.

Fenton, John H. "Underground Unit Will Hold Papers and Food Stocks." *New York Times*, December 2, 1960.

"Fire Horror in Pittsburg [*sic*]: Five Men Killed and Many Injured by an Explosion of 2,000 Barrels of Whisky." *New York Times*, February 10, 1898. https://www.nytimes.com/1898/02/10/archives/fire-horror-in-pittsburg-five-men-killed-and-many-injured-by-an.html.

Fishman, Charles. "The Dangerously Clean Water Used to Make Your iPhone." *Fast Company*, April 29, 2011. https://www.fastcompany.com/1750612/dangerously-clean-water-used-make-your-iphone.

Flynn, Meagan. "A Harvard Scientist Is Developing a DNA-Based Dating App to Reduce Genetic Disease. Critics Called It Eugenics." *Washington Post*, December 13, 2019. https://www.washingtonpost.com/nation/2019/12/13/genetics-george-church-dna-dating-app-reduce-disease-eugenics/. Accessed January 1, 2020.

Foer, Franklin. "Jeff Bezos's Master Plan." *Atlantic*, November 15, 2019. https://www.theatlantic.com/magazine/archive/2019/11/what-jeff-bezos-wants/598363/.

"For the Year 8113 A.D." *New York Times*, April 20, 1937, p. 24. ProQuest Historical Newspapers: The *New York Times* (1851–2009) with Index (1851–1993).

Foster, Catherine. "Desegregation of Pasadena Schools—12 Years Later." *Christian Science Monitor*, January 28, 1983.

"Freedom Train Documents Assured Fullest Protection." *Knickerbocker News* (Albany, N.Y.), July 23, 1948.

Fung, Esther, and Sebastian Herrera. "Amazon and Mall Operator Look at Turning Sears, J. C. Penney Stores into Fulfillment Centers." *Wall Street Journal,* August 9, 2020.

Gangitano, Alex. "The Long, Accident-Prone History of Getting the Library of Congress out of the Capitol." *Roll Call* (Washington, D.C.), August 8, 2017.

Germain, David. "Abandoned Iron Ore Mine Became Gold Mine for Savvy Developer." *Los Angeles Times*, April 19, 1992. https://www.latimes.com/archives/la-xpm-1992-04-19-mn-791-story.html.

Glaser, Susan. "Posh, Historical Greenbrier Resort Is at a Crossroads as Business Travel Slows." *Plain Dealer* (Cleveland, Ohio), March 13, 2009.

Greene, Dan, and Genevieve Patterson. "The Trouble with Trusting AI to Interpret Police Body-Cam Video." *IEEE Spectrum*, November 21, 2018. https://spectrum.ieee.org/the-trouble-with-trusting-ai-to-interpret-police-bodycam-video.

Gunn, Alistair. "Why Is There Poo on the Moon?" *BBC Science Focus*. https://www.sciencefocus.com/space/why-is-there-poo-on-the-moon/. Accessed October 7, 2021.

Gup, Ted. "The Doomsday Blueprints." *Time*, August 10, 1992. http://content.time.com/time/subscriber/article/0,33009,976187,00.html.

———. "The Ultimate Congressional Hideaway." *Washington Post*, May 31, 1992. https://www.washingtonpost.com/wp-srv/local/daily/july/25/brier1.htm.

Gustafson, Milton. "Travels of the Charters of Freedom." *Prologue* 34, no. 4 (Winter 2002). https://www.archives.gov/publications/prologue/2002/winter/travels-charters.html.

Hall, Dave. "Holograms: Are They Still the Preserve of Science Fiction?" *Guardian*, May 22, 2018.

Harwell, Drew, and Eva Dou. "Huawei Tested AI Software That Could Recognize Uighur Minorities and Alert Police, Report Says." *Washington Post*, December 8, 2020.

Hasdemir, Bilge. "Richard Beckett, Challenging the Aesthetics of Human Structures and Objects." *CLOT*, June 20, 2018. https://www.clotmag.com/design/richard-beckett.

Heaven, Douglas. "The First Detailed Look at How Elon Musk's Space Internet Could Work." *New Scientist*, November 7, 2017. https://www.newscientist.com/article/mg24032033-300-the-first-detailed-look-at-how-elon-musks-space-internet-could-work/.

"Henry Dreyfuss, Noted Designer, Is Found Dead with His Wife." *New York Times*, October 6, 1972.

Hesseldahl, Arik. "How to Preserve Photos for 500 Years." *Forbes*, April 14, 2005. http://www.forbes.com/2005/04/14/cx_ah_0414photo.html.

Hlavaty, Craig. "Texas' Lost 'Communist Invasion' of 1952." Chron.com (website of the *Houston Chronicle*), October 17, 2017. https://www.chron.com/news/houston-texas/texas/article/Central-Texas-lost-war-of-1952-11115386.php.

Jacobs, Thornwell. "Today—Tomorrow: Archeology in A.D. 8113." *Scientific American*, November 1936.

Johnson, Ted. "The Military Should Teach AI to Watch Drone Footage." *Wired*, November 26, 2017.

Kestler-D'Amours, Jillian. "Police Forces Keep Saying Body Cameras Are the Answer. Experts Say Otherwise." *Vice*, June 11, 2020.

Khan, Amina. "After a Bounce, Rosetta's Philae Lander Serves Up Cometary Surprises." *Los Angeles Times*, July 31, 2015. https://www.latimes.com/science/sciencenow/la-sci-sn-rosetta-philae-comet-67p-churyumov-gerasimenko-organic-bounce-20150730-story.html.

Klotz, Irene. "Tech Billionaires Bankroll Gold Rush to Mine Asteroids." Reuters, April 24, 2012. https://www.reuters.com/article/us-space-asteroid-mining-idUSBRE83N06U20120424.

Kluger, Jeffrey. "SpaceX's Starhopper Flight Test Is a Big Step Forward for Elon Musk's Moon Dreams." *Time*, August 28 2019. https://time.com/5663339/starhopper-spacex-flight/.

Koerner, Brendan I. "Inside the Cyberattack That Shocked the US Government." *Wired*, October 23, 2016. https://www.wired.com/2016/10/inside-cyberattack-shocked-us-government/.

Koselka, Rita. "Tasteful. Unprofitable. Microsoft?" *Forbes*, November 3, 1997. https://www.forbes.com/forbes/1997/1103/6010046a.html.

Lantz, Mark. "Why the Future of Data Storage Is (Still) Magnetic Tape." *IEEE Spectrum*, August 28, 2018. https://spectrum.ieee.org /why-the-future-of-data-storage-is-still-magnetic-tape.

Laurence, William L. "Cybernetics, a New Science, Seeks the Common Elements in Human and Mechanical Brains." *New York Times*, December 19, 1948.

Leahy, Emmett J., and Robert Weil. "Will One Fire . . . or Bomb . . . Ruin Your Company?" *Credit and Financial Management*, October 1951.

Lohr, Steve. "For Big-Data Scientists, 'Janitor Work' Is Key Hurdle to Insights." *New York Times*, August 18, 2014. http://www.nytimes.com/2014/08/18 /technology/for-big-data-scientists-hurdle-to-insights-is-janitor-work.html.

———. "Gates Acquires Rights to Adams Photo Images." *New York Times*, April 2, 1996.

Lombardi, Kate Stone. "Recalling the Glory Days of *Reader's Digest*." *New York Times*, October 1, 2010.

Lowry, Cynthia. "Mine Serves as Bomb Shelter." *Avalanche-Journal* (Lubbock, Tex.). June 15, 1952.

Lyons, Kim. "FCC Awards SpaceX $886 Million for Satellite Internet Network." *The Verge*, December 2020. https://www.theverge.com/2020/12/7/22159791 /fcc-awards-spacex-886-million-satellite-internet-broadband-rural.

Mack, Eric. "Are Physical Bitcoins Legal?" CNET. October 25, 2011. https://www .cnet.com/news/are-physical-bitcoins-legal/.

"Mannequins Visit Judge on Way to Atom Tests." *Las Vegas Sun*, March 9, 1953.

McCarten, John, and I. Dobell. "A Place to Hide." *New Yorker*, February 22, 1952.

McCoppin, Robert. "Who's Killing the Dewey Decimal System?" *Chicago Tribune*, February 18, 2011. https://www.chicagotribune.com/news/ct-xpm-2011-02-18 -ct-met-drop-dewey-20110218-story.html.

McInerney, Jay. "Brightness Falls." *Guardian*, September 15, 2001. https://www .theguardian.com/books/2001/sep/15/september11.usa1.

Mead, Margaret. "Are Shelters the Answer?" *New York Times Magazine*, November 26, 1961.

Mellis, Miranda F. "An Interview with Dyveke Sanne." *Believer*, December 1, 2008.

Mellon, DeForest. "Preserving Business Records for History . . . an Issue Raised by the NRA." *Bulletin of the National Retail Dry Goods Association*, June 1934.

"Mighty Midgets of Filmdom." *Popular Mechanics*, December 1942.

"Military Turns to ESPN to Help Analyze Drone Footage." *USA Today*, December 19, 2012. https://eu.usatoday.com/story/news/nation/2012/12/19 /drone-video/1770337/.

Mitchell, Paula Ann. "Kingston Cave Once Used as a Mine and to Grow Mushrooms." *Daily Freeman* (Kingston, N.Y.), July 31, 2014.

Molteni, Megan. "Scientists Upload a Galloping Horse GIF into Bacteria with Crispr." *Wired*, July 12, 2017. https://www.wired.com/story /scientists-upload-a-galloping-horse-gif-into-bacteria-with-crispr/.

Moskowitz, Clara. "DNA-Coded 'Lunar Library' Aims to Preserve Civilization for Millennia." *Scientific American*, September 28, 2018. https://www.scientificamerican.com/article/dna-coded-lunar-library-aims-to-preserve-civilization-for-millennia/.

"Most Interesting People." *American Magazine*, September 1937.

Mumford, Lewis. "The Sky Line in Flushing—Genuine Bootleg." *New Yorker*, July 19, 1939.

Nakashima, Ellen, and Craig Whitlock. "With Air Force's Gorgon Drone—'We Can See Everything.'" *Washington Post*, January 2, 2011.

Newton, Casey. "Speak, Memory." *The Verge*. October 6, 2016. https://www.theverge.com/a/luka-artificial-intelligence-memorial-roman-mazurenko-bot.

Nicholson, Catherine. "The Stone Engraving: Icon of the Declaration." *Prologue* 35, no. 3 (Fall 2003).

O'Dwyer, Gerard. "Datacenter Investment Boost as Norway's Government Reinstates Relief." *Computer Weekly*, June 18, 2020. https://www.computerweekly.com/news/252484792/Datacentre-investment-boost-as-Norways-government-reinstates-tax-relief.

"Parcel That Won't Be Delivered until 6939." *New York Times*, August 30, 1938.

Pardes, Arielle. "The Case for Giving Robots an Identity." *Wired*, October 23, 2018.

Pasternak, Alex. "AI Could Help Root Out Bad Cops—If Only the Police Allowed It." *Fast Company*, September 15, 2020.

Patterson, Thom. "US Airport Opens First Fully Biometric Terminal." CNN. December 3, 2018. https://edition.cnn.com/travel/article/atlanta-airport-first-us-biometric-terminal-facial-recognition/index.html.

Popper, Nathaniel. "How the Winklevoss Twins Found Vindication in a Bitcoin Fortune." *New York Times*, December 19, 2017. https://www.nytimes.com/2017/12/19/technology/bitcoin-winklevoss-twins.html.

Potter, Joseph C. "Herman Knaust Finds New Use for Old Mine: Anti-Atomic Storage." *Wall Street Journal*, October 24, 1952.

"Preserving Our History in a Tomb: 'Crypt of Civilization' Will Re-create Our Daily Life for People of 8113 A.D." *Popular Science*, December 1938.

Regalado, Antonio. "Here Are Some Actual Facts about George Church's DNA Dating Company." *MIT Technology Review*, December 11, 2019. https://www.technologyreview.com/2019/12/11/131611/actual-facts-about-george-church-dna-dating-company-digid8/.

Resnick, Brian. "Apollo Astronauts Left Their Poop on the Moon. We Gotta Go Back for That Shit." *Vox*, July 12, 2019. https://www.vox.com/science-and-health/2019/3/22/18236125/apollo-moon-poop-mars-science.

Rosenfeld, Everett. "Apocalypse Later: Largest Bunker Scrapped." CNBC. July 3, 2014. https://www.cnbc.com/2014/07/03/apocalypse-later-largest-bunker-scrapped.html.

Rothman, Joshua. "The Many Lives of Iron Mountain." *New Yorker*, October 9,
2013. http://www.newyorker.com/online/blogs/currency/2013/10/the-many
-lives-of-iron-mountain.html.

Sample, Ian. "Harvard Scientists Pioneer Storage of Video inside DNA."
*Guardian*, July 13, 2017.

"Sandra Legler Fiancee of Stuart Tucker." *Herald Statesman* (Yonkers, N.Y.), April
25, 1956.

Schiller, Dane. "Amazon.com Founder Has Plans for Massive Clock in West
Texas." *Houston Chronicle*, August 19, 2013. https://www.mrt.com/news/
article/Amazon-com-founder-has-plans-for-massive-clock-in-7442783.php.

Schlosser, Eric. "Nuns and Nuclear Security." *New Yorker*, March 9, 2015.

"Scientists of the World of Tomorrow." Advertisement for Westinghouse exhibits
at the New York World's Fair. *Life*, August 7, 1939.

Semerad, Tony. "NSA in Utah: Mining a Mountain of Data." *Salt Lake Tribune*
(Salt Lake City, Utah), July 1, 2013.

Sharpe, Tom. "Mountain of Mystery." *Albuquerque Journal*, January 23, 1994.

Sheets, Bill. "Kimberly-Clark Mill Leaves a Toxic Mess Behind." HeraldNet
(website for the *Daily Herald*, Everett, Wash.), May 4, 2012. https://www.
heraldnet.com/news/kimberly-clark-mill-leaves-a-toxic-mess-behind/.

Sheetz, Michael, "Satellite Start-Up Raises $100 Million to Put Cloud Data Storage
in Space." CNBC, December 20, 2018. https://www.cnbc.com/2018/12/19
/cloud-constellation-raises-100-million-to-store-cloud-data-in-space.html.

Slattery, Thomas J. "The Atchison Storage Facility." *Army Logistician Magazine*,
May/June 1999.

Sokol, David. "Coming Out of the Dark: A Former Federal Reserve Bunker
Protects a Different Kind of Currency." *Greensource: The Magazine of
Sustainable Design*, March 2009. http://greensource.construction.com
/features/solutions/0903/0903_FederalReserveBunker.asp.

Stein, Herbert G. "A Mine of Information: Plant Records Go Underground."
*Pittsburgh (Pa.) Post-Gazette*, January 30, 1961.

Stepanek, Maria. "Data Storage: From Digits to Dust." *BusinessWeek*, April 20,
1998. http://allanenterprises.net/articles-from-digits-to-dust.aspx.

Talley, Robert. "How Nation's 'Average Man' Is Meeting the Depression."
*Plattsburgh (N.Y.) Daily Press*, March 19, 1932.

Thorbecke, Catherine. "4 Astronauts Launch for ISS in Historic NASA-SpaceX
Mission." ABCNews, November 15, 2020. https://abcnews.go.com/US
/astronauts-set-launch-iss-historic-nasa-spacex-mission/story?id=
74134522.

"To Atomize Clothing in A-Bomb Test." *Las Vegas Review Journal*, March 8, 1953.

"To Execute Dog, a Thief." *New York Times*, April 10, 1939.

Trescott, Jacqueline. "A Sound Investment: Packard Heir Gives Library of
Congress Va. Facility for Audio and Film Treasures." *Washington Post*, July 27,

2007. http://www.washingtonpost.com/wp-dyn/content/article/2007/07/27
/AR2007072700160.html.

Tsukayam, Hayley. "How the Tupac 'Hologram' Works." *Washington Post*, April 18, 2012.

"'Typical Families' Greeted by Mayor: After Official Ceremony, He, His Wife and Children Have Private Visit with Them." *New York Times*, May 12, 1940.

United Press International. "Capital Slave Quarters Will Be Bomb Shelter." *New York Times*, December 7, 1950.

Upbin, Bruce. "Image Enhancement." *Forbes*, March 1, 2004.

Valéry, Paul. "The Spiritual Crisis of France." *Athenaeum* (London, England), April 11 and May 2, 1919.

Vincent, James. "'Five-Dimensional' Glass Discs Can Store Data for up to 13.8 Billion Years." *The Verge*, February 16, 2016. https://www.theverge
.com/2016/2/16/11018018/5d-data-storage-glass.

"Virtual Reality Game Helps Ease Pain for Burns Victims." BBC News, April 18, 2018. https://www.bbc.com/news/uk-england-south-yorkshire-43744009.

Vogel, Carol. "Leonardo Notebook Sells for $30.8 Million." *New York Times*, November 12, 1994.

von Busack, Richard. "Cinema Saver: David Packard of Stanford Theatre Gives Millions to National Film-Preservation Effort." Metroactive, September 5, 2007. http://www.metroactive.com/metro/09.05.07/film-restoration-0736.html.

Wallace, Amy. "Miss Millennium: Beyoncé." *GQ*, January 10, 2013.

Ward, Walter H. "Records Protection against Bombing: Your Storage Facilities." *Savings and Loan News*, May 1951.

Wharton, Don. "The Safest Place in the World." *Saturday Evening Post*, March 22, 1952.

"Wonders of Research: Aging of Films." *Christian Science Monitor*, July 14, 1938.

Yardley, William. "Willis Whitfield, Inventor of Clean Room That Purges Tiny Particles, Dies at 92." *New York Times*, December 4, 2012.

Yergin, Daniel. "Blood and Oil: Why Japan Attacked Pearl Harbor." *Washington Post*, December 1, 1991.

Zaleski, Andrew. "Why Bill Gates Is Betting on a Start-Up That Prints Synthetic DNA." CNBC, May 22, 2018. https://www.cnbc.com/2018/05/22/bill-gates-is
-betting-on-this-synthetic-biology-start-up.html.

Zapinski, Ken. "Mining the Hills for Storage: Butler County Hole in the Wall Becomes Acquisition Target." *Pittsburgh (Pa.) Post-Gazette*, June 12, 1998.

Zeitlin, Matthew. "This Iconic American Image Is Now Owned by China." *Buzzfeed News*, January 22, 2016. https://www.buzzfeednews.com/article
/matthewzeitlin/one-of-americas-most-iconic-photos-is
-now-owned-by-a-chinese.

## Multimedia

A Tribe Called Quest. "Space Program." *We Got It from Here . . . Thank You 4 Your Service*. Epic Records, 2016.

Catalog Technologies. "Introduction to DNA Data Storage and CATALOG."
YouTube video, 9:57. Posted November 1, 2018. https://www.youtube.com
/watch?v=IiPvJfbq2No.

Creative Time. "Trevor Paglen: The Last Pictures." Video. http://creativetime.org
/projects/the-last-pictures/videos/. Accessed March 15, 2014.

Ferris, Timothy. "Voyagers in Space & Time." *The Voyager Golden Record*. Mill
Valley, Calif.: Ozma Records, 2018.

Goebel, Johannes. "The Computer as Time Machine." Talk delivered at
Experimental Media and Performing Arts Center (EMPAC), Rensselaer
Polytechnic Institute, October 13, 2018. https://www.youtube.com
/watch?v=2rbGX4fdu8k.

"Go Inside Subtropolis." *The Today Show*. Aired October 16, 2016, on NBC.

Hennelly, Denis Henry, dir. *Goodbye World*. 2014; Culver City, Calif.: Sony
Pictures Home Entertainment, 2016. DVD.

Kassovitz, Mathieu, dir. *La Haine*. 1995; Sony Pictures Home Entertainment, 2012.
Blu-ray Disc.

Maness, Fred, narrator. "Civil Defense: Mock 'Alert' Tests Nation's Readiness." Los
Angeles, Calif.: Universal Pictures Company, 1954. YouTube video, "Operation
Alert 1954: Newsreel," 1:25. Posted by CONELRAD6401240. https://youtu.be
/m13zknLHF-8.

Mason, Christopher. "Discovering and Designing Genomes for Earth, Mars, and
Beyond." TEDMED Talk, 2015. Video, 12:49. https://www.tedmed.com/talks
/show?id=528172.

Morris, Errol, dir. *The Fog of War*. 2003; Culver City, Calif.: Sony Pictures Home
Entertainment, 2004. DVD.

Paglen, Trevor. "Invisible Images of Surveillance." Talk given at the Trevor Paglen
Studio, Germany, n.d. YouTube video, 12:46. Posted by World Economic
Forum, April 5, 2018. https://www.youtube.com/watch?v=ijVTdSoZEC4.
Accessed October 7, 2021.

———. "Trevor Paglen Photographs Classified 'Black Sites.'" San Francisco
Museum of Modern Art, n.d. Video, 03:26. https://www.sfmoma.org/watch
/trevor-paglen-photographs-classified-black-sites/.

Pescovitz, David, Timothy Daly, and Lawrence Azerrad. *The Voyager Golden
Record*. Mill Valley, Calif.: Ozma Records, 2018.

Pirat, Fred, dir. "Iron Mountain: Our Story." 2009. YouTube video, 3:59. Posted by
Webmaster Iron Mountain, November 14, 2009. https://www.youtube.com
/watch?v=rNU-L9c9nzs.

Snody, Robert R., dir. *The Middleton Family at the New York World's Fair*. 1939.
Audio Productions. https://archive.org/details/the-middleton-family-1939.

Tandon, Nina. "Could Tissue Engineering Mean Personalized Medicine?" TED
Talk, TEDGlobal 2012, June 2012. Video, 06:03. https://www.ted
.com/talks/nina_tandon_could_tissue_engineering_mean_personalized
_medicine?language=en.

Tarantino, Louis C., dir. *Life after People*. Season 2, episode 3, "Crypt of Civilization." Aired January 19, 2010, on History Channel. https://www.history .com/shows/life-after-people/season-2/episode-3.

## Online Sources

Aanika Biosciences. "Carverr Is Now Aanika Biosciences!" Medium (website). March 9, 2020. https://aanikabio.medium.com /carverr-is-now-aanika-biosciences-20c03a84758f.

———. "Scientific Advisory." https://www.aanikabio.com/about#our-advisors. Accessed October 10, 2021.

Alcorn, Paul. "Seagate Demos World's Fastest Hard Drive, Doubled Performance, HAMR Progress." *Tom's Hardware*, March 21, 2018. https://www. tomshardware.com/news/seagate-exos-hdd-hamr-mach.2,36719.html.

———. "Seagate Plans to HAMR WD's MAMR; 20 TB HDDs with Lasers Abound." *Tom's Hardware*, November 3, 2017. https://www.tomshardware.com/news /seagate-wd-hamr-mamr-20tb,35821.html.

———. "WD Plots a Course to 40TB HDDs with MAMR." *Tom's Hardware*, October 13, 2017. https://www.tomshardware.com/news/wd-mamr-hdd -hamr-drive,35682.html.

Apel, Jillian. "The Story of DeWitt Wallace: An Original Aggregator." DeWitt Wallace Center for Media and Democracy, Duke University. https://dewitt .sanford.duke.edu/the-story-of-dewitt-wallace-an-original-aggregator/. Accessed December 28, 2020.

Apple. "Airport Time Capsule." http://www.apple.com/airport-time-capsule/. Accessed April 1, 2014.

———. "Register Here." Apple Time Capsule Memorial Register. timecapsuledead. org. Accessed January 10, 2014.

AppliedVR. "About." https://appliedvr.io/about/. Accessed October 10, 2021.

Architect of the Capitol. "James Madison Memorial Building." https://www .aoc.gov/explore-capitol-campus/buildings-grounds/library-of-congress /james-madison-building.

Arthur, Charles, and Sebastian E. Payne. "Apple Finally Admits Problems with Time Capsule and Offers Replacement." *Technology Blog, Guardian*, July 12, 2010. http://www.theguardian.com/technology/blog/2010/jul/12 /apple-time-capsule-recall-replace-fault.

Atomic Heritage Foundation. "Hydrogen Bomb—1950." June 19, 2014. https://www.atomicheritage.org/history/hydrogen-bomb-1950.

Beckett, Richard. "Bioreceptive Façade Panels." http://www.richard-beckett. com/portfolio/items/bioreceptive-facade-panels-epsrc-funded-research -computational-seeding-of-bioreceptive-materials/. Accessed September 15, 2020.

Beldin, Sarah I., and Stephen S. Perakis. "Unearthing Secrets of the Forest." U.S. Geological Survey. Fact Sheet 2009-3078. https://pubs.usgs.gov /fs/2009/3078/.

Bennett, Todd J. "100 Years on Peachtree: Oglethorpe's Enduring Story of Persistence." Oglethorpe University. February 20, 2015. https://source .oglethorpe.edu/2015/02/20/enduring-story-persistence.

Bhan, Namita J., Jonathan Strutz, Joshua Glaser, Reza Kalhor, Edward Boyden, George Church, Konrad Kording, and Keith E. J. Tyo. "Recording Temporal Data onto DNA with Minutes Resolution." bioRxiv, Cold Spring Harbor Laboratory. July 3, 2019. https://www.biorxiv.org/content/10.1101/634790v3.full.

Binkley, Peter. *Robert C. Binkley | 1897-1940 / Life, Work, Ideas* (blog). https://www.wallandbinkley.com/rcb/. Accessed October 7, 2021.

Biosteel. http://www.biosteel-fiber.com/home/. Accessed October 10, 2021.

Blaustein, Jonathan. "Trevor Paglen Interview." A Photo Editor (website), November 4, 2015. https://aphotoeditor.com/2015/11/04 /trevor-paglen-interview/.

Bradsher, Greg. "The National Archives' Arthur Evarts Kimberly and the Allied Translator and Interpreter Section's Document Restoration Sub-Section, 1944–1945." *The Text Message* (blog). January 20, 2015. https://text-message.blogs. archives.gov/2015/01/20/the-national-archives-arthur-evarts-kimberly -and-the-allied-translator-and-interpreter-sections-document-restoration -sub-section-1944-1945/.

———. "The Travels of the Bill of Rights, Emancipation Proclamation, and Other National Archives Holdings on the Freedom Train, 1947–1949." *The Text Message* (blog). September 14, 2012. https://text-message.blogs.archives .gov/2012/09/14/the-travels-of-the-bill-of-rights-emancipation-proclamation -and-other-national-archives-holdings-on-the-freedom-train-1947-1949/.

Calandro, Daniel. "Hudson River Valley Icehouses and Ice Industry." Hudson River Valley Institute. May 9, 2005. https://www.hudsonrivervalley .org/documents/401021/1055071/NatIceIndustrydicehousepaper .pdf/105f65ae-77b3-4069-af5d-f153d733af56.

Cantu, Marissa, and Lee Reiners. "High-Frequency Trading Comes to Cryptocurrency." The FinReg Blog. Global Financial Markets Center, Duke University School of Law. April 24, 2019. https://sites.law.duke.edu /thefinregblog/2019/04/24/high-frequency-trading-comes-to-cryptocurrency/.

Cobblestone Software. "Welcome to the Paper Revolution!(TM)." Cobblestone Software website. http://www.paperdisk.com/index.html. Accessed December 28, 2020.

Cold Spring Harbor Laboratory. "Carnegie Institution of Washington." https:// www.cshl.edu/archives/institutional-collections/carnegie-institution-of -washington/. Accessed November 5, 2021.

Diamond Foundry. https://diamondfoundry.com/pages/technology. Accessed June 14, 2021.

Enterprise Storage Forum. "Storage That Really Lasts." September 11, 2008. http://www.enterprisestorageforum.com/print.php/3771001.

Facebook. "Managing a Deceased Person's Account." Facebook Help Center. https://www.facebook.com/help/275013292838654. Accessed October 7, 2021.

Good, Jonathan. "How Many Photos Have Ever Been Taken?" *1000memories blog*, September 15, 2011. http://blog.1000memories.com/94-number-of-photos -ever-taken-digital-and-analog-in-shoebox. Accesed January 25, 2013.

Guinness World Records. "Highest-Grossing Film at the Global Box Office (Inflation-Adjusted)." https://www.guinnessworldrecords.com/world -records/highest-box-office-film-gross-inflation-adjusted/. Accessed October 10, 2021.

Haynes, Gary. "Under Iron Mountain: Corbis Stores 'Very Important Photographs' at Zero Degrees Fahrenheit." National Press Photographers Association. February 1, 2005. https://nppa.org/news/257

HIVE Blockchain Technologies. "HIVE Blockchain Increases Bitcoin Mining Production Immediately with the Purchase of 1,240 Next Generation Miners While Upgrading Its GPU Chips to Mine Ethereum in the Cloud." News release. Cision, November 6, 2020. https://www.newswire.ca/news-releases /hive-blockchain-increases-bitcoin-mining-production-immediately-with -the-purchase-of-1-240-next-generation-miners-while-upgrading-its-gpu -chips-to-mine-ethereum-in-the-cloud-828763111.html.

Human Rights Watch. "Myths and Realities about Incendiary Weapons: Memorandum to Delegates of the 2018 Meeting of States Parties to the Convention on Conventional Weapons." November 14, 2018. https://www.hrw .org/news/2018/11/14/myths-and-realities-about-incendiary-weapons.

Internet Movie Database (IMDb). "The Ten Commandments." https://www .imdb.com/title/tt0014532/. Accessed October 4, 2021.

Iron Mountain. "Iron Mountain Announces 27 Megawatt Pre-Lease in Frankfurt with Fortune 100 Customer." Press release. June 8, 2020. https://www .ironmountain.com/about-us/news-events/news-categories/press -releases/2020/june/iron-mountain-announces-27-megawatt-pre-lease -in-frankfurt-with-fortune-100-customer.

———. "Welcome to Iron Mountain's National Data Center." https://www .ironmountain.com/resources/multimedia/w/welcome -to-iron-mountains-national-data-center.

Johnson & Johnson Innovation Labs. "EpiBone." https://jlabs.jnjinnovation.com /JLABSNavigator/company/EpiBone. Accessed October 11, 2021.

Kelly, Kevin. "Clock in the Mountain." The 10,000 Year Clock, Long Now Foundation. https://longnow.org/clock/. Accessed October 11, 2021.

———. "Very Long-Term Backup." *Long Now Foundation Blog*, August 20, 2008. https://blog.longnow.org/02008/08/20/very-long-term-backup/.

Library Journal. "Even Sasha Fierce Needs Archives/Archivists." Tumblr, January 10, 2013. https://tumblr.libraryjournal.com/post/40197756590 /even-sasha-fierce-needs-archivesarchivists.

Library of Congress. "'Packard Campus' Gift Ushers In Dawn of New Era for Audio-Visual Conservation." News release. July 26, 2007. http://www.loc.gov /today/pr/2007/07-149.html.

———. "Preservation Science." https://www.loc.gov/preservation/scientists/. Accessed October 6, 2021.

———. "Subject and Genre/Form Headings." Cataloging and Acquisitions. https://www.loc.gov/aba/cataloging/subject/. Accessed October 10, 2021.

———. "Torpedo Factory Art Center: A Local Legacy." America's Story from America's Library (website), Library of Congress. http://www.americaslibrary .gov/es/va/es_va_torpedo_1.html.

———. "2012 National Film Registry Picks in a League of Their Own." News release. December 19, 2012. http://www.loc.gov/today/pr/2012/12-226.html.

Lunt, Barry M., and Matthew R. Linford. "Long-Term Digital Data Storage." US 7613869B2, United States Patent and Trademark Office, issued November 3, 2009. Google Patents. https://patents.google.com/patent/US20090231978.

Mangomaterials.com. Accessed October 1, 2021.

Mansfield Memorial Museum. "ELEKTRO." http://www.themansfieldmuseum .com/elektro-1.html. Accessed October 7, 2021.

Mason Lab home page. www.masonlab.net.

Metropolitan Transity Authority (MTA). "The Train of the Future Now a Museum Piece." Press release. April 12, 2007. https://www.mta.info/press-release /mta-headquarters/train-future-now-museum-piece.

Miller, Rich. "NSA Building $860 Million Data Center in Maryland." DataCenter Knowledge. June 6, 2013. https://www.datacenterknowledge.com /archives/2013/06/06/nsa-to-build-860-million-hpc-center-in-maryland.

Naremco Services. "About Us." http://www.naremco.com/aboutUs.asp. Accessed June 10, 2013.

NASA. "Mars Terraforming Not Possible Using Present-Day Technology." Press release. June 30, 2018. https://www.nasa.gov/press-release/goddard/2018 /mars-terraforming.

National Archives and Records Administration. "The History of the National Archives at College Park." https://www.archives.gov/about/history /college-park.

National Institute of Standards and Technology. "Fiftieth Anniversary of First Digital Image Marked." May 24, 2007; updated August 13, 2020. https://www.nist.gov/news-events/news/2007/05/fiftieth -anniversary-first-digital-image-marked.

New York Public Library. "About the Dewitt Wallace Periodical Room." https://www.nypl.org/about/divisions/general-research-division /periodicals-room.

Nuclear Waste Partnership, for the U.S. Department of Energy. Waste Isolation Pilot Plant website. https://wipp.energy.gov/wipp-site.asphttps://wipp.energy.gov/wipp-site.asp. Accessed October 1, 2021.

Odell, Jenny. "The Satellite Collections." 2013. https://www.jennyodell.com/satellite-essay.html.

Officina Corpuscoli. "Caskia." https://www.corpuscoli.com/projects/caskia/. Accessed June 12, 2021.

Pike, John. "Dugway Proving Grounds." Global Security. https://www.globalsecurity.org/wmd/facility/dugway.htm. Accessed October 6, 2021.

Poponak, Noah, Matthew Porat, Michael Bishop, Chris Hallam, Brett Feldman, and Heath P. Terry. *Space: The Next Investment Frontier*. Profiles in Innovation. Goldman Sachs. April 4, 2017. https://www.gspublishing.com/content/research/en/reports/2017/04/04/49ead899-a05b-4822-9645-2948f2050a31.pdf.

ProQuest. "ProQuest Dissertation Publishing Preservation." http://www.proquest.com/en-US/products/dissertations/preservation. Accessed July 11, 2013.

———. "ProQuest Dissertations FAQ." https://about.proquest.com/products-services/dissertations/ProQuest-Dissertations-FAQ.html. Accessed June 2, 2021.

ProtonMail. "Pricing." https://protonmail.com/pricing. Accessed October 2, 2021.

"Questionnaire for Selecting the National Typical American Family." *Biblion: World's Fair* (online exhibit). New York Public Library. http://exhibitions.nypl.org/biblion/sites/exhibitions.nypl.org.biblion/files/imagecache/story-image/2H4-1_0.jpg. Accessed August 14, 2012.

Reader's Digest. "About *Reader's Digest*." https://www.rd.com/about-readers-digest/. Accessed December 28, 2020.

Riley, Rachele. "Researching the L.A. Darling Co. Mannequins." *Rachele Riley: Process and Research* (blog). September 6, 2012. https://blog.racheleriley.com/researching-the-l-a-darling-mannequins/.

———. "The Subject of My Archival Research, Appreciating Las Vegas." *Rachele Riley: Process and Research* (blog). January 7, 2013. https://blog.racheleriley.com/the-subject-of-my-archival-research-appreciating-las-vegas/.

———. "Update on the 'Annie' Test Mannequins." *Rachele Riley: Process and Research* (blog). January 8, 2013. https://blog.racheleriley.com/update-on-the-annie-test-mannequins/.

Ripley County, Indiana, Historical Society. "St. Magdelene Catholic Church Cemetery Records: New Marion, Shelby Twp., Ripley County, Indiana." January 25, 1998. http://rchslib.org/stmagdalene.html.

Sandia National Laboratories. "Modern-Day Cleanroom Invented by Sandia Physicist Still Used 50 Years Later." News release. November 26, 2012. https://newsreleases.sandia.gov/cleanroom_50th/.

Seagate. *HAMR Technology.* 2018. https://www.seagate.com/files/www-content
/innovation/hamr/_shared/files/tp707-1-1712us-hamr.pdf.

St. Germain, Joel. "Why Is Ashburn the Data Center Capital of the World?"
DataCenters.com. August 19, 2019. https://www.datacenters.com/news
/why-is-ashburn-the-data-center-capital-of-the-world.

Stillo, Stephanie. *Incunabula: The Art and History of Printing in Western
Europe, 1450–1500.* Rare Book and Special Collections Division,
Library of Congress. https://www.loc.gov/ghe/cascade/index
.html?appid=580edae150234258a49a3eeb58d9121c. Accessed September 29,
2021.

Sverdlik, Yevgeniy. "2021: These Are the World's Largest Data Center
Colocation Providers." DataCenter Knowledge. January 15, 2021.
https://www.datacenterknowledge.com/archives/2017/01/20
/here-are-the-10-largest-data-center-providers-in-the-world.

Tiseo, Ian. "Global Paper Production Volume from 2008 to 2018 by Type."
*Statista*, January 27, 2021. https://www.statista.com/statistics/270317
/production-volume-of-paper-by-type/.

UNESCO. "Bath's Roman Curse Tablets Added to the UNESCO
Memory of the World Register." https://en.unesco.org/news
/bath's-roman-curse-tablets-added-unesco-memory-world-register.

Vargas, Maria Tikoff. "10 Facts to Know about Data Centers." Office of Energy
Efficiency and Renewable Energy, U.S. Department of Energy. November 17,
2014. https://www.energy.gov/eere/articles/10-facts-know-about
-data-centers.

Vivos Global Shelter Network. https://terravivos.com/. Accessed October 1, 2021.

Weissman, Ken. "Library of Congress Unlocks Ultimate Archival system." Creative
COW. http://library.creativecow.net/print.php?id=12352.

Wilhelm Imaging Research. *Bettmann 100: Celebrating the Legacy of Dr. Otto
Bettmann.* May 17, 2004. http://wilhelm-research.com/corbis/Corbis
_Bettmann100_2003_11_preview.html.

Wilkins, Randall. "Art Directing Bomb Targets." *The Designer's Assistant* (blog),
December 6, 2011. https://thedesignersassistant.com/2011/12/06
/art-directing-bomb-targets/.

## Other Primary Sources

Allied Translator and Interpreter Section, South West Pacific Area. *Restoration of
Captured Documents.* ATIS Publication No. 10. June 28, 1945.

Bernays, Edward L. *The New York World's Fair—a Symbol for Democracy. Address
of Edward L. Bernays, Member of World's Fair Committee of the Merchants'
Association of New York at Luncheon under Auspices of the Association's
Members' Council at Hotel Pennsylvania, April 7, 1937.* New York City:
Merchants' Association of New York, 1937.

Bornholt, James, Randolph Lopez, Douglas M. Carmean, Georg Seelig, Luis Ceze, and Karin Strauss. "A DNA-Based Archival Storage System." In *ASPLOS '16: Proceedings of the Twenty-First International Conference on Architectural Support for Programming Languages and Operating Systems*, 637–49. New York: Association for Computing Machinery, 2016.

Cohen, E., and E. Laing. *Operation Plumbbob Preliminary Report: Project 30.4. Response of Protective Vaults to Blast Loading*. New York: Ammann and Whitney, 1957.

Conference of First Vice Presidents. *The Culpeper Switch: The Federal Reserve System*. Booklet. 1975. A Secret Landscape: America's Cold War Infrastructure (website). http://coldwar-c4i.net/Mt_Pony/culpsw01.htm. Accessed May 30, 2019.

Cutts, James A. *Conceptual Design of a Monitoring System for the Charters of Freedom*. JPL Publication 83-102. Pasadena: California Institute of Technology, 1984.

Davenport, C. B. *The Trait Book*. Eugenics Record Office Bulletin No. 6. Cold Spring Harbor, N.Y.: Eugenics Record Office, 1912.

"Directions and Lodging—Corbis Film Preservation Facility (FPF) Located at Iron Mountain." In author's possession.

Gale Group. "Pierce Leahy Corporation." In *International Directory of Company Histories*, 389–92. Farmington Hills, Mich.: Gale Group, 2006.

Hamilton, Alexander, John Jay, and James Madison. "No. 59. Concerning the Power of Congress to Regulate the Election of Members." In *Federalist Papers: Primary Documents in American History*. Library of Congress Research Guides. https://guides.loc.gov/federalist-papers/text-51-60#s-lg-box -wrapper-25493435. Accessed October 7, 2021.

Hengemihle, Frank H., Norman Weberg, and Chandru Shahani. *Desorption of Residual Ethylene Oxide from Fumigated Library Materials*. Preservation Research and Testing Series No. 9502. Washington, D.C.: Preservation Directorate, Library of Congress, 1995. Presented at the first meeting of the Pan-American Deterioration Society, Washington, D.C., July 1986.

Hornaday, William Temple. *Taxidermy and Zoological Collecting: A Complete Handbook for the Amateur Taxidermist, Collector, Osteologist, Museum-Builder, Sportsman, and Traveller; With Chapters on Collecting and Preserving Insects by W. J. Holland*. Illustrated by Charles Bradford Hudson. New York: Charles Scribner's Sons, 1891.

Jones, Neil R. "The Jameson Satellite." *Amazing Stories*, July 1931.

Kantrowitz, M. S., and R. H. Simmons. "The Technical Status of Permanence and Durability of Paper." Paper presented at the Graphic Arts Technical Conference, Washington, D.C., May 1936.

Kodak. *Recovering Silver from Photographic Processing Solutions*. Kodak Publication No. J-215. Rochester, N.Y.: Eastman Kodak, 1999.

———. *Sources of Silver in Photographic Processing Facilities*. Kodak Publication No. J-210. Rochester, N.Y.: Eastman Kodak Company, 1998.

Lupisella, Mark, et al. "Low-Latency Telerobotic Sample Return and Biomolecular Sequencing for Deep Space Gateway." Paper presented at NASA Deep Space Gateway Science Workshop, February 2018. Abstract 3032. https://www.hou.usra.edu/meetings/deepspace2018/pdf/3032.pdf.

Michelson, David M., and John W. Attig. *Laurentide Ice Sheet: Ice-Margin Positions in Wisconsin*. 2nd ed. Educational Series 56. Madison: Wisconsin Geological and Natural History Survey, 2017. https://wgnhs.wisc.edu/catalog/publication/000939/resource/es056.

"Microvivarium Portrays Life in a Drop of Water." *Westinghouse Fair World: Official News of Westinghouse Activities at the New York and San Francisco Fairs*. Pittsburgh, Pa.: Westinghouse Electric and Manufacturing, 1939.

Parmater, Richard, ed. *Communication Revolutions, Information Technology, and Libraries: Proceedings of the February 1, 1985 Symposium; Honoring Eugene B. Power and Vernon D. Tate*. Ann Arbor: University of Michigan University Library and School of Library Science, 1987.

*Project Greek Island: The Bunker*. Brochure. White Sulphur Springs: Greenbrier, undated.

Shahani, Chandru. "Preservation Research and Testing Series No. 9503: Accelerated Aging of Paper; Can It Really Foretell the Permanence of Paper." Paper delivered at the ASTM/ISR Workshop on the Effects of Aging on Printing and Writing Papers, Philadelphia, Pa., 1994.

Shapero, Natalie. "Our War." *failbetter*, December 1, 2009. http://www.failbetter.com/33/ShaperoOurWar.php.

Shehabi, Arman, Sarah Josephine Smith, Dale A. Sartor, Richard E. Brown, Magnus Herrlin, Jonathan G. Koomey, Eric R. Masanet, Nathaniel Horner, Inês Lima Azevedo, and William Lintner. *United States Data Center Energy Usage Report*. Ernest Orlando Lawrence Berkeley National Laboratory, LBNL-1005775. June 1, 2016. https://eta-publications.lbl.gov/sites/default/files/lbnl-1005775_v2.pdf.

Standard Oil Development Company. *Design and Construction of Typical German and Japanese Test Structures at Dugway Proving Grounds, Utah*. New Jersey: Standard Oil, 1943.

Wilhelm, Henry, with Ann C. Hartman, Kenneth Johnston, and Els Rijper and Thomas Benjamin. "High-Security, Sub-Zero Cold Storage for the PERMANENT Preservation of the Corbis-Bettmann Archive Photography Collection." In *Final Program and Proceedings: IS&T Archiving Conference*, 122–27. Springfield, Va.: Society for Imaging Science and Technology, 2004. http://www.wilhelm-research.com/subzero/Corbis_Bettmann_ColdStorage_preview.html.

Yokum, David, Anita Ravishankar, and Alexander Coppock. "A Randomized Control Trial Evaluating the Effects of Police Body-Worn Cameras."

*Proceedings of the National Academy of Sciences of the United States of America* 116, no. 21 (May 2019): 10329–32.

## SECONDARY SOURCES
### Journal Articles, Book Chapters, and Dissertations

Adams, Geoff W. "The Social and Cultural Implications of Curse Tablets [Defixiones] in Britain and on the Continent." *Studia Humaniora Tartuensia* 7 (2006). https://www.ut.ee/klassik/sht/2006/adams2.pdf.

"American Libraries." *Library Journal* 33, no. 11 (November 1908): 470–77.

Annunziato, Anthony T. "DNA Packaging: Nucleosomes and Chromatin." *Nature Education* 1, no. 1 (2008): 26.

Arendt, Hannah. "The Conquest of Space and the Stature of Man." In *Between Past and Future*, 265–80. New York: Penguin, 1993.

Auerbach, Jonathan, and Lisa Gitelman. "Microfilm, Containment, and the Cold War." *American Literary History* 19, no. 3 (2007): 745–68.

Baldwin, James. "Introduction: The Price of the Ticket." In *The Price of the Ticket: Collected Nonfiction, 1948–1985*, 1–12. Boston: Beacon, 1985.

Barcan, Arthur. "Records Management and the 'Paperwork Age.'" *Business History Review* 29, no. 3 (September 1955): 218–65.

Bazin, André. "The Ontology of the Photographic Image." In *What Is Cinema?*, 2 vols., translated by Hugh Gray, 1: 9–16. Berkeley: University of California Press, 1967.

Benjamin, Walter. "Theses on the Philosophy of History." In *Illuminations: Essays and Reflections*, edited and with an introduction by Hannah Arendt, 253–64. New York: Schocken Books, 1968.

———. "The Work of Art in the Age of Mechanical Reproduction." In *Illuminations: Essays and Reflections*, edited and with an introduction by Hannah Arendt, 217–52. New York: Schocken Books, 1968.

Billings, John Shaw. "Libraries in Washington." *Library Journal* 8, no. 10 (October 1883): 199–200.

Binkley, Robert C. "The Problem of Perishable Paper." In Fisch, *Selected Papers of Robert Cedric Binkley*, 169–78.

Bobinski, George S. "Carnegie Libraries: Their History and Impact on American Public Library Development." *ALA Bulletin* 62, no. 11 (December 1968): 1361–67.

Boothman, Barry E. C. "A Theme Worthy of Epic Treatment: N. S. B. Gras and the Emergence of American Business History." *Journal of Macromarketing* 21, no. 1 (June 2001): 61–73.

Borges, Jorge Luis. "The God's Script," translated by L. A. Murillo. In *Labyrinths: Selected Stories and Other Writings*, edited by Donald A. Yates and James E. Irby and with a preface by André Maurois, 169–73. New York: New Directions, 1964.

Brennan, Shane. "Making Data Sustainable: Backup Culture and Risk Perception." In *Sustainable Media: Critical Approaches to Media and Environment*, edited by Nicole Starosielski and Janet Walker, 56-76. New York: Routledge, 2016.

Brichford, Mayer. "The Relationship of Records Management Activities to the Field of Business History." *Business History Review* 46, no. 2 (Summer 1972): 220-32.

Buck, Solon J. "The National Archives and the Advancement of Science." *Science* 83, no. 2156 (April 24, 1936): 379-85.

Cady, Susan. "Machine Tool of Management: A History of Microfilm Technology." Ph.D. diss., Lehigh University, 1994.

Cardozo, Karen, and Banu Subramaniam. "Assembling Asian/American Naturecultures: Orientalism and Invited Invasions." *Journal of Asian American Studies* 16, no. 1 (February 2013): 1-23.

Carpenter, Kenneth. "Toward a New Cultural Design: The American Council of Learned Societies, the Social Science Research Council, and Libraries in the 1930s." In *Institutions of Reading: The Social Life of Libraries in the United States*, edited by Thomas Augst and Kenneth Carpenter, 283-309. Amherst: University of Massachusetts Press, 2007.

Carpenter, Kenneth, and Thomas Augst. "The History of Libraries in the United States: A Conference Report." *Libraries and Culture* 38, no. 1 (Winter 2003): 61-66.

Carruth, Allison. "The Digital Cloud and the Micropolitics of Energy." *Public Culture* 26, no. 2 (2014): 339-64.

Cartwright, Dorwin, and Francis Bradshaw. "Strikes Are Preventable." *Science News-Letter* 56, no. 18 (October 29, 1949): 277-78.

Chapman, Stephen. "Microfilm: A Preservation Technology for the 21st Century?" In *Archiving 2005*, 228-32. Washington, D.C.: Society for Imaging Science and Technology, 2005.

Chun, Wendy Hui Kyong. "Introduction: Race and/as Technology; or, How to Do Things to Race." *Camera Obscura* 24, no. 1 (2009): 6-35.

———. "Programmed Visions." *Vectors* 3, no. 1 (2007). http://vectors.usc.edu/issues/5/programmedvisions/.

Clynes, Manfred E., and Nathan S. Kline. "Cyborgs and Space." *Astronautics*, September 1960.

Coffey, Mary K. "The American Adonis: A Natural History of the 'Average American' (Man), 1921-32." In Currell and Cogdell, *Popular Eugenics*, 185-216.

Conaty, Matthew L. "The Atomic Midwife: The Eisenhower Administration's Continuity-of-Government Plans and the Legacy of 'Constitutional Dictatorship.'" *Rutgers Law Review* 62, no. 3 (Spring 2010).

Connor, R. D. W. "The National Archives: Objectives and Practices." *Bulletin of the American Library Association* 30, no. 8 (August 1936): 592-93.

———. "Our National Archives." *Minnesota History* 17, no. 2 (March 1936): 1-19.

Conway, Paul. "Preservation in the Age of Google: Digitization, Digital Preservation, and Dilemmas." *Library Quarterly* 80, no. 1 (January 2010): 61–79.

Cutter, C. A. "The Buffalo Public Library in 1983." *Library Journal* 8, no. 10 (October 1883).

Dain, Phyllis. "Harry M. Lydenberg and American Library Resources: A Study in Modern Library Leadership." *Library Quarterly*, 47, no. 4 (October 1977): 451–69.

Davis, Mike. "Berlin's Skeleton in Utah's Closet." *Grand Street* (Summer 1999): 92–100.

———. "Sunshine and the Open Shop: Ford and Darwin in 1920s Los Angeles." *Antipode* 29, no. 4 (October 1997): 356–82.

DeMarinis, Paul. "Erased Dots and Rotten Dashes, or How to Wire Your Head for a Preservation." In Huhtamo and Parikka, *Media Archaeology*, 211–38.

Detwiler, Kate. "'Belonging': Human/Archive/World." In Paglen, *Last Pictures*, 21–22.

Durrans, Brian. "Posterity and Paradox: Some Uses of Time Capsules." In *Contemporary Futures: Perspectives from Social Anthropology*, edited by Sandra Wallman, 51–67. London: Routledge, 1992.

Eales, Anne Bruner. "Fort Archives: The National Archives Goes to War, Part 2." *Prologue* 35, no. 2 (Summer 2003). https://www.archives.gov/publications /prologue/2003/summer/fort-archives-2.html.

Edwards, Elizabeth, and Janice Hart. "Introduction: Photographs as Objects." In Edwards and Hart, *Photographs Objects Histories*, 1–15.

Ehrhardt, J. D., Jr., Don K. Nakayama, and J. Patrick O'Leary. "Carbolic Acid before Joseph Lister—Rail Ties, Sewage, Manure, and the Great Stink." *American Surgeon* 86, no. 3 (March 2020): 176–83.

Ernst, Wolfgang. "Archives in Transition: Dynamic Media Memories." In Ernst, *Digital Memory and the Archive*, 95–101.

———. "Discontinuities: Does the Archive Become Metaphorical in Multimedia Space?" In Ernst, *Digital Memory and the Archive*, 113–46.

———. "Media Archaeography: Method and Machine versus History and Narrative of Media." In Huhtamo and Parikka, *Media Archaeology*, 239–55.

Fielding, Raymond. "Hale's Tours: Ultrarealism in the Pre-1910 Motion Picture." *Cinema Journal* 10, no. 1 (Autumn 1970).

Fisch, Max H. "Introduction: Robert Cedric Binkley, Historian in the Long Armistice." In Fisch, *Selected Papers*, 3–44.

Fitzgerald, Gerard J. "From Prevention to Infection: Intramural Aerobiology, Biomedical Technology, and the Origins of Biological Warfare Research in the United States, 1910–1955." Ph.D. diss., Carnegie Mellon University, 2003.

Galison, Peter. "Removing Knowledge." *Critical Inquiry* 31, no. 1 (Autumn 2004).

———. "War against the Center." *Grey Room* 4 (Summer 2001): 6–33.

Gladwell, Malcolm. "The 10,000-Hour Rule." In *Outliers: The Story of Success*, 35–68. New York: Little, Brown, 2008.

Goldbarth, Albert. "Both Definitions of Save." *Iowa Review* 21, no. 1 (Winter 1991): 59.

Griffith, Kevin. "The Night of the Living." In *Paradise Refunded*, 65. Omaha, Neb.: Backwaters, 1998.

Haraway, Donna. "Teddy Bear Patriarchy: Taxidermy in the Garden of Eden, New York City, 1908–1936." *Social Text* 11 (Winter 1984–85).

Harris, Wendy Elizabeth, and Arnold Pickman. "Towards an Archaeology of the Hudson River Ice Harvesting Industry." *Northeast Historical Archaeology* 29 (2000).

Hoffman, John. "When Pictures Came to Life." *American Cinematographer* 55 (February 1974): 184–86, 217–28.

Hogan, Mél. "Data Flows and Water Woes: The Utah Data Center." *Big Data and Society* (July–December 2015).

———. "Templating Life: DNA as Nature's Hard Drive." *PUBLIC 57: Archives /Anarchives/Counter-Archives* 29, no. 57 (June 2018).

Hogan, Mél, and Tamara Shepherd. "Information Ownership and Materiality in an Age of Big Data Surveillance." *Journal of Information Policy* 5 (2015).

Holbrook, Daniel. "Controlling Contamination: The Origins of Clean Room Technology." *History and Technology* 25, no. 3 (September 2009).

Holmes, Oliver Wendell. "The Evaluation and Preservation of Business Archives." *American Archivist* 1, no. 4 (October 1938): 171–85.

Horn, Jason. "Municipal Archives and Records Center of the City of New York." *American Archivist*, 16, no. 4 (October 1953): 311–20.

Hower, Ralph H. "The Preservation of Business Records: Why Business Records Should Be Preserved." *Bulletin of the Business Historical Society* 11, nos. 3–4 (October 1937).

Hudson, Paul Stephen. "The 'Archaeological Duty' of Thornwell Jacobs: The Oglethorpe Atlanta Crypt of Civilization Time Capsule." *Georgia Historical Quarterly* 75, no. 1 (Spring 1991): 121–38.

———. "'The End of the World—and After': The Cosmic History Millenarianism of Thornwell Jacobs." *Georgia Historical Quarterly* 82, no. 3 (Fall 1998): 594–607.

Iiams, Thomas M. "The Preservation of Rare Books and Manuscripts in the Huntington Library." *Library Quarterly* 2, no. 4 (October 1932): 374–86.

Jacobs, Thornwell. "Address at the Closing of the Crypt of Civilization." In Jacobs, *Step Down, Dr. Jacobs*, 911–14.

———. "Greetings to the Inhabitants of the World in the Year A.D. 8113: Recorded and Placed in the Crypt." In Jacobs, *Step Down, Dr. Jacobs*, 906–11.

———. "The Prophet on Parnassus." In Jacobs, *Step Down, Dr. Jacobs*, 1076–78.

———. "This Perilous Year: A Report on the State of the People of the Union; The Contents of This Pamphlet Comprise an Address Made by Dr. Thornwell Jacobs, President of Oglethorpe University, before the Committee of One Hundred at Miami Beach, Florida, January 28, 1936." In Jacobs, *Step Down, Dr. Jacobs*, 923–38.

———. "What Will the World Be Like in 8113?: When the Crypt at Oglethorpe University Is Opened." In Jacobs, *Step Down, Dr. Jacobs*, 915–19. Originally appeared in *Atlanta Journal Magazine*.

Jaeger, Paul T., Jimmy Lin, Justin M. Grimes, and Shannon N. Simmons. "Where Is the Cloud? Geography, Economics, Environment, and Jurisdiction in Cloud Computing." *First Monday* 14, no. 5 (May 4, 2009). http://journals.uic.edu/ojs /index.php/fm/article/view/2456/2171.

Jarvis, William E. "Do Not Open until 8113 A.D.: The Oglethorpe Crypt and Other Time Capsules." *World Fair* 5, no. 1 (Winter 1985): 1–4.

———. "Modern Time Capsules: Symbolic Repositories of Civilization." *Libraries & Culture* 27, no. 3 (Summer 1992): 279–95.

———. "The Time Capsule as a Way for the Future to Acquire Popular Culture Items." In *Popular Culture and Acquisitions*, edited by Allen Ellis, 33–46. Binghamton, N.Y.: Haworth, 1992.

Kevane, Michael, and William Sundstrom. "The Development of Public Libraries in the United States, 1870–1930: A Quantitative Assessment." *Information and Culture* 49, no. 2 (2014).

Kline, Wendy. "A New Deal for the Child: Ann Cooper Hewitt and Sterilization in the 1930s." In Currell and Cogdell, *Popular Eugenics*, 17–43.

Kluitenberg, Eric. "On the Archaeology of Imaginary Media." In Huhtamo and Parikka, *Media Archaeology*, 48–69.

Kratz, Jessie. "The National Archives Goes Underground." *Prologue* 48, no. 1 (Spring 2016).

Krumholz, Mark R. "Star Formation in Molecular Clouds." In *XVth Special Courses at the National Observatory of Rio de Janeiro*, 9–57. AIP Conference Proceedings, Vol. 1386. College Park, Md.: American Institute of Physics, 2011.

Lant, Antonia. "The Curse of the Pharoah, or How Cinema Contracted Egyptomania." *October* 59 (Winter 1992): 86–112.

Leahy, Emmett J. "Reduction of Public Records." *American Archivist* 3, no. 1 (January 1940): 13–38.

Little, Stuart J. "The Freedom Train: Citizenship and Postwar Political Culture, 1946–1949." *American Studies* 34, no. 1 (Spring 1993).

Lydenberg, Harry M. "Robert C. Binkley, 1897–1940." *American Council of Learned Societies Bulletin* 33 (October 1941).

Marte, Fernando, Amandine Péquignot, and David W. Von Endt. "Arsenic in Taxidermy Collections: History, Detection, and Management." *Collection Forum* 21, nos. 1–2 (2006): 143–50.

Masco, Joseph. "'Sensitive but Unclassified': Secrecy and the Counterterrorist State." *Public Culture* 22, no. 3 (2010): 433–63.

Massumi, Brian. "The Future Birth of the Affective Fact: The Political Ontology of Threat." In *Digital and Other Virtualities: Renegotiating the Image*, edited by Antony Bryant and Griselda Pollock, 79–92. London: I. B. Tauris, 2010.

Mattern, Shannon. "The Big Data of Ice, Rocks, Soils, and Sediments." *Places*, November 2017. https://placesjournal.org/article/the-big-data-of-ice -rocks-soils-and-sediments/.

Mbembe, Achille. "Necropolitics." Translated by Libby Meintjes. *Public Culture* 15, no. 1 (Winter 2003): 11–40.

Merz, Nancy M. "Archives and the One World of Records." In Jones and Cantelon, *Corporate Archives and History*, 153–62. Originally appeared in *INFORM: The Magazine of Information and Image Management*, April 1988.

Metcalf, Keyes. "Six Influential Academic and Research Librarians." *College and Research Libraries*, July 1976.

Mirzoeff, Nicholas. "The Shadow and the Substance: Race, Photography, and the Index." In Fusco and Wallis, *Only Skin Deep*, 111–27.

Montaño, Florence Gouvrit, and Jordi Vallverdú. "Hackable Bodies: An Unknown Error Has Occurred." *Media-N* 11, no. 2 (Summer 2015). http://median .newmediacaucus.org/?p=5753.

Nora, Pierre. "Between Memory and History: Les Lieux de Mémoire." *Representations* 26 (Spring 1989): 7–24.

Norman, Steve. "'The Library Quarterly' in the 1930s: A Journal of Discussion's Early Years." *Library Quarterly* 58, no. 4 (October 1988): 327–51.

Oyama, Hiroshi. "Virtual Reality for the Palliative Care of Cancer." *Studies in Health Technology and Informatics* 44 (February 1997): 87–94.

Paglen, Trevor. "Operational Images." *e-Flux* 59 (November 2014). July 24, 2019. https://www.e-flux.com/journal/59/61130/operational-images/.

"Parallel Computing Pioneers: W. Daniel Hillis." *Parallel Computing Research Newsletter* 4, no. 4 (1996).

Parikka, Jussi. "Archival Media Theory: An Introduction to Wolfgang Ernst's Media Archaeology." In Ernst, *Digital Memory and the Archive*, 1–22.

Parks, Lisa. "Around the Antenna Tree: The Politics of Infrastructural Visibility." *Flow*, March 6, 2009. https://www.flowjournal.org/2009/03/around-the -antenna-tree-the-politics-of-infrastructural-visibilitylisa-parks-uc-santa -barbara/.

———. "Drones, Infrared Imagery, and Body Heat." *International Journal of Communication* 8 (2014): 2518–21.

———. "'Stuff You Can Kick': Toward a Theory of Media Infrastructures." In *Between Humanities and the Digital*, edited by Patrik Svensson and David Theo Goldberg. Cambridge, Mass.: MIT Press, 2015.

Peck, Robert McCracken. "Preserving Nature for Study and Display." In Prince, *Stuffing Birds*, 11–25.

Pendray, G. Edward. "The Crucible of Change." *North American Review* 247, no. 2 (Summer 1939): 344–54.

———. "For 8113 A.D. Oglethorpe University Builds a Crypt to Preserve Culture of 1936." *Literary Digest*, October 31, 1936.

Persoz, Giulia. "One Small Step to Protect Human Heritage in Space Act as One Small Step Towards U.S. Space Dominance? The Case for a Multilateral Treaty Protection Regime." In *Protection of Cultural Heritage Sites on the Moon*, edited by Annette Froehlich, 41–52. Cham, Switzerland: Springer Nature, 2020.

Peters, T. K. "The Preservation of History in the Crypt of Civilization." *Journal of the Society of Motion Picture Engineers* 34, no. 2 (February 1940): 206–11.

Plantin, Jean-Christophe. "Data Cleaners and Pristine Datasets: Visibility and Invisiblity of Data Processors in Social Science." *Science, Technology, and Human Values* 44, no. 1 (2019): 52–73.

Plung, Dylan J. "The Japanese Village at Dugway Proving Ground: An Unexamined Context to the Firebombing of Japan." *Asia-Pacific Journal* 16, no. 3 (April 15, 2018).

Raffles, Hugh. "Jews, Lice, and History." *Public Culture* 19, no. 3 (2007): 521–66.

Raley, Rita. "Dataveillance and Countervailance." In Gitelman, *"Raw Data" Is an Oxymoron*, 121–46.

Renoir, Jean. "André Bazin's Little Beret." In *Jean Renoir*, by André Bazin and François Truffaut, 11–12. New York: Da Capo, 1992.

Rini, Regina. "Deepfakes and the Epistemic Backstop." *Philosopher's Imprint* 20, no. 24 (2020): 1–16, http://hdl.handle.net/2027/spo.3521354.0020.024.

Ritzenthaler, Mary Lynn, and Catherine Nicholson. "A New Era Begins for the Charters of Freedom." *Prologue* 35, no. 3 (Fall 2003). https://www.archives.gov/publications/prologue/2003/fall/charters-new-era.html.

Rosenthaler, Lukas. "Digital Archiving Tomorrow—a Foresight." In *Archiving 2005*, 244–48. Washington, D.C.: Society for Imaging Science and Technology, 2005.

Russell, Edmund. "'Speaking of Annihilation': Mobilizing for War against Human and Insect Enemies, 1914–1945." *Journal of American History* 82, no. 4 (March 1996): 1505–29.

Schwarzschild, Edward L. "Death-Defying/Defining Spectacles: Charles Willson Peale as Early American Freak Showman." In *Freakery: Cultural Spectacles of the Extraordinary Body*, edited by Rosemarie Garland Thomson, 82–96. New York: New York University Press, 1996.

Sekula, Allan. "The Body and the Archive." *October* 39 (Winter 1986): 3–64.

Shiff, Robert A. "The Archivist's Role in Records Management." *American Archivist* 19, no. 2 (April 1956): 111–20.

Shinozuka. Jeannie. "Deadly Perils: Beetles and the Pestilential Immigrant, 1920s–1930s." *American Quarterly* 65, no. 4 (December 2013): 831–52.

———. "From a 'Contagious' to a 'Poisonous Yellow Peril'?: Japanese and Japanese Americans in Public Health and Agriculture, 1890s–1950." Ph.D. diss., University of Minnesota, 2009.

Singh, Nikhil Pal. "Rethinking Race and Nation." In *American Studies: An Anthology*, edited by Janice A. Radway, Kevin K. Gaines, Barry Shank, and Penny Von Eschen, 9–16. West Sussex, U.K.: Wiley-Blackwell, 2009.

Spencer, Brett. "The Rise of Shadow Libraries: America's Quest to Save Its Information and Culture from Nuclear Destruction during the Cold War." *Information & Culture* 49, no. 2 (2014): 145–76.

Starosielski, Nicole. "Thermocultures of Geological Media." *Cultural Politics* 12, no. 3 (2016): 293–309.

Steffan, Will, Paul J. Crutzen, and John R. McNeill. "The Anthropocene: Are Humans Now Overwhelming the Great Forces of Nature?" *Ambio* 36, no. 8 (2007): 614–21.

Sterne, Jonathan. "The Preservation Paradox in Digital Audio." In *Sound Souvenirs: Audio Technologies, Memory, and Cultural Practices*, edited by Karin Bijsterveld and José van Dijck, 55–65. Amsterdam: Amsterdam University Press, 2009.

Susman, Warren I. "The Culture of the Thirties." In *Culture as History: The Transformation of American Society in the Twentieth Century*, 150–83. New York: Pantheon, 1984.

Tate, Vernon D. "From Binkley to Bush." *American Archivist* 10, no. 3 (July 1947): 249–57.

Taubes, Gary A. "The Rise and Fall of Thinking Machines." *Inc.*, September 15, 1995. https://www.inc.com/magazine/19950915/2622.html

Troyer, John. "Embalmed Vision." *Mortality* 12, no. 1 (February 2007): 22–47.

Tunc, Tanfer Emin. "Eating in Survival Town: Food in 1950s Atomic America." *Cold War History* 15, no. 2 (2015).

Valéry, Paul. "The Conquest of Ubiquity." In *Aesthetics*, edited by M. Jackson, 225–28. Vol. 13 of *The Collected Works of Paul Valéry*. New York: Pantheon, 1964.

Wardle, Brian L., and Karl Berggren. "Putting a Time Capsule in Orbit: What Should It Be Made Of?" In Paglen, *Last Pictures*, 183–85.

Weissman, Ken. "Film Preservation at the Library of Congress Packard Campus for Audio Visual Conservation." *AMIA Tech Review* 2 (October 2010). https://amianet.org/wp-content/uploads/Publication-AMIA-Tech-Review-V2-2010.pdf. Accessed September 19, 2021.

———. "Musings on 500 More Years of Film and Digits." *AMIA Tech Review* 3 (April 2011). https://amianet.org/wp-content/uploads/Publication-AMIA-Tech-Review-V3-2011.pdf. Accessed September 19, 2021.

Winter, Frank H. "The American Rocket Society Story, 1930–1962." *Journal of the British Interplanetary Society* 33 (1980): 303–11.

Wood, Andrew. "The Middletons, Futurama, and Progressland: Disciplinary Technology and Temporal Heterotopia in Two New York World's Fairs." *New Jersey Journal of Communication* 11, no. 1 (Spring 2003): 63–76.

Worboys, Michael. "Joseph Lister and the Performance of Antiseptic Surgery." *Notes and Records of the Royal Society of London* 67, no. 3 (2013): 199–209.

Wright, H. C. "Metallic Documents of Antiquity." *Brigham Young University Studies* 10, no. 4 (Summer 1970): 457–77.

Wright, H. Curtis, and Elisabeth R. Sutton. "Evidence of Ancient Writing on Metal: An Interview with H. Curtis Wright." *Religious Educator* 9, no. 3 (2008): 161-68.

Yablon, Nick. "Encapsulating the Present: Material Decay, Labor Unrest, and the Prehistory of the Time Capsule, 1876-1914." *Winterthur Portfolio* 45, no. 1 (Spring 2011): 1-28.

## Books

Amato, Joseph. *Dust: A History of the Small and Invisible*. Berkeley: University of California Press, 2000.

Atanasoski, Neda, and Kalindi Vora. *Surrogate Humanity: Race, Robots, and the Politics of Technological Futures*. Durham, N.C.: Duke University Press, 2019.

Baker, Nicholson. *Double Fold: Libraries and the Assault on Paper*. New York: Random House, 2001.

Bales, Kevin. *Blood and Earth: Modern Slavery, Ecocide, and the Secret to Saving the World*. New York: Random House, 2016.

Barnes, John H., and W. D. Sevon. *The Geological Story of Pennsylvania*. 4th ed. Harrisburg, Pa.: Pennsylvania Geological Survey, 2014.

Bartusiak, Marcia. *The Day We Found the Universe*. New York: Pantheon, 2009.

Batchen, Geoffrey. *Burning with Desire: The Conception of Photography*. Cambridge, Mass.: MIT Press, 1997.

Benjamin, Ruha, ed. *Captivating Technology: Race, Carceral Technoscience, and Liberatory Imagination in Everyday Life*. Durham, N.C.: Duke University Press, 2019.

Berg, A. Scott. *Max Perkins: Editor of Genius*. New York: E. P. Dutton, 1978.

Black, Edwin. *War against the Weak: Eugenics and America's Campaign to Create a Master Race*. New York: Four Walls Eight Windows / Turnaround, 2003.

Black, Megan. *The Global Interior: Mineral Frontiers and American Power*. Cambridge, Mass.: Harvard University Press, 2018.

Blouin, Francis X., and William G. Rosenberg. *Processing the Past: Contesting Authority in History and the Archives*. New York: Oxford University Press, 2011.

Bolter, J. David, and Richard A. Grusin. *Remediation: Understanding New Media*. Cambridge, Mass: MIT Press, 2000.

Bouk, Dan. *How Our Days Became Numbered: Risk and the Rise of the Statistical Individual*. Chicago: University of Chicago, 2015.

Brehm, William A., Jr., and Thomas H. Sutter. *The Kimberlys: A Glimpse at One Family's Years in North America*. Neenah, Wisc.: Palmer, 1989.

Brown, Joshua. *Beyond the Lines: Pictorial Reporting, Everyday Life, and the Crisis of Gilded Age America*. Berkeley: University of California Press, 2006.

Browne, Simone. *Dark Matters: On the Surveillance of Blackness*. Durham, N.C.: Duke University Press, 2015.

Burdick, Eugene, and Harvey Wheeler Jr. *Fail-Safe*. New York: McGraw Hill, 1962.

Campbell, Joseph. *The Hero with a Thousand Faces*. 3rd ed. Novato, Calif.: New World Library, 2008.

Caro, Robert A. *The Power Broker: Robert Moses and the Fall of New York*. New York: Knopf, 1974.

Carr, Nicholas. *The Shallows: What the Internet Is Doing to Our Brains*. Updated ed. New York: W. W. Norton, 2020.

Chandler, Alfred D., Jr. *The Visible Hand: The Managerial Revolution in American Business*. Cambridge, Mass.: Harvard University Press, 1977.

Cheney-Lippold, John. *We Are Data: Algorithms and the Making of Our Digital Selves*. New York: New York University Press, 2017.

Chong, Denise. *The Girl in the Picture: The Story of Kim Phuc, the Photograph, and the Vietnam War*. New York: Penguin, 1999.

Christianson, Scott. *The Last Gasp: The Rise and Fall of the American Gas Chamber*. Berkeley: University of California Press, 2010.

Chun, Wendy Hui Kyong. *Programmed Visions: Software and Memory*. Cambridge, Mass.: MIT Press, 2011.

Clark, Andy. *Natural-Born Cyborgs: Minds, Technologies, and the Future of Human Intelligence*. New York: Oxford University Press, 2004.

Cleaver, Nick. *Grover Cleveland's New Foreign Policy: Arbitration, Neutrality, and the Dawn of American Empire*. New York: Palgrave Macmillan, 2014.

Cogdell, Christina. *Eugenic Design: Streamlining America in the 1930s*. Philadelphia: University of Pennsylvania Press, 2004.

Cole, John Y. *America's Greatest Library: An Illustrated History of the Library of Congress*. London: GILES, 2017.

Colla, Elliot. *Conflicted Antiquities: Egyptology, Egyptomania, Egyptian Modernity*. Durham, N.C.: Duke University Press, 2007.

Conte, Robert S. *The History of the Greenbrier: America's Resort*. 2nd ed. White Sulphur Springs, W. Va.: Trans Allegheny Books, 2011.

Crawford, Kate. *Atlas of AI: Power, Politics, and the Planetary Costs of Artificial Intelligence*. New Haven, Conn.: Yale University Press, 2021.

Critical Art Ensemble, ed. *Digital Resistance: Explorations in Tactical Media*. New York: Autonomedia, 2001.

Crossen, Kendall Foster. *The Year of Consent*. New York: Dell, 1954.

Cubitt, Sean. *Finite Media: Environmental Implications of Digital Technologies*. Durham, N.C.: Duke University Press, 2017.

Currell, Susan, and Elizabeth Cogdell, eds. *Popular Eugenics: National Efficiency and American Mass Culture in the 1930s*. Athens: Ohio University Press, 2006.

Edwards, Elizabeth, and Janice Hart, eds. *Photographs Objects Histories: On the Materiality of Images*. London: Routledge, 2004.

Edwards, Gawain [G. Edward Pendray]. *The Earth-Tube*. New York: Appleton, 1929.

Eichhorn, Kate. *The End of Forgetting: Growing Up with Social Media*. Cambridge, Mass.: Harvard University Press, 2019.

Ernst, Wolfgang. *Digital Memory and the Archive*, edited and with an introduction by Jussi Parikka. Minneapolis: University of Minnesota Press, 2012.

Essinger, James. *Jacquard's Web: How a Hand-Loom Led to the Birth of the Information Age*. Oxford: Oxford University Press, 2004.

Ettinger, Robert. *The Prospect of Immortality*. Garden City, N.Y.: Doubleday, 1964.

Fanon, Frantz. *Black Skin, White Masks*. New York: Grove, 1952.

———. *The Wretched of the Earth*. New York: Grove, 1963.

Fant, Kenne. *Alfred Nobel: A Biography*. Translated by Marianne Ruuth. New York: Arcade, 1993.

Faust, Drew Gilpin. *This Republic of Suffering: Death and the American Civil War*. New York: Alfred A. Knopf, 2008.

Fisch, Max H., ed. *Selected Papers of Robert C. Binkley*. Cambridge, Mass.: Harvard University Press, 1948.

Fitzgerald, F. Scott. *The Great Gatsby*. New York: Scribner's, 1925.

Foucault, Michel. *Il faut defendre la société: Cours au collège de France, 1975–1976*. Paris: Seuil, 1997.

Frick, Caroline. *Saving Cinema: The Politics of Preservation*. New York: Oxford University Press, 2011.

Friedman, Lawrence Meir. *American Law in the 20th Century*. New Haven, Conn.: Yale University Press, 2002.

Fusco, Coco, and Brian Wallis. *Only Skin Deep: Changing Visions of the American Self*. New York: Harry N. Abrams / International Center of Photography, 2003.

Garrison, Dee. *Bracing for Armageddon: Why Civil Defense Never Worked*. New York: Oxford University Press, 2006.

Garrison, Fielding. *John Shaw Billings: A Memoir*. New York: G. P. Putnam's Sons, 1915.

Gates, Kelly. *Our Biometric Future: Facial Recognition Technology and the Culture of Surveillance*. New York: New York University Press, 2011.

Germain, Richard. *Dollars through the Doors: A Pre-1930 History of Bank Marketing in America*. Westport, Conn.: Greenwood, 1996.

Gilkeson, John S. *Anthropologists and the Rediscovery of America, 1886–1965*. Cambridge: Cambridge University Press, 2010.

Gitelman, Lisa. *Always Already New: Media, History and the Data of Culture*. Cambridge, Mass.: MIT Press, 2006.

———. *Paper Knowledge: Toward a Media History of Documents*. Durham, N.C.: Duke University Press, 2014.

Gitelman, Lisa, ed. *"Raw Data" Is an Oxymoron*. Cambridge, Mass.: MIT Press, 2013.

Goble, Mark. *Beautiful Circuits: Modernism and the Mediated Life*. New York: Columbia University Press, 2010.

Graeber, David. *Debt: The First 5,000 Years*. Brooklyn, N.Y.: Melville House, 2011.

Graff, Garrett M. *Raven Rock: The Story of the U.S. Government's Secret Plan to Save Itself—While the Rest of Us Die*. New York: Simon and Schuster, 2017.

Gugliotta, Guy. *Freedom's Cap: The United States Capitol and the Coming of the Civil War*. New York: Hill and Wang, 2012.

Hartman, Saidiya. *Scenes of Subjection: Terror, Slavery, and Self-Making in Nineteenth-Century America*. New York: Oxford University Press, 1997.

Hayles, N. Katherine. *How We Think: Digital Media and Contemporary Technogenesis*. Chicago: University of Chicago Press, 2012.

Heide, Lars. *Punched-Card Systems and the Early Information Explosion, 1880–1945*. Baltimore: Johns Hopkins University Press, 2009.

Hochman, Brian. *Savage Preservation: The Ethnographic Origins of Modern Media Technology*. Minneapolis: University of Minnesota Press, 2014.

Hong, Sun-Ha. *Technologies of Speculation: The Limits of Knowledge in a Data-Driven Society*. New York: New York University Press, 2020.

Huhtamo, Erkki, and Jussi Parikka, eds. *Media Archaeology: Approaches, Applications, and Implications*. Berkeley: University of California Press, 2011.

Hu, Tung-Hui. *A Prehistory of the Cloud*. Cambridge, Mass.: MIT Press, 2015.

Igo, Sarah. *The Averaged American: Surveys, Citizens, and the Making of a Mass Public*. Cambridge, Mass.: Harvard University Press, 2007.

——. *The Known Citizen: A History of Privacy in Modern America*. Cambridge, Mass.: Harvard University Press, 2019.

Jacobs, Thornwell. *The Law of the White Circle*. Nashville: Taylor-Trotwood Publishing, 1908. Reprinted with forward by W. Fitzhugh Brundage. Athens: University of Georgia Press, 2006. Page references are to the 2006 edition.

——. *Step Down, Dr. Jacobs: The Autobiography of an Autocrat*. Atlanta: Westminster, 1945.

Jarvis, William E. *Time Capsules: A Cultural History*. Jefferson, N.C.: McFarland, 2003.

Johnson, Victoria E. *Heartland TV: Primetime Television and the Struggle for U.S. Identity*. New York: New York University Press, 2008.

Jones, Arnita, and Philip L. Cantelon. *Corporate Archives and History: Making the Past Work*. Malabar, Fla.: Krieger, 1993.

Jones, Janna. *The Past Is a Moving Picture: Preserving the Twentieth Century on Film*. Gainesville: University Press of Florida, 2012.

Jonnes, Jill. *Conquering Gotham: A Gilded Age Epic; The Construction of Penn Station and Its Tunnels*. New York: Penguin, 2008.

——. *Empires of Light: Edison, Tesla, Westinghouse, and the Race to Electrify the World*. New York: Random House, 2003.

Katznelson, Ira. *Fear Itself: The New Deal and the Origins of Our Time*. New York: Liveright, 2013.

Kilgore, De Witt Douglas. *Astrofuturism: Science, Race, and Visions of Utopia in Space*. Philadelphia: University of Pennsylvania Press, 2003.

Kline, Ronald R. *The Cybernetics Moment, or Why We Call Our Age the Information Age*. Baltimore, Md.: Johns Hopkins University Press, 2015.

Koopman, Colin. *How We Became Our Data: A Genealogy of the Informational Person*. Chicago: University of Chicago Press, 2019.

Kuznick, Peter J., and James Gilbert, eds. *Rethinking Cold War Culture*. Washington, D.C.: Smithsonian Institution Press, 2001.

Lankevich, George J. *New York City: A Short History*. New York: New York University Press, 1998.

Latour, Bruno, and Steve Woolgar. *Laboratory Life: The Social Construction of Scientific Facts*. Beverly Hills, Calif.: Sage, 1979.

Learned, William S. *The American Public Library and the Diffusion of Knowledge*. New York: Harcourt, Brace, 1924.

Lears, Jackson. *Fables of Abundance: A Cultural History of Advertising in America*. New York: Basic Books, 1994.

———. *Rebirth of a Nation: The Making of Modern America, 1877–1920*. New York: HarperCollins, 2009.

Levenstein, Harvey. *Fear of Food: A History of Why We Worry about What We Eat*. Chicago: University of Chicago Press, 2012.

Lewis, Michael. *The Big Short: Inside the Doomsday Machine*. New York: W. W. Norton, 2010.

Lewis, Sinclair. *Arrowsmith*. New York: Harcourt, Brace, 1925.

Lipsitz, George. *The Possessive Investment in Whiteness: How White People Profit from Identity Politics*. Philadelphia: Temple University Press, 1998.

Lohr, Steve. *Data-Ism: The Revolution Transforming Decision Making, Consumer Behavior, and Almost Everything Else*. New York: HarperCollins, 2015.

Lowenthal, David. *The Past Is a Foreign Country*. Cambridge, England: Cambridge University Press, 1985.

Luther, Frederic. *Microfilm: A History, 1839–1900*. Annapolis, Md.: National Microfilm Association, 1959.

Lydenberg, Harry Miller, and John Archer. *The Care and Repair of Books*. 4th rev. ed. New York: R. R. Bowker, 1960.

Lye, Colleen. *America's Asia: Racial Form and American Literature, 1893–1945*. Princeton, N.J.: Princeton University Press, 2005.

Lynd, Robert S., and Helen Merrell Lynd. *Middletown: A Study in American Culture*. New York: Harcourt, Brace, 1929.

Marchand, Roland. *Creating the Corporate Soul: The Rise of Public Relations and Corporate Imagery in American Big Business*. Berkeley: University of California Press, 2001.

Masco, Joseph. *The Nuclear Borderlands: The Manhattan Project in Post–Cold War New Mexico*. Princeton, N.J.: Princeton University Press, 2006.

———. *Theater of Operations: National Security Affect from the Cold War to the War on Terror*. Durham, N.C.: Duke University Press, 2014.

Massumi, Brian. *Parables for the Virtual: Movement, Affect, Sensation*. Durham, N.C.: Duke University Press, 2002.

Mathias, Frank Furlong. *The GI Generation: A Memoir*. Lexington: University Press of Kentucky, 2000.

May, Elaine Tyler. *Homeward Bound: American Families in the Cold War Era*. Rev. and updated ed. New York: Basic Books, 2008.

Mayer-Schönberger, Viktor. *Delete: The Virtue of Forgetting in the Digital Age.* Princeton, N.J: Princeton University Press, 2011.

McClintock, Ann. *Imperial Leather: Race, Gender, and Sexuality in the Colonial Contest.* London: Routledge, 1995.

McCoy, Donald R. *The National Archives: America's Ministry of Documents, 1934–1968.* Chapel Hill: University of North Carolina Press, 1978.

McWilliams, John E. *American Pests: The Losing War on Insects from Colonial Times to DDT.* New York: Columbia University Press, 2008.

Milkman, Ruth. *L.A. Story: Immigrant Workers and the Future of the U.S. Labor Movement.* New York: Russell Sage, 2006.

Miller, Richard L. *Under the Cloud: The Decades of Nuclear Testing.* The Woodlands, Tex.: Two Sixty, 1991.

Mirzoeff, Nicholas. *The Right to Look: A Counterhistory of Visuality.* Durham, N.C.: Duke University Press, 2011.

Molina, Natalia. *Fit to Be Citizens? Public Health and Race in Los Angeles, 1879–1979.* Berkeley: University of California Press, 2005.

Monteyne, David. *Fallout Shelter: Designing for Civil Defense in the Cold War.* Minneapolis: University of Minnesota Press, 2011.

Mumford, Lewis. *The City in History.* New York: Harcourt, Brace and World, 1961.

———. *Technics and Civilization.* New York: Harcourt, 1934.

Murray, Stuart A. P. *The Library: An Illustrated History.* New York: Skyhorse, 2012.

Nadel, Alan. *Containment Culture: American Narratives, Postmodernism, and the Atomic Age.* Durham, N.C.: Duke University Press, 1995.

Ngai, Mae. *Impossible Subjects: Illegal Aliens and the Making of Modern America.* Princeton, N.J.: Princeton University Press, 2005.

Noblecourt, A. *Protection of Cultural Property in the Event of Armed Conflict.* Paris: UNESCO, 1958.

Oakes, Guy. *The Imaginary War: Civil Defense and American Cold War Culture.* Oxford: Oxford University Press, 1994.

Olegario, Rowena. *The Engine of Enterprise: Credit in America.* Cambridge, Mass.: Harvard University Press, 2016.

Paglen, Trevor. *The Last Pictures.* Berkeley: CreativeTime / University of California Press, 2012.

Parikka, Jussi. *A Geology of Media.* Minneapolis: University of Minnesota Press, 2015.

———. *What Is Media Archaeology?* Cambridge, U.K.: Polity, 2012.

Patterson, Orlando. *Slavery and Social Death: A Comparative Study.* Cambridge, Mass.: Harvard University Press, 1985.

Pederson, Jay P., ed. *International Directory of Company Histories.* Vol. 24. Farmington Hills, Mich.: St. James, 1998.

Pendray, G. Edward. *The Book of Record of the Time Capsule of Cupaloy: Deemed Capable of Resisting the Effects of Time for Five Thousand Years; Preserving an*

*Account of Universal Achievements; Embedded in the Grounds of the New York World's Fair, 1939*. New York: Westinghouse Electric and Manufacturing, 1938. https://archive.org/details/timecapsulecupsoowestrich.

Pernick, Martin. *The Black Stork: Eugenics and the Death of "Defective" Babies in American Medicine and Motion Pictures since 1915*. Oxford: Oxford University Press, 1999.

Peters, T. K. *The Story of the Crypt of Civilization*. Atlanta: Oglethorpe University, 1940.

Popenoe, Paul, and Roswell Hill Johnson. *Applied Eugenics*. New York: Macmillan, 1920.

Power, Eugene B. *Edition of One: The Autobiography of Eugene B. Power, Founder of University Microfilms*. Ann Arbor, Mich.: University Microfilms, 1990.

Prince, Sue Ann, ed. *Stuffing Birds, Pressing Plants, Shaping Knowledge: Natural History in North America, 1730–1860*. Philadelphia: American Philosophical Society, 2003.

Puleo, Stephen. *American Treasures: The Secret Efforts to Save the Declaration of Independence, the Constitution, and the Gettysburg Address*. New York: St. Martin's Press, 2016.

Raney, Llewellyn W., ed. *Microphotography for Libraries*. Chicago: American Library Association, 1936.

Rhodes, Richard. *The Making of the Atomic Bomb*. New York: Simon and Schuster, 1986.

Rinaldi, Thomas E., and Rob Yasinac. *Hudson Valley Ruins: Forgotten Landmarks of an American Landscape*. Lebanon, N.H.: University Press of New England, 2006.

Romo, David Dorado. *Ringside Seat to a Revolution: An Underground Cultural History of El Paso and Juárez, 1893–1923*. El Paso, Tex.: Cinco Puntos, 2005.

Rose, Kenneth. *One Nation Underground: The Fallout Shelter in American Culture*. New York: New York University Press, 2001.

Rosen, Philip. *Change Mummified: Cinema, Historicity, Theory*. Minneapolis: University of Minnesota Press, 2001.

Rotman, Brian. *Ad Infinitum . . . the Ghost in Turing's Machine: Taking God Out of Mathematics and Putting the Body Back In*. Stanford, Calif.: Stanford University Press, 1993.

Rydell, Robert. *World of Fairs: The Century-of-Progress Expositions*. Chicago: University of Chicago Press, 1993.

Schorer, Mark. *Sinclair Lewis: A Collection of Critical Essays*. New York: Prentice-Hall, 1962.

Schultz, Gwen. *Wisconsin's Foundations: A Review of the State's Geology and Its Influence on Geography and Human Activity*. 2nd ed. Madison: University of Wisconsin Press, 2004.

Schuster, E. Lincoln. *Eyes on the World: A Photographic Record of History-In-the -Making*. New York: Simon and Schuster, 1935.

Sellars, Nigel Anthony. *Oil, Wheat, and Wobblies: The Industrial Workers of the World in Oklahoma, 1905–1930*. Norman: University of Oklahoma Press, 1998.

Shah, Nayan. *Contagious Divides: Epidemics and Race in San Francisco's Chinatown*. Berkeley: University of California Press, 2001.

Solnit, Rebecca. *River of Shadows: Eadweard Muybridge and the Technological Wild West*. New York: Penguin, 2003.

Spears, Ellen Griffith. *Baptized in PCBs: Race, Pollution, and Justice in an All-American Town*. Chapel Hill: University of North Carolina Press, 2014.

Spector, Robert, and William W. Wicks. *Shared Values: A History of Kimberly-Clark*. Lyme, Conn.: Greenwich, 1997.

Spiro, Jonathan. *Defending the Master Race: Conservation, Eugenics, and the Legacy of Madison Grant*. Burlington: University of Vermont Press, 2009.

Srnicek, Nick. *Platform Capitalism*. Cambridge, England: Polity, 2017.

Starosielski, Nicole. *The Undersea Network*. Durham, N.C.: Duke University Press, 2015.

Stern, Alexandra Minna. *Eugenic Nation: Faults and Frontiers of Better Breeding in Modern America*. Berkeley: University of California Press, 2005.

Stoddard, Lothrop. *The Rising Tide of Color against White World-Supremacy*. New York: Scribner's, 1920.

Stott, William. *Documentary Expression and Thirties America*. Chicago: University of Chicago Press, 1973.

Strom, Susan. *Beyond the Typewriter: Gender, Class, and the Origins of Modern American Office Work, 1900–1930*. Champaign: University of Illinois Press, 1994.

Sugimoto, Hiroshi. *Hiroshi Sugimoto: Dioramas*. New York: Artbook, 2014.

Tapia, Ruby C. *American Pietàs: Visions of Race, Death, and the Maternal*. Minneapolis: University of Minnesota Press, 2011.

Theoharis, Athan. *Abuse of Power: How Cold War Surveillance and Secrecy Policy Shaped the Response to 9/11*. Philadelphia: Temple University Press, 2011.

Thomas, G. Scott. *A New World to be Won: John Kennedy, Richard Nixon, and the Tumultuous Year of 1960*. Santa Barbara, Calif.: ABC-CLIO, 2011.

Thoreau, Henry David. *Walden, or Life in the Woods*. 1854. Reprint. Boston: Shambala, 2010.

Thorpe, James. *Henry Edwards Huntington: A Biography*. Berkeley: University of California Press, 1994.

Thylstrup, Nanna Bonde. *The Politics of Mass Digitization*. Cambridge, Mass.: MIT Press, 2018.

Trafton, Scott. *Egypt Land: Race and Nineteenth-Century Egyptomania*. Durham, N.C.: Duke University Press, 2004.

Turner, Fred. *From Counterculture to Cyberculture: The Whole Earth Network, and the Rise of Digital Utopianism*. Chicago: University of Chicago Press, 2006.

Tye, Larry. *The Father of Spin: Edward L. Bernays and the Birth of Public Relations*. New York: Henry Holt, 1998.

Vanderbilt, Tom. *Survival City: Adventures among the Ruins of Atomic America.* Princeton, N.J.: Princeton Architectural Press, 2002.

Wakeham, Pauline. *Taxidermic Signs: Reconstructing Aboriginality.* Minneapolis: University of Minnesota Press, 2008.

Wark, McKenzie. *Capital Is Dead: Is This Something Worse?* Brooklyn, N.Y.: Verso, 2019.

Webb, Amy. *The Big Nine: How the Tech Titans and Their Thinking Machines Could Warp Humanity.* New York: PublicAffairs, 2019.

Wernimont, Jacqueline. *Numbered Lives: Life and Death in Quantum Media.* Cambridge, Mass.: MIT Press, 2018.

Wilhelm, Henry, with Carol Brower. *The Permanence and Care of Color Photographs: Traditional and Digital Color Prints, Color Negatives, Slides, and Motion Pictures.* Grinnell, Iowa: Preservation Publishing Company, 1993.

Winkler, Adam. *We the Corporations: How American Businesses Won Their Civil Rights.* New York: Liveright, 2018.

Wright, H. C. *Ancient Burials of Metallic Foundation Documents in Stone Boxes.* Champaign: University of Illinois, 1983.

Wright, H. C., and Thomas K. Edlund. *Modern Presentism and Ancient Metallic Epigraphy.* Salt Lake City, Utah: Wings of Fire, 2006.

Yablon, Nick. *Remembrance of Things Present: The Invention of the Time Capsule.* Chicago: University of Chicago Press, 2019.

Yergin, Daniel. *The Prize: The Epic Quest for Oil, Money, and Power.* 1991. Reprint. New York: Free Press, 2008.

Young, James Harvey. *Pure Food: Securing the Federal Food and Drugs Act of 1906.* Princeton, N.J.: Princeton University Press, 1989.

Zuboff, Shoshana. *The Age of Surveillance Capitalism: The Fight for a Human Future at the New Frontier of Power.* New York: PublicAffairs, 2019.

Zunz, Olivier. *Why the American Century?* Chicago: University of Chicago Press, 1998.

# Index

*Italic page numbers refer to illustrations.*

bitrot, 156

*Black Mirror*, 201-2, 203

black sites, 148, 157

blockchain, 170, 186

Blue Origin, 187, 190, 192

Bluffdale, Utah, 144

body, human, 10. *See also* biobodies

Boeing, Bill, 25

bombproof bunkers, 14, 90, 118-21, *122*; Bunker at Greenbrier, 134-37, 140; data bunkers, 128, 142; images of, 118-21; psychological effects of, 142; slave quarters made into, 148-49; storage facilities, 95-96, 97, 102, 138; as time capsules, 121; under World Trade Center, 123-24. *See also* Cold War; nuclear attack

bombproofing, 94; of data bodies, 105, 110, 116, 146; effectiveness of, 105; as fantasy, 111; preservation of Charters of Freedom and, 173; of telecommunications systems, 129-30

bombproofing investigations and bomb tests, 97-101, 103; data bodies in, 110; fallout from, 132; number of tests, 121; office equipment in, 104-5; as open time capsule, 112; Operation Cue, 109-13, *112*; Operation Plumbbob, 105; Operation Teapot, 104-5, 110, 124. *See also* Cold War

bomb shelters, 96, 118-21, *120*. *See also* bombproof bunkers

bombsight mirroring, 101-2

bombs, incendiary, 98-101

bomb tests. *See* bombproofing investigations and bomb tests

bone, growing, 199

*Book of Record, The* (Pendray), 70-75, *73*, 87, 146

book repair, 48

books: deterioration of, 46; fumigation of, 31, 32-33; insects in, 28-31 (*see also* bookworms; insects)

bookworms, 28-31, *30*, 33, 35, 36, 41. *See also* insects

Boston Athanaeum, 31

Brady, Matthew, 136

brain, technology's effects on, 10-11

Brand, Stewart, 192

Branson, Richard, 190

breeding, better, 36-37. *See also* eugenics; whiteness

Brigham Young University (BYU), 167

Brooks, Louise Cromwell, 148-49

*Brown v. Board of Education*, 76

Buck, Solon, 54

"Buffalo Public Library in 1983, The," 31

*Bulletin of the Business Historical Society*, 16

*Bunker Archaeology* (Virilio), 143

Bunker at Greenbrier, 134-37, 140

bunkers, bombproof. *See* bombproof bunkers

Burdick, Eugene, 148

Burdin family, 76-77, *78*

bureaucracy, expansion of, 15, 41. *See also* government, U.S.; records

Bureau of Entomology, United States, 31

Business Historical Society, 102

business history, 16

*Business History Review* (journal), 103

business records, 37, 41, 69-70, 102, 103, 104-5, 170. *See also* corporations; records management

*BusinessWeek*, 164

BuzzFeed News, 197

*Cahiers du Cinema* (journal), 7

California: eugenics in, 37, 75; San Francisco, 195; San Marino, 31, 75. *See also* Huntington Library

California Institute of Technology, 36, 75; Jet Propulsion Laboratory, 174

Calvert, Frederick C., 50

Cameron, James, 191

Campbell, Joseph, 175

data: aggregation and manipulation of, 12; attachment to, 142; materiality of, 21; profit from, 13; value of, 147; vulnerability of, 158

data, analog, 19, 172. *See also* backup culture

data, digital. *See* digital data

data banks, 135

data bodies: after death, 12–13; afterselves created with, 201–4, 206; as backup for human life, 21; biobodies and, 110, 181, 200; bombproofing, 105, 110, 116, 146; defined, 9; elements of, 97; growth of, 12; normalization of, 106; preservation of, 105; protection of, 97; searchability of, 147; survival of end of world, 129; value of, 147

data bunkers, 128, 142

data centers: carbon footprint of, 156; in cold environments, 186–87; Greenbrier Bunker, 135–37; location of, 140; for NSA, 144; number of, 8; repurposing of existing resources into, 140, 148, 150; security of, 1, 2, 14. *See also* Corbis Film Preservation Facility (CFF); infrastructure, data complex; Iron Mountain

data complex, 8, 20; air conditioner usage by, 17; in Cold War, 95–96, 121; control over, 11–12; crises and, 9, 19; emergence of, 8, 14, 15–19; expansion of, 121, 139–40, 148, 158, 191; features of, 19; impossibility of progress within, 166; infrastructure of, 134 (*see also* infrastructure, data complex); pervasiveness of, 11; power and, 56–57; profits and, 12; use of Cold War infrastructure, 140. *See also* preservation

Data Lock, 138

data storage, DNA, 179, 180, 193–94, 196–98

dating app, 194–95

Davenport, Charles, 68, 75

Davis, Jefferson, 86

days, length of, 24

death, data bodies after, 12–13, 202–4, 206

debt, profitability of, 70

Declaration of Independence, 172–74

deepfakes, 204–5

Defense, Department of, 166–67

democracy, 16, 94–95. *See also* government, U.S.

demolition, 124

Depression: beginning of backup loops during, 19; destabilization by, 16; effects of, 66; New Deal, 17, 41, 69, 70; records created by, 70; time capsules and, 9, 17 (*see also* Crypt of Civilization; time capsules; Westinghouse Time Capsule of Cupaloy)

desegregation, 76

design, streamline, 72

*Design and Construction of Typical German and Japanese Test Structures at Dugway Proving Grounds, Utah* (Standard Oil Development Company), 98

destruction, rehearsal of, 113. *See also* bombproofing investigations; civil defense

deterioration, 15–16, 41–43, 44–48. *See also* National Bureau of Standards (NBS)

Dewey decimal system, 8

diamonds, 165, 196

digiD8, 194–95

digital data: ephemerality of, 157, 158; lost, 164; preserving, 166–68; relation with analog, 19, 172 (*see also* backup culture); reliance on bombproof architectures, 150

digital technology: ecological unsustainability of, 156; manufacturing, 183–85; reliance on, 20

precursor, 168, 173; and 10,000-Year Clock, 192; use of stainless steel tickets, 86, 146. *See also* Crypt of Civilization

"Jameson Satellite, The" (Jones), 188

Japan: analyses of infrastructure of, 97–101; attack on Pearl Harbor, 98; Hiroshima, 105

Japanese Americans, 100

Japanese prisoners of war, 128

J. C. Penney's, 110, 111

*Jean Renoir* (Bazin), 7

Jefferson, Thomas, 155

Jet Propulsion Laboratory, 174

Jevons paradox, 182

Johns Manville Company, 76, 81, 184

Jones, Neil R., 188

Jonnes, Jill, 13

Jordan, David Starr, 75

Jorgenson, Ellen, 177, 195

J. P. Morgan (company), 124. *See also* Morgan, J. P. (person)

Kelly, Kevin, 192

Kennedy, John F., 124

"Key to the English Language, A" (Harrington), 71

Kimberly, Arthur, 16, 44, 47, 48, 53, 55–56, 57, 71, 158; Freedom Train, 173–74; international work of, 129; letters of, 50–51, 131; on library environments, 186; in World War II, 128

Kimberly, Harry Standish, 53

Kimberly, John Alfred, 52

Kimberly, Thomas, 51

Kimberly-Clark, 52–53, 57–58

Kimberly family, 51–52

Kirsch, Russell, 135

Klee, Paul, 165–66

Kline, Nathan S., 10

Knaust, Herman, 93

Knaust Cavern Mushrooms, 93

*Known Citizen, The* (Igo), 56, 106

Kodak, 87, 132, 180

Kolos, 186

Kuyda, Eugenia, 202–3

labor unrest, 80

LaGuardia, Fiorello, 77, 109

*La Haine* (film), 166

Lakeside School, 25

laminar flow clean room, 183–84

lamination, 54

Lampasas, Texas, 115

*Last Pictures, The* (Paglen), 157–58, *159*, 190, 197; connection to the *Golden Record*, 160, 161, 165; and deep time, 175. *See also* Paglen, Trevor

*Las Vegas Review Journal* (newspaper), 111

Latin America, national archives in, 55

Leahy, Emmett J., 110

Lee, Hillman, 111

Lefebrve, Henri, 120

Legler, John C., 118, 119

Legler, Mitchell, 119

Legler, Sandra, 119

Legler family, 118–21

LeMay, Curtis, 100, 101

Lewis, Sinclair, 62

librarians, 15, 26. *See also* Billings, John Shaw; Iiams, Thomas Marion; Lydenberg, Harry Miller

libraries: air conditioning and, 17, 47, 186; air in, 31, 33, 45, 47; contagious diseases and, 32–33; fumigation of, 31; Hoover War Library, 44; Huntington Library, 28, 36–37, 58, 67, 75, 96 (*see also* Iiams, Thomas Marion); hygiene and, 39; National Library of Medicine, 39; New York Public Library, 40, 41, 42, 45; preservation by, 16 (*see also* Iiams, Thomas Marion); public library system, 24, 31, 32, 40; Vatican, 29; ventilating systems, 47; World Library and Bibliographic Congress, 43

toxins, 50

traceability, 195–96

Treadway, Jim, 69

*Trinity Cube* (Paglen), 193

Truman, Harry S., 101

Tudor, Frederic, 92

UNESCO, 152

United Fiber and Data, 150

United States: after World War II, 88; institutional matrix in, 8. *See also* government, U.S.; *and individual agencies*

United States Strategic Bombing Survey (USSBS), 101, 102

Unity Glory International, 196–97

urban dispersal, 118

urbanization, 45, 92

urban renewal campaigns, 118

*U.S. News and World Report*, 135

USPHS (U.S. Public Health Service), 35

USSBS (United States Strategic Bombing Survey), 101, 102

U.S. Steel, 24

Utah Data Center (UDC), 144

Vanderbilt, Tom, 13, 140, 162

Vaporate Film Treatment, 83–84

Vatican library, 29

vectoralists, 12, 13

Venn, Couze, 18

ventilation systems, 47, 79–83, *82*, 183

Vicino, Robert, 141–42

Vietnam, 58

vinegar syndrome, 6

Virilio, Paul, 143

virtual reality (VR) technology, 205–6

*Vital Records* (journal), 16

vital statistics and records, 21, 23, 39; dog tags, 116; normalization of, 106; preservation of, 107, 109; protecting, 93; resistance to, 107; uneven documentation of, 56. *See also* records

Vivos Cryovault, 141–42

*Voyager Golden Record, The*, 160–61, 162, 165, 167

Voyager probes, 160, 161, 163–64, 174

VR (virtual reality) technology, 205–6

vulnerability, 140. *See also* security

*Walden* (Thoreau), 92

Walker, Nancy, 119

Walmart, 12

Walter, Thomas, 155

"War against the Center" (Galison), 101

Wark, McKenzie, 11

Warner Brothers, 3

Waste Isolation Pilot Project (WIPP), 162

water, ultrapure, 184–85

*We Are Data* (Cheney-Lippold), 147

Weather Bureau, U.S., 131

Weber, C. G., 71

Weissman, Ken, 139

Westchester, New York, 116

Western Digital, 182

Westinghouse, George, 24

Westinghouse Electric Corporation, 17; archives of, 60, 64; *The Book of Record*, 70–75, *73*, 87, 146; Kitchen Planning Section, 81; *The Middleton Family at the New York World's Fair*, 65–69, 79, 112, 114; Precipitron air filter system, 79–83, *82*, 183; time capsules, 88, *89* (*see also* Westinghouse Time Capsule of Cupaloy)

Westinghouse Time Capsule of Cupaloy (WTCC), 17, 103; American culture in, 64; amount of data in, 19; *The Book of Record*, 70–75, *73*, 87, 146; contents of, 110; context of, 79; inner crypt of, 80; microbooks in, 182; microfilm in, 69, 87; photograph of, *72*, *73*; reference to Crypt of Civilization in, 87; replica of, 60, *61*, 62–63, 68–69. *See also* time capsules

Whalen, Grover, 71